The Steep Climb

Essays on the Jewish Question

BOOKS FROM CLEMENS & BLAIR
— www.clemensandblair.com —

Myth and Sun, by Martin Friedrich
Unmasking Anne Frank, by Ikuo Suzuki
Pan-Judah! Political Cartoons of Der Stürmer, by Robert Penman
Passovers of Blood, by Ariel Toaff
The Poisonous Mushroom, by Ernst Hiemer
On the Jews and Their Lies, by Martin Luther
Mein Kampf, by Adolf Hitler
Mein Kampf (Dual English-German edition), by Adolf Hitler
The Essential Mein Kampf, by Adolf Hitler
The Myth of the 20th Century, by Alfred Rosenberg

BOOKS BY THOMAS DALTON
— www.thomasdaltonphd.com —

Debating the Holocaust
The Holocaust: An Introduction
The Jewish Hand in the World Wars
Eternal Strangers: Critical Views of Jews and Judaism
Hitler on the Jews
Goebbels on the Jews
Streicher, Rosenberg, and the Jews: The Nuremberg Transcripts

THE STEEP CLIMB

by
THOMAS DALTON

Clemens & Blair, LLC
— 2023 —

CLEMENS & BLAIR, LLC

Clemens & Blair, LLC, is a non-profit educational publisher.
www.clemensandblair.com

Library of Congress Cataloging-in-Publication Data

Dalton, Thomas B.
The Steep Climb: Essays on the Jewish Question

p. cm.
Includes bibliographical references

ISBN 979-8986-7250-48
(pbk.: alk. paper)

1. Jews
2. Jewish Question, the
3. Holocaust, the
4. National Socialism

Printing number: 9 8 7 6 5 4 3 2 1

Printed in the United States of America on acid-free paper.

CONTENTS

THE STEEP CLIMB

ESSAYS ON THE JEWISH QUESTION

INTRODUCTION

THOMAS DALTON

In early 1944, with the war going badly for Germany, Joseph Goebbels published a collection of his speeches and essays entitled *Der Steile Aufstieg*—The Steep Climb. It featured 51 entries from the years 1942 and 1943, coming to nearly 500 pages of text. Even in 1942, when the Germans were still very optimistic, they knew that their struggle would be a long haul, a grinding battle, a steep climb. As the situation progressively worsened, they realized that they were in a fight to the finish—no negotiations, no surrender, fight or die.

As we know, the global enemy, the Judeo-Capitalist-Bolshevist demon, would win that battle. In the end, all leading National Socialists would die; Hitler and Goebbels perished at their own hands. But their ideas have survived. Their words, their thoughts, and their dreams still persist, and still inspire people everywhere.

The outcome of World War Two was more or less as Hitler and Goebbels had predicted and feared: the Jewish enemy—in both capitalist and Marxist incarnations—would go on to dominate the world. In the 80-some years since the war, capitalist Jews in the US and the UK would control the Western sphere, and the Marxist-inspired Soviets would control the East—at least, until the demise of the USSR in 1991. After that momentous event, Russian Jews, in the form of the so-called oligarchs, would continue to have vast influence in their nation, but globally they were compelled to cede control to the Jewish-American 'superpower.'

By 2000, it was clear that the US, firmly under sway of the Jewish Lobby, was in a position to dictate events around the world. The following year, the highly contentious 9/11 attacks, with their extensive Jewish/Israeli entanglements, would serve as a pretext for attacking 'terrorism'—especially of the Islamic variety—everywhere. Israel, of course, profited immensely from all this, given that their natural enemies were now under mortal threat around the planet from a predominantly White America that had no obvious reason to fight them. The US initiated its illegal wars against Afghanistan and Iraq, dragging along its European lackeys; these conflicts led to a massive loss of life among some of the poorest people in the world.

And all throughout this time, American Jews were dictating events. It got to the point where the sitting prime minister of Malaysia, Mahathir Mohamad, could rightly say, "Today, Jews rule the world by proxy. They get others to fight and die for them".[1] This holds true in the US for all presidents and both parties; virtually all of the American political elite, left and right, are beholden to Jewish money, Jewish-run media, and Jewish interests. Forget about democracy; America truly is a Judeocracy.

Pernicious Jewish political influence, however, is not a recent phenomenon—not in the least. It goes back centuries, even millennia. As far back as 59 BC, famed Roman scholar and politician Cicero could complain about the influence of the Jews in Rome itself. In his speech *Pro Flacco*, he notes how the Jews "stick together," and "how influential they are in informal assemblies." Cicero then sarcastically states that he must speak in a low voice, lest he "incite them against me." In 41 AD, Emperor Claudius issued his *Letter to the Alexandrians*, condemning the Jews there for "fomenting a general plague which infests the whole world." Eight years later, Claudius was compelled to banish them from Rome. Not long thereafter, around the year 60, the great philosopher Seneca wrote:

> [T]he customs of this accursed race have gained such influence that they are now received throughout the world. The vanquished have given laws to their victors.[2]

Ten years later, though, Rome would crush the Jewish rebellion in Judea, dispersing the Hebrews and setting the stage for their later influence elsewhere around the world.

Since that time, much of the Middle Eastern and Western worlds have had to contend with Jewish influence and malevolent Jewish action. It has been a constant, 2,000-year battle against deceptive, destructive, and self-interested Jews who are willing to stoop to any measure, no matter how low and degrading, no matter how corrupt and unethical, to achieve their ends—ends which inevitably involve gains in money and power. It has, indeed, been a "steep climb" for humanity, precisely as Goebbels stated. That climb continues to the present day.

In the following essays, I present my case for the pernicious effects of Jews on Western society, and particularly in the US. I give special emphasis to the Holocaust because it is the keystone of Jewish duplicity; it is the true "Big Lie" of the present day, and something which is highly vulnerable to attack. In any case, anti-Jewish complaints are easy to state but harder to document and prove. Here, I tackle both historical and present-day issues, all of which intend to shine a harsh light on the Jewish Question.

---

[1] AP, 17 October 2003. Mohamad reconfirmed his view in 2016; see "Former Asian leader won't stop claiming Jews 'rule the world'," *Washington Post* (27 June).

[2] All the above quotations are cited in my book *Eternal Strangers* (2020).

Initial versions of all these essays have previously appeared; most only online, but a few in hard copy as well. The oldest pieces date to 2009 and 2010, but most of the essays were originally published in the past four years. The entries appearing here have been modified, updated, and slightly expanded, in order to address recent developments. All of them deal with the Jewish Question in one way or another—most directly, but some as incidental or tangential aspects of that larger problem. Pieces on White nationalism and White interests are inherently relevant to the Question, given that (a) Jews are not White in any relevant sense, and (b) Jews view White Europeans as their most formidable opponent and thus seek their ruination. Promoting White interests is a direct challenge to Jewish power and thus an ineliminable part of the solution to that problem.

*****

I, for one, am continually amazed at the ignorance, apathy, and naiveté of most people regarding the Jewish Question. There are very good reasons to believe that this is the single most vital issue facing the modern Western nations; and yet, to treat it as unimportant or nonexistent is stunning. I wonder about people: Do they really not know anything of this problem? Do they know, but not care? Or do they know and care, but feel powerless to do anything? I suspect that most fall in the first group, with lesser numbers in the second and third. In a way, all these people are the primary intended audience for this book. I hope to inform them, encourage them to care, and show that we do have viable options.

In any case, there are many people in society today—especially those in positions of influence and power—who would rather not see these essays ever appear in print. These are topics of which we are 'not allowed to think,' and words that we are 'not allowed to say.' Influential Jews actively suppress sales of such books, cancelling publishing accounts and banking services, and generally censoring these topics wherever possible. This makes a mockery of any alleged rights of free speech. And authors and publishers cannot publicize this suppression because the Jewish lobby stifles that as well! When you hold near-total control of the media and communications system, you can do almost anything you want. Most decent and well-meaning people would be outraged at such a situation, but then, most will never hear about it, and thus never have a chance to be outraged.

Many will call this book 'anti-Semitic hate speech.' This is a meaningless trifle, a mere *ad hominem*, nothing more than declaring "I hate what you say." As I have written, hate speech is speech that Jews (and their allies) hate. Jews are, after all, the master haters in world history—just as they are the master liars and master corrupters. Stating as much is not 'hate,' it is documented fact. Eminent German philosopher Martin

Heidegger called the Jews "planetary master criminals".[3] This is not hate speech; it is, more or less, established fact.

The message to all Gentiles, and especially to all Whites, is clear: We have a steep climb ahead. And yet, victory is attainable. History tells us that, at many places and times, nations have managed to solve—at least temporarily—their respective Jewish Questions. When they have done so, they have flourished. Nations that are unable to solve this problem have struggled and declined. In a way, it is just as Goebbels has said: Jews are like an infestation, a biological curse that inflicts itself upon the weak and vulnerable. They are a kind of test of nature. Those peoples with sufficient vision, strength, and will-power will be able to shake off the intruder and emerge stronger than ever; those unable to do so will suffer decay and collapse.[4]

The Western nations, those traditional lands of the White race, are under mortal threat. They are being tested to the utmost degree. White societies are collapsing as we speak. White physical health, mental health, life expectancy, and financial security are all in decline. Such occurrences are not accidents. They are the direct and indirect outcomes of specific policies created by specific people with a specific agenda in mind.

But as in all states of crisis, opportunities arise. Whites, and Gentiles more generally, will have increasing chances to rise up, organize, stiffen their collective spines, and take action. The path ahead is steep, but we will persevere, and we will succeed. Perhaps this book can be one more small contribution to that effort.

---

[3] Cited in P. Trawney, *Heidegger and the Myth of a Jewish World Conspiracy* (2015), p. 33.

[4] For details, see my book *Goebbels on the Jews* (2019).

PART I

HISTORICAL CONTEXT

— 1 —

BLOND HAIR, BLUE EYES: THOUGHTS ON THE ARYAN IDEAL

If there is one definitive historical contrast to the Jew, it is the Aryan—the northern European White. This contrast is not merely superficial; it is deeply-rooted and genetic. The distinction is manifest not only in physical appearance but also in values, culture, attitudes, and worldviews. It is one thing to be a White European and another, very different thing to be a Jew. For over two millennia, these two types of people have been locked in combat for social dominance. Today, the minority Jew has, in many ways, the upper hand; but White Europeans are not without their strengths and advantages. Today, we Whites are struggling with the historic Jewish Question: How can we respond to, and reign in, this troublesome minority in our midst?

Here, in this initial essay, I want to address the biological basis of this distinction, especially as revealed in physical appearance. Not to diminish the many differences between people, but we can say, in general, that White Europeans embody one characteristic set of physical features, sub-Saharan blacks another, and Jews yet another. If you like large noses, short stature, and wide ears, then the Jews are for you; as for myself, I'll take the traditional White qualities every time.

When we consider someone's physical appearance, the question of *beauty* naturally arises. What is beauty? Specifically, what is it to be a beautiful person? This has long been considered one of those imponderable questions, akin to asking about the meaning of life. But this does not mean that we cannot have a valuable and substantive discussion. Beauty, of course, is partly subjective, but it is also partly universal. There are good reasons, *biological* reasons, for this. Hence we can make a meaningful inquiry into the matter. This, despite the fact that discussing beauty in the context of the White race is politically incorrect in the extreme. Western political elites are currently doing all they can to push the supposed virtues of dark-skin aesthetics, and to offset or displace any visible presence of White beauty. Despite this, they will fail—for good biological reasons.

When we observe peoples all around the world, we find at least one thing in common: people everywhere value lightness. People want light-skinned partners, light-skinned children, and they do everything possible to lighten their own skin. Skin-whitening is big business globally, growing from around $8 billion to nearly $12 billion within the next few years.[1] (I set aside for the moment the desire of Whites for a tanned-body look; this is a special case that I will examine later.) Blacks, Hispanics, and Asians all seek light skin, either of their own races or of the truly White-skinned north Europeans.

Along with this come two ancillary values: blond hair and blue eyes. People of dark-skinned races frequently dye or lighten their hair, wear blond wigs or hairpieces, and otherwise employ various tactics to appear light-haired or blondish. Blond hair is indeed rare; only around 5% of White adults are naturally blond. And yet, some 60% to 70% of White women dye their hair blond at some point.

Blue eyes are more common, existing in something like a quarter of White Americans and perhaps half of White Britons. And they do appear in many other racial groups; approximately 10% of all humans globally have some shade of blue eyes. The percentage is highest, unsurprisingly, in the Scandinavian countries, where up to 90% are blue. As with blond hair, blue eyes are almost universally seen as attractive. We can rest assured, if there was some way to change eye color as there is with hair, millions would do it.

It is striking, then, that these universally-accepted qualities of beauty derive from, and primarily reside in, Whites of northern Europe. The White race, it seems, contains within itself the global standard of beauty. As we read in *The Color Complex*, "the pinnacle of ideal feminine beauty remains that of a White woman with pale skin, blond hair, and blue eyes".[2] This is, in fact, "the gold standard of femininity." Thus, Whites could indeed be justifiably seen as the most beautiful race in the world. This fact should be a source of pride for Whites everywhere, something they should never want to hide or diminish.

And yet, in our PC world of today, we are not allowed to speak this way. It sounds far too "supremacist," far too "racist," for sensitive ears. Our media and academic elites are far more concerned that the races and ethnicities lacking such qualities—virtually all blacks, and the vast majority of Arabs, Hispanics, Asians, and Jews—might "feel bad" if we highlight or praise White beauty, so they do everything conceivable to accentuate black, dark brown, and mulatto characteristics. The result is that White beauty is disparaged, and the world everywhere becomes that much uglier.

One might ask: Why is this even important? Why the emphasis on blueness of eye color? Or on blond hair? Are such things just "pretty"? And even if they are, why do so many people find blue eyes and blond hair

---

[1] See for example the CNN story "Skin whitening: What is it, what are the risks and who profits?" (25 Jan 2022).

[2] *The Color Complex* (2012; K. Russell et al.), p. 52.

attractive—as they undeniably do? These are pregnant questions. I will argue here that such features are not "just" appealing; or rather, they are appealing for very real and consequential reasons. In this essay, I want to examine a number of diverse but related aspects of the blond-haired, blue-eyed ideal—an ideal that also goes by such names as 'Nordic,' 'Scandinavian,' and more controversially, 'Aryan.' Let's first start by taking a look at the physiology of the Aryan people.

The Science of 'Aryanism'

The Aryans have an interesting history, no doubt. Consider the basic etymology involved here. The root of the word, *arya*, is Sanskrit. Originally, circa 2000 BC, it meant simply speakers of Sanskrit language; later it became associated with the lighter-skinned peoples of central Asia. Due to their superior abilities and intelligence, and capacity for culture-building, the term 'Aryan' became synonymous with 'the best' or 'the noble.' As they expanded southward and eastward, they became the dominant ruling people. In this sense, the Aryans are indeed rulers or masters of others; but it was by dint of their superior skills, intelligence, and morality. In a way, it was a justly-earned dominance.

Scientists today almost uniformly avoid all talk of Aryans, preferring to reserve that term for linguistic and perhaps cultural groups of people. And of course, the Nazi association makes the term largely taboo, in any case. But science, thankfully, has the power to overcome taboos. Recent scientific research has shed new light on the biological and historical origins of the light-skinned people of the north.

Let's take the long view for a moment.[3] The human legacy goes back at least 7 million years, to the earliest appearance of the genii Australopithecus and Ardipithecus. These were not yet of the genus Homo—'human'—which would appear only around 2.5 million years ago. But they were proto-humans, and were our common link to chimpanzees, who are our closest genetic relatives. These proto-humans were, like modern chimps, fully hair-covered, with silky black hair. Their skin, though, was light—even white. Even today, if we were to shave bare a chimpanzee, he would be white. The biological reasons for this are clear: dark skin, like dark hair, is an evolved characteristic to protect from strong sun. The dark pigmentation comes from melanin, which exists in two forms: *eumelanin* and *pheomelanin*. The former has a dark brown tone, the latter reddish. The amount and combination of these two determine the actual color of

---

[3] The following details were drawn from several academic sources, but a good recent summary is "Skin colour and vitamin D: An update" by A. Hanel and C. Carlberg (2020; *Experimental Dermatology* 29: 864-875).

one's skin, hair, and eyes. Functionally, melanin protects the body, the eyes, and specifically the DNA from damage by intense ultraviolet solar radiation. It can be produced in a short-term and temporary manner, as in tanning, but over millennia, it can come to be a genetically-heritable, and thus "permanent," change in skin tone or hair or eye color.

Melanin production, though, is biologically costly. It takes effort and energy for the body to produce and maintain melanin, something it would rather not do, so to speak. Having evolved in the equatorial regions of central Africa, proto-humans would have needed to incur the cost of heavy melanin production in their hair and eyes—but not their skin, being fully hair-covered. Hence they, like modern chimps, would have had white skin, black hair, and dark brown eyes.

By around 2 million years ago, the first humans began to appear, in the form of Homo habilis and Homo ergaster. They started to walk upright and to run, and perhaps as result, began to lose body hair—when the thermal cost became too high. (Rather like wearing a fur coat in summer.) But shedding hair exposed the skin. Thus, melanin production increased, and our skin became black.

Black-skinned early humans migrated into Eurasia around 1.8 million years ago, and as they moved north, likely experienced a lightening of their skin. They would have first travelled through the Middle East, at about 30- or 35-degrees north latitude, and then on into Europe, at 45- or 50-degrees north. There is a substantially weaker sun at such latitudes, and thus within a few thousand years, humans would have gradually lost melanin—in skin, in hair, and in eyes. In a sense, human skin began to revert to its evolutionary natural tone—white.

In the North, something else happened: humans first experienced *winter*. That is, cold weather, ice, and snow. As black Africans, we had no evolutionary experience with such things; but now, these intrepid northerners needed to adapt: to stay warm, to cook and preserve food, and to build suitable shelters. The intellectual and cognitive burden increased, and undoubtedly this new evolutionary pressure pushed us to think more, to think in more sophisticated ways, and thus to have more-evolved brain functions. It also increased the need to cooperate, to trust one's neighbors, and to create reliable and durable social networks. In short, the northerners became more sociable, and they became smarter.[4]

---

[4] Today this is known as the 'Cold Winters Thesis.' See, for example, "Only in America: Cold Winters Theory, race, IQ, and well-being" (2014; B. Pesta and P. Poznanski), *Intelligence* 46; and R. Lynn, *Race Differences in Intelligence* (2015). This idea is sometimes viewed as a modern reactionary theory, but in fact it goes back at least to Arthur Schopenhauer. In 1851, he said "Only after man propagated his stock during a long period of time outside his natural [African] habitat between the tropics and extended it…into the more frigid zones, did he become fair and

Today we have evidence of light-skinned, 'white' people that lived in the Middle East around 25,000 years ago. (Undoubtedly they existed long before that, but we lack the evidence to prove it.) A separate group of humans apparently entered Europe via Spain around 19,000 years ago, and we have evidence that they had bluish eyes; this is our earliest indication that eye color had begun to lighten, upon reaching 40 degrees latitude or so. (I note here that hominid eyes are "naturally" blue, that is, when lacking the protective melanin. Blue is not a pigment or color *per se*, not like a 'dye,' but rather simply the absence of the darkening melanin.)

As people pressed further north into central Eurasia—say, above 50 degrees north latitude—skin and eyes would have naturally continued to lighten, and eventually the hair as well. About the same time as bluish eyes appeared in Spain, blondish hair began to appear in north-central Asia. By 8,000 BC, the 'westerners' that had come up through Spain, and the 'easterners' that came via the Middle East, met and began to interbreed in north-central Europe. These people, now called Scandinavian Hunter-Gatherers, would have had all-white skin and a predominance of blue eyes and blond hair. A final wave of immigrants, the Yamnaya, arrived around 3,000 BC; as they blended into the existing hunter-gatherers and began to settle into fixed agricultural communities, they formed the core of modern-day north Europeans. These people, circa 3,000 BC, would have been the first true Aryans. Over the next 2,000 years, they would come to dominate the scene in all of north-central Europe. Later, these same people pressed southward, down into present-day Italy and Greece, serving as the leading ethnicity in the emergence of the ancient Greek civilization and the Roman Republic (later, Empire).

The result is striking, even today, and especially in the Nordic countries—those that lie above 55- or 60-degrees latitude. I have spent some time in these countries in recent years, and the predominance of very blond people, especially blond women, is obvious. (Women tend to have lighter blond hair than men, and children more than adults.) In my travels, it was not uncommon to see groups of three or four college-aged women, all of whom had long, flowing, pure blond hair. I have seen young Nordic children with astonishingly blond hair—so depigmented as to be almost white.

---

finally white. ... The highest civilization and culture, apart from the ancient Hindus and Egyptians, are found exclusively among the white races... All this is due to the fact that necessity is the mother of invention because those tribes that emigrated early to the north, and there gradually became white, had to develop all their intellectual powers and invent and perfect all the arts in their struggle with need, want, and misery, which in their many forms were brought about by the climate. This they had to do in order to make up for the parsimony of nature, and out of it all came their high civilization" (*Parerga and Paralipomena*, vol. 2, Oxford University Press, pp. 157-159).

They almost appear as albinos, but of course they are not. The effect of the sun on human appearance and human genetics is truly amazing.[5]

Divine Northerners

For all of recorded history, people have told myths and stories of others living in the far-off lands of the north. These stories would have been based on actual experience with these mysterious and striking people, some of whom would have traveled south. Hardened to the rigorous climate, intrepid, smart, and able to construct civilizations and cultures, it is no wonder that such people took on a mythic quality. And their striking physical appearance came to be the visible sign of such a noble personage.

In this way, blue eyes, blondness, and very white skin came to be seen as good, rare, desirable, and beautiful—perhaps divinely-inspired, perhaps even godly. This, in fact, was exactly Plato's view. In his *Republic* we find a telling passage in which he discusses various physical attributes of boys and young men, including skin tone. Some of the boys are swarthy and dark-toned, but "the pale ones are children of the gods (*leukous de theōn paidas einai*)" (474d). This is highly revealing; it suggests a rank-ordering in Greek society whereby light-skinned people were seen as better, higher, nobler, and more desirable—descendants of the gods themselves.

When it came to formalizing the official gods and myths of the various European cultures, then, it is unsurprising to find that the southern Europeans, in particular, would construct their gods and heroes in the image of these divine northerners. This is reflected, very explicitly, in their writings. Consider, for example, the incomparably important writings of Homer—the Iliad and the Odyssey, circa 800 BC.[6]

When we review the Iliad for relevant references, we find around 15 mentions of light-colored hair. Most of these are applied to the Spartan king Menelaus, but also to the gods Apollo and Demeter, to the demigod hero Achilles, and to the figures of Meleager and the woman Agamede. In all cases, Homer uses the same Greek word: *xanthos*. Formally, *xanthos* means 'yellow' or 'bright,' as in our English word 'xanthic' ("of, or relating to, a yellow color"). Technically, every usage by Homer of *xanthos* should be translated as 'blond.' But, for poetic effect, the various transla-

---

[5] In notable contrast to the native Scandinavians are the imported black African and Middle-Eastern "refugees" that are now quite visible in all major cities there. One cannot help but feel that there is something profoundly anti-natural about this situation, that somehow these recent immigrants simply do not belong there. It feels like a crime against nature.

[6] We believe that Homer lived sometime around 800 BC in the region called Ionia, comprising the far west coast of modern-day Turkey. This area had been part of the Greek proto-empire since at least the 1000s BC.

tors of Homer have chosen a variety of related terms and phrases. Thus, for example, we find reference to the "fiery hair" of Apollo (1.235), the "golden hair" of Meleager (2.737), the "red-haired Menelaus" (3.338), "blond Demeter" (5.575), "blond Agamede" (11.880), and the "red-gold" hair of Achilles (23.162)—all *xanthos*. And this, in a single translator's edition![7]

One also finds other translated references to "fair hair," which we might presume to mean 'blond.' But in these instances, Homer uses the word *eukomos*, which literally means "good hair." This, of course, need not be blond, so we are left with an uncertain picture in mind.

Regarding light-colored or blue eyes, we find in the Iliad a single reference: in chapter one, Homer refers to the goddess Athena and her "clear grey eyes." In Greek, the word is *glaukopis*—literally, blue or blue-green (*glaukon*) eyes. More often today we might refer to someone with "steel-blue" eyes, which is more flattering than "grey"—but the point is the same.

In the Odyssey, we find fewer references to *xanthos* hair (e.g. the "yellow locks" or "russet curls" of Odysseus [13.455]), but more to the *glaukopis* of Athena (e.g. 2.424, 2.475, 13.325). In all there are about half as many such references as in the Iliad. But notably, in both works, the characteristic features belong to gods, goddesses, and heroes. They are clearly marks of distinction and noble birth.

Homer's contemporary, Hesiod, makes a handful of similar references in his much-shorter Theogony. There we find four mentions of the *glaukopis* of Athena (lines 10, 575, 890, and 924), and he also writes of the "*xanthos* Ariadne" (line 950), presumably meaning her hair. He then adds one new term: *khrusokomes*, or 'golden-haired.' This is applied to the god Dionysus (line 950).

Other such 'Aryan' references would follow in subsequent centuries. Around 525 BC, the philosopher Xenophanes examined the customs of the Thracian people—modern-day Bulgarians, roughly. He wrote that "their gods are blue-eyed (*glaukos*) and red-haired (*pyrros*)".[8] The use of the word *pyrros*—from *pyr*, 'fire'—is interesting; the gods surely had "fiery-red hair," no doubt.

Into the 400s BC, two great lyric poets of the ancient world, Pindar and Bacchylides, made several relevant references. In Pindar we find mention of the *xanthos* Graces, *xanthos* Achilles, *xanthos* Danaans, *khrusokomes* Apollo, *xanthos* Menelaus, and for the first time ever, *xanthos* Athena—

[7] Robert Fagles' translation (1990). The line numberings of Fagles are slightly different than other translations, unfortunately.
[8] Fragment 3, from Clement, *Miscellanies*.

blond gods and heroes all.[9] Regarding blue eyes, Pindar makes only three such mentions, all of the *glaukopis* of Athena.[10] For his part, Bacchylides writes of *xanthos* Briseis, *xanthos* Athena, *khrusokomes* Apollo, *khrusean* Aphrodite, the surprisingly *xanthai* Spartans, and more generally of "the mortal men who crown their golden (*xanthan*) hair".[11] Bacchylides makes no reference to the blueness or greyness of anyone's eyes.

Pindar, furthermore, was among the first to give the mysterious blond and blue-eyed northerners a name; he called them *Hyperboreans*. This name means, literally, those dwelling beyond (*hyper*) the north winds (*boreas*). His first and oldest ode (Pythian 10), circa 498 BC, provides an extended and fascinating account of these people:

> Neither by ship nor on foot could you find the marvelous road to the meeting-place of the Hyperboreans. Once Perseus, the leader of his people, entered their homes and feasted among them, when he found them sacrificing glorious hecatombs of donkeys to the god. In the festivities of those people and in their praises, Apollo rejoices most, and he laughs when he sees the outright arrogance of the beasts. The Muse is not absent from their customs; all around swirl the dances of girls, the lyre's loud chords, and the cries of flutes. They wreathe their hair with golden laurel branches and revel joyfully. No sickness or ruinous old age is mixed into that sacred race; without toil or battles, they live without fear of strict Nemesis. Breathing boldness of spirit, the son of Danae [Perseus] once went to that gathering of blessed men, and Athena led him there. (lines 29-46)[12]

The Hyperboreans are thus beloved by the gods, happy and joyful, full of life, and free from pain and strife. They are, indeed, a "sacred race" (*hiera genea*).

---

[9] Source information: *xanthos* Graces (Nem 5.55), *xanthos* Achilles (Nem 3.45), *xanthos* Danaans (Nem 9.15), *khrusokomes* Apollo (Olym 6.42; Pyth 2.15; Olym 7.34; Isth 7.49), *xanthos* Menelaus (Nem 7.30), and, *xanthos* Athena (Nem 10.8).

[10] Source information: Nem 7.30; Olym 7.34; Nem 10.8. Note: If Athena is now both blond-haired and blue-eyed, she is surely the definitive Aryan goddess.

[11] Source information: *xanthos* Briseis (Ode 13.135), *xanthos* Athena (Ode 5.90), *khrusokomes* Apollo (Ode 4.1), *khrusean* Aphrodite (Ode 9.70), *xanthai* Spartans (Ode 20.1), and "the mortal men who crown their golden (*xanthan*) hair" (Ode 9.20).

[12] Further brief references to Hyperboreans occur in Isthmian 6 (circa 484 BC) and Olympian 3 (circa 476 BC).

Sometime around 425 BC, the great historian Herodotus issued his classic text, *Histories*. There he discusses the characteristics of many peoples and nations across the known world, including those of the Budinians, who were marked by their *glaukos* eyes and *pyrron* hair (4.108). The specific location of these people is unclear, but they apparently hailed from just north of the Black Sea, in the southern part of modern-day Ukraine.

Notably, Herodotus too elaborated on the Hyperboreans. In his same work, he details a story of two Hyperborean girls who travelled south bearing gifts for the Greeks, only to end up dead in Delos—accident or murder, we are not sure. A portion of his tale is as follows:

> Concerning the Hyperborean people, neither the Scythians nor any other inhabitants of these lands tell us anything, except perhaps the Issedones. ... But Hesiod speaks of Hyperboreans, and Homer too in his poem *The Heroes' Sons*, if that is truly the work of Homer.[13]
>
> But the Delians say much more about them than any others do. They say that offerings wrapped in straw are brought from the Hyperboreans to Scythia; when these have passed Scythia, each nation in turn receives them from its neighbors until they are carried to the Adriatic Sea, which is the most westerly limit of their journey; from there, they are brought on to the south, the people of Dodona being the first Greeks to receive them. From Dodona they come down to the Melian gulf, and [ultimately] to Delos. Thus, they say, these offerings come to Delos.
>
> But on the first journey, the Hyperboreans sent two maidens bearing the offerings, to whom the Delians give the names Hyperoche and Laodice, and five men of their people with them as escort for safe conduct... But when those whom they sent never returned, they took it amiss that they should be condemned always to be sending people and not getting them back, and so they carry the offerings, wrapped in straw, to their borders, and tell their neighbors to send them on from their own country to the next... I know that they do this. The Delian girls and boys cut their hair in honor of these Hyperborean maidens, who died at Delos... In this way, then, these maidens are honored by the inhabitants of Delos. ...
>
> I have said enough of the Hyperboreans. I won't tell the story of Abaris, alleged to be a Hyperborean, who carried an arrow over the whole world, fasting all the while. But if there

[13] Any such references by Hesiod or Homer are lost to history.

> are men beyond the north wind, then there are others beyond the south. (4.32-36)

Not quite the "sacred race" of Pindar, but still a people portrayed as generous, noble, and exceptional.[14]

By the late BC and early AD period, Roman writers were making note of the same distinctive qualities. Horace (23 BC) describes one Pyrrha in terms of her *flavam comae*—blond hair. And he speaks of a Phyllis as having similarly *flavae* hair.[15] In 100 AD, the great Roman historian Tacitus, in his highly consequential discussion of the Germanic people, refers to their *caerulei oculi* ("fiery blue eyes") and their *rutilae comae* ("red hair"). Two decades later, in his Satire 13, and speaking of the same people, Juvenal deployed the terms *caerula* and *flavam* to refer to the Germans' blue eyes and (now) blond hair. These were the first explicit historical connections between Germanism and Aryanism.

Such were the views of the ancient world. Little changed, biologically, over the next two millennia, given that there were no major waves of migrations, nor yet any high-speed transport that would have enabled rapid population movement. During this time, the superior Europeans set about creating Western civilization, advancing technology, and creating art and culture on an unprecedented scale. Into the mid-19th century, Aryanism had gained scientific credibility, and was taken mainstream by such men as Arthur de Gobineau, most notably in his *Essay on the Inequality of the Human Races* (1853). Some decades later, Houston Chamberlain's influential work *Foundations of the 19th Century* (1899) further advanced the Aryan thesis. Chamberlain placed particular emphasis on the Aryan-Germanic peoples who, he argued, had been responsible for the most significant advances in Western culture. It was this belief in German superiority that led him to join the National Socialist party early on; Chamberlain was in fact a great supporter and advocate of Hitler, until his death in 1927.

It was via such men as Chamberlain and, later, Hitler and Alfred Rosenberg, that the concept of 'Aryan' became so closely associated with 'Nazism.' Thus it was that both the culture-building, idealistic Aryan and the Nordic-Scandinavian blue-eyed blond aesthetic were blended into the overall National Socialist worldview—for good or bad. From then on, the

---

[14] I note in passing that no less a figure than Nietzsche was evidently inspired by this same northern people. At the very beginning of his landmark essay *Antichrist*, he states "We are Hyperboreans." "We"—Nietzsche and his followers—intellectually dwell among the ice and snow, far away from the comfortable, complacent, so-called civilized people; "we know very well how far off we live," he says.

[15] In Odes 1.5 and 2.4, respectively.

Aryan ideal of beauty was stained with the supposed Nazi conception of a master race.[16]

Closing Thoughts

What is the legacy of all this today? Firstly, I think it shows that the Nordic/Aryan aesthetic is not just a matter of "good looks." It is a reflection of a long genetic history in northern climates, and is a parallel marker with several positive human qualities: creative, trusting, culture-building, sociable, intelligent. The same evolutionary forces that gave people blond hair, blue eyes, and white skin also gave them a number of salutary virtues.

Second, it marks a sharp contrast with the popular, Jewish/Hollywood image of mixed races, blacks, Asians, mulattos, and generally "people of color." Jewish Hollywood wants to foist on Americans—and the whole world—an ideal of random race-mixing. They do this via many images and storylines that simultaneously promote racial mixing and disparage White ideals, especially the classic Aryan/Nordic aesthetic.

For example, Hollywood loves to play up the "dumb blonde" stereotype. Blondes are ok, but they have to be stupid, or naïve, or superficial. But as a factual matter, this seems to be untrue. In fact, there is some data for the contrary. In an interesting paper from 2016 titled "Are blondes really dumb?," author Jay Zagorsky draws from a large national database to show that "blonde women have a higher mean IQ than women with brown, red, and black hair." Furthermore, blondes "are more likely classified as geniuses" than people of other hair colors. The differences were more pronounced among women than men.[17]

Additionally, there is an old study—from almost 100 years ago—that argues for a similar result. Professor G. Estabrooks compiled data on nearly 1,000 boys and girls, ranging in age from 9 to 16. Based on a coarse sorting between "light" and "dark" hair, the light-haired children had an average IQ of 109, versus 106 for the dark-haired. He also looked at correlation with eye color, and by this measure, the blue-eyed group had an average of 109, versus 105 for the brown-eyed.[18] Obviously we would need further data to draw firm conclusions, but indications are that the ancient Aryan advantage has carried down, in some degree, to the present day.

And then we can look at entire nations. Not long ago, Lynn and Meisenberg (2010) calculated average IQs for 108 countries. Looking just within Europe, we find a significant difference between the four Nordic

---

[16] I address this matter in the 2nd essay of the present volume.

[17] In *Economics Bulletin*, 36(1): 401-410 (2016).

[18] "Intelligence and pigmentation of hair and eyes in elementary school children," *American Journal of Psychology* 41(1): 106-108 (1929).

nations (Norway, Sweden, Finland, Denmark) and, for example, four south-European nations (Italy, Greece, Spain, Portugal); the former average 99, and latter 95. Not a huge difference, but still significant.[19] Once again, this is in line with our expectations.

Let me also address here a couple of possible objections to my above analysis, especially the notion that solar intensity and latitude determine pigmentation. Recall my argument that, as humans migrated northward, the less intense sun allowed a decrease in melanin in skin, hair, and eyes, thus tending toward light skin, blond hair, and blue eyes. Some may reply to the contrary, that Inuit people (Eskimos) generally have a 'yellow' or ruddy skin tone, along with dark hair. But there are a couple of different factors at work here. First, Inuit came into North America relatively recently—perhaps only 5,000 years ago. This may not have been enough time to manifest the effects of lightening. Also, their heavy seafood diet, with its rich supply of vitamin D, may have mitigated the need for skin lightening.[20]

Another set of possible objections come from the animal kingdom. Lions, some may argue, live in intense African sun and yet are notably 'blond.' Why don't lions have the dark, protective melanin in their hair? But of course, a variety of environmental and evolutionary factors determine such things. Large predators benefit from blending into their backgrounds—all the better to sneak up on prey. Such animals have evolved different skin coloration: leopards and cheetahs evolved spotted fur, and lions evolved a blonder tone of hair, likely as a match to the yellow grasslands of the savannah. I have not claimed that solar intensity is the sole factor in hair and skin color, only that it is a major determinant.

Thus is my brief study of Aryan beauty. I have no grand and glorious conclusions to offer, other than the simple observation that *beauty matters*. Physical appearance is an expression of one's genetic inheritance, and thus reflects the kind of person one is. The same genes that give a certain physi-

[19] "National IQs calculated and validated for 108 nations," *Intelligence* 38:353-360 (2010). Particularly striking is a comparison of 'light-skinned nations' with 'dark-skinned nations.' But I will leave this for another time.

[20] Deng and Xu write, "One possible reason is that the dark skin could protect the Inuits from the severe UV exposure because of the long daylight hours in winter and high levels of UV reflection from the snow. While the dark skin is a disadvantage for vitamin D production, plenty of vitamins including vitamin D could be compensated from their diets. Another cause could be the founder effect of the ancient East Asian ancestry of the Inuits, who have inhabited the arctic region since nearly 5000 years ago, and had higher melanin production than the European ancestry" (2018; "Adaptation of human skin color in various populations," *Hereditas* 155:1).

cal appearance also give a certain state of mind, certain behavioral tendencies, and certain motivations and values. Beauty is not just "skin deep," as our PC crowd like to say. Beauty matters.

Classic markers of White, Aryan beauty have been valued for millennia, and this likely was for very real, very objective, and very evolutionary reasons. The blue-eyed blonds were smarter, more skilled, more industrious, and more robust. They were more creative. They were idealistic and altruistic. They knew how to build and sustain civilizations. They were, in short, *better people*.

Jews and leftist liberals don't want to hear any of this—especially Jews, who are notably lacking in blond hair, blue eyes, and Aryan personality traits. For leftists and Jews, everyone is "equal." For them, skin tone is little more than a biological paint, laid over a physical body that is otherwise identical in all humans. This is sheer nonsense. Privately, Jews know this, of course; but outwardly they all maintain a façade of egalitarianism because this significantly aids their cause among the Gentile majority. When you are a Jewish supremacist, it is best to make outward proclamations of equality even as you project supremacist thinking onto your primary opponents, Aryans and Whites.

Whites everywhere need to relearn about their own glorious legacy and to regain an appreciation for their outstanding physical and intellectual virtues. As a whole, Whites are the most beautiful, most productive, and most virtuous race on the planet. This is acknowledged, directly and indirectly, in a million different ways, by people all across the Earth. We are indeed "children of the gods," as Plato proclaimed. We are indeed a "sacred race," as Pindar recognized. We need to cast off those who would denigrate and debase us, reestablish our long-lost sense of self-confidence, and reclaim our rightful place in the world community.

— 2 —
THE ARYAN IDEAL, FROM FRANKLIN TO NATIONAL SOCIALISM

In the first essay of the present volume, I examined the physiology and history of the classic Nordic features. I argued that these hallmarks of beauty have been acknowledged and respected for millennia and around the world, and thus constitute a kind of universal aesthetic standard or benchmark for humanity. The Nordic/Aryan people furthermore have been proven to have a number of other virtues, including higher intelligence, higher moral and ethical standards, and a greater capacity for building cultures and civilizations.[1] It was not without good reason that Plato called light-skinned people "children of the gods"; it was not without good reason that Pindar called the northerners "a sacred race".[2] I concluded that the White race was the most beautiful and the most virtuous on Earth, based not on my own biased opinion but on testimony over centuries, scientific research, and on commonly-held views around the world today. Though representing only some 10% of humanity, Whites have good reason to be proud. We are exceptional, by most any measure.

Whites used to be proud. They used to speak openly and clearly about their love of one's own, about their sense of pride, about their hopes and dreams for a great future for their race. Take, for example, that wise and insightful Founding Father, Ben Franklin. In 1751 he wrote a short essay entitled "Observations concerning the increase of mankind." In it, he expresses concern about the need to fill up the "empty" lands of the nascent American colony—there being very little talk of independence yet. (This was still five years before the Seven Years' War, a conflict that set the stage for the later American revolution.) Franklin clearly understood the tradeoffs between native-born North European-American natural increases and the "importation" of foreigners of other ethnicities and races:

---

[1] Obviously, this does not imply that individual non-Whites cannot be beautiful or intelligent. Nor does it imply that Whites lacking in blue eyes or blond hair are in any way inferior. I am speaking here of generalized racial characteristics as they are realized in large populations. It says nothing about particular individuals.

[2] For Plato, see *Republic* 474d. He was referring specifically to boys and young men, but his statement was clearly in reference to "the pale ones" in general. For Pindar, see his ode Pythian 10, line 40.

> The Importation of Foreigners into a Country that has as many Inhabitants as the present Employments and Provisions for Subsistence will bear, will be, in the End, no Increase of People—unless the New Comers have more Industry and Frugality than the Natives [Whites], and then they will provide more Subsistence, and increase in the Country; but they will gradually eat the Natives out. Nor is it necessary to bring in Foreigners to fill up any occasional Vacancy in a Country; for such Vacancy will soon be filled by natural Generation. Who can now find the Vacancy made in *Sweden*, *France*, or other Warlike Nations, by the Plague of Heroism, 40 years ago; … or in *Guinea*, by 100 Years Exportation of Slaves, that has blacken'd half *America?* …
>
> Thus there are suppos'd to be now upwards of One Million *English* Souls in *North-America*, (tho' 'tis thought scarce 80,000 have been brought over Sea,) and yet perhaps there is not one the fewer in *Britain*, but rather many more… This Million doubling, suppose but once in 25 Years, will, in another Century, be more than the People of *England*, and the greatest Number of *Englishmen* will be on this Side the Water. …
>
> And since Detachments of *English* from *Britain*, sent to *America*, will have their Places at Home so soon supply'd and increase so largely here; why should the *Palatine Boors* [i.e. Germans] be suffered to swarm into our Settlements and, by herding together, establish their Language and Manners, to the Exclusion of ours? Why should *Pennsylvania*, founded by the *English*, become a Colony of *Aliens*, who will shortly be so numerous as to Germanize us instead of our Anglifying them, and will never adopt our Language or Customs any more than they can acquire our Complexion?

Clearly there was no love lost here for the Germans; the mere fact of their foreign language was enough to hinder true integration. Franklin then closes with these stunning thoughts:

> Which leads me to add one Remark, that the Number of purely white People in the World is proportionably very small. All *Africa* is black or tawny [i.e. light brown or yellowish]; *Asia* chiefly tawny; *America* (exclusive of the new Comers) wholly so [that is, Native Americans]. And in *Europe*, the *Spaniards*, *Italians*, *French*, *Russians*, and *Swedes*, are generally of what we call a swarthy Complexion; as are

> the *Germans* also, the *Saxons* only excepted, who, with the *English*, make the principal Body of White People on the Face of the Earth. I could wish their Numbers were increased.
>
> And while we are, as I may call it, *Scouring* our Planet...why should we, in the Sight of Superior Beings, darken its People? Why increase the Sons of *Africa*, by planting them in *America*, where we have so fair an Opportunity, by excluding all Blacks and Tawneys, of increasing the lovely White and Red [i.e. rosy-cheeked]? But perhaps I am partial to the Complexion of my Country, for such Kind of Partiality is natural to Mankind.[3]

A truly remarkable statement by the 45-year-old Franklin, and one we are not likely to see quoted in a textbook of American history. Given the amazing opportunity of a vast, productive, and largely open land, why, asks Franklin, would we import non-Whites? The creators of the American colony were Whites from England, who included a healthy admixture of "Saxons" (including Frisians, Angles, and Jutes) from the very north of mainland Europe—people who shared much genetic heritage with the Nordic Scandinavians. Why dilute the "very small" number of true Whites in the world with yet more dark-skinned races? If only we all were "partial to the complexion of our (native) countrymen"! Here is true pride in oneself and one's people, something utterly lacking in present-day Whites—thanks in part to relentless bashing by Jews and other PC-liberals. Today, Whites are becoming a minority in their native lands; "I could wish their numbers were increased"—indeed.

Back in Europe, a few brave individuals were proclaiming White virtues, including White/Aryan beauty. As I mentioned in my previous essay, the earliest prominent advocate was probably Arthur Schopenhauer, who, in his 1851 work *Parerga and Paralipomena*, wrote that

> The highest civilization and culture...are found exclusively among the white races... [N]ecessity is the mother of invention, because those tribes that emigrated early to the north, and there gradually became white, had to develop all their intellectual powers and perfect all the arts...

This was followed shortly by Arthur de Gobineau's influential work, *Essay on the Inequality of the Human Races* (1855), which made an explicit and extended case for the superiority of the Germanic/Aryan people.

---

[3] From *Benjamin Franklin: Representative Selections* (1936), F. Mott and C. Jorgenson, eds.; pp. 221-223.

Enter Nietzsche

By 1883, Friedrich Nietzsche had published his great work, *Thus Spoke Zarathustra*. There he famously introduced the idea of the *Übermensch*—the overman, the super-man, the being who would succeed today's human in the course of evolution. "I teach you the overman. Man is something that shall be overcome" (p. 124).[4] And a few lines later: "The overman is the meaning of the earth." The precise nature of the *Übermensch* is never clear, unfortunately, and he is certainly never described as white or Aryan. Nor is he a conqueror; he is, to be sure, "the lightning out of the dark cloud of man" (p. 132), but again, we are unclear of the implications. The overman is associated with "rainbows" and "bridges" (e.g. p. 163), and thus is clearly a transitional figure, a 'next phase' in some sense. But he is no world-destroyer, and nothing to be feared. In fact, he does *not yet exist* on the planet; he is still coming, still in the future. "Never yet has there been an overman" (p. 205). He is an aspiration, not a reality—certainly no "master race," certainly no proto-Nazi figurehead.

Nietzsche wrote little more on the *Übermensch*, and in truth, little at all on race, even the White race. Even Aryans are barely mentioned—though with two notable exceptions. In 1887, he released his book *On the Genealogy of Morals*, which contains a striking analysis of the origin of contemporary Judeo-Christian morality. Early in the book, Nietzsche makes some preliminary comments on the notions of good and evil as he contrasts the indigenous "pre-Aryan" people of Italy with the "blond, that is Aryan, conqueror race" that arrived from the north.[5] "The Celts," he adds, "were definitely a blond race." A few lines later, we find the one and only appearance in Nietzsche of the dreaded word: "who can say whether modern democracy…does not signify in the main a tremendous counterattack—and that the conqueror- and master-race, the Aryan, is not succumbing psychologically, too?" Here, for the only time, we find him explicitly describing the Aryan as the "conquerer- (*Eroberer-*) and master-race (*Herren-rasse*)." Clearly, though, he is describing a historical reality; this is no prescription for the present or future. If anything, he is implying that modern democracy has defeated any remnant of the old conquering Aryan.

Nietzsche picks up this same theme a few sections later, where writes, rather notoriously, of the "blond beast" (*blonde Bestie*). The phrase occurs three times in section 11: "One cannot fail to see at the bottom of all these noble races the beast of prey, the splendid blond beast prowling about avidly, in search of spoil and victory" (p. 40). He then speaks of "the raging

---

[4] Quotations and page numbers come from the standard Kaufmann translation in *The Portable Nietzsche* (1954).

[5] First Essay, sec. 6. Quoted here from Vintage Books edition (1989), pp. 30-31.

of the blond Germanic beast" in reference to German aggression over past centuries. Finally, and most ominously: "One may be quite justified in continuing to fear the blond beast at the core of all noble races, and in being on one's guard against it" (p. 43). It would seem, then, that Nietzsche locates an aggressive core within the historically conquering peoples of the world—which is undoubtedly true, given their various invasions and successes. In a European context, the successful invaders would often have been the Nordic/Aryan blonds from the north, hence the blond beast—the Viking, if you will—at the heart of the traditionally invading peoples.

Is this bad? Is this evil? Hardly. First, it is simply an acknowledgement of historical reality. Second, it suggests that something of the lion-hearted persists in the northern Europeans. If so, what of it? Perhaps we ought to treat them with respect, if true!

The second exception on the topic of Aryans comes in one of Nietzsche's final works, *Twilight of the Idols* (1888), where he has some important words to offer on the Aryans of India vis-à-vis the supposed Aryanism of Christianity. In India, the noble Aryans, the upper-caste Brahmins, stood in stark contrast to the lower ranks, especially to the "chandala"—the untouchables. In India, everyone understood the order of rank, and all knew where they stood. Christianity, by contrast, claims to raise up the lowest of the low, the untouchable chandalas, to turn even them into the "beloved of God"—and indeed, the *favored* of God.

For Nietzsche, this was sheer nonsense. Even more: it was sheer *Jewish* nonsense. The Jew, Paul, created his universalist church in the manufactured image of a perhaps mythical, and certainly dead, rabbi named Jesus. As a leading chandala, Paul hated the nobles: the Romans, the Aryans. It was Paul's hatred of Rome that sparked the creation of the Christian religion. As a result, Christianity is the enemy of Aryanism; it is the most anti-noble, "anti-Aryan" religion of all time:

> These regulations [of the Hindu Manu] are instructive enough: here we encounter for once *Aryan* humanity, quite pure, quite primordial—we learn that the concept of "pure blood" is the opposite of a harmless concept. On the other hand, it becomes clear in which people the hatred, the chandala hatred, against this "humaneness" has eternalized itself, where it has become religion, where it has become *genius*. Seen in this perspective, the Gospels represent a document of prime importance; even more, the Book of Enoch. Christianity, sprung from Jewish roots and comprehensible only as a growth on this soil, represents the counter-movement to any morality of breeding, of race, of privilege: it is the *anti-Aryan* religion par excellence. Christianity—the revaluation

> of all Aryan values, the victory of chandala values, the gospel preached to the poor and base, the general revolt of all the downtrodden, the wretched, the failures, the less favored, against "race": the undying chandala hatred as the *religion of love*. (VII.4, pp. 504-505)

What better cover for this religion of hatred—hatred of the noble, hatred of the Aryans—than to cast it as a "religion of love"? Paul: that master-hater and master-deceiver of all time.[6]

Into the 20th Century: National Socialism

All these ideas, then, were important precursors to the emergence of Adolf Hitler and his National Socialism, which first caught the public eye in 1920. For Hitler, Aryans were a major theme in many of his early speeches, and they were notably present in his *Mein Kampf*. His critics (Jews above all) were quick to distort things, decrying the Nazi conception of an Aryan "super-race" that would take over the world, slaughtering their way to total domination.

We all know the standard line: Hitler was allegedly obsessed with this super-breed of humans—which included Germans and most ethnicities of Northern Europe—throughout his alleged drive for world-domination. The 'master race' concept was closely linked, we are told, to his program of literal mass-murder of Jews, Slavs, and other "undesirables." Indeed, his alleged murder of some 6 million Jews, many in gas chambers, was seen as proof of his master-race ideology.[7] Furthermore, we are told that all of Hitler's top people subscribed to the same theory and actively worked on its behalf, which formed a cornerstone of the broader National Socialist worldview. Consequently, the entire concept of Aryanism is wrong, evil, and hateful. Most importantly, it still lingers today in the form of so-called "White supremacy" movements, White nationalism, and the dissident right more broadly. Therefore, it must be unconditionally opposed on all fronts.

The problem here, as usual, is that nearly all of this is wrong. The concept of a master-race (*Herrenrasse*) is nearly nonexistent in the actual writings of the leading NS personnel, Hitler included. If there was an "obsession," it was with the German people and German nationalism. Hitler was an ultra-nationalist, and this dictated most of what he did. Yes, he nat-

---

[6] For the full story, the reader is referred to Nietzsche's *Antichrist*. See also chapter 25 of the present book, "Christianity: The Great Jewish Hoax."

[7] For a recent elaboration on the Jewish death toll, see chapter 15, "The Holocaust of Six Million Jews—in World War One." Also of interest here is the book *The First Holocaust*, by Don Heddesheimer.

urally thought of the German people as the best and brightest among the nations of the world—and with good justification, given the vast cultural and scientific contributions of the Germanic people over the centuries. Yes, he felt that a nation that was unaffected by Jewish corruption would, in effect, lead the world by example. But this was not an intention for world domination or world rule—unlike, say, the United States of today, which strives, at the behest of the Jewish Lobby, to be a global hegemon via its trillion-dollar military and hundreds of foreign bases.

Furthermore, the "attack" on Jews and other minorities constituted a program of ethnic cleansing, not mass murder. Hitler and his staff wanted a Germany for the Germans, clear of other detrimental influences and conflicts that come with Jews and non-German ethnicities. All of Hitler's terminology in his speeches and writings indicates a need to forcibly remove Jews and others. Goebbels, too, in his vast private diaries, only and always spoke of removal and deportation, never—until the very end—of killing.[8] Obviously, amidst a major war, lots of Jews and other civilians did die, but none through a systematic process of industrial mass-killing.

If we proceed to cut through the nonsense, we will, first, set aside our obsession with a Nazi "master race" out to control the world. We will then bring to light, if we are diligent, a number of interesting facts on the truth about National Socialism and the Aryan ideal.

Rosenberg in his Own Words

Let me take a moment now to examine the thinking of the so-called "leading Nazi ideologue," Alfred Rosenberg. Four years Hitler's junior, Rosenberg was an early member of the NSDAP party, joining in early 1919, some eight months before Hitler himself. Rosenberg came to the Party with PhD in hand, marking him as one of the smartest and best-educated of all leading NS figures.

Throughout the 1920s, Rosenberg continued to support the emerging Party even as he continued his academic and publishing efforts. In 1930, he published his magnum opus, *The Myth of the 20th Century*—a stunning and far-reaching book, encompassing a vast range of knowledge.[9] He covers many aspects of what would come to be known as National Socialist ideology, and he touches in particular on the question of Aryanism and the blond, blue-eyed Aryan aesthetic. Consider the following passage from the initial chapter of the book, which examines this aesthetic as it relates to the culture of ancient Egypt:

---

[8] See my book *Goebbels on the Jews* (2019; Castle Hill).
[9] See the newly-edited and -translated version of this book, edited by myself (2021; Clemens & Blair).

> In predynastic Egypt, we find the Nordic boat with its swan neck and trefoil decor. But the rowers are the later-ruling Amorites, already recognized by [Archibald] Sayce as fair-skinned and blue-eyed. They once travelled North Africa as strictly homogeneous hunter-clans which gradually defeated the entire land. They then migrated somewhat further, across Syria and toward the future site of Babylon. The Berbers, among whom even today one finds light skins and blue eyes, do not go back to the Vandal invasions of the 5th century AD, but rather to the prehistoric Atlantic Nordic human wave. The Kabyle huntsmen, for example, are to no small degree still wholly Nordic—therefore, the blond Berbers in the region of Constantinople comprise 10% of the population; at Djebel Sheshor they are even more numerous. The ruling stratum of the ancient Egyptians reveals significantly finer features than the subject people. …
>
> Suddenly, around 2400 BC, reliefs of men with fair skin, reddish blond hair, and blue eyes begin to appear; these are the "blond Libyans" of whom Pausanias later reports. In the tomb paintings at Thebes, we find four races of Egypt represented: Asiatics, Negroids, Libyans, and Egyptians. The last are depicted with reddish pigmentation; the Libyans, on the other hand, are always shown bearded, with blue eyes and white skins. Pure Nordic types are shown on a grave of the Senye dynasty, in the woman on the pylon of Horemheb at Karnak, by the swan-boat people on the temple relief at Medinet Habu [in Egypt], and by the Tsakkarai who founded Phoenician sea travel. Light-skinned men with golden hair are shown on the tombs at Medinet Gurob. In the most recent excavations in 1927 in the mastabas at the pyramid of Cheops, the Princess and Queen Meresankh III (2633-2564 BC) were found depicted with blond hair. Queen Nitocris [c. 2180 BC], legendary and surrounded by myths, is likewise always said to have been a blonde. All these are racial memories of a prehistoric Nordic tradition in North Africa. (pp. 22-23)

There is a lot to unpack here, but if nothing else, one gets a feeling for the immense learning of the young Alfred Rosenberg, who was only in his late 30s when he wrote this. More to the point, he has much evidence that the divine northerners had a significant impact on southern culture as early as 3,000 BC. This, of course, is significantly older than the Homeric and pre-Socratic Greek texts that I cited in my prior essay. But it supports my main points: that waves of northerners pressed down into southern regions, successfully building culture and civilization in the process. Classical Greeks and imperial Romans were largely of Aryan stock. Consequently, the southern peoples would have been duly impressed by the appearance of the northerners, to the point that they cast their own heroes, royals, and gods in the Aryan image.

But what about the "master race"? Surely Rosenberg wrote extensively on that topic, did he not? Actually, no. *Myth* contains no explicit reference to the concept. He did write in an indirect fashion about human mastery, as in this passage: "As rugged masters and warriors, the Hellenic tribes supplanted the decaying civilization of the Levantine traders, and with the labor of the subjugated races, constructed an incomparable creative culture" (p. 29). In the second half of the book, he wrote:

> Today the German people begin to dream Eckhart's and Lagarde's dreams again. But many still lack the courage for this dream. Alien dream-visions still often hinder their spiritual effectiveness. For this reason, a modest attempt is undertaken here to lay down what, in the two preceding sections, was represented more analytically as our essence, as an image, insofar as this is permeated by the eternal Nordic-Germanic ideas… And where this must be outlined, it is done with the awareness that they could take a completely different appearance if new means of mastery over the Earth are found. (p. 273)

But this is clearly no program of racial domination by superhumans. Then we have a third indirect reference near the end of the book, where Rosenberg quotes a British military writer:

> The Englishman, Victor Germains, was therefore right when he declared: "The world-conquering Englishman who, glittering in his virtues and terrible in his passions, rough and brave simultaneously, raises his hand and…erects a world empire as a creative master people". (p. 409)

Perhaps surprisingly, it is the Brits who are the self-proclaimed "master people"—not the Germans.

At the end of the war, Rosenberg was captured and hauled before that mock-trial known as the Nuremberg Tribunal, where he testified extensively in his own defense. His personal attorney, Albert Thoma, queried him on certain key topics; Rosenberg gave thoroughly impressive and even heroic replies. One portion of the transcript is particularly relevant here:

DR. THOMA: Mr. President, National Socialism as a concept must be dissected into its constituent parts. ... Then I should like to ask the defendant how he will answer the charge that National Socialism preached a master-race.

ROSENBERG: I know that this problem is the main point of the indictment, and I realize that at present, in view of the number of terrible incidents, conclusions are automatically drawn about the past and the reason for the origin of the so-called racial science. I believe, however, that it is of decisive importance in judging this problem to know exactly what we were concerned with. I have never heard the word "master race" (*Herrenrasse*) as often as in this court room. To my knowledge, I did not mention or use it at all in my writings. I leafed through my *Writings and Speeches* again and did not find this word. I spoke only once of super-humans as mentioned by Homer, and I found a quotation from a British author, who in writing about the life of Lord Kitchener, said the Englishman who had conquered the world had proved himself as a creative superman (*Herrenmensch*). Then I found the word "master race" (*Herrenrasse*) in a writing of the American ethnologist, Madison Grant, and of the French ethnologist, Lapouge.

I would like to admit, however—and not only to admit, but to emphasize—that the word "superman" (*Herrenmensch*) came to my attention particularly during my activity as Minister in the East—and very unpleasantly—when used by a number of leaders of the administration in the East. Perhaps when we come to the question of the East, I may return to this subject in detail and state what position I took in regard to these utterances which came to my attention. In principle, however, I was convinced that ethnology was, after all, not an invention of the National Socialist movement, but a biological discovery, which was the conclusion of 400 years of European research. The laws of heredity discovered in the 1860s, and rediscovered several decades later, enable us to gain a deeper insight into history than many other earlier theories. Accordingly, race... [*President Lawrence interrupts, refusing to allow Rosenberg to finish his statement*][10]

[10] Cited from *Streicher, Rosenberg, and the Jews* (T. Dalton, ed.; 2020), p. 77. In the end, Rosenberg's defense failed. He was hanged on 1 October 1946.

Obviously, Rosenberg was attempting to save his own life; but nothing he said is evidently incorrect. As noted, his primary work includes no mention of the topic, as anyone can confirm. Of course, there was much discussion of race and racial issues, not only by Rosenberg but also by Hitler, Goebbels, and others; but this in no sense entails an endorsement of any master-race theory. In the end, the result seems clear: The concept of a world-dominating master race was not a central NS idea, but rather was mostly imposed upon them by their inquisitors.

Aryan Hitler

Consider, next, the views of Hitler and Goebbels. Let me start with the latter. As we know, Goebbels kept a highly detailed diary over nearly the whole of his adult life. It was recovered after the war, and ultimately published (in German). This massive documentation, covering 20 years, 29 volumes, and some 7,000 pages, details his intimate thoughts on every conceivable topic. When we scan the entire document for *Herrenrasse*, we find just two or three passing references—one of which (21 August 1938) refers, like Rosenberg, to the Britons; and another (26 December 1943) which quotes Roosevelt's stated desire to "liquidate the master race in Germany." Obviously Goebbels, at least, had no 'obsession' with the master-race concept.

In a similar vein, he had little preoccupation with the Aryan ideal. Only very few of Goebbels' diary entries even mention Aryans, and they are almost nonexistent in his speeches and published writings. Below are three of the most relevant passages in the entire diary, as brief as they are:

> The prophesy that the Führer made about [the Jews] for having brought on a new World War is beginning to come true in a most terrible manner. One must not be sentimental about these things. If we didn't fight the Jews, they would destroy us. It's a life-and-death struggle between the Aryan race and the Jewish bacillus. No other government and no other regime would have the strength to solve this question in general. (27 Mar 1942)

> Eden gave a speech in the House of Commons on the Jewish problem and answered planted questions. Rothschild, the "venerable MP," as the English press calls him, took the floor and delivered a tear-jerker bemoaning the fate of the Polish Jews. At the end of the session, the Commons observed a minute of silence; all members of Parliament rose from their seats as a silent tribute to Jewry. That was quite

> appropriate for the British House of Commons. Parliament is really a sort of Jewish exchange. The English, anyway, are the Jews among the Aryans. (19 Dec 1942)
>
> So we have to realize that, in this conflict between Aryan humanity and the Jewish race, we still have to fight very hard battles because Jewry has managed, consciously or unconsciously, to bring great tribes of the Aryan race into their service. … There is therefore also no hope of returning the Jews to the circle of civilized humanity through an extraordinary punishment. They will remain forever Jews, just as we are forever members of Aryan humanity. … On the basis of their very materialistic attitude, the English act similar to the Jews. They are the Aryans that have most acquired Jewish traits. (13 May 1943)[11]

Out of literally thousands of daily entries, these few are all but inconsequential. One could surmise that Goebbels, being short, club-footed, brown-hair, and brown-eyed, had little personal equity in the Aryan ideal.

And then, what about *the man himself?* Hitler indeed had much to say on the Aryans, but nothing on any 'master race'.[12] The same with the blue-eyed blond aesthetic, which almost passes without mention. This is notable, given that he himself had striking blue eyes. In an early diary entry, Goebbels recounts one of his first personal meetings with Hitler:

> We're going by car to see Hitler. He's just eating. He already jumps up and stands in front of us. Shakes my hand. Like an old friend. And these big, blue eyes. Like stars. He's pleased to see me. I am very happy. … Then he speaks here for another half an hour. With wit, irony, humor, sarcasm, with seriousness, with glow, with passion. This man has everything to be king. (6 Nov 1925)

In his important biography, historian John Toland quotes a number of people attesting to the same. Toland writes that, according to Josef Keplinger,

---

[11] For the full diaries entries as they relate to the Jewish Question, see *Goebbels on the Jews* (T. Dalton, ed; 2019).

[12] Even incidental references are rare. In all of *Mein Kampf*, for example, there are just a handful of appearances of variations on the term. For example: "It required the entire bottomless falsehood of the Jews…to lay blame for the collapse [of Germany] precisely on the man [Ludendorff] who alone had shown a superhuman will (*übermenschlicher Willens*) and energy…" Obviously, this is irrelevant to any Nietzschean *Übermensch*, let alone any 'master race.'

"[Hitler's] own eyes...were blue" (p. 16). A professor, von Müller, is quoted as speaking of Hitler's "remarkable large light blue eyes" (p. 89). Early enthusiast Kurt Lüdecke comments on his "intense, steel-blue eyes" (p. 123). And close personal friend Helene Hanfstaengl wrote in her memoirs of Hitler's "very blue eyes" (p. 142).[13] Despite this virtue, Hitler apparently placed little emphasis on eye color.

Regarding hair, again, almost nothing of substance on the blond ideal. In all of *Mein Kampf*, there is only a single mention; in volume two, Hitler writes against Jewish racial contamination of the noble German race. He elaborates:

> Look at the ravages that our people are suffering daily as a result of Jewish bastardization, and consider that this blood poisoning can only be eliminated from the national body after centuries, if ever. Think further of how the process of racial disintegration is debasing and often even destroying the fundamental Aryan values of our German people, such that our national cultural creativeness is regressing and we run the risk, at least in our large cities, of sinking to the present level of southern Italy. This pestilential contamination of the blood, blindly ignored by hundreds of thousands of our people, is being systematically conducted by the Jew today. These black parasites of our nation systematically corrupt our innocent blond girls and thus destroy something irreplaceable in this world. (vol 2, sec 10.6, p. 194)

But this is a mere passing reference to "blond girls," and it is not repeated. Even in his major speeches attacking the Jews, Hitler never refers to the blond-haired, blue-eyed aesthetic. Evidently for Hitler, as for Goebbels, the physical features were simply not that important.

The 'Aryan,' though, makes many appearances in Hitler's work, as in the above passage. In *Mein Kampf*, Aryans are a dominant theme in the highly-important chapter 11 of volume one ("Nation and Race"), where Hitler expounds on racial mixing, race and culture, idealism, and especially the contrast with the anti-Aryan, the Jew. The following passages are representative:

> Every manifestation of human culture, every product of art, science, and technical skill that we see today, are almost exclusively the creative product of the Aryan. This very fact

[13] *Adolf Hitler* (Doubleday, 1976), volume one. Incidentally, Toland also remarks in passing on Hermann Göring's "luminous blue eyes" (p. 129).

> fully justifies the conclusion that it was the Aryan alone who founded a superior type of humanity; therefore he represents the archetype of what we understand by the term 'man.' He is the Prometheus of mankind …
>
> If we divide mankind into three groups—founders of culture, bearers of culture, and destroyers of culture—the Aryan alone can be considered as representing the first group. It was he who erected the foundation and walls of every great structure in human culture. Only the shape and color of such structures can be attributed to the characteristics of the various peoples. The Aryan furnished the great building stones and plans for the edifices of all human progress; only the execution of these plans can be attributed to the qualities of each individual race. … [T]he real foundations are the enormous scientific and technical achievements of Europe and America; that is, of Aryan peoples. ….
>
> If, from today onwards, the Aryan influence on Japan ceased—if Europe and America collapsed—then Japan's present progress in science and technology might still last for a short while. But within a few decades, the inspiration would dry up, native Japanese character would flourish, and present civilization would become fossilized and fall back into the sleep from which it was aroused seven decades ago by Aryan culture. Therefore, just as present Japanese development is due to Aryan influence, so in the distant past, foreign influence and spirit awakened Japanese culture of that day. …
>
> This short sketch of the development of the culture-bearing nations gives a picture of the development and activity—and the decline—of those who are the true culture-founders on this Earth, the Aryans themselves. (vol one, sec 11.4, pp. 294-296)

The words are compelling, forceful, and clear. Notable is his reference to the Japanese as being an Aryan people; clearly he draws a larger circle than simply the White, blue-eyed blonds of northern Europe. Hitler adopts the broader, academic notion of the term—Aryans as culture-creating and noble northerners.

Our Jewish Masters

And we can hardly leave the topic of master-race theory without mentioning the oldest and most consequential of these: the Jewish master race.

Everything is documented in the Old Testament, for all to see: a Jewish god, Jehovah, the "creator of the universe," who selects, among all living beings in the cosmos, a small tribe of belligerent semi-nomads as his favored. "For you are a people holy to the Lord your God. The Lord your God has chosen you to be a people for his own possession, out of all the peoples that are on the face of the earth" (Deut 7:6).

As a consequence, the Old Testament is replete with self-important references to the claimed Jewish mastery over others. The Book of Exodus states, "we are distinct…from all other people that are upon the face of the earth" (33:16). Similarly, the Hebrew tribe is "a people dwelling alone, and not reckoning itself among the nations" (Num 23:9). In Deuteronomy (15:6), Moses tells the Jews "you shall rule over many nations"; "they shall be afraid of you" (28:10). Then we have Genesis: "Let peoples serve you, and nations bow down to you" (27:29); and Deuteronomy, where God promises Jews "houses full of all good things, which [they] did not fill, and cisterns hewn out, which [they] did not hew, and vineyards and olive trees, which [they] did not plant" (6:11). Outside the Pentateuch, we can read in Isaiah: "Foreigners shall build up your walls, and their kings shall minister to you…that men may bring you the wealth of the nations" (60:10-11); or again, "aliens shall stand and feed your flocks, foreigners shall be your plowmen and vinedressers…you shall eat the wealth of nations" (61:5-6). If we are to criticize the concept of a master race, we can start with the Jews; no need to dwell on the Nazis.

Closing Thoughts

The moral here is that European Whites have much to be proud of. All White Europeans have a more or less substantial genetic component of northern, Scandinavian, Aryan 'blood' (as they used to say), and this accounts for their broadly good looks, robust health, intelligence, morality, and ability to create civilization. Euro-Aryans, as we might call ourselves, are distinguished from all other races and ethnicities on the planet—especially from those white-appearing people of the Middle East or Latin America, who embody a different genetic heritage and thus a different moral, intellectual, and cultural outlook. We are different from Indo-Aryans, East Asian Aryans, and any others who have benefited from an admixture of northern genes.

This has two consequences for White Europeans. First, it explains why our physical standard of beauty—including light skin, blond hair, and blue eyes—is nearly a universal human ideal. Second, it ensures that peoples lacking in such qualities will be jealous, envious, and even hostile. In the most extreme case of the Jews, it yields a kind of burning hatred and resentment, and a desire to see us "brought down" to their level, or less.

Jews know that, ultimately, it is only White Euro-Aryans who pose a real threat to their domination of much of the globe. Ultimately, only we stand in their way.

Thus, in the end, all this comes down to a basic conflict: the future of Whites versus the dominance of the global Jewish Lobby. If it was true back in 2003 that, via the American superpower, that "Jews rule the world by proxy," as Mahathir Mohamad said,[14] then it is all the truer today, nearly two decades later. American Jews alone own or control some $75 trillion in assets—an astounding fact. Should the reader doubt this, consider that just the five richest Jews—Larry Ellison, Larry Page, Sergey Brin, Steve Ballmer, and Michael Bloomberg—collectively own about $425 billion. That's $425 billion dollars, for *just five individuals*; we can thus imagine the combined financial might of 6 million American Jews. Add to this the wealth of some 9 million other Jews around the world, and we get an idea of the situation.[15]

Even so, Whites globally are not without resources. There are around 800 million Whites in the world today, and their combined wealth and power exceed that of the Jews by a large margin. The problem is that our power is scattered and diffused, whereas theirs is focused and directed. Most Whites are ignorant of the Jewish Question and of the coordinated attack on their well-being. Many Whites are vaguely aware, in some very imprecise way, of "issues" with Jews, but they are too lazy or too distracted to bother investigating the matter. Being generally naïve and trusting—by nature—Whites have a very hard time believing that there is a hostile minority out there that is working collectively to undermine their very future. We have a huge educational task before us.

But as the old saying goes, it will probably have to get a lot worse before it gets better. And we can rest assured, it will get worse. As "America" continues to disintegrate, pockets of opportunity will open up.[16] The same holds with the "European Union," which is declining as we speak. The only path forward is for sub-groups of Whites in North America and Europe to break away completely from their Jewish overlords and establish truly independent political and financial structures that are completely free of Jews and Jewish influence. Only then will Whites be free from the constant cloud of Jewish obfuscation. When the fog clears, and when Whites realize the price that they have paid, the response will be ferocious.

As I have argued here and in the first essay of this book, Whites are a beautiful, noble, intelligent, and creative race. It is no boast to acknowledge that we are "children of the gods," that we are a "sacred race." This is

---

[14] "Malaysian Leader: 'Jews Rule World by Proxy'" (Fox News, 13 Jan 2015).

[15] See chapter 17, "A Brief Look at Jewish Wealth."

[16] See chapter 34, "America Must Die—So That the People Can Live."

the message from antiquity. In the past few centuries, though, we have failed to live up to that legacy. We have been, frankly, an embarrassment to the gods. We have allowed our better nature to be used against us by unscrupulous, malicious, corrupt minorities—Jews above all. The rare exceptions, like National Socialist Germany, have shown what can be accomplished when Whites are free from the Jewish yoke. The potential is breathtaking; we can scarcely imagine the bright future before us, should Whites regain true political autonomy.

The task is great, the climb is steep. But we are capable of meeting the severest of challenges. The looming crises will present many opportunities—for independence, for retribution, and for justice. Be prepared; a better future is coming.

— 3 —
NIETZSCHE ON THE JEWS

Philosophers, as a rule, are a rather low-key bunch. They generally discuss mundane, technical, or utterly abstract topics that cause little concern among society at large. Of course, there were exceptions, primarily during the Renaissance when the early humanists incurred the wrath of the Church—think of Bruno or Spinoza; this required some to publish their works either pseudonymously or posthumously. And Marx and Engels have certainly garnered their fair share of enmity. But by and large, philosophers throughout the ages have raised few serious hackles.

A major exception is the case of Friedrich Nietzsche, certainly one of the most controversial philosophers in history. As the epitome of non-political-correctness, Nietzsche clearly did not give a damn about whom he might offend. He was on a mission to uncover the fundamental flaws in Western society, to expose hypocrisy and moral corruption, and to undermine every aspect of degenerate modern society. Only by getting to the root of the problem, he thought, could we find our way forward—a path to the greatness that is human destiny.

Of Masters and Slaves

The sad state of modern life, he said, is a direct consequence of the overturning of classical values that occurred in the early post-Christian world. These classic values—originating in ancient Greece and embraced by the Romans—emphasized strength, robustness, nobility, self-determination, and personal excellence. These life-affirming values, the 'master' or 'aristocratic' values, were the foundation upon which the great civilizations of Athens and Rome were built.

One tangible manifestation of the Greek aristocratic values was the Roman Empire. An expansive and dominating institution, it reached Palestine by the year 60 BC, and held that territory for over five hundred years, until the fall of the Western Empire in 476 (though the Eastern, or Byzantine, Empire survived much longer). Roman incursion was welcomed by many commoners, though not of course by the local ruling authorities—which, in Judea, were the Jews. Having been conquered and driven out of power, the Jewish tribes naturally developed a deep and abiding hatred of the Romans and of all things European.

Violent resistance to Rome was unlikely to succeed, and so some Jews turned to more sophisticated and subtle forms of resistance. One such group centered around the Jew Paul of Tarsus (later, "St. Paul"), who evidently hit upon the plan of using a recently-martyred rabbi named Jesus as the central figure in a new pro-Jewish, anti-Roman religious outlook that could be promulgated among the pagan masses.[1]

As part of his new 'Christian' worldview, Paul, says Nietzsche, sought to counter and oppose the powerful Roman/Greek master value system with their very opposite. In place of a system based on life-affirmation, excellence, strength, and nobility, Paul substituted a new value system—one based on self-pity, oppression, revenge, and an obsession with freedom. Paul's Christians—through the figure of Jesus—preferred to emphasize the value of the down-trodden ("blessed are the meek"), faith in God to bring justice ("the meek shall inherit the earth"), salvation in the afterlife, and a fixation on love as a means for ameliorating suffering. Arising as it did out of the quasi-slavery imposed by the Romans, Nietzsche deemed this collective Judeo-Christian response a 'slave' or (Judaic) 'priestly' morality.

When the Western Empire, based in Rome, collapsed in the 5th century AD, the master morality collapsed with it. As the only real competitor, slave morality rose to take its place as the dominant European ethical system. And there it has remained for nearly two thousand years. In this sense, Nietzsche says, the slave has defeated the master, and become the new master.

But the actual outcome has been far from positive. Quite the contrary: it has been an absolute disaster for humanity. When combined with booming populations and advancing technology, there now exists a distinctly modern form of the priestly mindset, one based on subservience, conformity, 'equality,' pity, guilt, suffering, revenge, and self-hatred: *the herd morality*. One could scarcely devise a lower conception of man.

Which brings us to the question of the Jews. Nietzsche's position on the Jews is complex, ambiguous, but ultimately negative. On the one hand, they are the embodiment and product of the despised slave morality. Jews owe their very success to the promotion and exploitation of this way of thinking. On the other hand, they did succeed: they 'defeated' Rome, and thus were able to successfully pull off that inversion of values in which the slave eclipsed the master. Partly for this very reason they have been able to sustain themselves as a distinct ethnicity through the millennia. They are hardened survivors; they are (relatively) pure; they know how to succeed.

We see this ambivalent attitude in an early work, *Human, All Too Human* (1878). In a brief discussion of "the problem of the Jews," Nietzsche acknowledges their suffering: "I would like to know how much one must excuse in the overall accounting of a people which, not without guilt

---

[1] For more on this topic, see the second essay in the present volume, "Nietzsche and the Origins of Christianity."

on all our parts, has had the most sorrowful history of all peoples" (sec. 475). In a brief moment of praise—and in noted contrast to later writings—he hails the contributions of the Jews; they are the ones "to whom we owe the noblest human being (Christ), the purest philosopher (Spinoza), the mightiest book, and the most effective moral code in the world." This would be virtually his last unconditional praise for Jesus and the Bible.

The same passage, however, includes this observation: "Every nation, every man has disagreeable, even dangerous characteristics; it is cruel to demand that the Jew should be an exception." And there is no doubt that he is disagreeable: "the youthful Jew of the stock exchange is the most repugnant invention of the whole human race."

Nietzsche's next book, *Daybreak* (1881), offers provisional commendation for the Jews based on their long history of exclusion, isolation, and persecution. "As a consequence of this [history], the psychological and spiritual resources of the Jews today are extraordinary" (sec. 205). They are capable of the "coldest self-possession, ... the subtlest outwitting and exploitation of chance and misfortune." Mental acuity is of prime importance: "They are so sure in their intellectual suppleness and shrewdness that they never, even in the worst straits, need to earn their bread by physical labor." Still, "their souls have never known chivalrous noble sentiments."

But they do have a plan for Europe:

> [S]ince they are unavoidably going to ally themselves with the best aristocracy of Europe more and more with every year that passes, they will soon have created for themselves a goodly inheritance of spiritual and bodily demeanor: so that a century hence, they will appear sufficiently noble not to make those they dominate ashamed to have them as masters. And that is what matters! ... Europe may fall into their hands like a ripe fruit, if they would only just extend them.

In the end, not only Europe but America fell into their hands "like a ripe fruit."

The one other relevant passage in *Daybreak*, from section 377, introduces the important concept of Jewish hatred: "It is where our deficiencies lie that we indulge in our enthusiasms. The command 'love your enemies!' had to be invented by the Jews, the best haters there have ever been..." The (Judeo-) Christian commandment of love, Nietzsche thought, grew directly from the hatred of the enslaved Jews, as a kind of mask or cover. And even more than this—as a kind of deliberate deception. A 'bad hater' wears his anger on his sleeve, for all to see. A 'good hater' hides it inside. But the 'best' plots revenge using the very opposite—an image of divine love—as cover. "Even if you think of us as enemies," the Jews might say, "love us anyway. This is God's command." This whole idea, only hinted at here, would lie dormant for some six years; it reemerges strongly in his 1887 masterpiece *On the Genealogy of Morals*.

After *Daybreak* there was a long five-year stretch in which Nietzsche did not address the Jewish problem in any substantial way. *The Gay Science* (parts 1–4) focused instead on the nature of science, on power, and on the 'death of God.' His other book of this period, *Thus Spoke Zarathustra*, contained no reference to it.

But by 1886, with the release of *Beyond Good and Evil*, he had returned to the topic. He praises the flamboyance of the Old Testament: "In the Jewish 'Old Testament,' the book of divine justice, there are human beings, things, and speeches in so grand a style that Greek and Indian literature have nothing to compare with it" (sec. 52). (In fact, it was precisely this style that he mimicked so effectively in his *Zarathustra*.) Europeans are furthermore indebted to the Jews for their fantabulist conception of ethics: "What Europe owes to the Jews? Many things, good and bad, and above all one thing that is of the best and of the worst: the grand style in morality, the terribleness and majesty of infinite demands, infinite meanings" (sec. 250).

In part from this debt, and in part from their example as a tough, coherent, enduring race, the Jews should be allowed a role in Europe, Nietzsche thought. In section 251 he decries the "anti-Jewish stupidity" [*antijüdische Dummheit*] of the times. "I have not met a German yet who was well disposed toward the Jews." The common feeling — "that Germany has amply enough Jews" — was clearly holding sway. But the Jews need to be given due consideration, for their influence is not insignificant:

> A thinker who has the development of Europe on his conscience will…take into account the Jews as well as the Russians as the provisionally surest and most probable factors in the great play and fight of forces. … That the Jews, if they wanted it…could even now have preponderance, indeed quite literally mastery over Europe, that is certain; that they are not working and planning for that is equally certain.[2]

I would remind the reader at this point of the considerable influence that Jews in fact had in Germany in the late 19th and early 20th centuries. Their population hovered around one percent of the total during this time, but

---

[2] Nietzsche seems to have underestimated the Hebrews here. There were numerous signs, as early as 1875, that Jews had literal mastery over Europe. For several views on this, see *Classic Essays on the Jewish Question* (T. Dalton, ed.; 2022).

they were significantly overrepresented in a number of important fields. Sarah Gordon provides some relevant statistics:

> They were overrepresented in business, commerce, and public and private service... These characteristics were already evident in the Middle Ages and appeared in the census data as early as 1843. ... Jews were also influential in joint-stock corporations, the stock market, the insurance industry, and legal and economic consulting firms. Before the First World War, for example, Jews occupied 13 percent of the directorships of joint-stock corporations and 24 percent of the supervisory positions within these corporations. ...
>
> [D]uring 1904 they comprised 27 percent of all lawyers, 10 percent of all apprenticed lawyers, 5 percent of court clerks, 4 percent of magistrates, and up to 30 percent of all higher ranks of the judiciary. ... Jews were [also] overrepresented among university professors and students between 1870 and 1933. For example, in 1909-1910...almost 12 percent of instructors at German universities were Jewish... [I]n 1905-1906 Jewish students comprised 25 percent of the law and medical students... The percentage of Jewish doctors was also quite high, especially in large cities, where they sometimes were a majority. ... [I]n Berlin around 1890, 25 percent of all children attending grammar school were Jewish...[3]

Jewish influence was thus no idle matter.

"Meanwhile," Nietzsche continues, "[the Jews] want and wish rather...to be absorbed and assimilated by Europe...; and this bent and impulse...should be noted well and accommodated: to that end, it might be useful and fair to expel the anti-Semitic screamers from the country." Again, he sees the Jews as useful examples of racial toughness and coherence. And more importantly, they hold an important lesson in the creation of new value systems as a means of overcoming adversity, and exerting power. The typical German anti-Semite does not understand this; he just hates all Jews and wants to get rid of them. For Nietzsche, they are detestable but also useful and instructive. A truly strong German nation could easily accommodate a percent or two of Jews.

Nietzsche is emphatic that the value of the Jews and Jewish morality is purely educational; it is not to be emulated. He elaborates in section 195:

---

[3] *Hitler, Germans, and the Jewish Question* (1984), pp. 10-14.

> The Jews have brought off that miraculous feat of an inversion of values, thanks to which life on earth has acquired a novel and dangerous attraction for a couple of millennia. … Their prophets…were the first to use the word 'world' as a term of contempt. This inversion of values…constitutes the significance of the Jewish people: they mark the beginning of the slave rebellion in morals.

The 'inversion'—the defeat of the classic Greek/Roman values—was a remarkable accomplishment, and if we are now to move beyond the priestly Jewish slave values, we will need to perform yet another such act. Only by thoroughly understanding the previous inversion can we hope to accomplish the next.

The Anti-Semitic Turn

The year after *Beyond Good and Evil* was an exceptionally busy and productive one. In addition to keeping continuous notebook entries—many of which would later become part of *The Will to Power*—Nietzsche wrote an important fifth chapter for his earlier book *The Gay Science*, and published one of his greatest works, *On the Genealogy of Morals*.

Part 5 of *Gay Science* includes two relevant entries. First is a laudatory passage on the Jewish love of logic and analysis. "All of [the Jewish scholars] have a high regard for logic, that is, for compelling agreement by force of reasons… For nothing is more democratic than logic; it is no respecter of persons and makes no distinction between crooked and straight noses" (sec. 348). This has been a real benefit to all: "Europe owes the Jews no small thanks for making people think more logically and for establishing cleaner intellectual habits…"

As to their cultural influence, their presence in stage, theater, and press, Nietzsche offers the following critical thoughts:

> As for the Jews, the people who possess the art of adaptability par excellence, [my line of argument] suggests immediately that one might see them virtually as a world-historical arrangement for the production of actors, a veritable breeding ground for actors. And it really is time to ask: What good actor today is not — a Jew? The Jew as a born *Litterat* ['man of letters'], as the true master of the European press, also exercises his power by virtue of his theatrical gifts; for the man of letters is essentially an actor: he plays the 'expert,' the 'specialist.' (sec. 361)

Actors, of course, are professional deceivers; they make us think they are someone other than who they are. In a sense, actors are professional liars. Thus, if the Jew is a born actor, this is clearly a moral condemnation.

In *Genealogy*, Nietzsche begins to write in more overtly racial tones, speaking of the "blond Aryan" as the "master race," or the "conqueror race." On one occasion he again dismisses those who do not see instructive value in the Jews: "I also do not like these latest speculators in idealism, the anti-Semites, who today roll their eyes in a Christian-Aryan-bourgeois manner and exhaust one's patience by trying to rouse up all the horned-beast elements in people…" (III, sec. 26). But on the other hand, the Jews and their morality come in for severe criticism—not because of their ability to succeed, but because of what they inherently are:

> You will have already guessed how easily the priestly [i.e. Jewish] way of evaluating can split from the knightly-aristocratic, and then continue to develop into its opposite. … The knightly-aristocratic judgments of value have as their basic assumption a powerful physicality, a blooming, rich, even overflowing health, together with those things required to maintain these qualities—war, adventure, hunting, dancing, war games, and, in general, everything which involves strong, free, happy action. The priestly method of evaluating has, as we saw, other preconditions… As is well known, priests are the most evil of enemies—but why? Because they are the most powerless. From their powerlessness, their hate grows among them into something huge and terrifying, to the most spiritual and most poisonous manifestations. The truly great haters in world history have always been priests…

And we know who the true world-class haters in history are:

> Let us briefly consider the greatest example. Everything on earth which has been done against "the noble," "the powerful," "the masters," "the rulers" is not worth mentioning in comparison with what the Jews have done against them: the Jews, that priestly people, who knew how to get final satisfaction from their enemies and conquerors through a radical transformation of their values, that is, through an act of the most spiritual revenge. This was appropriate only to a priestly people with the most deeply repressed priestly desire for revenge. In opposition to the aristocratic value equations (good = noble = powerful = beautiful = fortunate = loved by god), the Jews, with an awe-inspiring consistency, dared to

> reverse things and to hang on to that with the teeth of the most profound hatred (the hatred of the powerless), that is, to "only those who suffer are good; the poor, the powerless, the low are the only good people; the suffering, those in need, the sick, the ugly are also the only pious people; only they are blessed by God; for them alone there is salvation.—By contrast, you privileged and powerful people, you are for all eternity the evil, the cruel, the lecherous, the insatiable, the godless; you will also be the unblessed, the cursed, and the damned for all eternity!"
>
> In connection with that huge and immeasurably disastrous initiative which the Jews launched with this most fundamental of all declarations of war, I recall the sentence I wrote at another time—namely, that with the Jews the slave revolt in morality begins... (I, sec. 7)

The means by which this revolt was carried out was none other than Christianity. Christian 'love,' according to Nietzsche, is little more than the "triumphant crown" of the Jewish tree of hatred. This love acted "in pursuit of the goals of that hatred—victory, spoil, and seduction—by the same impulse that drove the roots of that hatred deeper and deeper...into all that was profound and evil" (sec. 7). "What is certain," he adds, is that under the sign of Christianity, "Israel, with its vengefulness and revaluation of all values, has hitherto triumphed again and again over all other ideals, over all nobler ideals".[4]

After some two thousand years, this process continues, slowly but surely:

> The 'redemption' of the human race [from the classical master values] is going forward; everything is visibly becoming Judaized, Christianized, mob-ized (what do the words matter!). The progress of this poison through the entire body of mankind seems irresistible, its pace and tempo may from now on even grow slower, subtler, less audible, more cautious—there is plenty of time. (sec. 9)

Until we grasp this poisoning of modern man, we have no hope of liberating ourselves and attaining our higher destiny.

The many notebook entries that make up *The Will to Power* are difficult to interpret, both because the writings are a scattershot of ideas and observations, and also because these were never intended by Nietzsche to

[4] Again, this topic is much more fully elaborated in chapter two.

be published. They were a kind of intellectual laboratory where he worked through his various thoughts and theories. A small portion of the notes appeared in book form only after his death, at the behest of his sister. Still, we find a number of passages that are consistent with his published views, particularly on the subject at hand.

As might be expected, he writes in both laudatory and critical language. In section 175 (dating to 1888) we read:

> The reality upon which Christianity could be raised was the little Jewish family of the Diaspora, with its warmth and affection, with its readiness to help and sustain one another… To have recognized in this a form of power, to have recognized that this blissful condition was communicable, seductive, infectious to pagans also—that was [St.] Paul's genius.

Nietzsche is sympathetic to the few remaining 'noble-valued' Germans, and he understands their "present instinctive aversion to Jews: it is the hatred of the free and self-respecting orders for those who are pushing, and who combine timid and awkward gestures with an absurd opinion of their [own] worth" (sec. 186; 1887). Later he elaborates on this "Jewish instinct of the 'chosen'," in which the Jews "claim all the virtues for themselves without further ado, and count the rest of the world their opposites; a profound sign of a vulgar soul" (sec. 197; 1887). And if one thing is certain, it is that the Jews are, in some sense, deeply untrustworthy:

> People of the basest origin, in part rabble, outcasts not only from good but also from respectable society, raised away from even the smell of culture, without discipline, without knowledge, without the remotest suspicion that there is such a thing as conscience in spiritual matters; simply—Jews: with an instinctive ability to create an advantage, a means of seduction out of every superstitious supposition… *When Jews step forward as innocence itself, then the danger is great.* (sec. 199; 1887)

Rome Versus Judea

Nietzsche's overall view on Judaism and its Christian offshoot is nicely summarized in this passage from *Genealogy*:

> Let's bring this to a conclusion. The two opposing values "good and bad," "good and evil" have fought a fearful battle on earth for thousands of years. … The symbol of this battle,

> written in a script which has remained legible through all human history up to the present, is called "Rome against Judea, Judea against Rome." To this point there has been no greater event than this war, this posing of a question, this contradiction between deadly enemies. Rome felt that the Jew was like something contrary to nature itself, its monstrous polar opposite, as it were. In Rome, the Jew was considered "guilty of hatred against the entire human race." And that view was *correct*, to the extent that we are right to link the health and the future of the human race to the unconditional rule of aristocratic values, the Roman values.
>
> By contrast, how did the Jews feel about Rome? We can guess that from a thousand signs, but it is sufficient to treat ourselves again to the Apocalypse of St. John, that wildest of all written outbursts which vengeance has on its conscience…
>
> The Romans were indeed strong and noble men, stronger and nobler than any people who had lived on earth up until then or even than any people who had ever been dreamed up. Everything they left as remains, every inscription, is delightful, provided that we can guess what is doing the writing there. By contrast, the Jews were par excellence that priestly people of ressentiment, who possessed an unparalleled genius for popular morality…

The passage closes with a stunning conclusion:

> Which of them has proved victorious for the time being, Rome or Judea? Surely there's not the slightest doubt. Just think of who it is that people bow down to today in Rome itself, as the personification of all the highest values—and not only in Rome, but in almost half the earth, all the places where people have become merely tame or want to become tame—in front of three Jews, as we know, and one Jewess (in front of Jesus of Nazareth, the fisherman Peter, the carpet maker Paul, and the mother of the first-mentioned Jesus, named Mary). This is very remarkable: without doubt Rome has been conquered. (I, 16)

Judea thus "defeated"—or rather, outlived—Rome, establishing its own global headquarters for Judeo-Christianity in the Vatican; that is, in Rome itself. For those who may doubt that Christianity is truly Judaic at heart, Nietzsche asks us to consider the simple fact that all Christians everywhere worship not only the Jewish God, Jehovah, but four Jewish individuals:

Jesus, Mary, Paul, and Peter. Even Jews don't worship other Jews! Thus, in a sense, *Christians are more Jewish than the Jews themselves.* As Nietzsche writes elsewhere:

> In Christianity, all of Judaism, a several-century-old Jewish preparatory training and technique of the most serious kind, attains its ultimate mastery as the art of lying in a holy manner. The Christian, the ultima ratio of the lie, is the Jew once more—even three times a Jew. (*Antichrist*, sec. 44)

The Christian is the completion and culmination of the Paul's great Jewish lie. The Christian falls for the lie—hook, line, and sinker—and becomes, in the process, totally Judaized—a triple-Jew.[5]

Conclusion

I close with a final passage from one of Nietzsche's last works, *The Anti-Christ* (1888). As expected, religious themes dominate this book, and of particular interest are his comments on the origin of Christianity from its Jewish foundation. One can do little better than let Nietzsche speak for himself:

> The Jews are the most remarkable nation of world history because, faced with the question of being or not being, they preferred…being at any price: the price they had to pay was the radical falsification of all nature, all naturalness, all reality, the entire inner world as well as the outer. … Considered psychologically, the Jewish nation is a nation of the toughest vital energy which…took the side of all décadence instincts—not as being dominated by them but because it divined in them a power by means of which one can prevail against 'the world.' The Jews are the counterparts of décadents: they have been compelled to act as décadents to the point of illusion…. [T]his kind of man has a life-interest in making mankind sick, and in inverting the concepts of 'good' and 'evil,' 'true' and 'false' in a mortally dangerous and world-maligning sense. (sec. 24)

In order to survive as a people, Jews found it necessary to deceive both themselves and (via Christianity) others about the reality of the natural

[5] The fact that some Christians have been, and still are, anti-Jewish is no refutation of Nietzsche. Jews have always squabbled amongst themselves; anti-Jewish Jews ('self-hating Jews') are nothing unusual.

world. The Judeo-Christian worldview is grounded on a mythical creation story by a mythical god and his mythical return to Earth in human form. In viewing all of humanity as their enemy, they have always felt compelled to deceive, humiliate, degrade, and sicken others—morally, physically, and spiritually. Via Christianity, everything good and natural is detested, and the strong and noble type of man becomes evil. To win out in their perceived 'battle' with the rest of the human race, the Jews poisoned the very future of humanity itself.

I trust it is clear that Nietzsche's complex analysis of Judaism allows for multiple interpretations. Selective use of individual sentences or fragments can paint him either as a philo- or anti-Semite, and both have been done. But by examining his writings in detail we gain a reasonably coherent understanding of his position—of a strong dislike of Jews and a true hatred for the morality that Judaism (and Christianity) have brought, but also a qualified admiration for Jewish resiliency and 'success.' The bottom line, however, is clear: Judaism is something that must be overcome.

It is interesting to speculate on what Nietzsche would have thought of events of the 20th century. Had he not died of an indeterminate neurological disorder in 1900, he might well have lived to witness the early rise of Hitler and Nazism. (He would have been 89 in 1933 when Hitler took power.) He would likely have predicted the malevolent, global Jewish alignment against Hitler, a man who simply wanted a nation free of Jews. Like the Romans, Hitler defeated the local Jewish power structure; like Rome, he thus became the personification of evil for the Jews. Like Rome before it, Germany became "the evil enemy"—when, in reality, both were sources of power and greatness. The "good" became "evil," and via this inversion, the Jews rallied others to fight to the death. In both cases, the good was defeated and the Jews profited immensely.

Had Nietzsche miraculously lived to see the emergence of the Holocaust industry, AIPAC, and Jewish influence on American media and government, he surely would have felt vindicated. Through Hollywood, alcohol, illegal drugs, human trafficking, pornography, and overall cultural degradation, it is clear, as Nietzsche said, that Jews "have a life-interest in making mankind sick." The Jewish danger to a prosperous, healthy, and noble humanity can scarcely be overestimated.

Nietzsche's analysis of the Jewish problem is powerful, insightful, and utterly unique. It is of the sort that could never be conducted today by any mainstream philosopher. More, he has provided us with a timeless analysis of what is, arguably, the greatest problem facing humanity today: the Jewish Question. Let us be thankful that he lived and wrote in a time when such truly free thought was still possible.

— 4 —
Nietzsche and the Origins of Christianity

Over the course of two thousand years, Christianity has grown from nothing to the largest religion on the planet. Some 2.1 billion people now consider themselves Christian, about one third of all of humanity. It significantly outnumbers Islam, in second place with 1.5 billion members.[1] America is among the most religious of all industrialized nations; about 75 percent are Christians, and most of these are regular church-goers.

And yet few people, even Christians themselves, understand the origin of this most influential religion. In one sense, of course, we will never truly understand exactly what events transpired two millennia ago, in that land of shepherds, nomads, and dusty villages of the near Middle East. Archeology tells us some things, ancient documents others. But these give us only an outline of the facts of that place and time. If we wish to comprehend early Christianity and its implications for today, many gaps must be filled in—by analysis, probability, guesswork, and faith.

Friedrich Nietzsche took a great interest in Christianity and its allied religion, Judaism.[2] This interest, however, was strikingly—shockingly—negative. The title alone of his final book, *Antichrist*, gives a good indication. For Nietzsche, Christianity was decadent, weak, and nihilistic. It led to a sickly, subservient, herd morality, and suffocated the quest for human excellence. Worst of all, it replaced a life-affirming naturalness with an otherworldly, life-denying negativism. It has become, in fact, "the greatest misfortune of mankind so far" (*Antichrist*, sec. 51).[3] And this disaster of Christianity is impossible to understand, he said, without grasping its Jewish roots. Thus it is not simply Christianity, but Judeo-Christianity, that must be examined with a brutal honesty, if we are to overcome its weaknesses.

Before looking in detail at Nietzsche's critique, I want to briefly review the state of knowledge on the origins of this religion. We obviously

---

[1] Hinduism is number three, with about 900 million adherents, although those professing atheism or holding other explicit non-religious views are greater in number, now about 1.1 billion.

[2] For a detailed study of Nietzsche's complex views on Jews and Judaism, see my essay, "Nietzsche on the Jews" (section 1 of the present book).

[3] Most of the following quotations are from *Antichrist*, and this book is the source where I have indicated only section numbers. Quotations from other books will be explicitly cited.

know much more today than Nietzsche did in the late 1800s. But it is to his credit that the present facts seem, by and large, to bear out his analysis—though perhaps his conclusions remain as controversial as ever.

Historical Background

Consider, first of all, the ancient origins of Judaism and the corresponding events of the Old Testament (OT). The original patriarch, Abraham, apparently lived some time between 1800 and 1500 BC—he being the traditional father of not only Judaism (and thus Christianity) but a leading prophet of Islam as well.[4] The next major figure, Moses, lived around 1300 BC, and some time afterward the "Five Books of Moses" began to take shape, likely at first as an oral tradition. These books, as we know, would eventually form the Pentateuch (or Torah)—the beginning of the OT.[5]

The remaining 30-odd OT books were added over the next one thousand years, with the set becoming complete around 200 BC. These books were written in Hebrew, but a Greek translation—the Septuagint—was begun about this time, completed circa 50 BC. The Dead Seas Scrolls, which date to the first century BC, contain fragments from every book of the Hebrew OT, and thus are our earliest proof that the complete document existed by that time. Whether it appeared any earlier is a matter of pure speculation.

Dating of the OT texts is one thing; accuracy is another matter altogether. First of all, the earliest dates cited above are purely conjectural, since we have no recorded reference to the travails of Moses prior to 850 BC. Furthermore, prominent Israeli archeologist Ze'ev Herzog has shown the increasing discrepancies between archeological data and the biblical stories.[6] Efforts in the 1900s to confirm the OT yielded a plentitude of new information, but this "began to undermine the historical credibility of the biblical descriptions instead of reinforcing them." Scholars were confronted with "an increasingly large number of anomalies," among these: "no evidence has been unearthed that can sustain the chronology" of the Patriarchal age; of the Exodus, "the many Egyptian documents that we have make no mention of the Israelites' presence in Egypt, and are also silent about the events of the Exodus";[7] and the alleged conquest of Canaan (Pal-

[4] According to legend, Abraham had two sons: Isaac, who gave rise to the Jewish lineage, and Ishmael, the father of the Arabs.

[5] Genesis, Exodus, Leviticus, Numbers, and Deuteronomy.

[6] The following quotes are from his article "Deconstructing the walls of Jericho", *Ha'aretz Magazine*, 29 October 1999.

[7] "Most historians today agree that, at best, the stay in Egypt and the exodus events occurred among a few families, and that their private story was expanded and 'nationalized' to fit the needs of theological ideology." There is one later Egyptian

estine) by the Israelites in the 1200s BC is refuted by archeological digs at Jericho and Ai that found no existing cities at that time. Even the famed monotheism of the early Jews is undermined by inscriptions from the 700s BC that refer to a pair of gods, "Yahweh and his consort, Asherah." An overall picture thus comes into view: a kernel of true people and events magnified over time, acquiring legendary status. Disparate tribes of wandering and warring Jews become heroic freedom fighters, and ultimately the chosen people of the (eventually) one God.

Perhaps surprisingly, Nietzsche appreciated the Old Testament—in spite of his skepticism about its historical veracity. He liked the power of the language and the concept of a 'God of the Jews', a god appropriate for a given people and a given time, one who rewarded and punished in equal measures. "In the Jewish 'Old Testament,' the book of divine justice, there are human beings, things, and speeches in so grand a style that Greek and Indian literature have nothing to compare with it" (*Beyond Good and Evil*, sec. 52); and again: "all honor to the Old Testament!" (*Genealogy of Morals*, 3.22).

The New Testament—the Christian Testament—however, was a completely different matter. Again, the historical facts set the stage.

The Maccabean revolt of 165 BC, against the Seleucid Empire, reestablished Jewish rule over Palestine. The resulting Hasmonean dynasty was formed in 141 and ruled until the Roman Empire incorporated the region in 63 BC. Until that time the indigenous Jews had lived under many occupying powers—Persians, Babylonians, Alexander the Great—but apparently were able to accommodate their foreign rulers and still thrive.
Things were different under the Romans. Having been the ruling power in Palestine for 100 years, the Jews were rather quickly and dismissively subsumed into the Empire. Relatively benign at first, governance became increasingly callous and brutal.

In addition to passing judgment on Jesus, Pontius Pilate was known for his aggressive treatment of the Jews; but things grew even worse after his removal in 36 AD and the ascension of Emperor Caligula. Haim Ben-Sasson writes, "The reign of Caligula (37–41 AD) witnessed the first open break between the Jews and the Empire. … [R]elations deteriorated seri-

---

documentation of such an event, by the high priest Manetho from the third century BC, which comes to a similar conclusion. As recounted by Lindemann, "the Jews had been driven out of Egypt because they, a band of destitute and undesirable immigrants who had intermarried with the slave population, were afflicted with various contagious diseases." The Jews were thus expelled "for reasons of public hygiene." In sum, "the account in Exodus was an absurd falsification of actual events, an attempt to cover up the embarrassing and ignoble origin of the Jews." (*Esau's Tears*, 1997: 28).

ously during [this time]".[8] Tensions culminated in the first Jewish revolt, which began in 66 and ended in Roman victory and the plundering and destruction of the famed Jewish temple at Jerusalem (Herod's Temple) in the year 70—which had stood in place since 516 BC.[9]

Rome retained power over Palestine for nearly 400 more years, until the fracturing of the Empire in 395. The surviving Eastern (Byzantine) Empire continued to rule the region for another 240 years, until the Arab Caliphates took over in 638. Thus it is clear that Roman rule, beginning in 63 BC, was decisive for the emergence of Christianity. Nietzsche seems to have been the first scholar to grasp the significance of this fact: "Without the Roman Caesars and Roman society, the insanity of Christianity would never have come to rule" (*Will to Power*, sec. 874).

Nietzsche's Analysis of Christianity

So, how shall we understand Christianity? Nietzsche's analysis starts from three essential facts. "The first thing to be remembered if we do not wish to lose the scent here, is, that we are among Jews" (sec. 44). This much is obvious, but it bears repeating. Jesus was a Jew, as were his parents Joseph and Mary, and all 12 apostles. The three other main figures of the New Testament—Mark, Luke, and Paul—though not apostles, were also Jews. And the many unknown authors that contributed to the New Testament (NT) were almost certainly Jewish as well. This situation is not incidental, and not a question of individual character or action; "[it is] a matter of race."

This newly-constructed religion was intended not for the well-educated elite, but for the masses, and indeed for the lowest caste among the masses—the 'chandalas,' as Nietzsche calls them, the untouchables, the lumpenproletariat: "the people at the bottom, the outcasts and 'sinners', the chandalas within Judaism" (sec. 27). It was these men that gave strength to this great religion of redemption.[10] Even granting that Nietzsche exaggerates here, it is clear that they were the low class, 'blue collar' people of the day—the farmers, fishermen, carpenters, and laborers. Christianity was designed to appeal to the beleaguered people at the very bottom of society, whether Jew or Gentile.

This situation is important to grasp because it demonstrates that the proto-Christian Jews had, in effect, two sets of masters: the Romans, and their own elite Jewish priests, the Pharisees. Hence they were doubly en-

---

[8] *A History of the Jewish People* (1976), pp. 254-255.

[9] Future emperor Titus led the Roman attack. His victory was commemorated with the construction of the Arch of Titus, a striking monument that stands today aside the Colosseum.

[10] With the notable exception of Paul—details to follow.

slaved. In order to establish any sense of freedom and autonomy they would have to rebel against both parties—even as the Pharisees would be their allies against Rome. A difficult situation, to be sure.

His second fact—an unquestioned assumption, really—is that the entire concept of an actually-existing, transcendent, all-powerful God is utter nonsense. Stories about holy visions, miracles, redemption, and divine intervention are nothing more than *foeda superstitio*—vulgar superstition. This does not, however, mean that Nietzsche was opposed to 'God' in principle. He believed that every people and every culture need to create their own concept of religion, and of the divine. These things are a formalized recognition of respect and reverence toward that which embodies one's highest values. Each culture and each era needs to create its god(s) anew, appropriate to their situation in the world. Western Europeans have utterly failed in this task:

> There is no excuse whatever for their failure to dispose of such a sickly and senile product of decadence [as the Christian God]. But a curse lies upon them for this failure: they have absorbed sickness, old age, and contradiction into all their instincts—and since then they have not created another god. Almost two thousand years—and not one new god! (sec. 19)

A proper re-conception of religion, however, must be a truly uplifting, life-affirming, and ennobling enterprise—decidedly unlike Judeo-Christianity—and must never be taken as permanent and absolute truth. All superstitious, i.e. anti-natural, religions are out of the question. The human condition, and human 'salvation,' must be firmly rooted in the present, physical world—the real world.

The third basic fact, as explained above, is the historical context of the Roman occupation and persecution. Without this, the events of the Christian era are incomprehensible.

A Reconstruction

With this in place, let me reconstruct Nietzsche's conception of early Christianity. This is a difficult task in any case, due to the radically unsystematic nature of his writing. But a coherent picture emerges from his many disparate observations.

On Nietzsche's view, Jesus was a humble Jew, an ordinary man, though clearly a leader and moral preacher of some merit. He spoke of the value of humility and pity, and of a God who viewed with compassion even the lowliest slave. Jesus sought to relieve suffering through compassion—

the 'Kingdom of God' within each person. Simultaneously he opposed, via a path of nonviolent resistance, both the social oppression of the Pharisees and the political oppression of the Romans. To achieve all this, it was necessary to "spread the word," the Good Word of God. Jesus' life, his faith, and the faith of the real Christian were essentially pragmatic. His faith was the response of a lowly Jew struggling to assist other lowly Jews in the face of oppression. Thus follows the practice of true Christianity, which is its essence:

> [Christianity] projects itself into a new practice, the genuine evangelical practice. It is not a 'faith' that distinguishes the Christian: the Christian acts, he is distinguished by acting differently: by not resisting, either in words or in his heart, those who treat him ill… The life of the Redeemer was nothing other than this practice—nor was his death anything else. … [O]nly the evangelical practice leads to God, indeed, it is 'God'! (sec. 33)

This was absolutely appropriate for a man in Jesus' situation—namely, an underclass Jew fighting oppression and seeking to help his fellow sufferers. But this was a very specific situation, and appropriate only to a particular time, place, and culture. In a very real sense Jesus was, and could be, the only 'true' Christian: "in truth, there was only one Christian, and he died on the cross. The 'evangel' died on the cross" (sec. 39). But to exploit this singular example, to expand it, to universalize it, to use it as a generalized weapon against the powerful and noble classes, against nature and against life itself—this was the crime. Notably, the crime was not of Jesus' doing—though he too was a 'criminal'—but that of his followers; first and foremost, Paul.

The ground was ripe for exploitation in that first century of the new millennium. Traditionally the Jews had a long history of prophesies of coming saviors, of redeemers, and of a messiah who would deliver them from suffering and slavery, and restore the Kingdom of Israel as it was in the era of the so-called unified kingdom of David in 1000 BC. But for all this talk of saviors, there is surprisingly little textual basis in the OT. The Pentateuch contains no mention of a messiah. Neither do the 'historical' or 'poetic' books. Only the prophets speak of a savior, but rarely and obscurely; nearly all references of any specificity are found in just one book—Isaiah. In any case there was some extant tradition for such a man, and if there ever was a need for him it was during the Roman occupation.

However, there is strikingly little evidence that, during his lifetime, people considered Jesus to be 'the' Messiah. He was born around 4 BC, but we have astonishingly few details of his early life—apart from the miraculous virgin birth described in the Gospels, which are problematic in themselves, as I explain below. It has struck more than one commentator as extremely odd that this miracle child could be born and then all but drop out of sight for some 20 or 30 years.[11] Virtually nothing is known about the facts of Mary's life, and even less of Joseph; even the years and places of their deaths are a mystery.

Most surprisingly, there is virtually no recorded documentation about Jesus during his lifetime, or by anyone who personally knew him. Jesus himself wrote nothing, which, while not impossible, is counter to a long tradition of moral or spiritual teachers leaving a written legacy. (On the other hand, if he was in fact a poor uneducated Jew, he likely did not know how to write.) In spite of alleged miracles performed in front of thousands of people—recall the fishes and loaves story—no one at the time bothered to record such momentous events on paper. The men who knew him best, the 12 apostles, wrote nothing.[12] Of their lives we know almost nothing, other than some presumed years of death for five of them (John, Peter, Phillip, Thomas, and Judas). Again this is striking; once the true nature of the Messiah was confirmed by his resurrection, one would have expected his close followers to be revered in themselves, and for their every step to be noted and recorded.

At this point the student of the Bible will respond that two of the apostles, John and Matthew, wrote their corresponding Gospels. But few experts believe this today. The present consensus is that the four Gospel authors were anonymous individuals who did not personally know Jesus.[13] Based on events mentioned in them, however, scholars have assigned them approximate dates. The earliest was Mark, written about the year 70—some 40 years after the crucifixion. Again, this is an amazingly long time to wait to record the miracle of the Messiah, even if done by Mark himself (a man who did not personally know him).

Nor do we have any confirmation of Jesus' life story from contemporaneous non-Christian sources. One would certainly have expected his enemies to document his life, if he had been a person of substance or threat. But no such writings exist. The earliest mention is by the Jewish author

---

[11] The sole exception is an incident recorded in Luke (2:41-51), in which a 12-year-old Jesus escapes from parental oversight and is later found in the company of some spiritual teachers. Certainly nothing miraculous about that.

[12] As we recall: John, Matthew, Peter (aka Simon, aka Cephas), Andrew, James the Greater, James the lesser, Phillip, Bartholomew, Thomas, Jude (aka Thaddeus), Simon, and Judas.

[13] This fact should be widely known by now, but it's not. Even a quick glance at an encyclopedia confirms it: "Today, many scholars doubt that any of the writers of the Gospels knew Jesus during his lifetime. They also doubt that we know the actual names of the writers." (*World Book Encyclopedia*, 2003, 'Jesus Christ')

Flavius Josephus, in his *Antiquities of the Jews* from circa 93 AD. Pliny the Younger and Tacitus both refer to the Christians in their writings of the early 100s AD. Again, these sources come 60 to 70 years after Jesus' death—not what one would expect.

By all accounts, then, Jesus was a rather ordinary individual, a preacher of faith and action, and a consoler of troubled souls. He likely counseled his fellow down-trodden Jews to stick up for themselves, and perhaps to disobey the unjust Roman rule, and even the contemptuous dictates of their own Jewish elite. Such rabble-rousers were frequently exiled or put to death (recall Socrates), and so it is not surprising that the elite Jews would agitate for his execution—against the reluctant wishes of Pilate himself, if in fact he was ever truly involved. We know the result: "God on the Cross."

Then we come to Paul. For Nietzsche, as for many other scholars, Paul is the central figure in early Christianity—to the extent that 'Paulism' would be the more appropriate designation. In Paul's rendering, Jesus—the real Jesus—becomes virtually irrelevant, even counterproductive. Paul needed not Jesus' life, but his death; only this could work miracles. The entire story of Jesus' life was rewritten and altered, motivated not out of love but the very opposite: feelings of hatred and revenge toward the conquerors:

> In Paul was embodied the opposite type to that of [Christ]: the genius in hatred, in the vision of hatred, in the inexorable logic of hatred. ... The life, the example, the doctrine, the death...—nothing remained once this hate-inspired counterfeiter realized what alone he could use. Not the reality, not the historical truth! And once more the priestly instinct of the Jew committed the same great crime against history—he invented his own history of earliest Christianity.
>
> The Savior type, the doctrine, the practice, the death, the meaning of death, even what came after death—nothing remained untouched, nothing remained even similar to the reality. Paul simply transposed the center of gravity of the whole existence after this existence—in the lie of the 'resurrected' Jesus. At bottom, he had no use at all for the life of the Savior—he needed the death on the cross and a little more. ...
>
> Paul wanted the end, consequently he also wanted the means. What he himself did not believe, the idiots among whom he threw his doctrine believed. His need was for power; in Paul, the priest wanted power once again—he could use only concepts, doctrines, symbols with which one tyrannizes masses and forms herds. (sec. 42)

The real Jesus was thus reduced to a caricature, a trigger for some fictionalized grand narrative: "The founder of a religion can be insignificant—a match, no more!" (*Will to Power*, sec. 178). On Nietzsche's view, then, Paul repeated the trick of the Old Testament: He took the basic elements of a man's life and history, a kernel of truth, and wove out of this a fantastic story of miracles, immortality, and divinity incarnate. And precisely here was the source of the problem.

Recall the basic facts of Paul's life. He was born in Tarsus (modern-day Turkey) around the year 10 AD as 'Saul', a Jew like the rest though different in one important respect: He was not a chandala Jew, but rather a Pharisee, an elite Jew.[14] He never knew Jesus, and was in fact an early and harsh critic of the Christians, he tells us. Then on his travels to Damascus in the year 33, three years after the crucifixion, Saul encountered the 'risen Christ' in a revelatory vision and was immediately converted. Taking the name Paul, he became the foremost champion of Christianity—even more so, strangely, than any of the apostles who knew Jesus. He begins to create fledgling churches around the Mediterranean, and in the process writes a series of letters—the 13 "Pauline" epistles—encouraging and cajoling his recruits, and declaring his faith in Jesus the Messiah. These epistles—by far the earliest written Christian documents—would ultimately comprise nearly half the 27 books of the New Testament.[15] Like his Savior, Paul evidently acquired a reputation as a troublemaker. He was arrested and sent to Rome for trial, though we know few details. He was apparently executed, either by beheading or crucifixion, some time in the mid-60s AD.[16]

Nietzsche is rightly suspicious of Paul's conversion, and not only on grounds of 'superstition.' First of all, the two earliest epistles—Galatians and 1 Thessalonians—date to around 50 AD; this is a full 20 years after the crucifixion, and nearly as long after Paul's conversion. Granted, starting up a new religion is slow work, but one would expect some written record sooner than this, particularly from an elite, well-educated Jew. Second, Paul's conversion in or around the year 33 is virtually coincident with the initial outbreak of Jewish-Roman antipathy—during Pilate's reign, and just prior to the major break in relations attributed to Caligula. This suggests some causal link. Third, things worsened under the subsequent emperor, Claudius, as he expelled the Jews from Rome in the year 49 (see Acts

---

[14] See Philippians (3:5), and Acts (23:6) or (26:5).

[15] Seven of these 13 are considered to be genuinely authored by Paul; the other six are disputed.

[16] In another biblical oddity, one would expect details of his death to be recorded in Acts, which is otherwise so detailed about Paul's life. This is especially true given that this book dates to the years 80-100, well after his alleged execution. But it stops just short of describing his death.

18:2)—just about the time of the first epistles. Fourth, the epistles are strikingly lacking in details about Jesus' life: nothing on his birth, early life, ministry, or the apostles. This suggests that Paul either did not know, or did not care, about such trivial details.

Jewish Revenge

But Nietzsche's main contention, and his most controversial conjecture, was this: *Christianity as Jewish revenge*. He paints the following picture, to which I have added factual details as we understand them today.

Paul could see the growing oppression of the Jews. They had only limited ability to fight back militarily. They were increasingly frustrated and trapped, confronted by a larger and more powerful enemy than they had ever encountered before. So Paul, perhaps together with Luke, Mark (both educated, upper-class Jews) and Peter (the chandala apostle), concocted a plan. They could not use force against the Romans because the Jews were too few and too weak. The Romans were also few in number, and militarily strong. But the common man, the masses, especially the chandala Gentiles—*they* were many. If they could come to oppose the Romans then an overthrow, a revolution, might be possible; or at the very least, the iron-grip rule would be weakened. But the Gentiles did not have the same hatred that the Jews had; they were less oppressed, and had less to lose under Roman rule. And they were not naturally inclined to fight on the side of the Jews. Even if a leader were to emerge, the Gentiles would not follow a Jew—unless he was the Son of God.

A Jewish rebel, a fellow chandala, but a divine One sent by God—or better, the embodiment of God himself—might be able to win over the allegiance of the unthinking and superstitious Gentile masses. It would be a kind of 'charm offensive' against Rome—to steal away their moral authority and place it, ultimately, in the hands of a Jew who would sooth their suffering, and 'save' them. "Salvation is of the Jews" (John 4:22), as Nietzsche is fond of reminding us. This sort of stealth insurrection would avoid the kind of direct confrontation that would get the rebels imprisoned or killed, and it would be done in the name of nominally higher values like faith, hope, and love.

Tales of a Jewish messiah come to earth, however, would cause trouble with Paul's fellow Jews. First, the messiah was supposed to save *the Jews*, not the Gentiles. Second, despite the urgent need, the ancient prophetic signs were not yet in place; any alleged messiah would be false. Furthermore, Jesus apparently had a habit of working on the Sabbath, flouting Judaic law. These things were likely the source of Jewish antipathy toward him while he was alive.

The situation demanded a two-pronged strategy. One person—Peter—would work with his fellow Jews to convince them that, yes indeed, this savior would work to the benefit of the Jews; he could be a true 'redeemer' after all. The others—Paul, and perhaps Mark, Luke, and others[17]—would undertake to spread the 'Good Word' to the non-Jewish masses. How do we know this? *Paul tells us himself*:

- "Now I am speaking to you Gentiles. Inasmuch as I am an apostle to the Gentiles, I magnify my ministry..." (Rom 11:13);
- "[Jesus was revealed to me] in order that I might preach him among the Gentiles" (Gal 1:16);
- "Let it be known to you that this salvation of God has been sent to the Gentiles; they will listen" (Acts 28:28);
- "[Barnabas and Paul] related what signs and wonders God had done through them among the Gentiles" (Acts 15:12).

This conversion of the Gentiles was the core of the overall plan; without them the insurrection would fail: "I want you [Gentiles] to understand this mystery: a hardening has come upon part of Israel until the full number of Gentiles come in, and so all Israel will be saved" (Rom 11:25-26)—saved by the Redeemer from Zion.[18] To this end, the doctrine of 'original sin' was essential. Every man was condemned from birth, unless he accepted the Jewish savior: "all men, both Jews and Greeks, are under the power of sin" (Rom 3:9); "sin came into the world through one man [Adam] and death through sin, and so death spread to all men because all men sinned" (Rom 5:12).

Peter's assignment is made clear in Galatians (2:7-8):

> I [Paul] had been entrusted with the gospel to the uncircumcised [non-Jews], just as Peter had been entrusted with the gospel to the circumcised [Jews], (for He who worked through Peter for the mission to the circumcised worked through me also for the Gentiles)...

So the plan devised by the 'Apostle to the Gentiles' (Paul) and the 'Apostle to the Jews' (Peter) was well underway by the mid-50s AD. Nietzsche called it "the most subterranean conspiracy that ever existed" (sec. 62).

---

[17] Notably, "Barnabas." See Acts 14 and 15.

[18] The passage in Romans continues: "The Deliverer [Redeemer] will come from Zion," referring to the OT prophecy that "deliverance for Israel would come out of Zion" (Ps 14:7). See also Isaiah (59:20).

As far as we can tell, this small band of Jewish revolutionaries met with marginal success at first. Judging from the near complete lack of written documentation (apart from Paul's own letters), they had little immediate effect. Once again, the chronology is telling: Jesus lived for 30-some years; 20 years then passed with no written record at all; and for 20 *more* years we have only the Pauline epistles. So: 70 years gone by, and the *sum total* of recorded history for this group of Christian Jews is a handful of letters by their leader, Paul.

And then Paul dies—executed in Rome, so we are told. Coincidentally, it is just at this time (66 AD) that the first Jewish Revolt begins. The battle waxes and wanes for four years, until the Romans prevail in 70, destroying the great Jewish temple at Jerusalem. Suddenly, the game changes. The Jews are annihilated, defeated, and enraged. Their hatred knows no bounds. A burning resentment—*ressentiment*, according to Nietzsche—gives rise to a maniacal thirst for revenge: "The Romans will pay for this, if it takes a thousand years."

As luck would have it a nascent insurrection was already underway, thanks to Paul and his band of "little ultra-Jews" (sec. 44). Unfortunately, Peter and Mark both died during the Revolt, and with Paul already gone the movement was decapitated. The only survivors were Luke and the chandala apostles Phillip and John.[19] Someone then decided to launch a full-court press for Jesus. They decided that the story of his life needed to be written, clearly demonstrating his divine nature. Within a year of the destruction of the Temple, suddenly, *miraculously*, the Gospel of Mark appears.

As the first detailed account of Jesus, it was crucial that it reach and impress the non-Jewish masses. Hence it was written explicitly for them. Jewish terms and concepts are explained (5:41, 7:1, 13:46, 14:12, 15:42). Jesus employs simple-minded parables (4:10-12, plus many examples throughout). And the book is replete with miracles from the very first page; even the apostles performed them! (6:13). It no doubt had a great effect.[20]

The Gospel of Mark evidently sufficed, at least for some 10 years. Then, unknown persons for unknown reasons decided to embellish this text, but under different names. Thus came the Gospels of Matthew and Luke. (Again, expert consensus indicates that neither of these were written

---

[19] Thomas is alleged to have lived a couple more years, until 72. And several of the other apostles have unknown deaths, and thus may have been alive somewhere.

[20] Lindemann (*Esau's Tears*, 1997: 31) describes it this way: "Both Paul and the writers of the Gospels radically redefined the traditional Jewish notion of messiah, from [an ordinary man] to that of a supernatural figure much resembling the dying and reviving salvation gods that were common to many pagan mystery cults of the day. There were certainly many overlaps between those cults and early Christianity."

by their namesakes.) So by the year 90 we have the three 'synoptic Gospels' completed, all of which were constructed on a similar plan.

Finally, sometime in the final decade of that first century, the Gospel of John appears—again, authorship unknown. It is notably different, both in content and tone, from the other three: no mention of the virgin birth or baptism of Jesus, no 'casting out of demons' miracles, clear separation from orthodox Judaism, only rare mention of the suffering and downtrodden peoples, many first-person references by Jesus, and, oddly, Jesus now carries his own cross (previously, Simon). In general, Jesus is portrayed as more thoughtful and philosophical. It seems to have targeted a more upper-class audience, both Jews and non-Jews. Perhaps it was meant as 'Christianity for the intellectuals.'

By the early 100s, then, everything was in place. All NT books were complete, and they created—literally *created*—an image of Christ that was compatible with the OT, and, more importantly, suited the larger purpose of winning allegiance from the masses. The Pharisee Jews were not happy, because they understood that this Jesus was a false messiah, but they would come to accept the benefits of a Jewish Christ that could sway the public at large and undermine support for Rome. The plan was brilliant, and by all accounts, it worked. Christianity grew from being persecuted by Rome, to being tolerated under the reign of Constantine (306–337), to being installed as the official state religion by Theodosius in 380—coincidentally, just 15 years before the disintegration of the Empire.

Of course, it is very difficult to know the extent to which Christianity was a causal factor in the collapse—many other forces were at work, including imperial overstretch, economic inflation, growing attacks by outside powers, barbarization of the Roman military, depopulation from recurrent plagues, environmental degradation, lead poisoning, and corruption within the leadership. Notably, the first modern era account of Rome's collapse—Edward Gibbon's *The History of the Decline and Fall of the Roman Empire* (1776–1789)—was also the first to cite Christianity and Christian 'moral decay' as a leading cause; on this count Nietzsche was not original. Scholars since Gibbon's time generally prefer some combination of the other factors. But the actual cause is not really at issue here. Christianity was certainly very influential during the period of decline, and it undeniably filled the void created when Rome finally collapsed in 476. Even if Christianity was merely the opportunist of the time, Nietzsche's main contention holds.

An Incalculable Loss

Whatever the cause or causes, Christianity proved the victor. Unfortunately, says Nietzsche, this victory came at a tremendous cost. The Romans, in fact, *had the nobler values*. Having absorbed and assimilated the best of classical Greek culture, the Romans of that first century ad were the embodiment of strength, nobility, life-affirmation, and excellence—in short, all that was greatest in humanity.

> For the Romans were the strong and noble, and nobody stronger and nobler has yet existed on earth or even been dreamed of: every remnant of them, every inscription, gives delight... (*Genealogy*, 1.16).

> Greeks! Romans! The nobility of instinct, the taste, the methodical research, the genius of organization and administration, the faith in—the *will* to—man's future, the great Yes to all things, become visible in the *imperium Romanum*, visible for all the senses, the grand style no longer mere art but become reality, truth, *life*. (*Antichrist*, sec. 59)

The Empire could withstand almost anything—"but it was not firm enough against the *most corrupt* kind of corruption, against the *Christians*" (sec. 58). They were the revolutionaries and anarchists, pulling on the great pillars of the Empire by draining it of its greatest strength, its system of values:

> The Christian and the anarchist: both decadents, both incapable of having any effect other than disintegrating, poisoning, withering, bloodsucking; both the instinct of moral hatred against everything that stands, that stands in greatness, that has duration, that promises life a future. Christianity was the vampire of the *imperium Romanum*... (ibid.)

The defeat was total. "Which of them has won for the present, Rome or Judea?" Nietzsche answers:

> But there can be no doubt: consider to whom one bows down in Rome itself today—and not only in Rome but over almost half the earth, everywhere that man has become tame or desires to become tame: in front of *three Jews*, as is known, and *one Jewess* (Jesus of Nazareth, the fisherman Peter, the rug weaver Paul, and the mother of the aforementioned Jesus, named Mary). This is very remarkable: without doubt Rome has been conquered. (*Genealogy*, 1.16)

When they were defeated, nobility itself was destroyed, and the Jewish chandala morality, the *slave* morality, arose victorious. For the slaves and

Jews, this was a happy outcome; for humanity at large, it was a catastrophe of the highest magnitude.

How was this attack conducted? First, by countering every aspect of Roman morality and spirituality, and second, by establishing a system favorable to Jewish interests. Against Roman polytheism, the Jews placed monotheism (or "monotono-theism," as Nietzsche would have it). Against a sense of privilege, nobility, and hierarchy, the Jews placed 'equality before God,' and the notion of 'equal rights.' Against the ideal of human fulfillment and self-realization here on Earth, salvation now came in the afterlife. Against the gods of nature, who could be cruel and ruthless as well as beneficent, they placed a God of 'pure spirit' and love. Against the ideal of bodily strength and vigor, they placed the concept of spiritual health and bodily indifference. Against allegiance to men based upon leadership and the demands of the polity, they placed dependence on the priests. Against truth and reason, they placed *lies* and *faith*.

Nietzsche held out particular scorn for the three cardinal virtues of Christianity: faith, hope, and love (Paul, in 1 Cor 13:13). Faith is fundamentally opposed to truth, because one simply 'believes' for no rational reason, or worse, in spite of reason; "if faith is quite generally needed above all, then reason, knowledge, and inquiry must be discredited: the way to truth become the *forbidden* way" (sec. 23). Faith is a "form of sickness, and all straight, honest, scientific paths to knowledge must be rejected by the church as forbidden paths. Even doubt is a sin. … 'Faith' means not *wanting* to know what is true" (sec. 52). It engenders dependency, because one is not allowed to think critically, or for oneself; the believer becomes dependent on the priest, who in turn gains power over the believer. Hence "every kind of faith is itself an expression of self-abnegation, of self-alienation" (sec. 54).

Hope, Nietzsche reminds us, was the one evil that did not escape Pandora's box. It strikes the modern reader as odd to think of hope as an evil, but in the hand of the Christian it becomes merely "a hope for the beyond"—an unfulfillable (or at least unverifiable) promise of a blessed afterlife. As such, Christian hope is meaningless; worse still, a tool for manipulation, "precisely because of its ability to keep the unfortunate in continual suspense" (sec. 23). To repeatedly promise with no ability to deliver—this is the function of the priest.

Love is the most striking of the three, born as it is, paradoxically, out of Jewish hatred and revenge. Rather than teaching the non-Jews to hate the Romans—for which there was no real basis—Paul and his fellow Jews used 'God's love' to seduce the masses. This necessitated, first of all, a certain conception of God: "To make *love* possible, God must be a person," not merely some abstract metaphysical entity. To truly personalize God, he must come to Earth in human form—hence Jesus. 'Jesus' (of the

Pauline persuasion) now serves a specific purpose: to allow us to 'love God' more easily. Once we are in love, we both tolerate more, and are ripe for manipulation. "Love is the state in which man sees things most decidedly as they are not. ... In love man endures more, man bears everything" (ibid). So once the masses are drawn to the Jewish Messiah by love, they accept what he says unquestioningly, and are willing to submit to trials and hardship—a perfect combination for the Jewish priest. Accept the Jews, those chosen people of God; don't resist the Jews; *love thy neighbor*, the Jew (Rom 13:9)—this is the message:

> The Christian…is distinguished by acting *differently*: by not resisting, either in words or in his heart, those who treat him ill; by making no distinction between foreigner and native, between Jew and non-Jew ('the neighbor'—really the coreligionist, the Jew); by not growing angry with anybody, by not despising anybody… (sec. 33)

Because the goal was to convert and mobilize every available person, Jesus (God) must love all people equally. Paul thereby negated one of the most ancient realities of human society—the hierarchy of rank among individuals—with his doctrine of a God that gives his blessing to all. He also negated the existence and importance of ethnic and national differences and conflicts among different ethnic and national interests: All people are essentially the same in the eyes of God. All men have an immortal soul that can be saved, and thus are inherently equal: "For by one Spirit we were all baptized into one body—Jews or Greeks [i.e. non-Jews], slaves or free—and all made to drink of one Spirit" (1 Cor 12:13); "There is neither Jew nor Greek, there is neither slave nor free, there is neither male nor female; for you are all one in Christ Jesus" (Gal 3:28). In Nietzsche's paraphrase, "Everyone is the child of God…and as a child of God everyone is equal to everyone."

There could scarcely be a more pernicious lie than this, he argues. If no one is worse than anyone else, then *no one is better*—no one *can* get better. This is counter to the whole thrust of life and evolution, which is toward the greater, the higher, the more refined, the nobler. But it is as necessary as it is destructive, if the masses are to be mobilized.

Thus emerged the slave morality of the Christians, out of the hatred and revenge of the Jews. And it was all based upon lies: the lie of equality, the lie of the miracle, the lie of the resurrection, the lie of God, the lie of Christian love. It is so profoundly opposed to nature and the natural order of the world that it creates a deep sickness within humanity. This "world of pure fiction" and its "*hatred* of the natural…of reality!" actually has an interest in creating a sickness that only it can assuage:

> Christianity *needs* sickness just as Greek culture needs a superabundance of health—to *make* sick is the true, secret purpose of the whole system of redemptive procedures constructed by the church. (sec. 51)
>
> Christianity also stands opposed to every *spirit* that has turned out well; it can use only sick reason as Christian reason, it sides with everything idiotic, it utters a curse against the spirit, against the *superbia* of the healthy spirit… [S]ickness is of the essence of Christianity. (sec. 52)

The sickly, the weak, the enfeebled, the ignorant, the repugnant—we know these are the essence of a Jewish-contrived Christianity because…*Paul tells us*:

> God chose what is foolish in the world to shame the wise, God chose what is weak in the world to shame the strong, God chose what is low and despised in the world, even things that are *not*, to bring to nothing things that are… (1 Cor 1:27-28).

"This was the formula," says Nietzsche; under this sign, "decadence triumphed" (sec. 51). This, in a single passage, contains the essence of Christian depravity and decay.

> Decadence is only a means for the type of man who demands power in Judaism and Christianity, the priestly type: this type of man has a life interest in making mankind sick, and in so twisting the concepts of good and evil, true and false, as to imperil life and slander the world. (sec. 24)
>
> In Christianity all of Judaism, a several-century-old Jewish preparatory training and technique of the most serious kind, attains its ultimate mastery as the art of lying in a holy manner. The Christian, the *ultima ratio* of the lie, is the Jew once more—even *three times* a Jew. (sec. 44)

Nietzsche closes *Antichrist* with guns ablaze:

> Paul, the chandala hatred against Rome, against 'the world,' become flesh, become genius, the Jew, the *eternal* Wandering Jew par excellence. What he guessed was how one could use the little sectarian Christian movement apart from Juda-

> ism to kindle a 'world fire'; how with the symbol of 'God on the cross' one could unite all who lay at the bottom, all who were secretly rebellious, the whole inheritance of anarchistic agitation in the Empire, into a tremendous power. 'Salvation is of the Jews.' Christianity as a formula with which to outbid the subterranean cults of all kinds...*and* to unite them: in this lies the genius of Paul. His instinct was so sure in this that he took the ideas with which these chandala religions fascinated, and, with ruthless violence, he put them into the mouth of the 'Savior' whom he had invented... This was his moment at Damascus: he comprehended that he *needed* the belief in immortality to deprive 'the world' of value, that the concept of 'hell' would become master even over Rome—that with the 'beyond' one *kills life*. (sec. 58)

> The whole labor of the ancient world *in vain*...the whole *meaning* of the ancient world in vain! Wherefore Greeks? Wherefore Romans? All the presuppositions for a scholarly culture, all scientific methods, were already there... Everything *essential* had been found, so the work could be begun... *All in vain*! Overnight, nothing but a memory! ... [R]uined by cunning, stealthy, invisible, anemic vampires. Not vanquished—merely drained. Hidden vengefulness, petty envy become master. Everything miserable that suffers from itself, that is afflicted with bad feelings, that whole ghetto-world of the soul *on top*, all at once. (sec. 59)

> Parasitism as the *only* practice of the church; with its ideal of anemia, of 'holiness', draining all blood, all love, all hope for life; the beyond as the will to negate every reality; the cross as the mark of recognition for the most subterranean conspiracy that ever existed—against health, beauty, whatever has turned out well, courage, spirit, *graciousness* of the soul, *against life itself*. ... I call Christianity the one great curse, the one great innermost corruption, the one great instinct of revenge, for which no means is too poisonous, too stealthy, too subterranean, too *petty*—I call it the one immortal blot on mankind. (sec. 62)

What an incredible feat: to turn Europeans away from their own western heritage—a noble, life-affirming Greco-Roman culture—and toward a foreign, alien, decadent, *Oriental* worldview. And it was done as revenge, out of hatred, and built upon lies. An ancient religion—Judaism—born of falsehood and lies, creates another born of falsehood and lies. It is done for reasons of power, control, wealth, and survival. And the lie prevails.

Judaism never did fully accept Christian morality or the notion of a Christian Messiah—even if he were a Jew. Though there was considerable overlap in the two religions—both are variations on the slave morality—Judaism retained its insularity, suspicion of Gentiles, need for control, exploitation, and power, and inclination for revenge. As Christianity took flight it became, of course, a non-Jewish religion. Christian morals thus emphasized compassion, love, 'resist not evil,' 'turn the other cheek,' 'blessed are the meek.' There could obviously be no suspicion of non-Jews within Christianity, but this was replaced by a suspicion of all that was great, strong, and noble—the exemplar, the outstanding individual who put the lie to the notion of universal equality.

Implications for the Contemporary Scene

So what are the consequences of all this for today? There are many, of course. If indeed the essence of Pauline Christianity is sickness, and if it indeed is anti-natural and neglects all that is healthy and strong, then we should see some tangible evidence of this.

For example, given that ultimate value lies in spiritual salvation, we might expect that the more pious, church-going nations would have less concern about bodily health. And in fact, there seems to be a correlation between the two. Using obesity rates as a rough measure of physical health, an analysis of public survey data shows that the most religious Christian nations are also the most obese. Specifically, about 60 percent of the people in the US and Mexico consider Christianity "very important," and these same two nations have the highest obesity rates—30 and 25 percent, respectively. Conversely, France, Germany, and the Czech Republic are less than 20 percent religious, and are also less than 15 percent obese.[21] Of course, correlation is not causation, and we cannot say that Christian beliefs cause or promote ill health. But even if the converse is true—if the sick, the ill, the obese are drawn to Christianity—this does not speak well for the religion. Either way Nietzsche's point appears confirmed: Physical health is not a big deal; God loves us no matter what.

But on more philosophical points, four items in particular stand out as clear implications. First, a heavy emphasis on *freedom*. The Judeo-

---

[21] Obesity data from www.nationmaster.com. Religious attitudes are reported in the Pew Global Attitudes Project, 19 December 2002. Data from nine nations shows a strong linear correlation (R^2 value = 0.58). Interestingly, the correlation between obesity and religiosity seems not to be found in Islam; Turkey, for example, is very religious (65% consider it 'very important'), but has only a 12% obesity rate.

Christian slave morality arises from an extreme lack of personal and social freedom, and thus it should exhibit a clear preoccupation, or even obsession, with freedom. This seems transparently clear in the US, at least, where 'liberty' is a core value, along with 'life' and 'happiness.' One recalls President Bush (Jr.)'s 2002 State of the Union speech, peppered with some two dozen references to it. We could point to our 'war on terror,' of which a prime objective is to "bring freedom" to the oppressed. We could cite our military adventurism in the Middle East, with its "Operation Iraqi Freedom" and "Operation Enduring Freedom" (Afghanistan). Our leading enemies in the world today are those who "hate our freedoms."

The current, popular, governmental form of freedom is a debased concept. It is a freedom of capitalism, a freedom of exploitation, and a decadent, soft, amoral form of personal freedom; 'liberalism,' as Nietzsche would have it. Liberal institutions

> undermine the will to power, they set to work leveling mountains and valleys and call this morality, they make things small, cowardly, and enjoyable—they represent the continual triumph of herd animals. Liberalism: *herd animalization*, in other words… (*Twilight of the Idols*, sec. 38).

True freedom, on Nietzsche's view, is something different. It is the Greco-Roman conception of the idea—something felt, something lived. The Greeks and Romans did not speak of freedom or rights at all. They *were* free, they lived as free men, and thus did not obsess about it. And this is precisely the point: A truly free people does not obsess about freedom, or about rights. Only those enslaved, or those laboring under a slave morality, continue to do so. True freedom, Nietzsche says, is the struggle to maintain one's personal independence and integrity in the face of countervailing forces. "What is freedom? Having the will to be responsible for yourself. Maintaining the distance that divides us. Becoming indifferent to hardship, cruelty, deprivation, even to life. … A free man is a *warrior*" (ibid).

Second, the natural extension of 'equal before God' is 'equal before the law.' This implies a natural affinity to both democracy and equality of rights. Democracy is contemptuous precisely because it is the politics of the herd; it finds sustenance in the Judeo-Christian herd morality: "the *democratic* movement is the heir of the Christian movement" (*Beyond Good and Evil*, sec. 202). For Nietzsche, "the democratic movement is not only a form of decay of political organization but a form of the decay, namely the diminution, of man, making him mediocre and lowering his value" (ibid: 203). The Roman Empire flourished *because* it was anti-democratic.

On the general critique of democracy, Plato was in full agreement. For him (as for Aristotle), democracy was rule by the uneducated masses, and hence the lowest common denominator. Consequently it was nearly the worst form of government—surpassed only by tyranny.[22] The pre-Christian world knew that brute democracy was something to be avoided. Of course, the mere adoption of a Christian morality did not ensure democracy—as demonstrated by the Byzantine Empire, the Holy Roman Empire, and the many Renaissance dynasties of Europe. Nor is it the only path to modern democracy—witness the Hindu democratic system in India. But for Europe at least, large-scale industrial democracy was the "heir" to Christianity, and it took several centuries to become manifest. It represents only the latest stage in the decline of Western man.

The other implication of spiritual equality is that of equal rights. "The poison of the doctrine of 'equal rights for all'—it was Christianity that spread it most fundamentally" (sec. 43). It was a kind of gross flattery to tell even the lowest of the low—the chandalas, the masses—that they were equal to the highest, and deserved equal standing; this "miserable flattery of personal vanity" was a key element in the success of Christianity. It created the herd, and the herd would be led by their divine Shepherd. But this is not reality. In the real world there is *order of rank*, of lesser and greater individuals. Rights based on meaningless equality are themselves meaningless. Men are by nature unequal, and thus the only possible rights are those appropriate for each station—in other words, of unequal rights: "The *inequality* of rights is the first condition for the existence of any rights at all" (sec. 57). Rights are something one holds *against another*; when *all* have them, none have them.

Convinced of his equality and his rights, the chandala is willing to fight for them. Here the Christian rebel takes to work, inciting the masses against those stronger and nobler who would deny their equality—yet another justification for Nietzsche's contempt:

> Whom do I hate most among the rabble of today? The socialist rabble, the chandala apostles, who undermine the instinct, the pleasure, the worker's sense of satisfaction with his small existence—who make him envious, who teach him

---

[22] For Plato's critique see *Republic*, Book 8. On his view aristocracy was the ideal form, followed by timocracy and oligarchy; democracy and tyranny were the worst. Aristotle saw democracy as a degenerate form of 'rule by the masses'; see *Politics*, Book 3. This may strike some as odd, given ancient Greece's reputation for having invented democracy, and thriving because of it. And relative to barbarism or anarchy, it was superior. But it works best as participatory democracy, in a very small state. Large, modern nation-states, of the kind Nietzsche considered, brought out the worst aspects of democracy.

> revenge. The source of wrong is never unequal rights but the claim of 'equal' rights. ... The anarchist and the Christian have the same origin. (ibid)

The passions of the common man are inflamed, envy is fostered, and the result is discontent. Once the hierarchy of the strong (e.g. the *imperium Romanum*) is undermined, then the herd becomes the dominant force. It is thereby easily manipulated by the priestly shepherds.

Thirdly, under the dictate of equality of all men, and the moral prescription to love thy neighbor, one is compelled to accept some form of multiculturalism, and even cultural relativism. All of humanity is part of the great Christian herd, at least potentially so. Those not explicitly Christian are converts-in-waiting. God does not discriminate amongst souls, nor should we. All are welcome to our flock; the bigger the herd, the better.

Finally, the primary goal of the whole scheme: benefit to the Jews and the Jewish state. In this sense we have, on the whole, and in spite of periodic pogroms throughout the centuries, a tremendous success story for the Jewish people. It cannot be anti-Semitic to point this out. In fact it is to their credit that such a small and beleaguered people could achieve such influence in an uncertain and dangerous world.

Especially in recent times, Jews have profited immensely from public sympathy—a sympathy frequently rooted in Christian theology. With Christianity, "we are among Jews": Christ, the Virgin Mary, the Apostles, 'salvation is of the Jews'—*even God is a Jew*:

> When the presupposition of *ascending* life, when everything strong, brave, masterful, and proud is eliminated from the conception of God; when he degenerates step by step into a mere symbol, a staff for the weary, a sheet-anchor for the drowning; when he becomes a god of the poor, the sinners, and the sick par excellence...just *what* does such a transformation signify?
>
> To be sure, the 'kingdom of God' has thus been enlarged. Formerly he had only his people, his 'chosen' people. Then he, like his people, became a wanderer and went into foreign lands...until 'the great numbers' and half the earth were on his side. Nevertheless, the god of 'the great numbers,' the democrat among the gods, did not become a proud pagan: he remained a Jew, he remained a god of nooks, the god of all the dark corners and places, of all the unhealthy quarters the world over! (sec. 17)

Hence: to love Christ and to love God is to love God's chosen, the Jews—an ideal situation, if you are Jewish. How much the easier to exploit the sympathies of the masses; to curry favor and gain support; to manipulate and mislead. And as before, survey data show that the more Christian the nation, the greater its sympathy to Israel and Jews generally.[23]

As a practical consequence, Americans in particular seem satisfied to allow Jewish-Americans an unprecedented and hugely disproportionate role in their nation—in other words, to be their shepherds. Though less than 2 percent of the population, American Jews are extremely influential in the cultural and economic life of the nation.[24] Likewise in the political sphere, where the Israel Lobby—led by AIPAC (American Israel Public Affairs Committee) and the CoP (Conference of Presidents of Major American Jewish Organizations)—wields immense power.[25] The end result is that, through a hammer-grip on the American superpower, Jewish and Israeli interests are able to influence events throughout the world. As former Malaysian president Mahathir Mohamad said, "Today Jews rule the world by proxy. They get others to fight and die for them." Indeed—the sheep must occasionally be led to slaughter.

And yet...the system is not perfect. There is, as we know, a lingering anti-Semitism within Christianity. Some are angry that 'the Jews killed

---

[23] As the most religious nation (59% 'very important'), the U.S. is also most sympathetic: 48 percent of the population sympathizes more with Israel in the conflict in Palestine (Pew Research survey, 19 July 2006), a figure that rises to 57 percent among Christian Zionists. Conversely, the European countries are both less religious and less sympathetic to Israel (which run 38 percent in France, 37 percent in Germany, 24 percent in the UK, 9 percent in Spain).

[24] According to *Vanity Fair* (October 2007), they make up more than half of the "100 most powerful people" in the world. Of the top 400 richest individuals in the U.S., at least 149 (37%) are Jewish (top 400 reported in *Forbes*, 30 September 2009; Jewish count by Jacob Berman, www.blogs.jta.org [5 October 2009]). Fully half of the top 50 political pundits are Jewish (top 50 list from *Atlantic*, September 2009; Jewish count by Steve Sailer). Six of the top seven American newspapers have Jewish management. Virtually every major Hollywood studio exec is Jewish—see "How Jewish is Hollywood?", *Los Angeles Times*, 19 December 2008. For a recent update on wealthy Jews, see chapter 12 in the present volume.

[25] In the political sphere, some 80 to 90 percent of both the House and the Senate reflexively support Jewish interests. The reason: pro-Jewish individuals and lobbies supply half or more of political campaign contributions—*for both major parties*; see "Candidly speaking: Obama, Netanyahu and American Jews," *Jerusalem Post* (11 May 2009). The lobby AIPAC is among the top two or three most powerful in Washington, and they have absolute dominance in U.S. foreign policy. All major presidential candidates bend over backward to placate Jewish interests. For details on the American political scene, see Mearsheimer and Walt, *The Israel Lobby and U.S. Foreign Policy* (2007).

Christ.' Many dislike their dominance and corruption of American society. Others are dismayed at the criminal actions of Israel in the occupied territories. They are upset by the virtual apartheid that exists there today, the anti-Arab discrimination, and the driving out of Christians from the holy land. People are unhappy with Jewish manipulation of media and entertainment, with the billions of dollars in annual foreign aid to Israel, with the costly wars in the Middle East that serve primarily to protect Israel—and yet they cannot bring themselves to openly oppose the Jews. Such internal conflict is easily manifest in various forms of anti-Semitism.

I wonder if many Christians don't somehow know, deep inside, that their very faith is based on Jewish lies and resentment. I wonder if they know they have been duped. There are also, perhaps, subconscious worries that, just maybe, other popular legends might also be fanciful exaggerations built on hatred and lies.[26] When governmental and institutional leaders have proven themselves corrupt and unreliable, and occasionally outright liars, then one does not know whom to trust.

Even if Nietzsche was right—if Christianity was in fact "the most subterranean conspiracy that ever existed"—it still cannot go unexposed forever. People seem to be more willing than ever to challenge age-old (and not-so-old) religious myths. Perhaps the accumulated sense of manipulation, illness, and moral decadence will cause people to break out of their stupor, ask tough questions, and demand real answers. If so, then Dr. Nietzsche will have earned his keep.

---

[26] The Holocaust and the 9/11 attacks being the prime examples. For the Holocaust, see my books *Debating the Holocaust: A New Look at Both Sides* (2020; 4th ed.) and *The Holocaust: An Introduction* (2016), or G. Rudolf, *Lectures on the Holocaust*. On the 9/11 controversy, see D. Griffin, *Debunking 9/11 Debunking*.

— 5 —

SCHOPENHAUER AND JUDEO-CHRISTIAN LIFE-DENIAL

Vitam impendere vero ("Risk your life for the truth.")
—Juvenal, *Satire* IV, 91[1]

Every movement needs its icons, the dissident-right no less than any other social-political ideology. Any icon—a term deriving from the Greek *eikôn*, meaning a likeness or image—serves to embody key elements or aspects of a particular outlook, or to encapsulate certain key values. Within Christianity, the image of a crucified Jesus serves this purpose, as does an empty cross, which signifies his alleged resurrection. Within the dissident-right, we have our own secular heroes, often drawn from the great philosophers and intellectual figures of Western history. Among such men, I would include Socrates, Plato, and Aristotle; French thinkers like Rousseau, Diderot, and Voltaire; and leading German intellectuals like Kant, Goethe, and Nietzsche. All have contributed seminal and indispensable ideas to the Western project.

But special standing is reserved for Arthur Schopenhauer (1788-1860), a man of exceptional insight, intelligence, and courage. At once a brilliant metaphysician and a visionary social critic, Schopenhauer combined both aspects of his persona in his two main works, *The World as Will and Representation* (1818)[2] and *Parerga and Paralipomena* (1851)[3]. It is worthwhile examining his views on life and death, Christianity, and the Jews. There are valuable lessons here for us all.

---

[1] Opening quotation in Schopenhauer's *Parerga and Paralipomena* (Oxford University Press, 1851/1974; E. Payne, trans.). Original from Juvenal, circa 110 AD.

[2] *World as Will and Representation* (Dover, 1969; E. Payne, trans.) The German title is also rendered in English as *The World as Will and Idea*, owing to the ambiguity of the word *Vorstellung*.

[3] A 'parergon' is a supplement or addition, and a 'paralipomenon' is something omitted or overlooked. Hence this book comprises a number of essays and aphorisms on a variety of topics that are supplemental to Schopenhauer's main work. As an aside, I note that some of Schopenhauer's other "books," such as *Essays and Aphorisms* and *On the Suffering of the World*, are just extracts from *Parerga and Paralipomena*.

Metaphysics of the Will

Let's start with the big metaphysical picture. In its broad outline, Schopenhauer's worldview consists of a universe of struggle, strife, and conflict—of tension and opposition which is only ever temporarily relieved, except to resume once more later on, in new and more potent forms. We see this clearly, he said, in the human realm, in the guise of war, oppression, and criminality. We see it in the mundane struggles of daily life, for money, friends, influence, power. We see it in countless minor actions and decisions that we all make, every day, aiming at something new, something better, something more. Every human action, even the most trivial, is a manifestation of a want, a desire, an urging, a striving—in short, of the *will*. As such, all social conflict reduces, ultimately, to a battle of wills.

But this situation is not limited to humans. We see a comparable picture in the animal kingdom, in the struggle for existence, for mates, for food, and for survival. We see it in plants, in their battle for sunlight and water, and for nutrients in the soil. And we see it even in inanimate nature, via such forces as gravitation, magnetism, and electrostatics. All the world, said Schopenhauer, is comprised, in its essence, of struggle, strife, frustration, and opposition; all the world is a manifestation of the will. The metaphysics here are fascinating and strikingly original, but I won't elaborate for now. Here, we are most concerned with the social realm and the far-reaching implications of seeing "the world as will."

For we humans, as mentioned, our daily life is a constant expression of our will. We *want*: want food, want drink, want material goods, want sex, want prestige, want power. Different people express their wills differently, but the essential nature of all people is the same: a constant striving or desiring for something.

This has two important consequences. First, since we all are constantly striving—often for the same limited things—we are thereby engaged in an endless competition with others. As in any competition, there are (a few) winners and (many) losers. The losers become frustrated, disappointed, depressed, perhaps angry, perhaps aggressive. They either vow to try harder next time, or they give up altogether. Even the winners—and we all do win, from time to time—are not really satisfied. After a short-lived sense of relief or satisfaction, we immediately settle into a new sense of desiring and wanting. The sweetness of victory is fleeting. Soon we are either fending off jealous rivals, or we are constructing new, higher desires that we hope to fulfill. At best, we are simply bored.

Hence the second consequence: the basic reality of human life is a condition of unsatisfied want, endless craving, relentless competition, and unfulfilled desire—in other words, of *suffering*. Our lot in life is a constant striving for things that we can never really possess, least of all 'happiness.'

Therefore, the tangible reality of life is pain, suffering, and want. 'Happiness' or 'satisfaction' are merely temporary releases from such pain; consequently, happiness and pleasure are *negative* in their nature, and pain and suffering are the positive realities of the world.

Thus we arrive at Schopenhauer's infamous pessimism. Life is a task, a chore, indeed, a punishment. We are all condemned to lives of greater or lesser suffering, sometimes physical, sometimes psychological, sometimes intense, sometimes mild—but ever-present and always looming greater in the future. The end of this life of suffering comes only with the 'great suffering' of physical death, which we all dread, and which therefore weighs upon our heads as yet more suffering. It would have been better, he concludes, if we had never been born.

What to do? Such a depressing picture almost inclines one to suicide. And yet Schopenhauer masterfully turns the picture around for us, finding a way through the morass of existence. First, he says, we are strangely fortunate that the world is as it is. Were it otherwise, if we somehow attained fulfillment and satisfaction on a regular basis, life would become truly pointless. We would either be driven insane by boredom, or would create artificial conflicts and struggles, wars and mass atrocities, simply to have a reason for being. Failing these, we might simply end our own lives—ironic, that the suicidal person is the one who has all his desires satisfied, not the one, like us, condemned to a life of struggle and pain. Suffering, said Schopenhauer, was like the ballast of a ship; it keeps us on the straight-and-narrow, keeps us focused, and drives us forward. Paradoxically, we ought to be grateful for our condition; if nothing else, it leads us to the ultimate metaphysical truths about the world.

Be that as it may, we still need to live our lives, preferably with a minimum of suffering. Hence we are faced with a profound dilemma: Life is desire, and desire leads to the very suffering that we seek to avoid. On the one hand, then, we ought logically to minimize or reduce ("deny") our desires. But this is tantamount to *denying life*. This may be a theoretical possibility for a saint or a god, but it is an unworkable plan for the real world. At its worst, a 'life of life-denial' is an incoherent and self-annihilating concept, one appropriate only for a pathological individual.[4]

Therefore, to live, we must accept the struggle and pain of life, keep our expectations low, press ahead, and hope for the best. This is the only

---

[4] Nietzsche recognized and acknowledged this very point: "For an ascetic, life is a self-contradiction. … [For such a man,] life somehow turns against itself, denies itself" (*Genealogy of Morals* III, sec. 11). And again: "Morality, as it has so far been understood—as it has in the end been formulated once more by Schopenhauer, as 'negation of the will to live'—is the very instinct of decadence, which makes an imperative of itself. It says: '*Perish!*'" (*Twilight of the Idols* V, sec. 5).

practical conclusion. Yes, we ought to minimize our desires where possible: avoid a fixation on money, material things, status—all those things that Jews, for example, obsess about, and thus foist upon the public mind as the ultimate goals in life. We should not be too concerned about a nebulous and facile goal like 'happiness,' which in any case is virtually impossible in a world of perpetual strife. We ought not expect that things will necessarily turn out well, and therefore not be disappointed when they don't. Life goes on, the struggle goes on—such it is.

It is a striking moral picture that Schopenhauer paints for us, one that is hard to refute. I think we all can relate to such thinking in our everyday experience. Much of this rings true, and yet we rarely follow the logic out to the full implications.

If it all sounds vaguely Buddhist, that's because it is. One of Schopenhauer's great surprises, and greatest satisfactions, was his discovery of Buddhist philosophy in the 1830s, well after he had written volume one of his monumental work, *World as Will and Representation*. There are many obvious affinities, and Schopenhauer viewed himself as independently coming to the same eternal truths as the Buddha but from an entirely different route, and with a much firmer philosophical foundation. Their prescriptions were essentially the same: end suffering via an elimination of desire and attachment, which is the source of that suffering.[5] But Buddhism was entangled in a mythological schema involving *samsara* or a cycle of endless reincarnation and rebirth, and of *nirvana*, conceived as an end to that cycle. Schopenhauer had no patience for such mythology but he respected the metaphysical insight, and placed it, in his mind, on a superior rational footing.

'One True Christian'

But it wasn't only Buddhism that Schopenhauer found affinity with; it was also there, to a surprising degree, in Christianity. In fact, his alignment with 'original' or 'true' Christianity was so strong that Schopenhauer considered himself, ironically, the 'one true Christian,' and in fact the *only* such person in all of modern history: "my teaching could be called Christian philosophy proper, paradoxical as this may seem to those who do not go to the root of the matter, but stick merely to the surface".[6] This astonishing conclusion demands some examination.

Consider, he says, the basic creation myths of the major religions. In Hinduism, the god Brahma is said to have created the world "through a

[5] Putting an end to personal desires and attachment to material things was in fact the third of the Buddha's "four noble truths."

[6] *Parerga and Paralipomena* (hereafter, P&P), vol. 2, p. 315.

kind of original sin"[7]—a mistake or error, one in which Brahma himself must atone for. ("This is quite a good idea!", Schopenhauer adds with emphasis.) Buddhism, for its part, sees the world as coming into being "in consequence of an inexplicable disturbance in the crystal clearness of the blessed…state of Nirvana." ("An excellent idea!") The ancient Greeks saw the formation of the cosmos as an act of "unfathomable necessity," that which simply *had to be*. This too was reasonable. All such views saw the act of cosmic creation as a negation, as a failing—an error, a mistake, or an unfortunate necessity.

But the Judaic view was altogether different. There, the Jewish god Jehovah creates this world "of misery and woe," stands back on the seventh day, and declares it "all good"—what is this? Utter nonsense, says Schopenhauer, and more, "something intolerable." Recall the key passage from Genesis 1:31: "And God saw everything that he had made, and behold, it was very good." Schopenhauer repeatedly mocks this idea, drawing from and paraphrasing the Greek Septuagint version by use of the phrase πάντα καλὰ λίαν (*pánta kalá lían*),[8] "all was very good." This was pure nonsense, utterly disproven by common sense, philosophical insight, and even a modicum of a realist view of the world. Indeed, says Schopenhauer elsewhere, the world could hardly be any *worse* than it is.[9] To proclaim the opposite is sheer stupidity.

As a putative religion, however, Judaism is even worse. There is a god in it, of course, but this deity is merely a brutal enforcer of the Law. He praises and cajoles his "chosen" and smites their enemies, nothing more. In this metaphysical system there is no immortal soul, no real afterlife, no heaven, no hell; all such things are utterly lacking in the Old Testament. Schopenhauer thus concludes,

> And so in this respect, we see the religion of the Jews occupy the lowest place among the dogmas of the civilized world, which is wholly in keeping with the fact that it is also the only religion that has absolutely no doctrine of immortality, nor has it even any trace thereof.[10]

---

[7] P&P, vol. 2, p. 300.

[8] The full phrase in Genesis is: *kaí eíden o theós tá pánta ósa epoíisen kaí idoú kalá lían kaí egéneto espéra kaí egéneto proí iméra ékti.*

[9] "Now this world is arranged as it had to be, if it were to be capable of continuing with great difficulty to exist; if it were a little worse, it would no longer be capable of continuing to exist. Consequently, since a worse world could not continue to exist, it is absolutely impossible; and so this world itself is the worst of all possible worlds. … Consequently, the world is as bad as it can possibly be, if it is to exist at all." (WWR, vol. 2, pp. 583-584).

[10] P&P, vol. 2, p. 301.

Not that Schopenhauer endorsed the concept of an immortal soul; far from it. But he realized that any honest religion must include some such doctrine. Judaism, as we will see, evidently served a different purpose.

Nor did he accept anything like a moral, omnipotent, all-good god. "Such a view…is too flagrantly contradicted by the misery and wretchedness that fill the world, on the one hand, and by the obvious imperfection and even burlesque distortion of the most 'perfect' phenomenon…of man." The evil inherent in worldly existence, and the many failings of humanity, decisively disprove the existence of any such god. In fact, the great suffering of the world is proof of the opposite, namely, that it came into being in "sin," as the other religions have it. There remains a trace of this original sin, of course, in the Bible, in the myth of the Fall, of Adam and Eve—which stands as the only philosophically valid insight in Judaism: "it is only the story of the Fall of Man that reconciles me to the Old Testament. In fact, in my eyes, it is the only metaphysical truth that appears in the book…"

Schopenhauer next turns to a central issue: the view of earthly life in the various religions. For emphasis, he contrasts the ancient Greek view with that of Christianity. Consider first the distinction between Greek and Christian views of death as seen in images engraved on ancient sarcophagi. For the Greeks, the dead man's life is depicted in happy, optimistic terms: his birth, family, marriage, occupation, and so on. It is, says Schopenhauer, an essentially positive, *life-affirming* outlook; life is good, life is to be lived to its fullest, and people can indeed attain happiness. Then look at the Christian coffin: draped in black, and topped by the cross, the symbol of ultimate suffering and death. This, he said, is an essentially *life-denying* outlook. But it is fitting: for the Christian, this temporal life of sin and suffering is superseded by eternal life in heaven. What is life for a Christian, after all, but a test, a burden, indeed, a "cross to bear"?

From the perspective of a modern-day secular philosopher, one looks at this distinction and says: "Of course, the Greeks were right; you have one life, it can be good, so live it to the fullest. Those foolish Christians, with their mindless belief in an afterlife, disavow the value of earthly existence. They are always looking ahead, to heaven, never to the here and now." But Schopenhauer again turns the tables on us:

> Between the spirit of Graeco-Roman paganism and that of Christianity is the proper contrast of the affirmation and denial of the will-to-live, according to which, in the last resort, Christianity is fundamentally right.[11]

[11] P&P, vol. 2, p. 314.

(I note here parenthetically that he frequently clarified his concept of the will as, more specifically, the will-to-live [*der Wille zum Leben*].) Christianity is "right" in the sense that the world *is* suffering, it *is* 'sin'—not for Christian reasons, of course, but because that is the nature of a world of pure willing. Even more, the Christian 'solution' is nearly the same as Schopenhauer's: *deny the will, be life-denying.* Will is will-to-live, and thus to deny the will is to deny life. Deny your material desires, deny bodily pleasures. Become an ascetic. "Take up your cross and follow me".[12] This is the path of redemption.

Hence Schopenhauer sees his philosophical worldview as aligned with the Christian New Testament and its 'pessimism' about the world, whereas other philosophers are inherently more consistent with the 'optimistic' view of Judaism and the Old Testament:

> My ethics is related to all the ethical systems of European philosophy as the New Testament to the Old, according to the ecclesiastical conception of this relation. Thus the Old Testament puts man under the authority of the Law [of Moses] which, however, does *not* lead to salvation. The New Testament, on the other hand, declares the Law to be inadequate, in fact repudiates it. On the contrary, it preaches the kingdom of grace which is attained by faith, love of one's neighbor, and complete denial of oneself; this is the path to salvation from evil and the world. For in spite of all protestant-rationalistic distortions and misrepresentations, the ascetic spirit is assuredly and quite properly the soul of the New Testament. But this is just the denial of the will-to-live…

He then places his own outlook in historical context:

> Now all the philosophical systems of ethics prior to mine have kept to the spirit of the Old Testament, with their absolute moral law and all their moral commandments and prohibitions, to which the commanding Jehovah is secretly added in thought…
>
> My ethics, on the other hand, …frankly and sincerely admits the abominable nature of the world, and points to the denial of the will as the path to redemption therefrom. It is, accordingly, actually in the spirit of the New Testament, whereas all the others are in that of the Old, and thus theoretically amount to mere Judaism (plain despotic theism). In

[12] Mark 8:34; Matthew 16:24.

> this sense, my teaching could be called Christian philosophy proper, paradoxical as this may seem to those who do not go to the root of the matter, but stick merely to the surface.[13]

…thus arriving back at the quotation I cited above. Judaism, with its *pánta kalá lían*, an all-good God, and a promise of material prosperity, is a pathetic form of optimism, utterly at odds with the real world. (Of course, for the Jews themselves over the past century at least, and excepting a few years during WW2, the world has been exceptionally good; it's good to be king. I will return to this idea shortly.) Christianity, with its sufferings of the world, its sin and misery and death, and its "you will be hated by all",[14] is realistic pessimism—albeit, as with Schopenhauer, with an escape route, namely, denial of the will and the consequent asceticism. The analogy is imperfect but sufficient to allow for an instructive comparison. It permitted Schopenhauer to draw out some fascinating implications but it also blinded him to a likely deeper truth about Christianity.

Sexual Abstinence as Jewish Ethnic Strategy

Among many other things, Schopenhauer was fascinated by human sexuality, which for him assumed deep metaphysical importance. The human essence, the will-to-live, finds "as its kernel and greatest concentration, the act of generation"—which is to say, sexual reproduction. Here is the beginning of everything, not only of biology but of the whole great charade that is human existence. With a biting sense of humor, he explains it this way:

> Seriously speaking, this is due to the fact that sexual desire, especially when, through fixation on a definite woman, it is concentrated to amorous infatuation, is the quintessence of the whole fraud of this noble world; for it promises so unspeakably, infinitely, and excessively much, and then performs so contemptibly little.[15]

Appropriately, then, sexual desire is the prime urging that must be suppressed by any real ascetic. Hence, by rights, we should find this admonition in the New Testament; and in fact, we do. Schopenhauer examines this matter in his exceptionally important Chapter 48 of Volume Two of *World as Will and Representation*:

---

[13] P&P, vol. 2, p. 314.
[14] Matthew 10:22, Luke 6:22, John 15:19.
[15] P&P, vol. 2, p. 316.

> The ascetic tendency is certainly unmistakable in genuine and original Christianity… We find, as its principal teaching, the recommendation of genuine and pure celibacy (that first and most important step in the denial of the will-to-live) already expressed in the New Testament.[16]

And he means, not only for single men and women, *but for the married as well*. Schopenhauer's astonishing claim, that he proceeds to adduce from primary evidence, is that *good Christians should not have sex—ever*. He then dedicates the next several pages to building his case for this "perpetual chastity." He begins with these lines from an 1832 book by the Catholic author Friedrich Carove:

> By virtue of the Church view…perpetual chastity is called a divine, heavenly, angelic virtue… [Quoting a Catholic periodical,] "In Catholicism, the observance of a perpetual chastity, for God's sake, appears in itself as the highest merit of man." … To both [Paul and the author of Hebrews], virginity was perfection, marriage only a makeshift for the weaker… The self should turn away and refrain from everything that contributes only to its pleasure… We agree with Abbe Zaccaria, who asserts that celibacy…is derived above all from the teaching of Christ and of the Apostle Paul.[17]

At this point we want to exclaim: Can this be true? Could original Christianity actually expect its followers to adhere to "perpetual chastity," even when married? And what would prompt such a call?

Evidence for this claim must ultimately come from our primary source, the New Testament. We further know that the earliest NT writings are the letters of Paul, which predate the four Gospels by two or three decades, at least. Let's briefly look at the evidence, both that which Schopenhauer offers and that which we may supplement on our own.

Schopenhauer cites two passages from Paul. The first and earliest is 1 Thessalonians (4:3), an oddly cryptic passage. Paul says, "For it is the will of God, for your sanctification, that you abstain from *porneias*." I cite here the Greek original—but what is *porneias*? Among the 70-odd English translations we find a range of terms, such as "immorality" (RSV), "sexual immorality" (NKJV), and "fornication" (KJV), all of which suggest illegitimate sex, perhaps unmarried sex, perhaps adultery. But we also find broader terms, like "all sexual vice" (AMPC), "sexual sins" (ERV), "sexu-

[16] WWR, vol. 2, p. 616.
[17] WWR, vol. 2, p. 619-620.

al defilement" (TPT), and even "unchastity" (RSV). Paul goes on to say that "each one of you knows how to take a wife in holiness and honor, not in the passion of lust like a heathen." Can he be suggesting that men take wives as "partners in Christ" all while abstaining from the sexual lust of heathens?

The second passage is a lengthy portion from 1 Corinthians 7. Again, it is oddly conflicted. At the start of the chapter, Paul says, bluntly, "It is good for a man not to have sexual relations with a woman" (7:1, ESV). But owing to "the temptation to immorality"—presumably meaning sexual intercourse—a man may take a wife. Affirming his own unmarried status, Paul then says "I wish that all were as I myself am. ... To the unmarried and the widows, I say that it is well for them to remain single as I do" (7:7-8). "But if they cannot exercise self-control"—that is, if they are weak—"they should marry."

Later on, Paul returns to the subject: "Are you free from a wife? Do not seek marriage" (7:27). Two lines later he warns, "those who marry will have worldly troubles (!), and I would spare you that." Paul goes on to state that married people are worried about worldly matters and about pleasing each other, which distracts them from their "undivided devotion to the Lord." A married man may do well, says Paul, "but he who refrains from marriage will do better" (7:38). These are striking words from our "Apostle." The conclusion seems clear—Paul will accept you if you marry, but he would much prefer that you did not.

There are other Pauline passages that Schopenhauer might have cited. For example, Colossians 3:5: "Put to death, therefore, whatever belongs to your earthly nature: sexual immorality, impurity, lust, evil desires and greed, which is idolatry" (NIV). Or Galatians 5:16-19: "Do not gratify the desires of the flesh. For the desires of the flesh are against the Spirit… The acts of the flesh are obvious: sexual immorality, impurity and debauchery…" Or 1 Corinthians 6:18: "Flee from sexual immorality. All other sins a person commits are outside the body, but whoever sins sexually, sins against their own body." Or Romans 13:14: "Rather, clothe yourselves with the Lord Jesus Christ, and do not think about how to gratify the desires of the flesh." We might also include the pseudepigraphic Ephesians 5:3: "But among you there must not be even a hint of sexual immorality, or of any kind of impurity, or of greed, because these are improper for God's holy people." This is prudish Puritanism in the extreme. Paul, indeed, seems to strongly prefer that his fellow Christians have no sexual relations at all.

There are other related suggestions in the Gospels. Schopenhauer refers to Matthew 19:10, where the disciples offer to Jesus the idea that "perhaps it is better not to marry." Jesus gives a typically cryptic reply, suggesting that chastity may be best:

> Not everyone can accept this word, but only those to whom it has been given. For there are eunuchs who were born that way, and there are eunuchs who have been made eunuchs by others—and there are those who choose to live like eunuchs for the sake of the kingdom of heaven. The one who can accept this should accept it.

The apparent suggestion here is that we all should 'be like a eunuch' and not have sex. In Luke 20:34 Jesus addresses the future resurrection of married people: "The people of this age marry and are given in marriage. But those who are considered worthy of taking part in the age to come, and in the resurrection from the dead, will neither marry nor be given in marriage…" Indeed, the unmarried are "equal to angels and are sons of God." It's clear who the preferred people are.

Outside the Gospels and the Pauline Epistles, we have 1 John 2:15: "Do not love the world or the things in the world. … For all that is in the world, the lust of the flesh and the lust of the eyes, is not of the Father but is of the world." Or we could cite 1 Peter 2:11: "Beloved, I urge you as aliens and exiles to abstain from the desires of the flesh that wage war against the soul" (NSRV). And in the late-written Revelations, we read that the Lamb of God will return to Earth only with those "who have not defiled themselves with women, for they are chaste" (14:4).

What is one to conclude? It seems that Schopenhauer is indeed correct—that perpetual chastity is the prescribed course of action for all good Christians.

But why? Why would Paul, for example, encourage his would-be followers to abstain from sex? Obviously he did not get this suggestion from "Jesus" or from God; it was clearly his own doing. Obviously he did not get it from the Old Testament, with its many calls to "be fruitful and multiply".[18] The idea itself of a celibate religious group was not unknown to him, as it was characteristic of a number of esoteric cults and secretive groups over the centuries. But Paul wasn't aiming at some clandestine cult; he wanted a mass movement. He must have known that it was poor organizational strategy to ask people to commit to chastity. Clearly he had some compelling reason for introducing this component into his new religion.

Schopenhauer had no real knowledge of evolution, having been born a few decades too early, and so it is understandable that he had no idea of group evolutionary strategy. If he had, he might have discerned something in Paul's motive—an overriding concern for the welfare of his fellow Jews. As an elite Pharisee Jew, Paul (born Saul) clearly resented the incur-

---

[18] Genesis 1:28, 9:1, 9:7, 17:20, 28:3, 35:11; Exodus 1:7; Leviticus 26:9; Jeremiah 23:3.

sion of the Roman Empire into Palestine, in the decades prior to his birth. He also surely shared the long-standing Jewish antipathy for his neighboring Gentile masses—Arabs, Greeks, and Egyptians.[19] Seeing the futility of violent resistance to Rome, Paul was surely searching for nonviolent, indirect, psychological or moral means of undermining the enemy.

Then he hit upon a plan: Why not play up the alleged divinity of a recently-crucified Jewish rabbi, Jesus of Nazareth, turning him into the savior of all humanity? This way, all of Paul's exhortations—in his self-assigned role as "Apostle to the Gentiles"—could be turned into an anti-Gentile morality and placed into the mouth of God himself. 'It's not my idea,' implies Paul; 'God wants you to be chaste—forever.'

But is "perpetual chastity" anti-Gentile? Yes—if, by proscribing future children, it erodes Gentile families. This, in fact, is the only practical consequence: *fewer Gentile children.* Seen this way, as a Jewish ethnic evolutionary strategy, Paul found a way to inhibit the growth of the non-Jewish population. If there is any historical basis to the concept of "White genocide," this is it.

And it wasn't only Paul. Above I gave two chastity quotations from the Gospels of Matthew and Luke. Those same two books also contain, unsurprisingly, a number of explicitly anti-family passages. In Matthew 10:21, Jesus says, "Brother will betray brother to death, and a father his child; children will rebel against their parents and have them put to death." At Matthew 19:29, Jesus proclaims, "And everyone who has left houses or brothers or sisters or father or mother or wife or children or fields for my sake will receive a hundred times as much, and will inherit eternal life." In the Gospel of Luke (12:52) we read, "From now on, there will be five in one family divided against each other, three against two and two against three." And later (14:26) we find that Jesus says, "If anyone comes to me and does not hate father and mother, wife and children, brothers and sisters—yes, even their own life—such a person cannot be my disciple." What is this but a family-destroying message, an admonition to tear apart familial ties, all while staying chaste, simply for the sake of "Jesus"? The Jewish Gospel writers seem to have clearly endorsed Paul's anti-Gentile strategy.

In the end, of course, this anti-family stance had to be abandoned, as Schopenhauer makes clear. Beginning with Clement of Alexandria, circa 200 AD—especially in book 3 of his *Stromata*—Gentile Christian Fathers

---

[19] Jewish misanthropy is notorious and well-documented. It dates back at least to Hecateus of Abdera, circa 300 BC, who observed that "Moses introduced a way of life [for the Jews] which was to a certain extent misanthropic and hostile to foreigners." Apollonius Molon, circa 75 BC, "reviled the Jews as atheists and misanthropes." In 50 BC, Diodorus Siculus remarked that "the nation of Jews had made their hatred of mankind into a tradition." The list of such commentaries is extensive; for details, see my work *Eternal Strangers* (2020).

rejected the anti-marriage, anti-family, and anti-child stance of the early Jewish Christians. Clement rails against earlier Fathers like Marcion and Tatian, who held to the literal, anti-natalist reading: "they teach that one should not enter into matrimony and beget children, should not bring further unhappy beings into the world, and produce fresh fodder for death".[20] Writing two centuries later, Augustine too recognized this dilemma in the early Christian Fathers: "They reject marriage and put it on a level with fornication and other vices." By way of modest defense, and with perhaps a touch of irony, he adds that, with mass abstention, "the kingdom of God would be realized far more quickly, since the end of the world would be hastened".[21]

Still, it was clear that mass perpetual chastity was not a practical way to build a worldwide religion, and in the end it had to be abandoned or "reinterpreted" by Catholics and Protestants alike. They had to adopt the Jewish optimism, the *pánta kalá lían*, and surrender the central aspect of Christian asceticism, its perpetual chastity. But in doing so, they drained away the key elements of their own religion. As Schopenhauer says, summing up the situation, "From all this, it seems to me that Catholicism is a disgracefully abused, and Protestantism a degenerate, Christianity".[22]

On the Jews

Where, then, does all this leave us? For Schopenhauer, Christianity had an original and profound core in its inherently life-denying outlook, something which was consistent with his own philosophical stance. But it got subverted and contaminated with the detestable Jewish optimism, and thus lost to history. For all his skepticism, Schopenhauer seems to believe that an historical (but non-miraculous) Jesus really existed, and that Paul was an honest interpreter of his message.

In retrospect, this seems utterly naïve. Far more likely is that Paul and the Jewish Gospel writers were master deceivers—"artful liars," as Hitler might have put it[23]—who were only interested in Jewish power and Jewish well-being, and who thus instituted an effective Jewish group-strategy to confuse and weaken the Gentile masses. And in the end, and even though some aspects had to be jettisoned, it worked. Rome collapsed and Christian-

[20] Cited by Schopenhauer in WWR, vol. 2, p. 622 note.
[21] Cited in WWR, vol. 2, p. 618 note.
[22] WWR, vol. 2, p. 626.
[23] In *Mein Kampf*, vol. 1, section 2.25, he expresses his amazement at the Jews' "art of lying" (*Kunst der Lüge*). And later in chapter 10 (section 10.4), he employs the explicit phrase "artful liars" (*Lügenkünstler*). See my translation (Clemens & Blair, 2022).

ity went global. Given that we have some 2 billion Christians on Earth today, the implications are enormous.

Schopenhauer's many reflections on religion, and his negative assessment of Judaism in particular, furthermore allowed him the opportunity to offer a number of critical comments on Jews generally. Even in his early writing, in volume one of *World as Will and Representation*, he offered harsh commentary. In a passage on the development of the arts, he briefly addresses "the history of a small, isolated, capricious, hierarchical (i.e. ruled by false notions), obscure people, like the Jews, despised by the great contemporary nations of the East and of the West".[24] "It is to be regarded generally as a great misfortune," he adds, "that the people whose former culture was to serve mainly as the basis of our own were not, say, the Indians or the Greeks, or even the Romans, but just these Jews."

For the next three decades, he said little about them. But he returned to the topic, in a very pointed manner, in *Parerga and Paralipomena*. Volume 1 begins with a sketch of the history of idealism and the limitations of that metaphysical view. The classic idealists are closely allied with Judeo-Christian theology, and thus "are all marred by that Jewish theism which is impervious to any investigation, dead to all research, and thus actually appears as a fixed idea".[25] But the subsequent essay, on the history of philosophy, brings the occasion for an extended digression on the subject:

> The real religion of the Jews, as presented and taught in Genesis and all the historical books up to the end of Chronicles, is the crudest of all religions because it is the only one that has absolutely no doctrine of immortality, not even a trace thereof. ... The contempt in which the Jews were always held by contemporary peoples may have been due in great measure to the poor character of their religion. ... Now this wretched religion of the Jews does not [offer any conception of an afterlife], in fact it does not even attempt it. It is, therefore, the crudest and poorest of all religions and consists merely in an absurd and revolting theism. ... While all other religions endeavor to explain to the people by symbols and parables the metaphysical significance of life, the religion of the Jews is entirely immanent, and furnishes nothing but a mere war-cry in the struggle with other nations.[26]

---

[24] WWR, vol. 1, p. 232.
[25] P&P, vol. 1, p. 15.
[26] P&P, vol. 1, p. 125-126.

Here we see real insight: Judaism is not a religion at all, but rather a war-manual in the competition with other peoples. It serves to sustain and promote the Jewish race in their material well-being, nothing more.

Volume 2 elaborates on these ideas, especially in the chapter titled "On Religion," which brings this observation:

> Also we should not forget God's chosen people who, after they had stolen, by Jehovah's express command, the gold and silver vessels lent to them by their old and trusty friends in Egypt, now made their murderous and predatory attack on the 'Promised Land,' with the murderer Moses at their head, in order to tear away from the rightful owners, by the same Jehovah's express and constantly repeated command, showing no mercy, and ruthlessly murdering and exterminating all the inhabitants, even the women and children.[27]

A footnote to the above passage adds this widely-cited remark:

> Tacitus and Justinus have handed down to us the historical basis of the Exodus… We see from the two Roman authors how much the Jews were at all times and by all nations loathed and despised. This may be partly due to the fact that they were the only people on Earth who did not credit man with any existence beyond this life and were, therefore, regarded as beasts… Scum of humanity—but great master of lies [*grosse Meister im Lügen*].[28]

The ultimate tragedy, for Schopenhauer, is that the pathetic *Judeo*-Christian culture dominated the history of Europe, rather than the nobler Greco-Roman: "The religion of the Greeks and Romans, those world-powers, has perished. The religion of the contemptible little Jewish race [*verachteten Judenvölkchens*], on the other hand, has been preserved…"[29]

But, as noted, the Hebrew tribe is not simply defined by a religion; "[i]t is an extremely superficial and false view to regard the Jews merely as a religious sect. … On the contrary, 'Jewish Nation' is the correct expression".[30] Like Johann Fichte and Johann Herder, Schopenhauer was also concerned about the political consequences of integrating, and granting

---

[27] P&P, vol. 2, p. 357.

[28] Payne mistranslates this sentence, interpreting the final phrase as "past master at telling lies."

[29] P&P, vol. 2, p. 393.

[30] P&P, vol. 2, p. 263.

rights to, this Jewish Nation. The Jews were a "*gens extorris*" (refugee race), eternally uprooted, always searching for but never finding a homeland:

> Till then, it lives parasitically on other nations and their soil; but yet it is inspired with the liveliest patriotism for its own nation. This is seen in the very firm way in which Jews stick together...and no community on earth sticks so firmly together as does this. It follows that it is absurd to want to concede to them a share in the government or administration of any country.[31]

Schopenhauer was more moderate than Fichte; banishment was not necessary. He was willing to grant them limited rights, *provided* they took no role in government. "Justice demands that they should enjoy with others equal civil rights; but to concede to them a share in the running of the State is absurd. They are and remain a foreign oriental race..."[32] The race could be tolerated, but the corrupt ideology had to go: "We may therefore hope that one day even Europe will be purified of all Jewish mythology".[33]

Finally, Schopenhauer found much use in an intriguing little phrase, *foetor Judaicus*—the 'Jewish stench.' From ancient times, Gentiles held a longstanding belief that Jews literally smelled bad; this likely derived from a true and persistent Jewish tendency to avoid or minimize bathing. For Schopenhauer, though, the stench represents not so much a literal smell but rather an intellectual odor of stale Jewish thought, arising primarily from the Old Testament. Oddly enough, he applies it most often in his critique of Jewish approaches to animal rights.[34] In the *Parerga* he criticizes Spinoza (and his view of animals) as a man who speaks "just as a Jew knows how to do, so that we others, who are accustomed to purer and worthier doctrines, are here overcome by the *foetor Judaicus*".[35] Of the Genesis account that God created animals for man's use, Schopenhauer exclaims, "Such stories have on me the same effect as do Jew's pitch and *foetor Judaicus!*"[36] Somewhat later he refers to "Europe, the continent that is so permeated with the *foetor Judaicus*..."[37] And on the same subject: "It is

[31] P&P, vol. 2, p. 262.
[32] P&P, vol. 2, p. 264.
[33] P&P, vol. 2, p. 226.
[34] Schopenhauer was a passionate advocate for animal welfare, far ahead of his time on that count. He was the first major philosopher to incorporate them into his ethical schema.
[35] P&P, vol. 1, p. 73.
[36] P&P, vol. 2, p. 370. "Jew's pitch" is a naturally-occurring bituminous asphalt, found in ancient times around the Dead Sea and other parts of Judea.
[37] P&P, vol. 2, p. 372.

obviously high time that in Europe, Jewish views on nature were brought to an end... A man must be bereft of all his senses or completely chloroformed by the *foetor Judaicus* not to see [this]".[38]

Members of the dissident-right, no longer "chloroformed by the *foetor Judaicus*" nor deceived by the "great master of lies," can see the evident truth in such statements—statements that were years ahead of their time, and written in a period when a great thinker could still speak the truth. Sadly, and thanks to Jewish domination of our society, we can no longer openly say such things without harsh recriminations. True free speech no longer exists. Hence we are locked into a long struggle with the Jewish race, simply to achieve basic freedoms of speech and expression, and to live our lives out from under the dominance of the Jewish hand.

Perhaps this is our lot in life—and indeed, the lot of all people everywhere today. This calls to mind a well-known quotation from Schopenhauer, which I cite here in context:

> History shows us the life of nations and can find nothing to relate except wars and insurrections; the years of peace appear here and there only as short pauses, as intervals between the acts. And in the same way, the life of the individual is a perpetual struggle, not merely metaphorically with want or boredom, but actually with others. Everywhere he finds an opponent, lives in constant conflict, and dies weapon in hand.[39]

Less known is that the concluding thought appears earlier in the book, in different form, and is attributed to Voltaire. The words are apt:

> In this world where "the dice are loaded," we need a temper of iron, armor against fate, and weapons against mankind. For the whole of life is a struggle, every step contested, and as Voltaire rightly says, *on ne réussit dans ce monde qu'à la pointe de l'épée, et on meurt les armes à la main* ("In this world, we succeed only at the point of the sword, and we die with weapons in hand.")[40]

In such a world, says Schopenhauer, our motto should be (quoting Virgil): *tu ne cede malis, sed contra audentior ito* ("Do not give way to evil, but face it more boldly"—*Aeneid* 6.95). The situation demands courage and

---

[38] P&P, vol. 2, p. 375.
[39] P&P, vol. 2, p. 292.
[40] P&P, vol. 1, p. 475. The original source for Voltaire is *Les pensées et maximes* (1821).

resolve; "we should not think of nervousness or hesitation, but only of resistance." We must harden ourselves, and stiffen our resolve; he cites Horace: *Si fractus illabatur orbis, Impavidum ferient ruinae* ("Even if the world collapses over a [just] man, its ruins would leave him undismayed"—*Odes* III, 3.7). The future is there for those who are willing to face the battle head-on: *Quocirca vivite fortes, Fortiaque adversis opponite pectora rebus* ("Live on with courage, and with courage in your heart, stand up to the blows of fate"—*Satires* II, 2.135). As they say, timeless wisdom is eternally valuable.

But perhaps we leave the last word to Schopenhauer himself. His pessimistic realism held true to the end. In volume two of the *Parerga*, he sums up all the strivings of our lives:

> A happy life is impossible; the best that man can attain is a *heroic life*, such as is lived by one who struggles against overwhelming odds in some way and in some affair that will benefit the whole of mankind, and who, in the end, triumphs—although he obtains a poor reward, or none at all.[41]

The message is clear: Have low expectations of life; as a rule, things will not go as we wish. Any victories will be rare, hard-fought, fleeting, and unacknowledged. Life is perpetual struggle; therefore, never give up. Above all, strive to be heroic.

Words to ponder, for all those who would fight for justice in this unjust world.

[41] P&P, vol. 2, p. 322.

— 6 —
RETHINKING *MEIN KAMPF*

On 1 January 2016, *Mein Kampf* came out of copyright. It had been over 70 years since the author's death, and by international copyright law, legal protection for the book expired. Thus it is a good time to reconsider and reexamine this most notorious work—and perhaps to banish some of the many myths surrounding it to history.

In fact, we are long overdue for a revisionist treatment of this work. In my experience, very few people really understand what is in it. The common man, and even the well-educated one, likely knows little more than the title and the author. Revisionists who work on the Holocaust or either of the world wars often bypass the book completely, as if it had no relevance at all; most likely, they have never read it. Traditional journalists, academics, and alleged experts frequently display their ignorance by taking passages out of context, overlooking key facts, or simply failing to cite the author appropriately. More generally, the mainstream approach to *Mein Kampf* seems be rather similar to its tactics with regard to Holocaust revisionism: ignore, censor, or disparage. It is simply too problematic to discuss this work in a fashion that might lead readers to ask tough questions, or to seek out the book itself.

A large part of the reason for the book's obscurity is the sorry state of its many English translations. These will be discussed and critiqued below. This is also one of the reasons that I am currently working on a new, parallel German-English translation—the first ever, in fact. I will attempt to remedy many of the shortcomings in current versions, and provide something of a revisionist perspective on the entire work. In the present essay, I examine the translations, discuss some main themes of the book, and argue for its relevance in the present day.

A Most Consequential Work

Mein Kampf is the autobiography and articulated worldview of one of the most consequential and visionary leaders in world history. It is also one of the most maligned and misrepresented texts of the 20th century. There have been so many obfuscations, deceptions, and outright falsehoods circulated about this work that one scarcely knows where to begin. Nonetheless, the time has come to set the story straight.

That Adolf Hitler would even have undertaken such a work is most fortunate. Being neither a formal academic nor a natural writer, and being fully preoccupied with pragmatic matters of party-building, he might never have begun such a major task—were it not for the luxury of a year-long jail term. In one of the many ironies of Hitler's life, it took just such an adverse event to prompt him to dictate his party's early history and his own life story. This would become Volume One of his two-part, 700-page magnum opus. It would have a dramatic effect on world history, and initiate a chain of events that has yet to fully play out. In this sense, *Mein Kampf* is as relevant today as when it was first written.

Display of Copies of Hitler's *Mein Kampf*
(Documentation Center in Congress Hall – Nuremberg)

Perhaps the place to begin is with the rationale for the book. Why did Hitler write it at all? Clearly it was not a requirement; many major politicians in history have come and gone without leaving a personal written record. Even his time in prison could have been spent communicating with party leaders, building support, soliciting allies, and so on. But he chose to spend much of his stay documenting the origins and growth of his new movement. And this was a boon to history as well as to understanding of the human spirit.

The work at hand seems to have served at least four purposes for its author. First, it is autobiographical. This aspect consumes most of the first two chapters, and is repeatedly woven into the remainder of Volume One. For those curious about the first 35 years of Hitler's life, this aspect is invaluable. It gives an accurate and relevant account of his upbringing, his education, and the early development of his worldview. Like any good autobiography, it provides an irreplaceable first-hand description of a life. But as well, it offers the usual temptation to cast events in a flattering light, to downplay shortcomings, or to bypass inconvenient episodes. On this count, Hitler fares well; he provides an honest and open life story, devoid of known fabrications or omissions—one that is essential for understanding his thinking and attitudes on social, economic, and political matters.

Second, *Mein Kampf* is a kind of history lesson on Europe around the turn of the 20th century. Hitler was a proximate observer—and often first-hand witness—to many of the major events of the time. He served in the trenches of World War One for more than four years, which was virtually the entire duration of the war. Serving on the 'losing' side, he naturally gives a different interpretation of events than is commonly portrayed by historians of the victorious nations. But this fact should be welcomed by any impartial observer, and in itself makes the book worth reading. With rare exceptions—such as Jünger's *Storm of Steel*—no other non-fiction contemporary German source of this time is readily available in English. For those interested in the Great War and its immediate aftermath, this book is irreplaceable.

In its third aspect, the book serves to document the origins and basic features of Hitler's worldview. This, unsurprisingly, is the most distorted part of the book, in standard Western versions. Here we find the insights and trigger events that led a young man without formal higher education to develop a strikingly visionary, expansive, and forward-looking ideology. Hitler's primary concern, as we read, was the future and well-being of the German people—*all* Germans, regardless of the political unit in which they lived. The German people, or *Volk*, were, he believed, a single ethnicity with unique and singular self-interests. They were—indisputably—responsible for many of the greatest achievements in Western history. They were among the leading lights in music, literature, architecture, science, and technology. They were great warriors, and great nation-builders. They were, in large part, the driving force behind Western civilization itself. Hitler was justly proud of his heritage. Equally is he outraged at the indignities suffered by this great people in then-recent decades—culminating in the disastrous humiliation of World War I and the Treaty of Versailles. He seeks, above all, to remedy these injustices and restore the mantle of greatness to the German people. To do this, he needs to identify both their primary opponents and the defective political ideologies and structures that bind them. Then he undertakes to outline a new socio-political system that can carry them forward to a higher and rightful destiny.

Finally, in its fourth aspect, *Mein Kampf* is a kind of blueprint for action. It describes the evolution and aims of National Socialism and the *NSDAP*, or Nazi Party, in compelling detail. Hitler naturally wants his new movement to succeed in assuming power in Germany and in a future German Reich. But this is no theoretical analysis. Hitler is nothing if not pragmatic. He has concrete goals and specific means of achieving them.

He has nothing but disdain for the *geistige Waffen*, the intellectual weapons, of the impotent intelligentsia. He demands results, and success.

Importantly, his analysis is, in large part, independent of context. It does not pertain only to Germans, or only to the circumstances of the mid-1920s. It is a broadly universal approach based on the conditions of the modern world, and on human nature. As such, Hitler's analysis of action is relevant and useful for many people today—for all those who might strive for national greatness in body and spirit.

This complex textual structure of *Mein Kampf* explains some of the complaints of modern-day critics who decry Hitler's lack of 'coherence' or 'narrative flow.' He has many objectives here, and in their implementation, many points overlap. Perhaps he should have written four books, not one. Perhaps. But Hitler was a doer, not a writer. We must accept this fact, take what we have, and do our best to understand it in an open and objective fashion. He was not striving for a best-selling novel. He wanted to document history and advance a movement, and to these ends he succeeded most admirably.

Origins and Context

Born on 20 April 1889 in present-day Austria, Hitler grew up as a citizen of the multi-ethnic state known as the Austro-Hungarian Empire. This disparate amalgamation was formed in 1867, with the union of the Austrian and Hungarian monarchies; thus does Hitler refer to the state as the "Dual Monarchy." Throughout its 50-year history, it was always a loose conjunction of many ethnicities, and never a truly unified state. The ethnic Germans in it were a minority, and had to struggle to promote their own interests. This fact caused Hitler no end of distress; he explicitly felt more attachment to the broader German *Volk* than to the multi-ethnic state into which he was born.

As a youth, his interests tended toward the arts, painting, and history. This led to conflict with his obstinate father, who envisioned a safe, comfortable bureaucratic career for his son. But his father's death on 3 January 1903, when Adolf was 13, allowed the young man to determine his own future. Two years later, he moved to Vienna, scraping by with menial jobs to survive. In late 1907, his mother died. At the age of 18, he then applied to enter the Viennese Arts Academy in painting, but was diverted to architecture. He worked and studied for two more years, eventually becoming skilled enough to work full-time as a draftsman and painter of watercolors.

All the while, he studied the mass of humanity around him. He read the various writings and publications of the political parties. He observed the workings of the press. He watched how unions functioned. He sat in on Parliament. He followed events in neighboring Germany. And he became intrigued by the comings and goings of one particular minority in Vienna: the Jews.

Gradually he became convinced that the two dominant threats to German well-being were Marxism—a Jewish form of communism—and the international-capitalist Jews. The problems were compounded by the fundamentally inept workings of a representative democracy that tried to serve diverse ethnicities. In the end, the fine and noble concept of democracy became nothing other than a "Jewish democracy," working for the best interests of Jews instead of Austrians or Germans.

Upon turning 23 in 1912, Hitler went to Munich. It was his first extended contact with German culture, and he found it invigorating. He lived there for two years, until the outbreak of World War I in July 1914. Thrilled at the opportunity to defend the German homeland, he enlisted, serving on the Western front in Belgium. After more than 2 years of service, he was slightly wounded in October 1916 and sent back to Germany, spending some time in a reserve battalion in Munich. Appalled at both the role of Jews there and the negative public attitude, he returned to the front in March 1917.

By this time, the war had been dragging on for some two and a half years. It had effectively become a stalemate. Even the looming entrance of the Americans into the war—President Wilson would call for war the next month, and US troops would soon follow—would have little near-term effect. As Hitler explains, however, the Germans actually had reasons for optimism by late 1917. The Central Powers (primarily Germany and Austria-Hungary) had inflicted a decisive defeat on Italy in the Battle of Caporetto, and the Russians had pulled out of the war after the Bolshevik Revolution, thus freeing up German troops for the Western front. Hitler recalls that his compatriots "looked forward with confidence" to the spring of 1918, when they anticipated final victory.

November Revolution, and a New Movement

But things would turn out differently. Germans' dissatisfaction with the prolonged war effort was being fanned by Jewish activists calling for mass demonstrations, strikes, and even revolution against the Kaiser. In late January 1918 there was a large munitions strike. Various workers' actions and riots followed for months afterward. The Western front held, but Germany was weakening internally.

In mid-October of 1918, the German front near Ypres, Belgium was hit with mustard gas. Hitler's eyes were badly affected, and he was sent to a military hospital in Pasewalk, north of Berlin. In late October, a minor naval revolt in Kiel began to spread to the wider population. Two major Jewish-led parties, the Social Democrats (SPD) and the Independent Social

Democratic Party (USPD), agitated for the Kaiser to abdicate—which he did, on November 9. Jewish activists in Berlin and Munich then declared independent "soviet" states. Germany formally capitulated on November 11. After the dust had settled, a new 'Weimar' government was formed, one that was notably susceptible to Jewish influence.[1]

Hearing about the revolution from his hospital bed, Hitler was devastated. All the effort and sacrifices made at the front had proven worthless. Jewish agitators in the homeland had succeeded in whipping up local dissatisfaction to the point that the Kaiser was driven from power. The revolutionaries then assumed power and immediately surrendered to the enemy. This was the infamous "stab in the back" that would haunt German nationalists for years to come. And it was the triggering event that caused Hitler to enter politics.

In September 1919, working for the government, he was assigned to follow and report on a little-known group called the *Deutsche Arbeiterpartei*, or German Workers' Party (*DAP*). He ended up joining the group, and quickly assumed a leadership role. By early 1920, Hitler's speeches were drawing hundreds or thousands of people. On February 24, he announced that the party would henceforth be known as the National Socialist German Workers' Party, or *NSDAP*—'Nazi,' in the parlance of its detractors. It is with this "first great mass meeting" that Hitler closes Volume One of his book.

The new movement grew rapidly. Hitler formalized his leadership in July 1921. A series of stormy and occasionally violent public events occurred in the following months. In November 1922, ideological compatriot Mussolini took power in Italy, which served to bolster both National Socialist efforts domestically and their international reputation. It was on November 21 that the *New York Times* printed its first major article on Hitler: "New Popular Idol Rises in Bavaria." Calling the National Socialists "violently anti-Semitic" and "reactionary" but "well-disciplined," the *NYT* viewed them as "potentially dangerous, though not for the immediate future." Indeed—it would not be for another 10 years that they would assume power in Germany.

Soon thereafter, other events would favor the National Socialists. France had occupied the Ruhr Valley in January 1923, claiming a violation of Versailles; this was taken as a grave insult to German sovereignty. It was also at this time that the infamous German hyperinflation took hold, wiping out the savings of ordinary Germans and forcing them to haul around bushels of cash for even the smallest purchases. By the end of the year, Germany was in a full-blown financial crisis. This led Hitler and

[1] For an elaboration on this matter, see T. Dalton, *The Jewish Hand in the World Wars* (2019).

the *NSDAP* leadership to plan for a revolutionary take-over of Munich on 9 November 1923.

This attempted *Putsch*, or coup, would fail. In a brief shoot-out, 16 Nazis and four policemen were killed. Hitler and the other leaders were arrested within days, put on trial in February 1924, and sentenced to light prison terms. In all, Hitler spent some 13 months in confinement, obtaining release in December of that year. It was during this time that he dictated what would become Volume One of his book.

Hitler reportedly wanted to call his new book "Four and a Half Years of Struggle against Lies, Stupidity, and Cowardice." The publisher adroitly suggested a shorter title: "My Struggle," or *Mein Kampf*. It would initially be published in July of 1925.

Hitler then began a second, shorter volume to complete his program. This appeared in December of 1926. The next year, the two volumes were slightly revised and combined into one work. This so-called 'second edition' of *Mein Kampf* was published when Hitler was 38 years old.

Adolf Hitler at the inauguration of the renovation of the "Brown House," Munich 1930.

Chapter Synopses

It will be useful to provide a very brief summary of the main themes of each of the 27 chapters.

Volume 1

Chapter 1: Hitler's early life. Relationship with parents. Early education. Interest in history and art. Budding nationalism. Covers birth in 1889 to mother's death in late 1907, when Hitler was 18 years old.

Chapter 2: Time alone in Vienna. Marxism and international Jewry as main threats. Assessment and critique of Viennese government. Life of the working class. Study of the Social Democratic party, and its Jewish influence. Role of unions. Burgeoning anti-Semitism. Study of the destructive role of Marxism.

Chapter 3: General reflections on Austrian politics, and representative democracy. Failings of multi-ethnic states. Critique of Western democracy. Failings of 'majority rule.' Demise of the pan-German movement. Unfortunate conflict with the Catholic Church. Anti-Semitism and religion. Covers period up to age 23 (1912).

Chapter 4: Moves to Munich. Critique of German alliances. Four possible paths of German policy. Population growth, and the need for land. Need for alliance with England. Initial discussion of the role of Aryans. Marxism as mortal foe. Covers up to mid-1914.

Chapter 5: Outbreak of World War One. Hitler enlists, at age 25. "Baptism by fire."

Chapter 6: Role and need for propaganda. Effective use by England; failure by Germany.

Chapter 7: Course of the Great War. Wounded in late 1916. Jews and negative attitudes rampant in Munich. Munitions strike in early 1918. Poisoned by mustard gas in October 1918, at age 29. November Revolution.

Chapter 8: Postwar time in Munich. Need for a new party. Negative role of global capitalism.

Chapter 9: Encounters German Workers' Party (*DAP*). Early meetings. Joins *DAP*, as member #7, at age 30.

Chapter 10: Analysis of the collapse of the German Empire in 1918. Dominance of international capitalism. Effect of the press on the masses. Jewish control of press. Combating the syphilis epidemic. Cultural decay in modern art. Ineffective parliament. The army as a source of discipline.

Chapter 11: Detailed racial theory. Nature strives to improve species. Racial mixing between 'higher' and 'lower' types yields physical, moral, and cultural decay. Aryans as true founders of civilization. Aryan tendency for self-sacrifice. Aryan versus Jew. Jews as parasites. Fake Jewish 'religion.' Extended examination of "the way of Jewry"—historical, sociological, political. Marxist worldview. Jewish subversion of democracy. Ill effects of racial impurity.

Chapter 12: Evolution of *DAP*. Extended discussion of the need to nationalize the masses. How to organize a party. Gaining publicity. Second major meeting in October 1919. Growing success. Rejection of 'intellectual' weapons. First true mass meeting in February 1920. Transition to *NSDAP*.

Volume 2

Chapter 1: Corruption of democracy. Concept of 'folkish.' Transforming ideals into practice. Marxism pushes race equality. State must serve racial function: to promote the best.

Chapter 2: Three conventional concepts of state. State as means to end: advancing human race. Must maintain racial integrity. Strong minorities end up ruling. Racial mixing leads to decay. State must promote healthy children. Basic eugenic theory. Folkish education, for physical, mental, and moral strength. Promote willpower, determination, responsibility. Meritocracy.

Chapter 3: Citizenship based on race. Three classes: citizen, subject, foreigner.

Chapter 4: Aristocratic principle. Value of the individual. Marxism promotes mass thinking. Government rule by the best individuals, not majority.

Chapter 5: Need for an uncompromising worldview. Need for decisive leadership. 25-point *NSDAP* program is unshakable. Only *NSDAP* is truly folkish.

Chapter 6: Resumes autobiography. *NSDAP* must dominate mass opinion. Must fight against common views. Brest-Litovsk and Versailles. Importance of spoken word. Marxism flourished with speeches. Need for mass meetings.

Chapter 7: Lame bourgeois mass meetings. Need for publicity. Control of mass meetings. Violent protests. Party flag and symbol: swastika. First use in summer 1920. Party strength by early 1921. Mass meeting 3 Feb at Circus Krone. Attempted disruption.

Chapter 8: Right of priority. Many folkish movements. Futility of compromise and coalition.

Chapter 9: Three pillars of authority. In warfare, survival of the inferior. Deserters and Jewish revolutionaries in November 1918. Bourgeois capitulation. Need for a great ideal. Creation of the *SA* (storm troops). *NSDAP* is neither secret nor illegal. *SA* as trained fighters. March to Coburg in Oct 1922. French occupation of the Ruhr.

Chapter 10: War industries in World War I. Bavaria versus Prussia as diversion. Kurt Eisner, Jewish revolutionary. Growth of anti-Semitism from 1918. Catholic versus Protestant as diversion. Federation versus unification. Opposition to Jewish Weimar.

Chapter 11: Role of propaganda. Supporters and members. Need for restricted growth. Leadership principle versus majority rule. Acquisition of *Völkischer Beobachter*. Building the party. Dissolution on 9 Nov 1923.

Chapter 12: Question of trade unions. Necessity of unions. *NSDAP* must form a union. Union in service to the people. Priority of worldview.

Chapter 13: Foreign policy as means for promoting national interest. Unification of German people. England against Germany. France against England. Need for alliance with England and Italy. Jews seek world conquest, racial contamination. Question of South Tyrol. Jews oppose German-Italian alliance. Only fascist Italy is opposing Jews. Jews gain power in America.

Chapter 14: Russia policy is foremost. Top priority: need for land, living space. Victory goes to the strong. No colonies, but only an expanded Reich. Look to the East. Russia is ruled by Jews, and cannot be an ally. Only possible alliances: England and Italy.

Chapter 15: German submission. Locarno Treaty as further submission. France seeks to dismember Germany. War with France is inevitable. France occupies Ruhr, opposes England. Must confront and destroy Marxism. Failure of Cuno's passive resistance.

Previous English Translations

For the first several years of its existence, there was no real need for English publishers to produce a translation of *Mein Kampf.* The Nazi movement was small, limited more or less to Bavaria. It had little prospect for growth or real power. There was simply not much interest in an obscure Bavarian politician.

All this changed when Hitler took power in 1933. Suddenly there was a need to understand this man who had risen to power at only 44 years of age. A British translator, Edgar Dugdale, undertook the initial effort to produce an English version. It was a highly abridged edition, covering only some 45 percent of the full text. It was published in England by Hurst & Blackett, and in the US by Houghton-Mifflin, in late 1933.

In 1936, the German government decided that they would sponsor their own, complete, English translation. They hired a British writer and journalist, James Murphy. There not yet having been a second world war, and the worst excesses of Nazism still in the future, Murphy was inclined to produce a favorable and sympathetic translation. Unfortunately, there was a falling out with National Socialist officials and Murphy was 'fired' sometime in 1938, his project incomplete. Through some obscure process, the Germans completed Murphy's draft version on their own, and published it in the late 1930s. Today this is known as the Stalag edition, and is currently available in print in two forms: one by Ostara Publications, and one by Elite Minds (the "official Nazi English translation"). To call this version 'unpolished' is an understatement; more below.

By 1939, four new versions had appeared. After his dismissal, Murphy returned to England and revised and completed his translation, which was published by Hurst & Blackett in 1939. This is 'the' Murphy translation; it is widely available on the Internet, and through various reprints. Under the Hutchinson imprint, the Murphy translation was republished in 1969 with a lengthy and hostile introduction by British historian D. C. Watt.

Secondly, the British firm Reynal & Hitchcock enlisted a team of people, headed by Alvin Johnson, to do their own translation. It was notably hostile to the content of the book and the National Socialist movement generally.

Third, an American publisher, Stackpole and Sons, produced a version under the direction of a Jewish editor, William Soskin. They hired a Jewish socialist, Ludwig Lore, to write the preface. Unsurprisingly, this too was a hostile effort. Soskin was successfully sued by Houghton-Mifflin for copyright infringement, and production was halted after only a few months.

The final work of 1939 was a second abridgment, produced by American journalist—and future senator—Alan Cranston. Cranston was also sued; he too lost, but not before allegedly selling several hundred thousand copies.

Dissatisfied with the abridged Dugdale translation, Houghton-Mifflin embarked on a new, full translation, by Jewish-German writer Ralph Manheim. They also solicited a short introduction by a Jewish-German journalist, Konrad Heiden. As expected, it was another blatantly hostile production. The book appeared in 1943, and has been continuously in print since then. To the present day, the Manheim version functions as the 'official' translation of *Mein Kampf*; it is the one quoted by nearly all academics and journalists. The latest Houghton edition, issued in 1998, includes an introduction by notorious Jewish Zionist Abraham Foxman. Clearly, little has changed in the intervening years.

For several decades, these were the extant English translations. Then in 2009, a little-known writer, Michael Ford, published his own translation through Elite Minds. This edition has several shortcomings, as explained below.

Something of the flavor of these efforts can be seen in the very first words of the book. In my 2022 translation, Chapter 1 is titled "In My Parents' House." (Original: *Im Elternhaus*.) The first sentence: "I consider it most fortunate today that destiny selected Braunau-on-the-Inn to be my birthplace" (*Als glückliche Bestimmung gilt es mir heute, dass das Schicksal mir zum Geburtsort gerade Braunau am Inn zuwies*.) The list below gives the chapter title and the first few words, in the various translations:

Translation	Chapter 1	Initial words
Dugdale	My Home	It stands me in good stead today that Fate…
Johnson	At Home	Today I consider it my good fortune that Fate…
Murphy (Stalag)	My Home	To-day I consider it a good omen that destiny…
Murphy ('standard')	In the Home of my Parents	It has turned out fortunate for me to-day that…
Manheim	In the House of my Parents	Today it seems to me providential that Fate…
Soskin	Childhood Home	Today I regard it as a happy change that Fate…
Ford	Childhood Home	Today, I am pleased that Fate chose the city…

The variability of even this simple leading sentence is striking. One can imagine the issues involved with the many more-complicated thoughts that follow.

Why a New Translation?

As it happens, every one of the previous translations has major problems and disadvantages, for a modern English reader.

The two primary versions—Murphy and Manheim—are written in the style of early-20th-century British writers. They use a wide array of archaic 'British-isms' and British spellings that make reading awkward, particularly for Americans in the present day. Worse, they attempt to follow too closely Hitler's original style. Like most Germans of the time, Hitler wrote long sentences, fashioned into long, complex paragraphs. Manheim follows this style scrupulously, to the detriment of the reader; Murphy at least occasionally breaks up long sentences into more readable segments.

Worst of all, both major translations are simply poor efforts. They do not read well. One repeatedly encounters passages that are awkward, incoherent, or incomprehensible. There is little of the fluidity and lyrical power of the German original. For his part, Murphy takes a considerable amount of 'translator's license,' interjecting unwarranted terminology and wording, or simply leaving things out. Manheim is more literal, but in the end is scarcely more readable. The reader simply needs to scan a sampling of either text to understand the situation.

This is unfortunate, to say the least. It is almost as if the publishers intended, or at least preferred, that the translations be difficult to read. Certainly this limits the circulation of Hitler's ideas, and makes it easier to dismiss them—a convenient situation for the book's many critics.

With the exception of Murphy, all of the standard editions betray their intentions with aggressive, hostile, and slanderous comments in their introductions. Consider this selection of remarks:

> Johnson: Hitler is "no artist in literary expression," and "often indifferent to grammar and syntax." The book is "a propagandistic essay by a violent partisan" that "warps historical truth" or "ignores it completely." Hitler's discussions on race can be safely dismissed, because "the greatest anthropologists of the 20th century are agreed that 'race' is a practically meaningless word."
>
> Lore: "I cannot conceive of any book of which I more positively disapprove." The book has an "atrocious style" and "countless contradictions." In essence, the book is "an outpouring of willful perversion, clumsy forgery, vitriolic hatred, and violent denunciation."
>
> Manheim: Hitler is a "paranoiac" who offers us "disjointed facts" and "largely unintelligible flights of Wagnerian fantasy." He creates "a dream-world," one "without color and movement."

> Heiden: *Mein Kampf* was written "in white-hot hatred." It is "ill-founded, undocumented, and badly written." "The book may well be called a kind of satanic Bible."
>
> Watt: The book is "lengthy, dull, bombastic, repetitious and extremely badly written." "Most of its statements of fact…are demonstrably untrue." It yields "an intolerably prolix German style and a total lack of any intellectual precision." As a work of political philosophy, "it has no claims whatever to be taken seriously." Hitler's racial theory—a "mystical racist mumbo-jumbo of Aryanism"—is a "revolting mixture of pseudo-science and bogus historicism." The work is self-consistent, but this only betrays "the terrible consistency of the insane." In the end, Hitler is nothing more than a "master of the inept, the undigested, the half-baked and the untrue."
>
> Foxman: Hitler's "theories have long since been discredited." The book is "a work of ugliness and depravity." It is "unreliable as a source of historical data," full of "lies, omissions, and half-truths." The book's "atrocious style, puerile digressions, and narcissistic self-absorption" are obvious. Its theories are "extremist, immoral, and seem to promise war." Hitler's "lunatic plan" is "absurd" and even "comical." All in all, "a ridiculous tract."

Any translator, editor, or publisher who would include such words can hardly be trusted to do an honest job. The intent to bias the reader is plain. Certainly there is no concern here for the author to obtain a fair and objective reading. In fact, precisely the opposite.

The recent Ford translation, while not overtly hostile, has several other major flaws. Ford has no discernible credentials, no publishing record, nor any documented history with such academic works. His 'in text' notes are awkward and distracting. The book includes many amateurish and cartoonish 'photos.' There is no index. And his so-called publishing house, Elite Minds, appears to be some kind of obscure environmental group. This is unfortunate; the last thing the public needs is another misleading, ill-conceived, and unqualified version of *Mein Kampf.*

The 'Nazi' or 'Stalag' edition of Murphy has its own problems. The version published by Elite Minds claims to be authentic, which means that they retained all the original flaws of grammar, punctuation, and spelling. The result is nearly unreadable. The edition published by Ostara fixes many of these problems, but still reads poorly. It does break up the long paragraphs, but to an extreme degree; one typically finds single-sentence paragraphs, as in a newspaper. This move destroys all flow and connection of ideas. And neither version has an index or explanatory footnotes.

It was for all these reasons that I embarked on a new translation, which was initially released in 2017 and then revised in 2022. My edition addresses and resolves many of these unfortunate drawbacks. First, by including the full and original German text, in a parallel translation, the English wording can be easily verified. This technique has often been used with classic Greek and Latin authors, but never before with *Mein Kampf.* Section headings have been added, in text, in bold. The German original employed such headings, but only at the top of each page; the reader thus never knew where a new section actually began. These headings have been translated and inserted at the appropriate points, in my estimation, and directly in the text. My translation also has helpful and relevant footnotes, a useful index, and a bibliography of relevant secondary source material. Most important of all, though, is the fact that the English reads smoothly and naturally. Obviously I am not unbiased here, but based on reader feedback, my edition is perhaps the best English version in existence.

Some Contentious Topics

It goes without saying that this book is controversial. In fact, it may well be named as the single most controversial book in history. As such, the typical reader is more or less guaranteed to get a slanted and biased account of it. Of Hitler's many controversial statements and topics, four subjects warrant a brief mention here: *National Socialism, race theory, religion*, and *the Jews*.

Of the many simplistic and overused hyperboles in modern usage, the use of 'Nazi' surely ranks among the worst. It is a crude and almost comical synonym for evil, hateful, cruel, tyrannical, and so on. This is consistent with the general demonization of everything Hitler.

'Nazi' is, of course, an abbreviation for National Socialist (*Nationalsozialist*). It was prompted by an earlier term, 'Sozi,' which was short for *Sozialdemokrat*, referring to the Social Democrat party that had been in existence since the mid-1800s. Hitler and colleagues rarely used 'Nazi,' generally viewing it as derogatory—although Goebbels did write an early essay and short book titled *The Nazi-Sozi*.

As an ideology, National Socialism is utterly misunderstood. In fact, surprisingly, many people around the world today implicitly endorse some form of it. Most European countries, and many other nations globally, are to some degree socialist. Socialism—loosely defined as government control and oversight of at least certain key portions of the economic sector—stands in contrast to free-market capitalism, in which for-profit corporations control such things. Suffice it to say that socialism is a respected political and economic system around the globe.

Nationalism places high priority on the well-being of the nation-state and its traditional residents. It is inward-looking, rather than outward. It tends toward economic independence and autonomy rather than globalization and inter-connectedness. It typically supports and strengthens the dominant ethnicity and culture, and largely ignores that of minorities. This, too, is hardly unknown; there are strong nationalist movements in many countries around the world today.

As it happens, the United States is neither nationalist nor socialist. Thus, its media and its economic and political elite tend to dismiss or abuse both concepts. Americans are functionally brainwashed to believe that socialism is evil and that nationalism is the hallmark of crude and primitive autocrats, and racist as well. This fact is revealing; the American power elite wants no one to get the idea that anything like nationalism or socialism—or, God forbid, national socialism—should become a credible ideology.

Now, it is true that Hitler's form of national socialism went further than these basic concepts. It explicitly targeted Marxists, Jews, and global capitalists as enemies of the German people. It also sought to replace representative democracy with a more efficient and accountable centralized governance. Hitler had rational arguments for all these issues, as he explains in his book.

In sum, Hitler's National Socialism is essentially the product of German nationalism and progressive socialism, combined with a mild form of anti-Semitism—hardly the embodiment of evil.

Racial Theory

Mein Kampf contains numerous references to 'blood' (*Blut*) and 'race' (*Rasse*). This is always portrayed in the worst possible terms, as some kind of demonic, hate-filled, blind racism. But we must first realize that such talk was commonplace in the early 20th century; Hitler's terminology, though shocking today, was actually quite conventional at the time. Not being a scientist, and few having much understanding of genetics at the time, it is understandable that he would use such terms.

Therefore, a literal interpretation of such words is misleading. In modern terminology, Hitler's 'race' is better viewed as 'ethnicity.' He was more an *ethnicist* than a racist. His call for justice for the "German race" is really on behalf of *ethnic* Germans—the *Volk*. Thus understood, his view is much less threatening than commonly portrayed. Yes, he viewed ethnic Germans as superior. Yes, he wanted the best for his people. Yes, he was not much interested in the welfare of minorities or other nationalities. This is hardly a sin. Many people around the world today fight for precisely such things, for their own ethnicities. And they are right to do so.

Even today, it is reasonable and appropriate to discuss issues of race. It is a relevant term in biological taxonomy, indicating the highest-level sub-grouping within the species Homo sapiens. By some accounts, there are three races: White/Caucasian, Black/Negroid, and Mongoloid/Asian. These are then subdivided into ethnicities, of which there are some 5,000 in total.

By this measure, Hitler cared little about race. He made a few dismissive comments about Blacks, but nothing that wasn't standard at the time. He actually admired certain people of the Asian race, especially the Japanese. But his primary concern was among the various White ethnicities. He sought a position of strength and influence for ethnic Germans; he sought alliances with ethnic Britons; and he sought to oppose ethnic Jews.

Then there is Hitler's infamous talk of 'Aryan.' Apart from passing mention elsewhere in the book, it is discussed in detail only in Chapter 11 of Volume 1. While there is no talk of any 'superman'—no reference to Nietzsche's *Übermensch*, for example—it is clear that Hitler views the Aryan as the highest human type, the greatest ethnicity, mover and creator of civilization. Notably, he never defines Aryan. Rather, we learn only what the Aryan is *not*: he is not Black, not Oriental, and certainly not Jewish. The Jew is the anti-Aryan, his dark and corrupting opposite. The Aryan builds, the Jew destroys. The Aryan produces, the Jew consumes. The Aryan is idealistic, the Jew materialistic.

In the end, the Aryan is distinguished not by his superior intelligence, nor his great creativity, but mainly by his altruism: the Aryan is a self-sacrificing person, more willing than any others to work on behalf of society. Thus he builds civilization and culture, and spreads it to the world. Non-Aryans, to the extent that they have a culture, get it from the Aryans, even as they customize it to their own needs. But the original source and sustainer is the self-sacrificing Aryan.

The word 'Aryan' has an interesting origin, and it has nothing to do with the Germans. It comes from the Sanskrit *arya*, meaning 'noble.' It originally referred to the people and language that moved into India from the north around 1500 BC. In the Indian caste system, the Aryans became the Brahmans—the highest and noblest caste. It was they who cultivated the Sanskrit language, and ultimately developed Indian culture. And a final point of interest: Those immigrants from the north came from the region that is known today as the Iranian plateau. In fact, the word 'Iran' derives directly from 'Aryan'; the Iranians were the original Aryans.

Not being a scholar of ancient history, and having no Internet at hand, Hitler knew little of all this. He simply picked up on prior German and European usage. In fact, talk of Aryans as a superior race predated Hitler by several decades. It was a main theme of Frenchman Arthur de Gobineau's book *Essay on the Inequality of the Human Races*, of 1855. And it was prominent in Briton-turned-German author Houston Stewart Chamberlain's book *Foundations of the Nineteenth Century*, published in 1899. By the time Hitler picked up on the term, it was old hat.

On Religion

Among other calumnies, Hitler is often portrayed as a godless atheist, a devil worshipper, the antichrist, or some kind of maniacal pagan. In fact he was none of these. Rather, Hitler was broadly supportive of Christianity. He called it "the Religion of Love," and referred to Jesus, indirectly, as its "sublime founder." He argued that the masses are not and cannot be philosophical; their ethics must come from traditional religious sources. And he believed in separation of church and state: "political parties have no right to meddle in religious questions." He condemned the Jews because they mock religion, and portray ethics and morality as "antiquated sentiment."

His view on God is quite intriguing. Frequently he refers to a kind of cosmic deity or divine power, but in a variety of unconventional terms. We find many references, for example, to *Schicksal*—fate or destiny. We read of the "Goddess of Destiny" (*Schicksalgöttin*). He writes of "Providence" (*Vorsehung*), "Doom" or "Fate" (*Verhängnis*), and "the Lord" (*Herr*). Elsewhere we find reference to "Chance" (*Zufall*) and "the eternal Creator" (*ewige Schöpfer*). Volume 1 closes with a reference to "the Goddess of Inexorable Vengeance" (*die Göttin der unerbittlichen Rache*). These are not mere metaphors. It seems to be a kind of recognition of higher powers in the cosmos, but not those of traditional religions.

In the end, Hitler was most offended by crude materialism: the quest for money and material power. This view has no concept of idealism, no notion of spirituality, no vision of higher powers in the universe. Materialism was the essence of both Marxism and capitalism—and both were embodied in the Jew. That is why these things were, according to Hitler, the mortal enemy of anyone seeking higher aims in life.

Hitler himself was no fan of religious dogma, but seems to have envisioned a future that moved toward a new kind of spirituality, one aligned with the workings of nature. We may perhaps best view him as a 'spiritual but not religious' sort of person—a view that is notably widespread today.

On the Jews

If nothing else, Hitler is inevitably depicted as a confirmed anti-Semite and Jew-hater. We should be clear: this is absolutely true. There are many lies spread about Hitler, but this is not one of them. The key is understanding why he held this view.

In the second half of Chapter 2 (Volume 1), he describes in striking detail his gradual discovery of the role and effects of Jews in society. He recalls that, as a youth, he had only known one Jewish boy, but had no particular feelings toward him one way or the other. He hadn't even heard them discussed much until his mid-teens, and then only in a vaguely negative political context. When he moved to Vienna at age 15, he encountered a city of 2 million that was 10 percent Jewish. At first, he barely noticed them. When he did, he viewed them as representatives of a rather strange religion, but since he was generally tolerant of religious diversity, he gave them little thought. He was put off by the "anti-Semitic" press. As he says, "on grounds of human tolerance, I opposed the idea that [the Jew] should be attacked because he had a different faith."

But then Hitler began to pay attention to the mainstream press. They were informative and liberal, but yet often flamboyant and garish. They seemed anxious to curry favor with the corrupt monarchy. And they were uniformly critical of the German Kaiser and his people. He noticed that some of the anti-Semitic papers were actually more skeptical of Viennese authority, and more open-minded regarding the Germans. At the same time, he realized that the Jews were more numerous than he previously believed. In fact, certain districts of Vienna were 50 percent Jewish, or more. And they all seemed to endorse a strange ideology: Zionism.

Furthermore, they were visually and physically repellent. Their black caftans and braided hair locks looked comical. They had their own odd concept of 'cleanliness': "That they were not water-lovers was obvious upon first glance." They smelled bad: "The odor of those people in caftans often made me sick to my stomach." This was topped off by "the unkempt clothes and the generally ignoble appearance." All in all, a sorry sight.

Worst of all, hidden away inside, was their "moral rot." Jews seemed to be involved in all manner of shady, unethical, and illegal activities. Hitler began to study the situation in more detail. "The fact was that 90 percent of all the filthy literature, artistic trash, and theatrical idiocy had to be charged to the account of a people who formed scarcely one percent of the nation. This fact could not be denied." Pornography, lewd art and theater, prostitution, human trafficking…all could be tied to the Jews.

The famed mainstream Viennese press, Hitler discovered, was almost completely a Jewish enterprise. Jewish writers repeatedly praised Jewish actors, authors, and businessmen. People, events, and policies favorable to Jews were lauded, and those that were disadvantageous were condemned. Even the dominant political party, the Social Democrats, was found to be led by Jews. Upon this realization, says Hitler, "the scales fell from my eyes." The whole pattern came together: a Jewish press supporting a Jewish political system, even as other Jews profited from the moral corruption of the people. Profit and power at all cost; lies and deceit without compunction; and an utter lack of concern for fairness, democracy, human welfare or even human decency. "I gradually came to hate them," he said.

Considered globally, the situation was even worse. Marxism—the product of a Jew, Karl Marx—was promulgated by Jews in Europe and around the world. It sought to dominate and control nature. It sought to level all social differences, thereby subverting the natural order in which the truly best people rightly flourish. In essence, it was a teaching and a means by which Jews could ruthlessly assume control of entire nations. Once that happened, thousands or even millions of natives would die. The 1917 Bolshevik Revolution in Russia was proof enough.

In other parts of Europe, the dominant ideology was capitalism. Here, money ruled. Here, the bankers and corporate moguls dictated even to kings. Markets must be opened, international trade promoted, and loans used to extract wealth from the masses. And when these titans of capital were investigated, they were found to be, more often than not, Jews.

For Hitler, these realizations were devastating. The recognition of the insidious role of the Jews was "the greatest inner revolution that I had yet experienced." Indeed: "From being a soft-hearted cosmopolitan, I became an out-and-out anti-Semite." No hidden views here.

Hitler's conversion to anti-Semitism was remarkable. In contrast to the common view, it was neither arbitrary nor irrational. He was not a born Jew-hater. It was a step-by-step process, taken over a long period of time, and based on his data and observations about the real world. His was a "rational" anti-Semitism. As he saw it, any person of dignity and self-respect, anyone with a concern for human life, anyone committed to the integrity of the natural world, would of necessity be an anti-Semite. In their ruthless pursuit of their own self-interest, Jews, said Hitler, become the enemy of all mankind. Anyone not recognizing this fact—and acting accordingly—he thought a fool.

The modern person today winces at such talk. "A monster!" we say. "Hate speech!" "The devil!" And yet, these are not rational responses. The modern man is conditioned to say such things. We must be objective here. Hitler was not inventing facts. His observations were largely true, even if he had no access to formal data or statistics. Jews did dominate in Vienna, and even more so in Germany. Consider the following numbers, cited by Sarah Gordon:

> The reader may be surprised to learn that Jews were never a large percentage of the total German population; at no time did they exceed 1.09 percent of the population during the years 1871 to 1933… [In spite of this, Jews] were overrepresented in business, commerce, and public and private service… Within the fields of business and commerce, Jews…

> represented 25 percent of all individuals employed in retail business and handled 25 percent of total sales...; they owned 41 percent of iron and scrap iron firms and 57 percent of other metal businesses....
>
> Jews were [also] prominent in private banking under both Jewish and non-Jewish ownership or control. They were especially visible in private banking in Berlin, which in 1923 had 150 private (versus state) Jewish banks, as opposed to only 11 private non-Jewish banks....[2]

This trend held true in the academic and cultural spheres as well: "Jews were overrepresented among university professors and students between 1870 and 1933.... [A]lmost 19 percent of the instructors in Germany were of Jewish origin.... Jews were also highly active in the theater, the arts, film, and journalism. For example, in 1931, 50 percent of the 234 theater directors in Germany were Jewish, and in Berlin the number was 80 percent..." Hitler was not imagining things.

Furthermore, Jews did in fact curry favor with the monarchy when it was in their interest, but they were quick to revolt if that could yield a greater gain. Jewish Marxists had succeeded in Russia, and were prominent in the November Revolution in Germany, making them responsible, in part, for Germany's defeat in World War I. Jews were eager to profit by any means possible: war, corruption, immorality, exploitation, deception. And many were Zionists: committed to creating a Jewish state in Palestine, and willing to do whatever it took to achieve this.

What to do? For Hitler, there was only one logical conclusion: Drive them out. This meant pushing them out of society, out of the economy, and restoring control of the media and government to non-Jews. It meant creating a *Judenrein*, or Jew-free, society, one that was free from internal and external manipulation by Jewish interests. This, in fact, was Hitler's conclusion years before he began *Mein Kampf*. In late 1919, as he was just becoming acquainted with the DAP, he wrote a letter to one of his officers regarding how to respond to the Jewish question. This striking early letter concludes as follows:

> Rational anti-Semitism...must lead to a systematic and legal struggle against, and eradication of, the privileges the Jews enjoy over the other foreigners living among us (Alien Laws). Its final objective, however, must be the total removal of all Jews (*die Entfernung der Juden überhaupt*) from our midst. Both

[2] *Hitler, Germans, and the Jewish Question* (1984), pp. 10-14.

> objectives can only be achieved by a government of national strength, never by a government of national impotence.[3]

His view did not change in *Mein Kampf*, nor evidently anytime later in his life. His solution was always the same: drive them out. Total removal. Ruthlessly if necessary, but out they must go.

Here is one striking point, however: With one minor exception, Hitler never called for killing the Jews. Though his terminology shifted over time, his words always referred to some form of removal: Jews should be "deported," "expelled," "rooted out." Their role and their power in the German Reich must be "destroyed" or "liquidated." But explicit words like 'killing,' 'shooting,' 'murder,' 'gassing,' virtually never appear in his speeches, writings, or even private conversations.

The one exception is at the very end of *Mein Kampf*. There were about 600,000 Jews in Germany at the start of World War I, a war that ended in the deaths of over 2 million Germans. Hitler argues that killing "12 or 15 thousand Hebrew corrupters" at the start of the war, by a poison gas such as fell on the German troops in the battlefield, would have spared a million lives and led to German victory. Not *all* the Jews, or even most of them; just one or two percent would have sufficed, to derail their pernicious aims. But this seems to be the last such reference by Hitler, in any documented writing or speech.

English sources always translate Hitler's wording as wanting to "exterminate," "destroy," or "annihilate" the Jews; but this is another deception. None of his actual words demands mass killing—or even any killing at all. If the Jews have been driven out of Germany, they have indeed been 'exterminated' (lit. 'driven beyond the border'). If their control over the economy has been terminated, their power has indeed been 'annihilated,' or 'reduced to nothing.' If Jewish society has been removed, it may rightly be said to have been 'destroyed' (lit. 'un-built' or 'deconstructed'). Hitler's tough talk was never any different than that of any world leader when confronting a mortal enemy. President Obama often speaks of "destroying" the "cancer" of the Islamic State, but no one accuses him of attempted genocide.

Thus we find no talk of mass murder (with the lone exception), extermination camps, genocide, or anything like this in *Mein Kampf*. Hitler's opponents search in vain for signs of an impending 'Holocaust' in which the mass of German Jewry would be murdered. The reader is invited to do the same. It is simply not there—much to the chagrin of his critics.

From all this, it should be clear that Hitler had only one real enemy in the Jews. He was not some all-purpose hater of humanity. He disliked the French, respected the British and Americans, and sympathized with the

---

[3] Cited from W. Maser, *Hitler's Letters and Notes* (1974), p. 215.

Russians, but didn't hate them. Even the "lesser" races were never a target of contempt, but rather, if anything, pity. Today we are under the impression that, in 1940, the entire world quivered at the thought of a Nazi takeover. But this was never more than trumped-up propaganda. Hitler wanted to be a world *power*—like all major nations—but never a world *ruler*.

In short, unless you were a Jew, you had nothing to fear. Whites had nothing to fear—unless they allowed themselves to be ruled by Jewish Marxists or Jewish capitalists. Hispanics, Blacks, and Orientals, though of lower status, had nothing to fear. France and England had nothing to fear—until *they* declared war on Germany. America never had anything to fear—until Roosevelt made the unwise decision to harass Germany and Japan into conflict. It was always and only the Jews who were his enemy.

From the Jewish perspective, of course, this is the ultimate evil: a man who seeks to destroy Jewish power, confiscate their obscene wealth, and create a Jew-free society. Should he succeed, and should his new society flourish, it would mean catastrophe for Jews worldwide. People everywhere might begin to perceive treachery in Jewish influence.

This is why *Mein Kampf* is so dangerous.

Hitler's Legacy

Hitler had a great and noble vision for his people. He desperately wanted Germany to assume its rightful place in the world, and to set an example for all those who aspired to something better than a crude material existence. By contrast, the social vision of virtually every other world leader of the 20th century—or the 21st—pales.

Hitler had concrete goals in mind for his nation, and concrete plans to get there. He faced three fundamental challenges: (1) to restore the economy, (2) to achieve security and independence by becoming a world power, and (3) to create an idealistic, uplifting, and sustainable German society. He put his plan into action as soon as he came to power in 1933. And it worked. It worked so well that a beleaguered, beaten-down, hyper-inflated, emasculated German nation rose up to become a world power with astonishing speed. Consider: After just three years, Hitler's Germany had conquered inflation, driven down unemployment, and put industry back to work—all in the midst of a global depression. After six years, it was a world power. After eight years, his nation was so powerful that it took the combined effort of virtually the entire rest of the world to defeat it.

The first two aspects of his plan were attained. But the rest of the world, driven in part by Jewish hatred, jealousy, and spite, could not bear this, and so they sought to crush him and his German nation—which they did. The real tragedy of Hitler's story is that he never had time to tackle his third great challenge: to create a flourishing German society. Sadly, we will never know the long-term potential consequences of National Socialism, or whether a truly great society could have been constructed.

But what about the Holocaust? What about the death camps and gas chambers? Isn't this the terrible, inevitable outcome of Hitler's warped vision?

Here we have perhaps the greatest deception of all. In order to show the world the horrible outcome of a potent anti-Semitism, a tale of monumental human disaster had to be constructed, promoted, and sustained. The undeniable and tragic death of several hundred thousand Jews—which included many deaths by old age, disease, injury, suicide, and in combat situations—would have to become "6 million." Tough talk against Jews, aimed at driving them out of Germany, would have to become "euphemisms for mass murder." Rooms designed to disinfest clothing and bedding against disease-carrying lice would have to become "homicidal gas chambers." Hundreds of thousands of Jewish bodies would have to be burned down to ash, and then made to completely vanish. Transit camps constructed to move Jews out of the Reich—Treblinka, Belzec, Sobibor—would have to become "extermination camps" designed for mass-murder; and with diesel-engine exhaust, no less. And a forced-labor camp in which thousands of Jews died from typhus—Auschwitz—would have to become "the greatest death camp of all time."

Clearly there is much more to be said here.[4] Suffice it to say that the Holocaust, as commonly portrayed, is an unsubstantiated, unwarranted, and unjustified exaggeration of epic proportions. Nearly every aspect of the story crumbles as soon as it is put to the test. The alleged horror of the Holocaust becomes, in the end, a story of the dispossession and expulsion of one particular minority community that held disproportionate power in a nation that did not want them, and that bore disproportionate guilt for that nation's misfortunes. That they themselves should have suffered as a result is unsurprising.

Mein Kampf is one man's assessment of history and vision for the future. It is blunt; it is harsh; it is unapologetic. It does not comply with contemporary expectations of politeness, objectivity, and political correctness. It sounds offensive to sensitive modern ears. But the book is undeniably important. It is more consequential than perhaps any other political work in history. It deserves to be read. And each reader will then be free to determine its ultimate value and meaning for themselves.

---

[4] For more on the decisive Jewish role in WW2, see my book *The Jewish Hand in the World Wars* (2019). For more on the many issues with the Holocaust narrative, see my books *The Holocaust: An Introduction* (2016) or *Debating the Holocaust* (2020; 4th ed.).

— 7 —
IN DEFENSE OF 'NAZISM'

For an intelligent and well-educated man, Barack Obama says some incredibly stupid things. Speaking to a college campus on 7 September 2018, on the topic of the many failings of the Trump presidency, and in particular his response to the White nationalist Charlottesville rally of 2017, Obama denounced Trump for not clearly and unconditionally denouncing the marchers. The participants, who represented a range of views and political opinions, were uniformly condemned by the mass media as "Nazis." At the time, Trump said there were "good people" among the marchers. Obama disagreed, saying, "We're sure as heck supposed to stand up clearly and unequivocally to Nazi sympathizers. How hard can that be? Saying that Nazis are bad?"[1]

Now, it's unclear if Obama is ignorant, brainwashed, bribed, or coerced into saying such simple-minded and facile things. The degree of distortion, deception, and propaganda in this short statement is quite amazing—and likely deliberate. It is worth taking a moment to dissect this situation, and draw some plausible conclusions.

First, it's not evident that there was much 'Nazism' in Charlottesville at all. A few Nazi flags were to be seen, and a few random swastikas—from unknown perpetrators, possibly engaged in a false flag operation—but they were vastly outnumbered by American flags, Confederate flags, and a range of dissident-right and nationalist symbolism. I don't recall seeing any stiff-arm salutes, pro-Hitler chants, or anything of the sort. And yet Obama and the media—left and right—loved to call the marchers 'Nazis' or 'neo-Nazis,' as if this were some magic incantation with the power to ward off evil. Calling someone a Nazi is evidently viewed as an effective all-purpose slur intended to stifle discussion and demonize one's target. And in our present politically-correct, Jewish-media-dominated world, it works—at least, on the unthinking masses.

But any thoughtful person understands that there is much more going on here. Any thinking person would ask at least two questions: 1) What

---

[1] A similar situation occurred a year earlier, when comedian Stephen Colbert interviewed former Trump communications director Anthony Scaramucci. Colbert opened the interview with this line: "I promised you no gotcha questions, but I'm going to lead with one: Nazis, good or bad?" Scaramucci gave the politically-correct answer: "Super-bad."

exactly is a 'Nazi'? and 2) Why are they 'bad'? Let me start with these elementary issues, because even here, there is much to be revealed.

Most people, I hope, know that 'Nazi' is a slang shorthand for the National Socialists of Hitler's Germany (*Nationalsozialisten* in German, hence the 'z'). It was coined by his opponents, along the lines of an earlier term, 'Sozi,' that was applied to the Social Democrats (*Sozialdemokraten*). Hitler himself apparently never used the term 'Nazi,' and others, such as Goebbels, did so only rarely. They preferred the full German term, or would use the acronym NSDAP (for *Nationalsozialistiche Deutsche Arbeiterpartei*, or National Socialist German Workers' Party). For the true National Socialists, 'Nazi' was a derogatory insult.[2]

But beyond this simple terminology, we have the striking fact that no one today—virtually no one—knows what a 'Nazi' is. Are they Jew-haters? No, that's an anti-Semite. A Hitler-lover? Perhaps, but that's not a definition, and certainly not a requirement. A violent right-winger? Hardly. A racist? More likely a 'racialist,' but again, that's no definition.

Let's start with the actual phrase, 'national socialism.' The first term refers simply to *nationalism*—that is, a tendency to favor one's own nation or nationality, as opposed to outsiders, foreigners, or those of other ethnicities or races. It typically involves national independence, self-reliance, self-determination, and a robust sense of patriotism. A nationalist is usually concerned to have a military force capable of self-defense, an economy and a currency that operates independently of other nations, and places an emphasis on traditional culture and social norms. A 'nation,' in turn, is literally a breed, stock, or 'race' of people. The word derives from the Latin *nasci* or *natus*, 'to be born.' A nation, then, is a group of people who are genetically related, of common ancestry, and who comprise a unified ethnicity.

The opposite of nationalism would be, of course, 'internationalism'—that is, globalism. Internationalists, such as those who predominate in the US and Europe today, promote global trade, global treaties and business pacts, currency unification, and active involvement in foreign affairs. In the old days, they pushed for colonialism. Today they promote international business practices (such as low-cost labor in poor, third-world countries), and they like to project military power around the world. Being unconcerned with ethnic unity or homogeneity, they advocate for mass immigration, interracial marriage, and multiculturalism—none of which are historically or biologically natural, and which are proven to be detrimental to the national majority.

What about socialism? Certainly nothing evil there. Socialism—loosely defined as a system in which the government owns or controls

---

[2] Today, many sympathetic commentators will use 'NS' as a shorthand for 'National Socialist' or 'National Socialism.'

large sectors of the economy—is widely practiced around the world, often in a kind of partnership with capitalist activities. Socialism is not 'a' system, but rather a spectrum of political and economic positions that can range from relatively unobtrusive to highly active and controlling. Most European countries today are mildly socialist and are able to produce very high qualities of life. American capitalists love to bash socialism primarily because it tends toward higher taxes (especially on the rich) and because it tends to restrict otherwise unrestrained business practices and speculations. In a nutshell, socialism tends to benefit society as a whole, especially the middle and lower classes, whereas capitalism tends to benefit *capital*—i.e. the wealthy. In crude terms, we can say that capitalism is 'money-ism' and socialism is 'people-ism.'

Hitler, then, found virtue in both nationalism and socialism. He decided that it was necessary, early in his career, to take the small existing German Workers' Party (DAP) and make it both nationalist and socialist. This was neither radical nor evil; it was simply common sense, for someone who was concerned about the well-being of his fellow native German speakers.[3] 'National socialism' is thus nothing intrinsically evil or "bad," despite what the media or government—or Barack Obama—would have us think.

The context for all this, and for the rise of the NSDAP, was Germany's defeat in World War I in 1918 and the subsequent rise of the Weimar regime that ruled that country. As a frontline soldier, Hitler knew firsthand the sacrifices that were made in the war. And he also knew—or came to discover—the dominant role played by Jews in the German Revolution of November 1918, and in the postwar Weimar government. On his view, Jews were the leading elements in the Revolution that fatally undermined support at home; they were leaders among all the various revolutionary groups that were active at that time; and they benefited the most from the formation of the Weimar government.[4] Thus it was that Hitler's special form of national socialism came to take on an anti-Semitic outlook.

But the movement itself, National Socialism in itself, was in many ways a remarkably progressive and benign system. It was codified in the famous 25 Points established by Hitler in 1920. They called for equal rights for German people (Points 2 and 9). They gave citizens the right to select the laws and governmental structure (6). They abolish war-profiteering (12). They called for corporate profit-sharing with employees (14). They supported retirement pensions, a strong middle class, free high-

---

[3] Hitler, of course, was a native Austrian, but identified strongly with the Germanic peoples, regardless of which political unit they happened to live in.

[4] For more on the extensive Jewish presence and causal role in both World Wars, see my book *The Jewish Hand in the World Wars* (2019).

er education, public health, maternity welfare, and religious freedom, including explicit support for "a positive Christianity" (15, 16, 20, 21, 24). And they explicitly endorsed the principle of "Common good before individual good" (24). Certainly nothing outlandish or extreme here.

On the other hand, only a relative few—albeit important—points appear threatening or aggressive. These points assert that the interests of ethnic Germans should be the first priority of the government. Unlike (say) Israel, where the ethnic majority is in a dominant position politically, economically, and culturally, in Germany during this period, a small ethnic minority held vastly disproportionate power, resulting in proposals intended to redress this situation—as, one might reasonably imagine, would also occur in Israel if the Palestinians had vastly disproportionate power in Israel.

The points grant citizenship only to ethnic Germans, explicitly denying it to Jews (4). They block further immigration, and compel recent immigrants to leave (8). They seek to prohibit all financial speculation in land (17), though this can hardly be called a negative. More harshly, the plan calls for the death penalty against "traitors, usurers, and profiteers" (18). It demands that the German-language press be controlled only by ethnic Germans—but doesn't restrict press in other languages (23). And it calls for "a strong central authority in the State" (25), thus being unsympathetic to anything like parliamentarian democracy.

As anti-Semitic as Hitler was, it's surprising how lightly the Jews get off. They are banned from citizenship, and therefore from any role in government or the German-language press. Recent (since August 1914) Jewish immigrants, like all immigrants, must leave. And the National Socialist view of religious freedom "fights against the Jewish materialist spirit" (24). But apart from these two references, there is no explicit mention of Jews or other minorities. There are no threats to imprison or kill Jews. Longtime Jewish residents can stay in the country. No confiscation of wealth, with the stated exceptions. Also, incidentally, no repression of Gypsies or gays. And certainly nothing that sounds like a looming 'Holocaust.'

In sum, Hitler's National Socialism, as described in the 1920 document and as enacted through the 1930s, was essentially the product of German nationalism and progressive socialism. These were combined with an anti-Semitism that was fundamentally concerned with enacting a program that would limit Jewish influence, particularly in the media, and restore ethnic Germans to a dominant position in the German economy and culture.

In practice, National Socialism was, of course, 'bad' for some people. It was bad for those who would exploit the masses through financial chicanery—disproportionately Jews. It was bad for those who wanted to accumulate unrestricted wealth. It was bad for globalists and internationalists. It was bad for those who were happy to see African Blacks streaming into Europe from former colonies—or Jews streaming into Germany from Eastern Europe. It was unsupportive of non-Christian religions, but this can hardly be considered a major fault. But for the vast majority of people, National Socialism was a benevolent, supportive, uplifting, and visionary political ideology. *In short, unless you were a Jew or other financial exploiter of the people, you had nothing to fear from National Socialism.*

In the end, National Socialism, or 'Nazism,' was really only bad for one small group of people: the Jews. Throughout the early part of the twentieth century, Germany never had more than around 1 percent Jews—about 600,000. And yet they were massively overrepresented in business, commerce, finance, media, academia, and the arts. Major sectors of German society were dominated by non-Germans, and Hitler was determined to put an end to this. Hence, upon coming to power in 1933, he proceeded to push the Jews out of these aspects of social life, and encouraged them to emigrate. We should note that this was not inherent in the National Socialist platform; rather, it was a consequence of the particular implementation that Hitler enacted. There is nothing intrinsic to National Socialism that compels abuse, torture, or murder of Jews. But of course, his formal policies did put an end to Jewish domination of society, and for many Jews, that was simply intolerable—the greatest of all evils, in fact.

And so it is today. The specter of Nazism is raised whenever anyone or any movement threatens to disrupt Jewish power or Jewish control over society. The dissident-right movement has the temerity to examine and criticize Jewish power, and thus is equated to stereotypical "Nazism," and thus slandered in the highest degree. Dissident-rightists, White nationalists, Confederates—these people threaten to upset Jewish influence in the media, academia, and in the political realm. Hence the Jews, and their establishment lackeys, do everything possible to attack and condemn such movements.

Despite what we universally hear from media and government, the dissident-right movement threatens virtually no one—apart from Jews and those reliant upon them. Even if they were true Nazis—and very few are—they pose no risk to society at large. And in fact, *the opposite*: By exposing and criticizing Jewish power and influence, they promise to make things vastly better for society. Disproportionate Jewish influence in government, media, business, and academia inevitably serves to benefit Jewish interests—and not society at large, let alone the world, let alone nature.

Why do we relentlessly push globalism? Because it serves Jewish financial interests. Why do we engage in endless wars against Arabs and Muslims, at the cost of trillions of dollars? Because they attack and kill the enemies of Israel. Why do we support unlimited and unrestricted immigration? Because a multiracial, multicultural society makes Jews feel more comfortable, primarily by weakening the natural, national cohesion of Whites or other ethnic groups.

Imagine a society not dominated by Jewish interests. Imagine a nationalist America that was primarily concerned with the White European peoples who established this country. Imagine a socialist America in which the media did not continually spout anti-White messages and in which the needs of the true middle class, and the truly underprivileged, were addressed. Imagine, that is, a *national socialist America*: an America more concerned with the problems at home than with running a global empire; an America more concerned about justice and fairness than with crude power politics; an America that regained something of its original idealism; an America not content to allow its culture to be debased by crude Jewish appeals to common human vices.

When Trump called on us to "make America great again," it wasn't just a slogan. There is something to it. America has the potential, the resources, the intelligence, and the initiative to become, again, a truly great nation. We need only recall what Hitler achieved in Germany with his National Socialism and his derailing of Jewish power: he took a beleaguered, defeated, bankrupt nation and raised it up to the heights of prestige and power in just six short years, and amidst a global Depression. Had he not over-reached in his military aims, Germany might well have gone on to become a true leading light in the world.

Germany could do it again. America could do it. Other nationalities could do something similar. There are lessons here for all peoples of the world: *banish the Jews and Jewish influence, purge your nation of minorities, and the sky is the limit.*

So, explain it to us again, Mr. Obama, about how, precisely, "the Nazis are bad." And this time, tell us the truth.

PART II

THE HOLOCAUST

— 8 —

Holocaust Revisionism in 60 Seconds

On the traditional view, the Holocaust was the deliberate murder of some 6 million Jews by the Nazi regime during World War II. Hitler's intention all along was to kill the Jews, and many died in special-constructed gas chambers. The corpses were burned in crematoria or on pyres, and the ashes scattered. Some of the most infamous extermination camps—Treblinka, Sobibor, Belzec—were completely dismantled and have all but vanished, as have the remains of the victims.

Scholars known as "Holocaust revisionists" challenge this view. They believe that there was never an intention to kill the Jews; rather, Hitler simply wanted them out of Germany. They believe that there were no homicidal gas chambers, and that the number of Jews who died during the war, from all causes, comes to far less than a million—and perhaps only 500,000 or so.

Traditionalists call revisionists "Holocaust deniers," because, they say the revisionists deny that the Holocaust happened. But this is obviously a misleading claim. Revisionists accept that Hitler wanted a Germany free of Jews, and that he forcibly removed many of them, seized their property, and sent many others to labor camps. They also accept that Hitler knew that many Jews would die in the process. Depending on your definition, this could certainly count as a "holocaust." Revisionists do deny, however, that 6 million died, and they do deny that the Germans constructed homicidal gas chambers. They do not deny that a tragedy happened to the Jews, nor do they deny that many thousands of them died. No serious revisionist claims that "the Holocaust never happened."

Some Troubling Facts

So, how can the average person begin to check these claims, to see where the truth lies? Start with the "6 million" figure. How plausible, in general, is this number? The war in Europe ran for roughly 2,000 days (or 5½ years: September 1939 to April 1945). If the Germans killed 6 million Jews, then they must have averaged 3,000 per day—every day, 365 days a year, for five and a half straight years. And of course, they also must have burned, buried, or otherwise disposed of those same 3,000 bodies per day.

This fact, in itself, is highly implausible, especially given all the other urgencies of a world war.

But isn't the "6 million" figure documented in hundreds of history books? The number itself is, but not the details. Given all we supposedly know about this event, one would expect that there would be a clear and concise breakdown of the number, showing roughly where, and how, 6 million died. Experts like Raul Hilberg claim that there are three main categories of deaths: death camps, shootings, and ghettos. So, the experts should be able to show us how many died in camps, how many by shooting, and how many in the ghettos—such that the numbers add up to 6 million. But they cannot do this. The reader is invited to look at any mainstream published source for this information; it does not exist. One can find numbers individually for each camp, or each ghetto, but virtually never any totaling 6 million. This strongly implies that there are serious problems with the overall picture.

Furthermore, the "6 million" number has a history that long precedes WW2. One can find various accounts of "6 million suffering Jews" as far back as the 1880s. In major newspapers like the *New York Times* and the *Times of London*, we find about two dozen occurrences of that number in the six decades before Hitler even came to power in 1933. And it shows up another two dozen times before the end of the war. All this strongly suggests that the number was more symbolic than factual. It would be a miracle if the actual death toll were 6 million.

The Context

The situation in Germany prior to 1933, back to at least the 1850s, was of a powerful Jewish minority, vastly disproportionate to their size of 1% to 2% of the population. This is very well-documented, for the German media, entertainment, academia and several sectors of business. Furthermore, German Jews played an active role in causing Germany to lose WWI, and they were the first to attempt to seize power after its defeat. Given the tragedy of WWI and the crushing war debt that followed, it is understandable that Hitler and others wanted to completely remove the Jews from German society. And in fact, this is all they ever wanted—ethnic cleansing. Hitler's first letter on the topic, from 1919, speaks directly to this need to remove them. The same holds with all his speeches through the 1930s, even into the war years.

Hitler, Goebbels, and others used words like *Vernichtung* and *Ausrottung*, which are flamboyant terms for removal or elimination. But they do not entail murder. The Western press always translated these terms in English as 'extermination' or 'annihilation,' in a literal or physical sense. But the press was doing that for decades before Hitler. *New York*

Times articles dating back to the 1880s decry the "extermination," "annihilation," and even "holocaust" against the Jews in various countries—it really is striking how common this theme is. Again, one sees how any action against Jews is portrayed in the harshest possible terms.

The Gas Chambers

The standard gassing story is rife with problems. At Auschwitz, the Germans allegedly crammed up to two thousand people into enclosed rooms—some partly underground—and dumped cyanide pellets on them from above. But this is senseless, because (a) the rooms generally had neither windows or ventilation, to later vent the poisonous gas, (b) the pellets would keep emitting poison for hours, killing anyone who went inside, and (c) there is no plausible way to remove the bodies in a timely manner. The Germans would never have designed such a preposterous scheme.

And for all that, cyanide gas killed only about 1 million Jews, we are told—all at Auschwitz. By contrast, more than 2 million were allegedly gassed in other camps with "exhaust gas from diesel engines." This, unfortunately, is even more ridiculous than the Auschwitz scheme. Diesel engines, it turns out, produce very little carbon-monoxide gas—far too little to kill people in any reasonable time. Even if the Germans used regular gasoline engines, it would have been hugely impractical and inefficient to try to use exhaust gas to kill millions of people.

Body Disposal

Killing thousands per day is one major problem; even more difficult is disposing of the bodies. How do you completely eliminate a corpse? The usual line is: burned in a crematorium. But the cremation furnaces were all equipped with single-body muffles, and each took about an hour to burn one body. All of Auschwitz had a total of 46 muffles, and thus could dispose at best of perhaps 900 bodies per day. But at its peak, the camp was allegedly gassing 6,000 or 7,000 Jews per day. What happened to the bodies?

And that's at the largest of the death camps. Smaller camps like Treblinka, Sobibor, and Belzec had no furnaces at all. Hence all the bodies, we are told, were burned in the open air, over big log fires. But this would have been technically impossible at the rate claimed—again, up to 7,000 or more per day. The Germans would have needed a mountain of chopped wood for fuel each day, and would have had to dispose of another mountain of ash at the end of each day. Large bones, furthermore, cannot be burned to ash when using pyres. Where are these remains today?

Additionally, crematoria and open-air fires create a lot of smoke—smoke that would be visible from both ground and air. As it happens, we have ten reconnaissance air photos of Auschwitz from 1944. Of all these, not one photo shows even a single smoking crematorium chimney. Four photos show small fires burning, but only from a very small corner of the camp. Evidence of mass burning is strikingly absent. Again, what happened to the bodies?

Survivors?

But what about all the Holocaust witnesses? Hundreds survived the camps, and lived to tell their stories. Well—what, after all, did the victims witness? Enforced evacuation and confinement (true), people dying *en route* (true), people catching typhus and dying in the camps (true), dead bodies stacked in and around the crematoria (true), corpses being burned (true), people separated from family members and disappearing (true). And all this amidst a major war. Such true facts get mixed with rumor and wild speculation, and suddenly we get crazy stories: 2,000 Jews being gassed in a crematorium cellar, "5 million dead at Auschwitz" (*NY Times*), "6 million exterminated," etc.

Given all these issues, and many more, revisionists conclude that no mass gassings ever occurred, and that the total number of Jews killed comes to perhaps 500,000—a tragic figure, but far less than 6 million. Jews thus constitute about 1 percent of the 50 million people killed globally during the war. Their "holocaust" was perhaps not so special after all.

Evidence, logic, and common sense all suggest that the revisionists are right. If so, this has huge implications for the present world. It would mean that people everywhere have been given a false story of human suffering. It would fundamentally discredit the powerful Jewish interests in media and academia that promote the conventional story. And it would mean an end to the many privileges given to Jews and to Israel, based on the standard account. These are the kinds of issues that true Holocaust researchers should be investigating.[1]

[1] A much fuller elaboration of these issues can be found in my books *The Holocaust: An Introduction* (2016) and especially *Debating the Holocaust* (2020; 4th ed.).

— 9 —
Reexamining the 'Gas Chamber' of Dachau

Of the Dachau crematorium called "Barrack X," one can read the following on the Website of the US Holocaust Memorial Museum: "There is no credible evidence that the gas chamber in Barrack X was used to murder human beings".[1] A strange situation indeed, given that the facility, built in late 1942 and completed by May 1943,[2] allegedly contained a dedicated homicidal gas chamber of substantial size—about 39 square meters (425 square feet), sufficient to gas nearly 400 people at a time, on the traditional view. Why would the Germans build such a dedicated facility, and then never use it?—not a single mass gassing, in nearly two years?[3] Is there perhaps another story here? And what can we learn from examining the facility today?

The following study is the result of my personal visit to Dachau over a period of three days. All photos included below are my own.

Let me start with the main crematorium building known as Barrack X. Photo 1 shows the exterior of the building, with the external wall of the gas chamber on the left (behind the water downspout). Photo 2 is the current floor plan.

Photo 1: Crematorium exterior (gas chamber area at left).

[1] www.ushmm.org (accessed 1 April 2022).

[2] *The Holocaust Encyclopedia* (2001; p. 240) claims that "The Germans built a gas chamber in the second crematorium building of Dachau…in March 1942."

[3] The camp was occupied by the Americans on 29 April 1945.

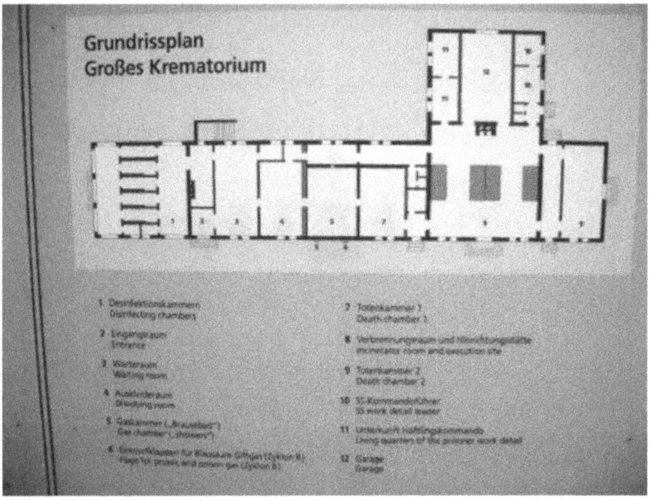

Photo 2: Crematorium floor plan (room 5 = gas chamber).

In the immediate aftermath of the war, no one had any doubt that the crematorium contained a homicidal chamber. An official US Army report, issued within days of takeover of the camp, was unequivocal. In Dachau the Germans conducted a "systematic policy of extermination"—though today we know that no such thing ever occurred or was even planned. There were "a total of five gas chambers," the largest disguised as a shower. In it, 15 fake shower heads were installed, "from which gas was then released".[4]

The Nuremberg Tribunal proceedings contain two important references, the first in the so-called Chavez Report, dated 7 May 1945:

> The new [crematorium] building had a gas chamber for executions… The gas chamber was labeled 'shower room' over the entrance and was a large room with airtight doors and double-glassed lights, sealed and gas proof. The ceiling was studded with dummy shower heads. A small observation peephole, double-glassed and hermetically sealed, was used to observe the conditions of the victims. There were grates in the floor. Hydrogen cyanide was mixed in the room below, and rose into the gas chamber and out the top vents.

Now, the showerheads no longer supply the deadly gas, but it emanates from the floor. There is indeed a cellar room below the gas chamber, but we have no evidence at all that it was a 'Zyklon mixing room,' or that such

[4] *Dachau Liberated: The Official Report by the US Seventh Army* (2000), pp. 14-15, 44, and 52, respectively.

gas entered the room from below. Today there are six floor vents in the room, and by all accounts they are, and have always been, actual water drains (photo 3). This is logical, because the room was likely built from the start as an ordinary inmate shower facility.

Photo 3: Gas chamber floor.

American newspapers were quick to report the gruesome news. A visit by some prominent journalists on May 2, arranged by General Eisenhower, was reported in the *New York Times*:

> One of the worst death traps seen by the party was a gas chamber at Dachau disguised as a bathhouse. Mr. [Gideon] Seymour described it as a room about 30 by 20 feet square, with 25 rows of perforated pipes overhead. There were no water connections to the showers, but instead the pipes were supplied from the same gas pipes that led to the cremation chambers. … In the chamber walls, Mr. Seymour said, were small glass 'peepholes' through which the German guards could observe the dying agonies of the condemned. (9 May 1945, p. 17)

Here we see an immediate contradiction with the first two reports: no gas from showerheads, no gassing through floor vents, but rather rows of overhead perforated pipes. Also, the alleged connection with the ductwork of the cremation chamber (room #8 in Photo 2) is absurd; there is no conceivable reason to run Zyklon gas, which is flammable, into a furnace room. And the reported floor area of roughly 600 square feet—versus today's figure of 425—is a significant overestimate.

Further confusion would come soon after the Chavez report, when, in an American investigation report of May 15, it was stated that "The supply of gas into the chamber was controlled by means of two valves on one of the outer walls… The gas was let into the chamber through pipes terminating in perforated brass fixtures set into the ceiling".[5] No gas from the floor, no rows of perforated pipes, but now "perforated brass fixtures." Today, incidentally, there is no evidence whatsoever of brass fixtures. Significantly, the May 15 report also stated that "the ceiling was some 10 feet in height." Today it is about 2.15 meters, or 6 feet 10 inches. This is a huge discrepancy, and not attributable to misjudgment; clearly the ceiling was lowered after takeover by the Americans.

The second Nuremberg reference came in testimony by Dr. Franz Blaha, a Czech prisoner and four-year inmate. He stated:

> Many executions by gas or shootings or injections took place right in the camp. The gas chamber was completed in 1944, and I was called by Dr. Rascher to examine the first victims. Of the eight or nine persons in the chamber there were three still alive… Many prisoners were later killed in this way.

A puzzle: Blaha claims the chamber was completed only in 1944, but experts today insist that it was part of the original construction that began in 1942. The NYT reported on Blaha's testimony in November 1945, dramatically stating that he was "assigned to work in the death chamber of the hospital"—meaning, of course, the mortuary. Blaha told of decapitations and the creation of shrunken heads, and of skin made into "gloves, lampshades, riding breeches, house-slippers, handbags" and other items (all such claims have since been completely discredited, putting Blaha's credibility into serious doubt). He also recalled "the wholesale execution of Russian prisoners in a gas chamber… He declared that a quick death in the gas chamber had been meted out to the sick prisoners transferred to Dachau from other camps" (Nov. 17, p. 7).

Meanwhile the NYT continued to report on the alleged gassing atrocities. For example, it reported statements by one Colonel Jaworski that "Jews had been 'ruthlessly wiped out' by hanging and firing squad and gas chambers at Dachau. Frequently they were paraded into a gas chamber, told to strip for shower and then left to die when the gas was turned on" (21 October, p. 11)—as if the gas chamber were like some household oven.

---

[5] IMT document L-159, vol. 37, p. 621.

As one can imagine, questions eventually arose regarding the veracity of these gas chamber reports.[6] The first challenges appeared in 1950, with Paul Rassinier's book *Le mensonge d'Ulysse* (The Lies of Ulysses) and Maurice Bardèche's *Nuremberg*, both in French. In 1954, the German Ludwig Paulin published an article, "The lie of the 238,000: What happened in camp Dachau?" in which he disputed the existence of a gas chamber.[7] Two months later, another article appeared in the same journal, pseudonymously written by American military attorney Stephen Pinter. Pinter claimed to have visited all the western camps, including Dachau, without finding any credible evidence for homicidal gas chambers.[8]

In 1958, Louis Marschalko published the book *The World Conquerors*. He argues that, upon takeover by the Americans, captive Germans "were ordered subsequently to build various additional buildings with the greatest possible speed" (p. 155). They constructed "blood-pits" and a "hanging tree," and destroyed gardens and flowerbeds that might detract from the 'death camp' image. Marschalko adds, "The shower-baths, dressing rooms, and reception halls had to be rebuilt so that they should appear like gas-chambers" (p. 156).

In June of 1959, Pinter spoke out again, publishing the follow statement in a letter to a Catholic periodical:

> I was in Dachau for 17 months after the war, as a US War Department Attorney, and can state that there was no gas chamber at Dachau. What was shown to visitors and sightseers there and erroneously described as a gas chamber was a crematory. Nor was there a gas chamber in any of the other concentration camps in Germany.[9]

Former inmate and Catholic bishop Johannes Neuhäusler claimed, in 1960, that no gas chamber had ever been put into use at the camp.[10] Two months later, orthodox German historian Martin Broszat issued a letter confirming that "Neither in Dachau nor in Bergen-Belsen nor in Buchenwald were Jews or other prisoners gassed".[11]

Admission of no gassing at the camp was an important milestone, but the much more serious charge of deliberate deception continued to appear.

---

[6] The following sources are detailed by Thomas Kues, "A Chronicle of Holocaust Revisionism, Parts 2 and 3," *Inconvenient History* (2010).
[7] *Der Weg*, vol 8, no. 5-6.
[8] *Der Weg*, vol 8, no 8. Under byline "Warwick Hester."
[9] *Our Sunday Visitor*, June 14, p. 15.
[10] *Deutschen Wochenzeitung*, 18 June 1960, as reported by Kues (2010)
[11] Letter to *Die Zeit*, 19 August 1960.

In 1961, the journal of the British National Party, *Combat*, published an article titled "Jewish Deceit at Dachau":

> When Dachau fell into Western hands in 1945, it had to look the part, so…it was transformed into a showplace of horrors. … The camp had to have a gas chamber, so, since one did not exist, it was decided to pretend that the shower bath had been one. Previously it had flagstones to a height of about four feet [on the walls]. Similar flagstones were taken [from the adjacent room] and put above those in the shower bath, and a new lower ceiling was created at the top of this second row of flagstones, with iron funnels in it (the [fake] inlets for the gas)".[12]

Indeed, the gas chamber ceiling today is 2.15 meters high, but the adjacent room height is 2.9 meters—a full 75 cm (30 inch) differential.

Whoever lowered the ceiling and installed the 'fake showerheads' did a remarkably crude job. Today it appears as a poured concrete ceiling, smooth and white, into which someone roughly chiseled several funnel-shaped holes. Of the 15 such holes, 13 have an open metal funnel, one is complete with perforated head, and the last is fully exposed—see Photos 4, 5, 6. In most cases, one can faintly see evidence of rework to the ceiling after the 'shower heads' were installed—see Photo 7 for an example.

Photo 4: "Fake shower heads."

[12] Jan/Feb 1961, issue #10, p. 4.

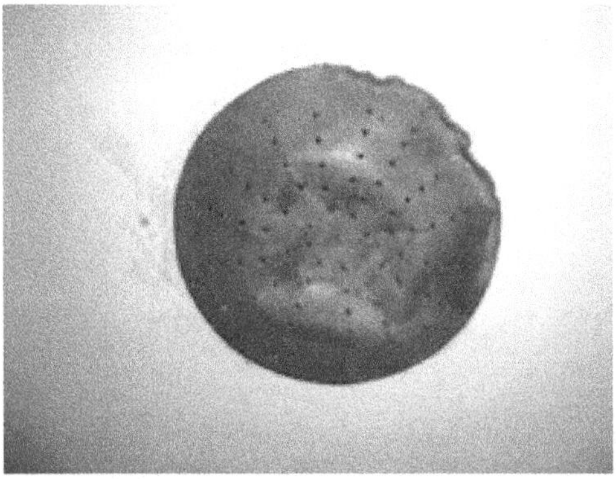

Photo 5: Sole remaining intact head.

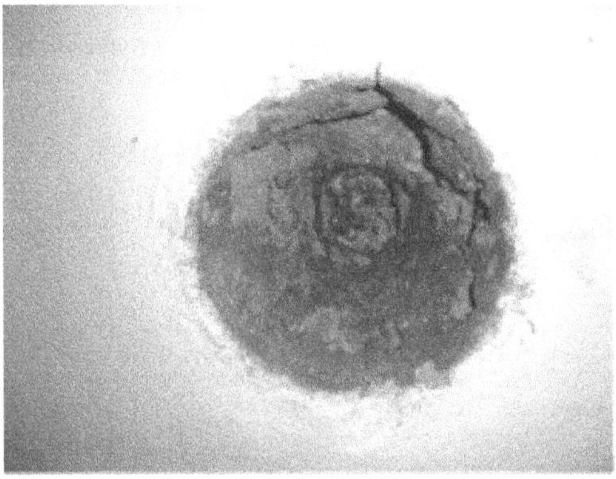

Photo 6: Missing funnel.

Photo 7: Rework to ceiling around shower head (faint).

By the 1960s, talk of mass killings in a "Dachau gas chamber" subsided significantly. Raul Hilberg's magnum opus, *Destruction of the European Jews*, contains virtually no mention of such a gas chamber—either in his first (1961) edition or in his massive, 3-volume 2003 edition. Paul Berben's *Dachau 1933-1945: The Official History* states flatly that "the Dachau gas-chamber was never operated" (1975: 8).[13] *The Holocaust Encyclopedia* (p. 240) briefly discusses the Blaha testimony and his claim that "several executions were carried out in the Dachau gas chamber." The editor concludes that, because of the "mantle of secrecy" that surrounded Barrack X (the crematorium) and the fact that we have "only one unequivocal testimony"—that of Blaha—that therefore "it is difficult to corroborate Blaha's statements and say with certainty whether the Dachau gas chamber was ever used for its designed purpose."

The most definitive recent study is Harold Marcuse's *Legacies of Dachau* (2001). This 590-page book contains numerous details on the camp construction and history, and yet has scarcely a mention of the infamous gas chamber. He claims, without evidence, that "only trial gassings" were conducted at the camp.[14] He cites a 1960 exhibit in the crematorium that included a sign with a striking admission: "This room would have been used as an undressing and waiting room if the gas chamber had worked" (p. 254). Marcuse dismisses this claim, stating, again without evidence, that it was in fact used "on at least two groups of prisoners." He quickly adds that "it was indeed never used for systematic gassings…"

Other recent works seem to completely overlook Dachau, as if it played no role whatsoever in the Holocaust. Peter Longerich's authoritative *Holocaust: The Nazi Persecution and Murder of the Jews* (2010), for example, has only passing mention of the camp on three or four scattered pages (out of 645 total), and no reference to a gas chamber there at all.

Even as late as 2003, there was an official sign there stating: "GAS CHAMBER: disguised as a 'shower room'—never used as a gas chamber." Today there is one wall sign that says, "This was the center of potential (!) mass murder." Another sign states that the chamber "was not used for mass murder. Survivors have testified that the SS did, however, murder individual prisoners and small groups here using poison gas".[15] Evidently the story of a 'homicidal gas chamber' must be maintained at all costs.

---

[13] The point is reiterated later in the book: "As is well-known, the crematorium was enlarged by a gas-chamber, however this was never put into operation." (p. 176)

[14] Page 46. He adds that "death by other causes supplied enough raw human material for the ovens"—as if the Germans needed dead bodies for fuel!

[15] To gas individual persons in a room of 425 square feet is ludicrous.

Further Complications

There are other reasons to be suspicious, and other indications that something is not quite right with the official history.

Let's return to the room itself. Photo 8 shows the interior entrance door and the infamous "Brausebad" ('shower') sign, looking on through to the exterior exit door. Both entrance and exit have similar, heavy, vault-like metal doors. The entrance door is wedged in place against the floor and cannot move, but the exit door swings freely. The problem is that it does not close. The following two photos (9 and 10) show that this door hits on the locking pin; it cannot close and cannot seal 'gas tight'. In fact, the door is roughly half an inch too wide for the pin. This is no minor adjustment; the doorway was significantly altered since its original construction. But we do not know when, or for what purpose. It may have been as part of covert American alterations immediately after the war, or it could have simply reflected the general conversion of the camp to a 'memorial' and tourist destination in the early 1960s—it clearly would not do to have tourists locking each other in the room. (But of course, with one door wedged open, this could not happen…another strange fact.)

Photo 8: Entrance to gas chamber.

Photo 9: Exit door obstruction.

Photo 10: Exit door obstruction.

During my visit, I came prepared to do a unique bit of analysis: I brought along a hand-held wall metal detector.[16] I cannot claim any astounding new discoveries, but I did a fairly careful scan of all four interior walls and the ceiling. The walls had virtually no metal at all, at least to the scanning depth of three inches. The ceiling, by contrast, showed extensive metal content, almost throughout the entire extent. There was no evident pattern, just a more or less continuous positive reading. This would suggest some kind of heavy wire mesh, perhaps associated with the poured concrete.[17] It was not possible to detect the presence or absence of individual pipes in the ceiling.

Another feature of interest is the pair of "Zyklon gassing ports." In the (one) exterior wall we find two large (70 x 40 cm) openings, with a

[16] Zircon "Videoscanner" 5.5.

[17] The block wall construction would not require supporting wire mesh, and thus the negative reading is not surprising.

heavy metal grating on the interior—see Photos 11 and 12. Allegedly, the Zyklon pellets were dumped into a chute on the exterior of the building (Photo 13) and then either were trapped by the grill, or spilled through onto the floor. The grill was there to prevent the victims from interfering with this process.

Photo 11: Two Zyklon ports.

Photo 12: Zyklon port and grill.

Photo 13: Two Zyklon chutes.

There are several problems with this set-up. First, the chutes are welded open, so that no one can verify the closure, air-tight seal, etc. Second, the process is very crude—hardly better than just tossing an open Zyklon can into the room as the door is being slammed shut. Third, the first few dead bodies could have easily blocked the grates, putting a quick end to the gassing process. Then there is the problem of cleanup: How were the operators supposed to collect up those deadly Zyklon pellets, which would continue to emit gas for two hours or more, long after the victims were dead? To this we have no answer.

Furthermore, it is a very inefficient scheme at best; the poison gas would only slowly and unevenly diffuse into the room. Far better would be to employ some kind of heated, forced-air system that would quickly circulate the deadly gas. And in fact, the Germans had precisely such a system—and only three rooms away. Room #1 (see Photo 2) contains four actual Zyklon disinfesting chambers, with sophisticated dispensing systems. Photo 14 shows the exterior of these chambers, and Photo 15 the machine for opening and retaining the pellets, and forcing hot air through them. These rooms were very effective at delousing linens, clothing, and personal items, and thus preventing the spread of the deadly typhus disease. Evidently the Germans wanted to spare lives in the camp, not end them.[18]

Photo 14: Delousing chamber.

Photo 15: Hot-air fumigation device.

[18] Traditionalist writer Harry Mazal counters that delousing requires high air concentrations of Zyklon gas, whereas the gassing of people requires a much lower concentration to be fatal. This, he claims, accounts for the dispensing machines for delousing but not for murder. However, the Germans would clearly have wanted to kill everyone in a crowded room, in short order, and this would necessitate a high-concentration, forced-air system, just like in the delousing chambers. Mazal's claim that the chutes made it "simpler and less expensive" to kill people, rather than using the "costly" dispensing machines, is ridiculous. ("The Dachau gas chambers," www.holocaust-history.org)

And one further oddity: The Zyklon chutes show clear signs of being installed *after* the original building construction. In close-up views of the chutes, we can see that the concrete mortar is clearly different than that used for the remainder of the wall—finer quality, more viscous, and of different composition. See Photos 16 (left chute), 17 (right chute), and the detail in Photo 18.

Photo 16: Left Zyklon chute.

Photo 17: Right Zyklon chute.

Photo 18: Mortar variation in right chute.

There would not be such a discrepancy in the construction material if the gas chamber and chutes were installed at the time of construction, as the experts insist to this day. Evidently someone broke into the completed brick wall at a later date to install the chutes—perhaps at the direction of the occupying Americans.

While they were at it, someone, at some later date, significantly altered the crematorium chimney. Compare Photo 19, from the summer of 1944, with Photo 1, which I explicitly took from the same perspective. The new chimney is significantly shorter, and thus, at the very least, someone removed the top 10 or 20 feet. They also added some sort of white banding strips at two points. There is no obvious explanation for this reconstruction. Well-built brick chimneys survive for literally hundreds of years. More riddles.

Photo 19: Crematorium in summer 1944.

Finally, there is a huge question mark around the piping and ductwork that runs above and behind the room. Various drawings and studies over the years indicate numerous changes, alterations, additions, and reconstructions—to the point where the present system is nonsensical. A properly-designed chamber would be clear and simple: a single air duct connected at opposite ends of the room (to recirculate the poison gas), an in-line air heater (to improve gasification), a remote (attic or backroom) Zyklon introduction device, and a simple pair of inlet/outlet chimneys for cleansing the chamber of the deadly gas. Instead we find, by all indications, an absurd, jury-rigged system of pipes, valves, and condensers, one that bears all the marks of a series of postwar constructions. In all likelihood, the room was designed and built as an actual shower, which was then reconstructed, with the lower ceiling, to meet American expectations of what a 'gas chamber' should look like.

One can imagine what visitors learn of all this when they see the camp today. Entrance is free and there are no official guides, so various groups pass through with various self-appointed 'expert' guides. However, when it comes to the crematorium (Barrack X), there seems to be a set routine. The group gathers outside the building as the guide briefly explains the 'assembly-line process' of undressing, gassing, cremating, etc. He then sends them in at one end, and they pass through the several rooms of the building (see again the floor plan in Photo 2), emerging from the furnace room, where the guide is dutifully waiting. No guide accompanies the groups inside—all the better to avoid any pointed and difficult questions that may arise. Perhaps it was a coincidence, but in the several hours that I was in the chamber and building, not one guide entered the gas chamber.

Traditional historians would undoubtedly like to see the infamous Dachau gas chamber simply fade away. Playing no role in the Holocaust, it serves no real purpose. The many problems and inconsistencies make it more of an embarrassment than asset to the orthodox view.

And in truth it is more than an embarrassment; such deception threatens to undermine major aspects of the entire Holocaust story. A purpose-built gas chamber, right on German soil, sitting for two years…but 'never used'? So maybe all those other gas chambers in Poland were likewise 'never used'? All those indications of reconstruction, alteration, fraud… perhaps recurring in places like Auschwitz and Majdanek?[19] A complicit mass media, happy to play along, unwilling to ask tough questions or conduct an impartial investigation…could that happen today? And a situation rife with American lies to justify Allied war crimes… What shall we make of that? Best not to ask too many questions.

---

[19] For more on the story of those camps and their gas chambers, see my book *Debating the Holocaust* (2020; 4th ed.).

— 10 —
A Postcard from Auschwitz

The following is a true account of my personal visit to the camp. All photos are my own.

Krakow is a beautiful city in early summer, the stand-out among southern Polish cities. Miraculously, the old city center survived both world wars unscathed. The huge central square is a sight to behold, and with no less than three major universities, Krakow bristles with youthful energy. Coming down by train from Warsaw, I was able to arrange a two-night stay before continuing on my way to Vienna. As with most major European cities, one quickly learns of the "must-see" sites: St. Mary's Basilica, Wawel Castle, the salt mines, and of course, Auschwitz.

This being my first visit to Auschwitz, I decided to see it as a tourist would.[1] This was not only easier—I was travelling alone—but allowed me to better understand the "official" portrayal of the camp and of events there. Auschwitz is the number one tourist destination in all of Poland; about 1.3 million visit the camp every year—coincidentally, about the same number as is alleged to have been killed there. The official guided tours dictate a particular image of the camp, and I was as interested in this image as the camp itself. I wanted to see what the public sees.

So I went to one of the many tourist information offices around town and purchased a standard "day trip" to Auschwitz. The package, which included free pickup and return delivery to my hotel, cost 90 złoty, about $30—quite a deal. My pick-up time was set (8:30 am), and the van would be at my hotel the next morning, for the "6-hour tour." Plenty of time to see the place, I thought, given that Oswieçim—the Polish name of Auschwitz—was only some 70 kilometers (about 40 miles) from Krakow.

The van dutifully arrived the next morning. But I soon realized that, as at Auschwitz itself, the tour was not quite as expected. The vehicle—a bit larger than I anticipated, more like a small bus—had a capacity of about 25 people. I was one of the first in, and the driver proceeded to cover much of the city in order to pick up our remaining guests. But between rush hour traffic, construction delays, and people slow getting out to the bus, a good hour went by before we were even ready to depart Krakow. So my "6-hour tour" was now down to five. And of course it would require another hour or so to return everyone; in other words, I was really getting a "4-hour tour." Not sure that that counts as a "day trip," but such is the life of a tour-

[1] Some years later, I would visit the camp again over a period of several days.

ist in Poland. (I'm no tour planner, but it seemed to me that, if everyone simply walked to the central tourist office and met the bus there, we could have saved a couple hours…)

It turned out that this little time crunch would impact our tour itself, and, in my suspicious mind, served an ulterior purpose. But I come to that matter in due course.

There are three distinct and roughly parallel paths from Krakow to Oswieçim: the (longer) expressway route, and two cross-country routes via two-lane roads. In good traffic, as I learned, all three take about one hour—a rather long time for a mere 40 miles. But Poland has only two kinds of roads: expressways and two-lane roads, and the latter are painfully slow. Our driver opted for one of the scenic country rides.

As soon as we were clear of Krakow city, the driver pulled out a DVD and popped it into a dashboard player. A small screen above us lit up: this was our complimentary 20-minute documentary about the camp (in English). No surprises here. We were treated to the usual recounting of the "extermination camp" history, the appalling conditions, the emaciated inmates, the gas chambers, and the "over one million" Jewish deaths. Horror awaits, it seemed to say.

The remainder of the journey was uneventful. The forecasts called for rain that day, but supposedly not until later in the day; with luck it would hold out for our visit. Around 10:30 am—a good two hours after my pickup—we rolled into the town of Oswieçim. It was a typical smallish European town, nicely maintained, with the usual amenities. We drove only a few minutes through the town when, suddenly, we arrived at the main camp, Auschwitz I. For those not familiar, "Auschwitz" is comprised of three primary facilities, and dozens of smaller sub-camps. The original and main camp is Auschwitz I, also called the *Stammlager*. It opened as a Nazi camp in 1940, but was originally built by the Polish army as a military barracks complex, apparently during World War I. This camp allegedly had a single gas chamber, which we were about to see. But the vast majority of the gassings are said to have occurred at Auschwitz II, known as Birkenau. This would come later in the day. The third facility, Auschwitz III (Monowitz), was located some three kilometers from the town, and served as an industrial facility; no mass murder is alleged to have happened there, and consequently it receives few tourists.

Knowing all this, I was still surprised at how integrated the main camp was into the town. This, I think, is not the usual image we have: the dreaded "Auschwitz death camp" located in the heart of a civilian village. But we have a good explanation for this, of course. Its original function, as a Polish military camp, had nothing to hide. And even as a German camp, when constructed in 1939 and 1940, it was not originally intended, even on the traditional view, as an extermination camp. The Germans were simply making good use of a captured military barracks.

Pulling into the parking lot, we were immediately confronted with a mass of vehicles: passenger cars, taxis, small tour buses like our own, and full-size long-haul buses packed with people. The place was a frenzy of activity—see Photos 1 and 2. Our bus disembarked, we merged with another small group, and then were assigned a tour guide: a cheerful young woman with a good knowledge of English and of the standard story she was scripted to present.

Photo 1: Auschwitz parking lot.

Photo 2: Auschwitz Museum entrance.

We pushed through the mob into the entrance building, past the gift shop, and on into a small alcove. There we were given our headsets and radio receivers. It is a rather high-tech affair: with all the commotion and simultaneous tours in multiple languages, the Poles gave the tour guide a radio voice transmitter; each of us could then hear her speaking through our headsets. Thus each group heard only their personal guide. On the one hand, this was a clever and useful solution. No confusing cross-talk, and even if you drifted away from the group, you could still hear your guide speaking loud and clear. On the other hand, it had a noticeable (and to me, suspicious) side effect: questions from individuals to the guide *could not be heard by the group*. They were necessarily individual questions between you and the guide. When I did this on a couple of occasions, she answered me personally, but *shut off the transmitter*. No one else in the group heard either my questions, or the answers. Very clever, I thought to myself.

Moving into the camp grounds, we immediately came upon the famous "*Arbeit Macht Frei*" sign— "Work Makes You Free" (Photos 3 and 4).

Photo 3: "*Arbeit Macht Frei.*"

Our group wandered through the camp, following the guide as she made stops in various barracks to tell us stories of the appalling conditions faced by the inmates. The buildings were mostly empty. Some contained walls of inmate photos; others, simulated sleeping bunks. One final barrack was set up rather as a standard museum. It had exhibits displaying inmate suitcases, personal items, and hair (cut from inmates as a precaution against lice). One large glassed-in exhibit showed an apparent mound of "thousands" of shoes—though, as Germar Rudolf has noted, the mound is displayed on an unseen elevated board, which is empty beneath. This is the same trick that grocers use to display fruit, to give the illusion of a vast quantity. The shoe mound was not so vast after all.

Photo 4: "*Arbeit Macht Frei.*"

At one point the guide mentioned the total Auschwitz death count as roughly 1 million Jews and thousands of others. I caught up to her and asked if the toll wasn't previously claimed to be 4 million. (Microphone *off*.) Yes, she said, but better research in the 1980s and 1990s had confirmed the new, lower figure. "Any chance it would be lowered still in the future?" I asked. "Unlikely," she said.

By this time, people were beginning to talk among themselves about the as-yet-unseen gas chambers. The guide then reminded us that, indeed, we were about to come to the gas chamber itself. "And oh, by the way," she added, "most of the gassings were at Birkenau. But we'll see that later." It was already approaching 12:00 noon.

Finally, we arrived at "the" gas chamber in the main camp, also called Krematorium #1 (or Krema 1, for short). It was a partially underground structure with a flat roof and sloping, grassy side walls with large trees—see Photo 7. Few statistics were given on the details of the gassings: no start or finish date (in fact, February to November 1942), no details on the gassing procedure (Zyklon pellets thrown in through roof vents), and only rough numbers of Jews allegedly gassed there (about 20,000—a mere two percent of the claimed Auschwitz toll). We could not enter via the "inmate entrance," as this was blocked off (Photo 8), so we went around to the other side (Photo 9).

Photo 7: Alleged Gas Chamber (Krema 1).

Photo 8: "Inmate entrance."

Photo 9: Entering Krema 1.

Upon entering the building, we were treated to what must have been the world's shortest tour of a gas chamber. We walked in, took a hard right turn into a small room, then a hard left into the gas chamber itself. It was a windowless, rectangular room, about 25 x 5 meters. The guide said little more than "this is the gas chamber, no photos please," and then she was off into the adjoining room with the cremation ovens. Rebel that I am, and not wanting to miss an opportunity, I lagged behind the group and then snapped a quick photo (#10). But the guide was gone—no chance to ask about the many post-war modifications to the room (chamber size, door location, chimney), nor about its history as a morgue and an air raid shelter. No chance to ask how 800 to 1000 people were jammed into that room, nor how the deadly Zyklon pellets were collected up without killing the guards handling the dead bodies. No chance to ask why the four Zyklon vents appeared to be added later than the original construction. No chance to ask about French traditionalist Eric Conan's claim that "everything there is false."

In the oven room (Photo 11), we had about one minute to view the ovens themselves—"no photos please"—and our guide was off. No chance to ask why the reconstructed chimney was not attached to the ovens. No chance to ask why the six cremation muffles, which could handle six bodies per hour, were such a capacity mismatch with a gas chamber that could kill 800 to 1,000 at a shot. Note: it would have taken roughly 150 hours—or more than 6 days working round the clock—to dispose of all the bodies from a *single* gassing.

Photo 10: Alleged Gas Chamber Krema 1.

Photo 11: Krema 1 oven.

Outside again, our guide was suddenly much more relaxed. Now we have time for a break, for bathrooms, for a visit to the gift shop, she informed us. "Be out front at the bus at 12:30, for the ride over to Birkenau." Finally, I thought—the highlight of the trip.

Again, the "ride to Birkenau" was surprising—all of about five minutes. Out of the small village, across a field, and there we were, at the famous entrance building, complete with train tunnel (Photo 12). There we were, at the site of the greatest mass killing in human history: 1.1 million people, the vast majority Jews, killed over two years (1943 and 1944), 90 percent of whom were gassed in the four Birkenau crematoria.

Photo 12: Birkenau main gate.

I was very anxious to get inside and look around. Then another surprise. "Because we are running late," said our guide ("late"?), "we will only have time to see the main guard tower and one of the barracks. Unfortunately we won't be able to see the gas chambers." What?! You must be kidding me, lady! No gas chambers?! Like hell!, I said to myself. "How much time do we have until the bus leaves?," I asked our guide. "About 25 minutes." "I'm going to the gas chambers." "Ok," she said as she headed off with the group. I didn't care if I had to *walk* back to Krakow; I was going to see the Birkenau gas chambers.

Inside the main gate, one sees the train tracks going out into the distance, to a dead end, and flanked by guard towers and a loading area (Photo 13). Being familiar with the camp layout, I knew that the main objectives were Kremas 2 and 3, and that they were straight ahead of me, at the end of the tracks, about 800 meters—almost half a mile—away. Quick calculation: I can walk there in 10 minutes, and 10 minutes back, leaving 5 minutes for the chambers—or I can run, and have a few more precious minutes. I ran.

Photo 13: Train tracks heading to gas chambers.

So, after an earnest five-minute run, I could at last see the ruins of the infamous Krema 2—site of the single greatest death toll at Auschwitz: some 300,000 people, on the conventional view (Photo 14). Across the way, its twin facility, Krema 3—site of another 275,000 gassings (Photo 15). Both buildings were destroyed by the Germans upon abandoning the camp, though Krema 2 retains some very relevant and important structures.

Photo 14: Krema 2 ruins.

Photo 15: Krema 3 ruins.

Standing there in front of the remains of both buildings, one gets a real sense of the improbability of the conventional story. Each building had an almost completely underground chamber, roughly 30 x 7 meters, at right angles to the main building, which contained the cremation ovens. On the revisionist view, this chamber was a morgue—a large, unventilated, but cool, place to store dead bodies (many infectious) until they could be cremated. On the standard view, this room was the gas chamber—a place in which 2,000 people were collectively gassed in less than 20 minutes. Photo 16 shows the collapsed roof of the Krema 2 chamber as it exists today.

Photo 16: Alleged Krema 2 gas chamber.

Now, imagine this: You are somehow able to pack 2,000 frightened, sick, angry people, wall to wall, into this underground room—a room with only a single narrow doorway from the main building. You then kill them all by sprinkling pellets of Zyklon-B over their heads, through openings in the roof. Now you have to *quickly* extract the dead bodies, steeped in poisonous gas, without killing yourself or your fellow workers. No problem—if you could peel the roof off and scoop them out with a backhoe. Lacking that option, it would be *nearly impossible* in any reasonable amount of time. And yet the experts, like Francizek Piper, claim that it took only three or four hours. Incredible—that they can make such claims, and no one (except the few revisionists) challenges them.

There are other stories in these remains. One is the search for residue of the deadly cyanide gas. If the chambers were used on as many people as claimed, the remaining bricks should have detectable cyanide compounds still in them. And yet none are to be found. Another story is the search for the roof openings into which the Zyklon pellets were poured—supposedly four per chamber. Krema 2's roof is sufficiently intact that we should be able to find evidence of these holes. And yet they are not to be found—not one single indisputable hole.

But my time was running short. A quick dash over to Krema 3 for a last shot or two (Photo 17), and then back to the bus. The other two crematoria, Kremas 4 and 5, were across the camp, a good 600 meters away, in the wrong direction; they would have to wait for my next visit—destined to be around seven years hence. So too would the two "bunkers," or small converted farm houses, that were allegedly used to pilot the Birkenau gassing project in 1942. Almost nothing remains of them, yet one day I would hunt them down—the sites of some 250,000 Jewish gassings, it is said. But now it's time to go.

Photo 17: Alleged Krema 3 gas chamber.

I arrived back at the bus just as the crowd was loading up—perfect timing. After an hour ride, we returned to Krakow around 2:00 pm. But rather than sitting it out for another hour circuit of the city as we returned my fellow riders, I opted to hop out at the first stop and walk home. A good move. I was back at my hotel for less than an hour when the skies unleashed a pounding rain. Luck was with me after all, that day—my day in Auschwitz.

— 11 —
A Postcard from Treblinka

The following is a true account of my personal visit to the camp. Certain names and dates have been changed to protect privacy. All photos are my own.

Mid-summer, Warsaw. Partly sunny, mild—a nice day to visit a death camp. I had just finished with an academic conference in the suburbs of Warsaw, and had one free day, a Tuesday, before moving on to my next European engagement. This was very fortunate, as I knew that the Treblinka concentration camp was only some 100 km away, and I was very much hoping for a chance to see it. My local Polish contacts were supportive, if slightly puzzled why an American professor of humanities would bother visiting a place "with nothing there to see." But I insisted, and so they complied. A Polish colleague, Lech, agreed to travel with me. He had no car, so we booked a taxi—reasonably priced, considering the distance—and by 9:30 am we were on our way to Treblinka.

We would not be arriving as mere tourists. Another colleague previously contacted the camp and spoke with museum director Edward Kopowka. He agreed to meet with us, show us the small museum, and then walk the camp grounds with us for two full hours. Good luck for us, though perhaps not for him.

We made good time, arriving in Malkinia before 10:30 am, and only some 10 km from the camp. But then a problem: the bridge over the Bug River was out of service. We would have to go down to the next crossing at Leg Nurski, about 20 km away, and then work our way back to the camp. This little detour threw our Warsaw-based cabbie for a loop, and with signage virtually nonexistent, I knew we were in a bit of a fix. So we crossed the river, worked our way down to Kosow Lacki, stopped two or three times for directions, drove up past Wolka Okraglik, and on to the entrance of the camp—after 45 extra minutes. But we were there. We drove right in—no gate, no guard, no entrance fee—and parked. Only two other cars in the lot, a relief; no Auschwitz-style Disneyland here.

Lech and I walked over to the small museum (Photo 1). Edward was in his office, ready to see us. He was a clean-cut fellow, probably in his late 40s, and seemed happy to have us. Lech introduced us (in Polish), and I immediately learned that Edward "spoke no English." Lech would have to translate back and forth—a bit of an inconvenience, I thought, and strange for someone whose job it is to interact with many visitors. But here I was the foreigner, so I couldn't much complain.

Photo 1: Treblinka Museum.

Inside the museum we viewed a large wall map, showing both the labor portion of the camp (Treblinka I), and the "extermination" zone, Treblinka II—see Photo 2. We were presently located at the far right, near the parking "P", with the museum marked "M".

Photo 2: Camp layout.

Edward then introduced to us—with Lech patiently translating—a large scale model of the extermination camp (Photo 3). Edward explained the standard extermination process: the arriving train cars, the separation by sexes, the "tube" pathway to the gas chambers, and then the gassing itself—with diesel engine exhaust. Not being your typical ignorant tourist, I asked if diesel exhaust had enough carbon monoxide to efficiently kill masses of people. Edward's answer: the Germans used "dirty fuel"! This was a new one for me; I am unaware of any witness or perpetrator describing the deliberate use of contaminated diesel fuel in order to increase CO content, nor do I know if it would even work. But it was an interesting response. Evidently he knew that ordinary diesel exhaust cannot kill masses of people, so the story had to be modified. But who am I to challenge the director of the Treblinka Museum himself?

Photo 3: Scale model of extermination camp.

Edward then explained that a total of 912,000 people were killed over the brief, 11-month lifetime of the camp. In fact, this is precisely the figure offered by Manfred Burba in his 1995 German book, *Treblinka*. Why Edward preferred this number over the other "expert" estimates—including van Pelt's 750,000, Hilberg's 800,000, Arad's 870,000, or Benz's 974,000 —he did not say.

Of the 912,000, the first 700,000 were initially buried in mass graves, he said, and then later exhumed for cremation on open-air pyres—the usual story, but rife with problems. He pointedly did not discuss the timeframe, so I asked (knowing already) if *all* 700,000 were buried first, prior to exhumation. He hesitated, but finally answered 'yes.' So I asked: where *exactly* were these 700,000 bodies buried? He pointed to a few areas marked "mass grave" on the model. And how much space did they require? A lot, he said. How deep were the graves? I asked. Eight meters—some 26 feet, a very impressive hole. Isn't there a ground water problem here, I asked, being a flat landscape so close to the Bug River? Not a concern, Edward replied; the water table is some 10 meters deep. No problems here!

We then proceeded to walk to the extermination camp. One quickly notices that many things about the camp are "symbolic": symbolic camp entrance (Photo 4), symbolic fence (Photo 5), symbolic railroad tracks

(Photo 6). Necessary, Edward says, because the Nazis obliterated every trace of the original camp. How convenient, I thought to myself.

Photo 4: Symbolic camp entrance.

Photo 5: Symbolic camp fence.

Along the way we passed a large map of the camp area (Photo 7). Unfortunately it bore little resemblance to the present memorial layout, and it was nearly impossible to locate the various "symbolic" markers that we had seen. But perhaps it was just as well—fewer difficult questions to answer this way.

Photo 6: Symbolic railroad tracks.

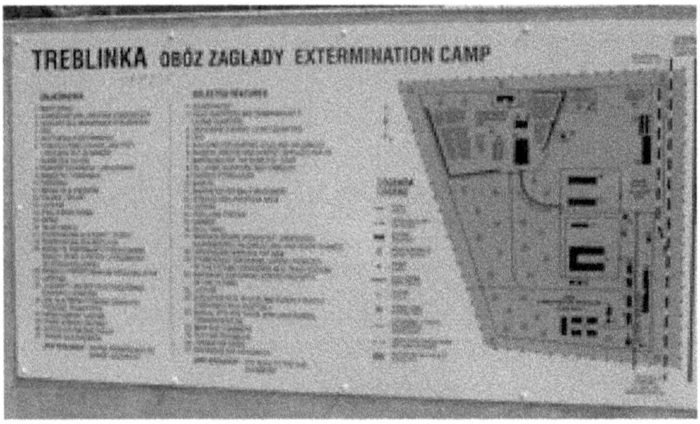

Photo 7: Camp layout.

Soon enough we arrived at the pathway (the symbolic "tube") that led to the famous central monument: a toadstool-like monolith located at the very spot of the alleged gas chambers (Photo 8). Here we were, at the heart of Treblinka, the site of the most horrendous kill rate of the entire Holocaust: of the 912,000 victims, 837,000 were killed in just six months of 1942, according to the camp's (and Burba's) "official" tally. (The remaining 75,000 died in 1943.) This works out to nearly 140,000 per month, 35,000 per week, or *5,000 per day*, every day, rain or shine, for six months. Not even Auschwitz during the alleged Hungarian massacre could match this rate.

Surprisingly, gassing that many people per day was no problem, on the traditional view. Treblinka had, for most of its existence, 10 chambers with a combined capacity of nearly 40,000 gassings per day; 5,000 would have been a walk in the park.

Corpse disposal, on the other hand, would have been a nightmare. Burying the first 700,000 victims would have required astoundingly huge graves. If we accept Arad's claim of four such graves, each would have had to be something like 15 x 120 meters in area, and 8 meters deep (as Edward claimed), to hold all those bodies. Combined, this is an area equivalent to 1.4 times as large as a professional American football field, and 26 feet deep. (And where did they put all that dirt, by the way?) Upon dumping the bodies for nine months, the Germans then, allegedly, covered the whole mess up—just in time to *change their minds* and decide to burn them all.

Photo 8: Central monument, marking the gas chambers.

So they uncovered the graves, dredged up 700,000 rotting, decaying corpses, and dragged them over to…a fire pit. To burn them all. Down to *pure ash*, down to *nothing*. In the open air. Using wood logs.

I asked Edward where this miracle happened. He walked us over to the "symbolic" pit where the Germans had constructed grills of elevated railway rails, on which they could stack the corpses—see Photos 9 and 10. Wood was placed underneath, ignited, and the bodies all but vaporized. And not only did they have the 700,000 exhumed corpses, but they also had to contend with the ongoing supply of 212,000 "fresh" bodies that were still being gassed—at a rate of 5,000 per day. All 912,000 bodies, reduced to ash, in the very spot we were standing. And they did this in *just 16 weeks*, according to the experts—more than 8,000 per day, every day. Those Germans were brilliant indeed, and *efficient*.

"Where is the ash?" I asked. "It's still in the ground," said Edward. He reached down, scraped around in the dirt with his hand, and said, "Here is some." He handed me 5 or 6 bits of something that certainly looked like ash: two were black (wood ash?), one was grey, and two white—bone fragments, perhaps? I was quite impressed: here in my hand were the likely remains of actual Treblinka victims. I stuffed the bits of ash in my pocket. I have them to this day.

Photo 9: Symbolic cremation pit.

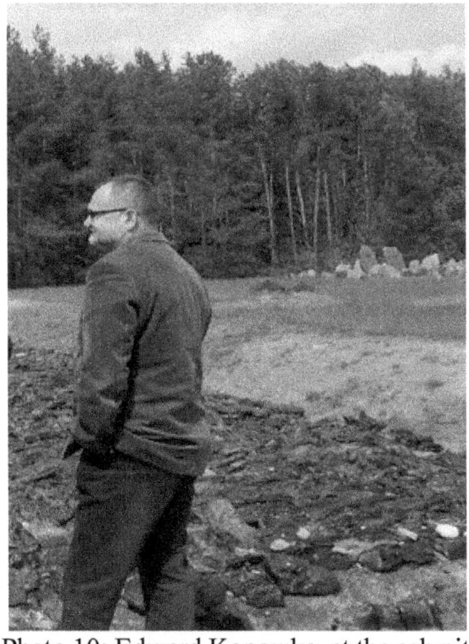

Photo 10: Edward Kopowka, at the ash pit.

During our discussion the question of excavations arose. On the traditional view, the ash was reburied in the graves that held the bodies; even today, there would be literally tons of it remaining. But as we know, there have been no attempts to unearth evidence of mass graves, or to measure or quantify ashes or human remains—not one single attempt, in nearly 70 years. It is almost as if the powers that be did not want to confirm the truth. Perhaps they suspected, in the back of their minds, that the conventional storyline would not hold up. So, I was quite surprised to hear that a team from Birmingham University (UK) was preparing to conduct a non-invasive study of the mass graves, using a ground-penetrating radar. I made a note to myself to follow the progress of this very interesting development (see Postscript below for an update).

Our time about up, we walked on back to the museum. Along the way we stopped at a little gift-shop kiosk and purchased two small books: a photo album titled *Treblinka: The Stones Are Silent* (2007) and a historical overview, *Treblinka II – The Death Camp* (2007). The latter reiterated that "around 900,000" Jews were killed there, but it included a surprising statistic: "one third of the deportees were dead or on the verge of death when they reached [the camp]" (p. 9). This was a shock: something like 200,000 or 250,000 of the Treblinka victims were all but *dead on arrival?* I am unaware of this estimate in any conventional academic work; it would significantly alter the whole story.

The book also mentions the 10 gas chambers, each of 16 square meters in area, which could collectively gas "up to 5000 victims at a time" (p. 13). So: 500 victims per room, which works out to *31 persons per square meter of area.* Evidently the authors count on the reader being incapable of basic math—otherwise they wouldn't put forth such obvious nonsense.

Thus was my day in Treblinka. Back in the parking lot, our cabbie was waiting—arising from a little nap. Heading back to Warsaw, we took "the direct route," meaning, we got lost three more times. Finally, two hungry hours later, we arrived back at our hotel. Quite a day. I wouldn't have missed it for the world.

Postscript: For a long time after my visit, I heard nothing at all about any Birmingham study of the camp using ground-penetrating radar. I was disappointed, but not surprised. Then one day, to my astonishment, came a blazing headline in the British paper *The Daily Mail*: "British archaeologist destroys Holocaust deniers' argument with mass grave find at Treblinka" (18 January 2012). The short article reads, in part:

> A British forensic archaeologist has unearthed fresh evidence to prove the existence of mass graves at the Nazi death camp Treblinka—scuppering the claims of Holocaust deniers who say it was merely a transit camp. … Forensic archaeologist Caroline Sturdy Colls has now undertaken the first coordinated scientific attempt to locate the graves.

Ms. Colls is quoted as follows: "I've identified a number of buried pits using geophysical techniques. These are considerable in size, and very deep, one in particular is 26 by 17 meters." This is the full extent of the details that we are offered—a very strong sign that Ms. Colls did not, in fact, "destroy" the revisionists' arguments. The presumably largest grave is 26 by 17 meters, or 442 square meters in area. Recall above where I noted that the orthodox story requires a total grave area of roughly 7200 square meters. So Ms. Colls's one large grave is about 6% of the necessary area. She claims to have found "a number" of graves, but unless this number was something like 30 or 40, she is far short of the mark. More likely, of course, the "number" was quite small, or we would surely have been given specifics.

I would further add that, on the revisionist thesis, many thousands of people did indeed die in the camp, of various causes. A high-volume transit camp would have received thousands of incoming dead (recall the "one third" statistic above), and many more would have died of disease and, yes, execution (likely by bullet) at the camp. So it is fully expected that mass graves exist in the camp. But the anticipated number of victims is much smaller—perhaps 10% of those claimed. Thus we might expect to see a total grave volume of around 10,000 to 12,000 cubic meters, rather than the 120,000 required by the conventional account.

So what grave volume did Ms. Colls find? BBC Radio 4 ran a 30-minute exclusive story on this event, on 23 January 2012. Colls spoke several times, but offered very few additional details. She confirmed that a "number" of graves were found, with the largest as mentioned above. But of course, we also need to know how deep they are. The newspaper article quoted her as saying they were "very deep." But it turns out that her high-tech ground-scanning system cannot record the depth! All she knows is that the graves are "at least 4 meters deep"—evidently the scanning limit of her system. Unbelievable. This is a case of either blinding incompetence, or willful neglect. Any serious attempt to understand the graves would have obviously recorded their depth, at least to the full 8 meters claimed by Edward Kopowka. As it is, and for all she knows, the graves may indeed be *no more than* 4 meters deep—in which case, her large "26 x 17" grave is a mere 3% of the required size.

Colls added one further fact on the radio program: the "main area" for graves, right behind the presumed gas chambers, showed evidence of "five graves in a row." And all five, presumably, are significantly smaller than her largest. This again suggests that she has found only a small fraction of the necessary grave area. The conventional story, and the 700,000 buried corpses, may well have been fatally undermined by this latest discovery. But we won't know until we see the details of her report—if they ever reach the light of day.

Lacking the details, it is hard to draw firm conclusions. But all signs point in one direction. They imply that, as at Belzec, ground surveys provide far more support for the revisionist thesis than the traditional one. Things are looking up; the truth is at hand.[1]

---

[1] For more details on radar scans at Treblinka and Belzec, see my book *Debating the Holocaust* (2020).

— 12 —
The Importance of Holocaust Revisionism

A few years ago, the online website *Veterans Today* published three pieces on Holocaust revisionism by former BBC journalist Alan Hart,[1] and one set of reflections by Jim Dean and Paul Eisen. Any discussion of this topic is welcome, given its central importance in American life today. However, Hart, in particular, perpetuates some false and misleading ideas about the matter, and thus a brief reply is called for.

Let me begin with a few points that Hart has correct. There are, in fact, three essential elements to the event called the Holocaust:

(1) intention to mass murder the Jews, by Hitler and the Nazi elite;
(2) the use of gas chambers; and
(3) the 6 million deaths.

If any one of these three should undergo substantial revision, then, technically speaking, we no longer have "The Holocaust"—at least, not in any meaningful sense. (Broadly speaking, of course, any mass fatality is a holocaust.) Holocaust revisionism contends that, not one, but *all three* of these points are grossly in error, and thus that "The Holocaust," as such, did not occur. Obviously, this is not to deny that a tragedy happened to the Jews, nor that many thousands died, directly and indirectly, as a result of the war. But the conventional account is an extreme exaggeration.

Hart's treatment of these issues is woefully inadequate. On the first point, he claims that the Nazis did indeed have a program of mass murder, and that they deliberately and systematically implemented it—but only after the British abandoned their commitment to Zionism in May 1939. And yet, he offers no evidence that this was a major turning point in German policy. I am unaware that any such evidence exists.

In fact, all available evidence suggests a consistent policy of enforced evacuation and deportation, throughout the Nazi era. The Germans wanted a Reich free of Jews, and thus they corralled them into camps, and then systematically evacuated them to the Eastern regions. Yes, many would die

---

[1] "The Nazi holocaust: My response to my critics" (10 Feb 2013), "WANTED – A psychiatric diagnosis of Nazi holocaust denial" (7 Feb), and "Understanding the real significance TODAY of the Nazi holocaust" (5 Feb).

in the process; a regrettable loss. But this is ethnic cleansing, not genocide—something the Israelis are eminently familiar with.

To argue for mass killing, Hart relies almost entirely on ten entries from the Goebbels diary. Unfortunately he has a very superficial knowledge of this subject. Had he done even a bit of research, he would have found my on-line article, "Goebbels on the Jews".[2] There I examine 132 separate entries, covering the final nine years of his life. Roughly 90% refer only to evacuation and deportation. There is *not one entry* on industrial mass killings, *not one entry* on gas chambers, *not one entry* on Auschwitz. Even in the most damning cases, Goebbels uses ambiguous wording such as *Vernichtung* and *Ausrottung*, which refer simply to complete elimination or removal; neither term entails killing.

In fact, only a single late entry, in March 1945, refers explicitly to the killing of Jews—which is inexplicable if his policy was indeed one of mass murder. He had no reason to cover up the truth in his own private diary.

Hart's one other bit of evidence, Himmler's well-known Posen speech of 1943, explicitly equates deportation with *Ausrottung*, or "extermination." The full phrase is, "I am now thinking of the evacuation of the Jews, the *Ausrottung* ['extermination'] of the Jewish people. … [I]t is in our program: deactivation [*Ausschaltung*] of the Jews…" It was their *presence* and their *power* that was to be eliminated.

Regarding the gas chambers, very little can be determined from the Jewish Auschwitz survivors, even ones we trust. What, after all, did they see? Jews forcibly sent to the camp, under appalling wartime conditions. Families separated, never to meet again. People dying from typhus, dysentery, and other diseases. Cans of deadly Zyklon poison (for fumigation of lice). Dead bodies. Corpses being burned in crematoria. But all these things are completely comprehensible—and in fact expected—in a wartime concentration camp. *None of this entails mass murder in gas chambers*.

What none of the survivors have seen is 2,000 live Jews forced into an underground chamber, Zyklon pellets dumped on their heads, and then 2,000 dead bodies hauled out. And the fact that no one has seen this strongly suggests that it never happened.

Independently, it is an utterly ludicrous way to kill masses of people: packing victims into an underground room with military-like precision, dumping cyanide pellets on them (that continue to out-gas for two or three hours), and then gingerly hauling out dead body after dead body without killing yourself or your worker-slaves. And the job's not done yet: now load four or five dead bodies at a time on a small freight elevator, to send them up two floors to the crematoria ovens, where it takes one full hour to

[2] Later published in book form as *Goebbels on the Jews* (2019).

incinerate one body—hardly the streamlined industrial killing operation that we've been sold.

Furthermore, few (including Hart) realize that Zyklon was the alleged murder weapon for 'only' one million Jews; another *two million* were allegedly killed in carbon monoxide gas chambers, primarily at Treblinka and Belzec. Unfortunately this is yet an even more ridiculous scheme: to pump engine exhaust into a sealed, airtight room packed with people. The alleged diesel engines put out far too little CO gas to be effective, and in any case one cannot pump exhaust gas into a sealed space. For that matter, with an airtight room available, one has only to shut the door and wait 30 minutes—and all would suffocate! The entire gassing scheme collapses into absurdity.

As to the third point, that the "6 million" figure might be a considerable exaggeration, Hart simply says, "so what!" In fact, the best revisionist estimates suggest that perhaps 500,000 Jews died during the war years—a staggering 90% reduction from the claimed number. Well—so what? Historical accuracy, for one; when speaking of the "greatest crime in the history of humanity," we should at least get our numbers straight. Secondly, this would reduce the Jewish death toll to barely 1% of the total war dead, turning it into a mere footnote of history.

But most importantly, it makes starkly clear the degree to which the world has been bamboozled by the international Jewish Lobby. The sheer fact that large portions of the public and academia have been cowed into accepting a patently false storyline—one that serves only to benefit a small Jewish minority—is beyond reprehensible. It is criminal; and the criminals ought to be called to account.

Hart is right to say that the Holocaust is used to bully America and the European nations into subservience, and to cast a collective guilt upon all parties involved in the war. The guilt trip works best, incidentally, on the level of the individual, and it keeps otherwise knowledgeable and ethical people from speaking out against Israeli crimes. It keeps Americans from demanding that their government stop supplying some $6 billion per year in aid to Israel; stop providing diplomatic cover in the UN; and stop the stranglehold on Congress and our foreign policy. By exposing this fraud, Germany and the other extorted nations would be right to demand repayment of hundreds of billions of dollars; now there would be a first step on the path to justice.

All this is only the tip of the Holocaust iceberg. The full story is spelled out in my book, *Debating the Holocaust.*[3] There, the reader is invited to judge for himself.

---

[3] Latest edition: *Debating the Holocaust: A New Look at Both Sides* (2020, 4th ed.).

Finally, as to Hart's contention that the truth-seeking revisionists are evil, and the lying, fraudulent, Holocaust blackmailers ought to get a free pass—well, that speaks for itself.

— 13 —
"GATES OF HELL": AUSCHWITZ IN THE MASS MEDIA

It has now been more than 75 years since Auschwitz labor camp was captured by the advancing Soviet Army. Since then, we have seen the growth of a monstrous propaganda machine focused on this one, small location in the vast global theater of WW2. Imagine: some 60 million people killed all around the world, across hundreds of thousands of square kilometers and in dozens of nations; and yet today, in film and television, on radio and the Internet, popular media gives a hugely disproportionate amount of war coverage to one small location, a mere pinpoint on the map, in southeast Poland—the alleged site of the murder of one million Jews.

Since the media machine uses every opportunity to further advance its propaganda, we may as well turn the picture around and analyze the media itself. The on-going system of obfuscation and brainwashing about the Holocaust is endlessly instructive.

But let us first recall the early days of the Auschwitz myth. Reports about a German camp at Oswiecim—the Polish name for Auschwitz—first appeared in the *New York Times* as early as 30 March 1941. In November 1942, the NYT was reporting on "gas chambers in which thousands of Jews have been put to death" there. In August 1943 we read of the "Oswiecim camp, where 58,000 persons are believed to have perished." June 1944 saw the first reference to Birkenau and to "gas chambers" there, where "800,000 persons had been killed or allowed to die." The first explicit reference to Auschwitz came on 3 July 1944, where "more than 1,715,000 Jewish refugees were put to death." Several other stories followed in quick succession. Thus by the end of 1944, the groundwork for the Auschwitz myth had been fully laid.

Into 1945, even more outrageous claims emerged after the camp was "liberated" on 27 January. In February, a Jewish newspaper, the *Palestine Post*, reported that "truckloads of children were burnt alive by the Germans at Auschwitz concentration camp." On 3 April, the NYT reported on 35 Jewesses from Auschwitz who claimed that "women…too weak to work were taken to a gas chamber and asphyxiated." Then the astonishing headline of 12 April: "5,000,000 reported slain at Oswiecim." And in just 10 months![1]

---

[1] This comes to nearly 18,000 per day, every day, for almost a full year—sheer nonsense.

This ridiculous claim came from the Jew Bela Fabian, president of the former "Hungarian Independent Democratic Party." In the AP's version of the same story, it was added that "Dr. Fabian told a story so horrible as to be almost unbelievable"—indeed!

Nonetheless, claims of 4 million killed at Auschwitz appeared in the Nuremberg Trials, and this figure henceforth became the official statistic, surviving all the way until 1990, when it was unceremoniously dropped to around 1 million. Today, the new "official" story is that around 1.1 million people were killed there, of whom about 1 million were Jews. And of these Jews, around 900,000 allegedly died in one of the Zyklon gas chambers.

Those who study Holocaust revisionism know that there are many holes in the conventional story. I recount these in detail in my book *Debating the Holocaust*, but in brief, these are some of the many issues:

- The "gas chamber" in the Auschwitz main camp was massively reconstructed after the war, in order to fit public expectations of a homicidal facility. In fact, it was never more than a standard crematorium and, later, an air raid shelter.
- Despite all the public attention today on the main camp, 98% of all alleged Jewish deaths occurred at Birkenau camp, located a few miles from the main camp. But 98% of all tourists see only the main camp, where the story is much easier to control.
- Nearly 250,000 Jews are claimed to have been gassed at two Birkenau farm houses, or "bunkers," despite the fact that these buildings had no logical way of introducing the Zyklon pellets, nor did they have exhaust fans to clear the rooms after gassing. Oddly, we have virtually no tangible evidence of these structures today; only the outline of the foundations remains.
- Details of the gassing scheme rely on highly dubious testimony from just a handful of Jewish ex-inmates, and from three captive Germans (Rudolf Hoess, Johann Kremer, and Pery Broad). The Jews had every reason to lie or exaggerate, and the Germans were likely tortured or threatened into saying almost anything their captors wanted.
- The most common gassing scheme—Zyklon pellets dumped on top of Jews trapped in 'gas chamber' rooms—is ridiculous, because it could not have killed all the people in a timely manner. It furthermore would have been nearly impossible to clean up, with the deadly pellets emitting gas for hours. How could anyone get in there to get the bodies out, without themselves dying?
- The ruins of Crematorium #2 today have no obvious candidates for ceiling holes by which the Germans could have dumped in the Zyklon.

- Samples of "gas chamber" walls taken by Fred Leuchter and Germar Rudolf were chemically analyzed, showing little or no exposure to Zyklon gas.
- After the alleged gassings, the crematoria were utterly incapable of burning the bodies at the rate needed. The four Birkenau crematoria could have burned a maximum of around 1,100 daily, and yet the "gas chambers" were allegedly killing, at their peak, 200,000 per month, or some 6,600 per day.
- The so-called "Hungarian Operation," which supposedly gassed the Jews of Hungary, claimed to have killed about 450,000 Jews in just eight weeks during the summer of 1944. This represents nearly half of the total Auschwitz toll, *in just eight weeks*—in a camp that allegedly gassed Jews for almost three years.
- The Hungarian gassing would have required that the Germans burn huge amounts of bodies in the open air, on large log fires—at the rate of 6,000 to 10,000 per day, every day, for weeks on end. This whole concept is both ludicrous and utterly impractical.
- Open air fires, and even crematoria smoke, would have been visible from the air. But despite a series of air photos taken mid- to late-1944, none show supporting evidence. As explained below, a few photos show very small open-air burnings, but these are consistent with the incineration of perhaps a few hundred bodies, at most.

All this points to an Auschwitz death toll far below the claimed numbers. Leading revisionists argue that all evidence suggests a figure of perhaps 140,000. This is still a tragic number, it's true, but far less tragic than the 1 million trumpeted by the media machine.

An Example of Fine British Media

How, then, do Western media handle these tricky issues? Virtually without exception, they do so by obfuscation, selective omission, inuendo, implication, and outright lies. Let's take one specific example. On 12 January 2020, the British paper *The Guardian* published a lengthy story entitled "The gates of hell: Auschwitz 75 years on." It is a case study in how major media manipulate and distort the Auschwitz story, in service to the traditional account, and to the benefit of Jews and Israel. Let's look at their account with a critical eye to the truth.

The news story is centered on a 90-year-old Jewish woman, Renee Salt, a camp survivor and first-hand witness to events there. Now, the most basic questions about any Auschwitz survivor are (a) when did they arrive at the camp? (b) how long did they stay? and (c) when did they leave? This is critical because it allows us to compare their claims of events with what the orthodox experts tell us occurred at that time. Then we can better assess the validity and value of the survivor's account.

Here, for the most part, the *Guardian* leaves us guessing. Currently 90 years old, Salt arrived at Auschwitz when she "had just turned 15." Why say it this way? Why not just state when she arrived? Does she not remember her own birthday? Apparently we have to calculate dates for ourselves. Depending on Salt's birthday, she could have arrived anytime between February and December 1944. But later in the article we get another clue: "Salt and her mother had been moved [from Auschwitz] about four months earlier" than the arrival of the Soviets on 27 January. Therefore, she left the camp around mid-September 1944.

But when did she arrive? Was she there for months—beginning February or March—or just weeks? We are not told. At one point, the story implies that the Salts were imprisoned "for several weeks," which suggests perhaps two months. This seems about right. Any longer and the story surely would have mentioned their "months" at the camp; but this is not said. So let's assume that Salt arrived in mid-July 1944, and departed around two months later, in mid-September. Shortly I will return to what she might have witnessed at that time.

The Salt family arrived via a "cattle truck," along with "hundreds" of other Jews, during which they were deprived of "food, water, or air for 24 hours." (We note that no one can live without air for 24 hours, so clearly there was some exaggeration going on here.) Most Jews, however, arrived via train, not truck, in train cars also designed for cattle; perhaps Salt was confused here.

Upon arrival with her parents, she and her mother were separated from their father, whom she "never saw again"—presumably gassed, but the story does not say. Standing in the selection line, she and her mother were confronted by none other than Josef Mengele, the notorious doctor of Auschwitz. (Encounters with Mengele are standard fare for most every Auschwitz survivor tale.) Mengele allegedly decided who went "to the right" (gas chambers) and who "to the left" (labor camp). By "God's will," Salt and her mother were sent to the left.

"I remember everything," says Salt. "I can see everything." They were taken to a hall and had their heads shaved—standard procedure for likely lice-infested Jews. The Germans took all their possessions—obviously, since they were now in a forced labor camp. "We thought this was our last hour," says Salt. Instead she was given prison clothes, and presumably set to work.

Camp conditions must always be portrayed as inhumanly as possible, to keep with the conventional myth. The story claims that "for several weeks, the prisoners sat in rows on the stone floor of a hut, day and night." This is a ridiculous statement; no one could, or would, be made to sit, 24/7, on a stone floor. And yet, Salt insists that "we had to sleep as we were sitting." (Right.) "Twice a day we had roll calls outside the hut. Very often people collapsed from weakness." "We were treated like animals," she says.

But this, oddly, is all we hear from poor Ms. Salt about the "hell" of Auschwitz. No more statements about the camp appear in the article. No explicit mention of gas chambers, nothing on piles of corpses, nothing on huge open-air fires to burn the bodies, no smoke from crematoria chimneys—*nothing*. Instead, we read that Salt and her mother left Auschwitz, were sent to Hamburg "to do back-breaking demolition work" (how much demolition work could the Germans have demanded from a 15-year-old girl?), and then on to Bergen-Belsen, until that camp's "liberation" in April 1945.

Salt's lack of discussion of the gas chambers and disposal of bodies is hugely revealing. If she arrived in July 1944, this was during the final phase of the infamous Hungarian Operation (mentioned above). In the month of July, on the standard view, some 100,000 Jews were gassed. And another 60,000 in August. This would have meant something like 3,000 Jews per day being paraded to the gas chambers—an event Salt could never have overlooked, especially since she "remembers everything."

Even more striking, this rate of killing far exceeded the existing crematoria capacity, and therefore the Germans must have had to burn thousands of corpses a day on huge open-air fires. In July, the figures would have been staggering: around 80,000 burned in the open. This, along with another 45,000 in August and 20,000 in September. This would have required some 10 or 20 active fire pits, burning bodies around the clock. The smell and the smoke would have smothered the camp for weeks. And yet nothing on all this from Ms. Salt—the woman who "remembers everything," and who, even today, "can see everything."

What this suggests, of course, is that there was nothing to see. No parade of Jews to homicidal gas chambers, no massive burning of bodies on open-air fires. Instead, the bodies of the few hundred Jews who died in Auschwitz each month—most of typhus or other disease—would have been discretely disposed of, either in the three operating crematoria or in a small firepit in the far corner of Birkenau. Either way, nothing for young Ms. Salt to see.

And in fact, we have objective, positive evidence to suggest that there was nothing for her to see: air photos. As it happens, we have four or five air photos of Auschwitz during precisely the time that Salt was there.[2] And they show—*almost nothing*. The photo of 8 July has no smoking crematoria, and no parades of people heading to the "gas chambers"; but it does show a wisp of smoke from a small pit near Crematorium #5, consistent with the burning of perhaps a few dozen bodies, or perhaps some unknown

[2] Photos reproduced and discussed in my *Debating the Holocaust* (pp. 229-237).

debris. Three photos in August (20, 23, 25) show either the small smoking firepit (20, 23) or no smoke at all (25). The photo of 13 September shows no smoke, no pits, nothing—nothing but a calm prison facility on a clear fall day. We can understand Salt's failure to comment.

Compliant Authorities

The article supplements Salt's story with other bits on information on the camp's then-upcoming 75th "anniversary." At Auschwitz, Salt and "200 other Holocaust survivors" would return and commemorate the liberation. (Salt, we read, has personally returned to the camp "dozens of times" in the past 15 years—implausible, to say the least.) She would be accompanied by "scores of heads of state, political leaders and dignitaries," including England's own Camilla, Duchess of Cornwall. Later in the piece, we read that heads of no less than 22 countries would be participating. Truly an impressive show of support.

Meanwhile another event would take place at Yad Vashem in Israel. This one would be "attended by dozens of world leaders," including Britain's Prince Charles, Mike Pence, Emmanuel Macron, Vladimir Putin, and German president Steinmeier—all in all, "more than 40 state leaders, royals, and other dignitaries." (One wonders: What kind of political influence does it take to make such things happen?)

The article goes on to write of suffering by 2nd- and 3rd-generation "survivors"—that is, children and grandchildren of actual camp inmates. Incredibly, the trauma seems to have passed on to future generations of Jews, who struggle with "clinical depression, anxiety, addiction, and eating disorders"—all thanks to those evil Nazis. Such "survivors" naturally demand reparation money. Back in 2015, it was reported that British Jews were lobbying for a "campaign to support the grandchildren of Holocaust survivors across the world".[3] Astonishingly, some actually claim that "the breast milk of survivors was affected by stress hormones that impacted on the physiology of the next generation"—even to the point that it may have "altered the DNA of victims' descendants." This, of course, is the stuff of science fiction, not reality.

Meanwhile, the wonderful British media continued to unquestioningly promote the conventional view of Auschwitz and the wider Holocaust. The article notes that the BBC produced a documentary featuring Salt back in 2005 ("Grandchild of the Holocaust"). Late in the piece, the article states that the BBC will be "broadcasting a range of documentaries and dramas," along with a feature "Songs of Praise" from the UK National

[3] "Holocaust survivors' grandchildren call for action over inherited trauma" (*The Guardian*, 3 Aug).

Holocaust Centre, as well as providing live coverage of the Polish commemoration. The key man behind this propaganda is cited as Tony Hall, then-director general of the BBC, who evidently takes it as his personal mission "to ensure that the millions of lives lost in the Holocaust are not forgotten." Hall, incidentally, has been criticized as serving as a leading Israeli apologist and advocate, and whose top staff reflect similar attitudes.[4] So much for fairness and objectivity at the BBC.

Those Evil "Deniers"

At two points in the *Guardian* article, we read of the true fear of those in power: that the evil "Holocaust deniers" might continue to persuade people of the falsity of large parts of the conventional story. UK Holocaust Centre's chief executive, Marc Cave, is quoted as saying "In a climate of ignorance, trivialization, and denial, the primacy of first-hand testimony cannot be overstated"—as if ambiguous, exaggerated, or obviously false testimony is worth anything. Thus he is undertaking to create "The Forever Project," which will recreate bizarre "life-sized images of survivors" that can "answer" questions from future generations. And he has produced a short film "through the medium of hip-hop" to reach the younger crowd—nothing like rappin' Nazis! The propaganda machine spares no effort.

The article ends with a quotation from Ms. Salt: "There are still people who say it didn't happen, there are still deniers. But you can't hide people like me away." There are two problems with this statement. First, no rational Holocaust skeptic claims that Auschwitz, or the Holocaust, "didn't happen." This is a classic strawman fallacy repeatedly presented by traditionalists. All revisionists admit that Hitler and the top Germans hated the Jews and wanted them out of the greater Reich; that they implemented a ruthless plan of deportation by which many thousands of Jews would die; and that upwards of half a million Jews lost their lives in the process. Revisionists *do* deny that homicidal gas chambers were used at Auschwitz (or elsewhere), and they *do* deny that anything like 6 million Jews died. But this is not saying that "nothing happened." Any claim otherwise is pure propaganda.

Second, why would revisionists want to "hide away" survivors like Ms. Salt? We love people like her. They either tell the truth—as Ms. Salt has largely done—and thus support the revisionist cause. Or they lie through their teeth, in which case their duplicity and maliciousness are

---

[4] For one assessment, see "Apologists for Israel take top posts at BBC" (*Electronic Intifada*, 23 Apr 2013).

transparent to all, which again aids revisionism. By all means, let's hear from the survivors now; within a few years, there won't be any left at all.

In sum, the "hell" of Auschwitz is not what happened at that camp—horrible things happen everywhere in a world war—but rather it is the present-day propaganda media machine, aided and abetted by wealthy and influential Jews, who radically distort history for their own benefit. They effectively divert billions to Jews and Israelis, they sustain a pathological guilt complex over Germany and much of the West, and they use the Holocaust as a weapon against free speech and against all those who might speak up against Jewish hegemony. This is the true "hell" of the Holocaust, and millions of us continue to live with the consequences of this artificially-constructed reality every day. Its costs are incalculable.

But with the ongoing good work of revisionists everywhere, its days are surely numbered. With luck, our time in the Jewish-constructed Auschwitz hell may soon be over. And perhaps then, with luck, our tormentors will get their due. One can only hope.

— 14 —
JASENOVAC UNMASKED

Funny how it goes with the Holocaust story: time and again, an ugly bit of truth slips out. When that happens, yet one more piece of the charade comes to light, for all to see. For a brief moment, one more embarrassing truth catches the public eye, only to quickly be cast into the depths of the memory hole. Only through diligence, hard work, and a bit of luck do such things come to assume a greater significance.

This time, sharp eyes caught the slip-up. The issue in question is an obscure World War II concentration camp in present-day Croatia, by the name of Jasenovac. The camp—which operated for around three and a half years, from mid-1941 until war's end—is, by any reasonable accounting, all but irrelevant to the Holocaust story. Even according to the US Holocaust Memorial Museum, only some "12,000 to 20,000 Jews" died there, which means that the camp accounts for, at best, 0.33% of the presumed Jewish death toll of 6 million. Were it not for a blunder by the *Jerusalem Post*, I would likely never have spent a moment on the topic. In the grand Holocaust narrative, there are much larger fish to fry. But the latest gaff gives us a chance to shine a light on the on-going fraud that is the Holocaust. When the Jews themselves put a foot in their collective mouths, we should make the most of it.

The subject at hand is an article that briefly appeared on the *Post* website, titled "This disgraceful mocking of the Holocaust needs to stop now".[1] Written by an Australian journalist named David Goldman, the short essay obsesses over a three-year-old Croatian television interview in which historian and Croatian Jew Ivo Goldstein expounds on the "increasingly problematic" camp at Jasenovac. The interview, from 2018, included this question of Goldstein: "Many have commented on the lack of forensic evidence from this particular camp. Can you explain why this is the case?" (meaning, why there is an absence of evidence). Goldstein then dropped his "bombshell" reply: "Because in April 1945, Hitler flew in special machines to Jasenovac. These machines were used to dissolve the bones that were left."

Several points here: One, in all of Holocaust historiography, there is no actual or even rumored documentation of any such "bone dissolving

---

[1] Available at: https://jpost.pressreader.com/jerusalem-post/20210815 (p. 10). The original URL has been deleted.

machines." There were alleged bone *crushers*, driven by diesel engines; a photo of one such machine is shown below:

But these have been shown to be fraudulent.[2] The Germans also allegedly used chlorinated lime (quicklime) to try to decompose corpses at Treblinka and Belzec, but this chemical, when used, only reduces the odor; it does nothing to hasten decomposition. "Dissolving," especially for bones, implies the use of acid or some other strong chemical process, but again, such claims are completely unknown in the literature. Hence Goldman rightly refers to these as "hitherto unheard-of machines." Perhaps there was some confusion on Goldstein's part, and he actually meant 'crushing,' not 'dissolving.' But again, we have no reliable evidence that such crushing machines were ever used by the Germans.

Two, this idea seems to be a pure invention by Goldstein to explain away a troublesome fact, namely, lack of forensic evidence at Jasenovac—that is, any corpses, ash, or other human remains. And by "pure invention," I mean an outright lie. By all accounts, Goldstein lied to cover up a critical and damning fact. Anyone who has studied the Holocaust story knows that such lies are legion.[3]

---

[2] All alleged use of Nazi 'bone crushers' to eliminate bodily evidence has been refuted in recent years. The machines in the few extant photos are likely conventional gravel ball mills used in the early 20th century. See the discussion in *The Einsatzgruppen in the Occupied Eastern Territories* (2018, C. Mattogno, Castle Hill), pp. 481-484. See also the online article "The bone mill of Lemberg" (2013).

[3] My all-time favorite Holocaust liar is Herman Rosenblat, who fabricated the whole "angel at the fence" story in the 1990s. His television interview in 2009, in

Three, the whole premise that the Germans, in the final throes of defeat, would take the trouble to send anything like "bone dissolving machines" to an obscure camp in Croatia is patently absurd, as Goldman points out. The whole idea is nonsense.

Perhaps most significantly, this little episode brings to mind similar claims about the more important camps like Auschwitz, Treblinka, and Belzec. Lacking physical evidence, how can we justify claims of thousands, or hundreds of thousands, or a million Holocaust victims at these camps? For the journalist Goldman, however, the lies about Jasenovac only "contaminate" the larger Holocaust story, which he accepts unquestioningly. As he says, "Why allow the contamination of Holocaust history with a place [Jasenovac] that cannot provide any independent forensic evidence past a few thousand victims, and that has an ever-increasing—including in 2021—victim list that has been repeatedly proven to have been doctored?" Indeed; and we can ask *the same question* about virtually all the conventional Holocaust sites. The implications are dire for Jews everywhere.

A Short Course on Jasenovac

It is worthwhile taking a moment to review the conventional history of this camp, given the many lessons it offers here. It is undisputed that Jasenovac was established under the auspices of the Nazi-aligned government of occupied Croatia known as the Ustasa (or Ustase, or Ustashi). The camp was constructed in August 1941, not long after Hitler began his invasion of the Soviet Union. It consisted of five separate facilities, two of which were short-lived, but the other three—Ciglana, Kozara, and Stara Gradiska—operated right until the virtual end of the war in April 1945. The purpose of the camp is disputed; some claim it was strictly a detention and work camp, whereas others declare it to be an extermination center on par with the worst camps of Poland. By all accounts, several thousand people died there—mostly Serbs, but also Jews, Roma, and scattered numbers of Muslims and Croatian political enemies.

The numbers of victims, and especially the numbers of Jews, are the main points of contention. Like most Holocaust camps and death sites, the range of estimates is vast. Individuals sympathetic to the Ustasa regime, like former president Franjo Tudjman, regularly gave figures of just 3,000 to 4,000 total. Such numbers date back to the first forensic examinations of the camp in 1947. But by the 1970s and 1980s, the numbers were rising;

---

which he openly confesses to the lie, is so audacious, so brazen, and so deluded that it stands as a monument to Jewish mendacity. It can be found here: www.dailymotion.com/video/x2qusht

the 1990 *Encyclopedia of the Holocaust* (p. 189) claimed, without evidence, that around 300,000 bodies were discovered and exhumed there.

Yet even this number was insufficient for our Holocaust propagandists. One recent article notes that, over past decades, "historians have estimated that between 700,000 and 1,000,000 people were killed at Jasenovac".[4] Serbian publications of the 1990s cited figures as high as 1.2 million.[5] Of these, around 15% are claimed to have been Jews—meaning, potentially 100,000 to 150,000. At that upper estimate, this would put Jasenovac well ahead of Majdanek in terms of Jewish death toll, and approaching the status of a Sobibor. If, on the other hand, Jews were 15% of, say, 3,000 fatalities, it would mean an utterly inconsequential 400 or 500 deaths. Much is at stake.

Today, though, the more commonly accepted estimates are much closer to the low end than the high. The current Croatian government seems to accept a figure of 83,000 total deaths. The US Holocaust Memorial Museum claims that "the Ustasa regime murdered between 77,000 and 99,000 people in Jasenovac between 1941 and 1945." Of these, some 12,000 to 20,000 are claimed to have been Jews. Still, the USHMM is not very sanguine about their own estimates:

> Determining the number of victims for…Jasenovac is highly problematic, due to the destruction of many relevant documents, the long-term inaccessibility to independent scholars of those documents that survived, and the ideological agendas of postwar partisan scholarship and journalism, which has been and remains influenced by ethnic tension, religious prejudice, and ideological conflict. The estimates offered here are based on the work of several historians who have used census records as well as whatever documentation was available in German, Croat, and other archives in the former Yugoslavia and elsewhere.[6]

As I noted above, even 20,000 Jewish deaths are largely irrelevant to the broader Holocaust narrative.

---

[4] "Jasenovac, the forgotten extermination camp of the Balkans," *New Europe* (31 Jan 2020).

[5] Benčić, A. (2018). "Koncentracijski logor Jasenovac: konfliktno ratno nasljeđe i osporavani muzejski postav." *Polemos* XXI (41): 37–63.

[6] From www.encyclopedia.ushmm.org, entry on 'Jasenovac.'

A Rebuttal

Goldman's short essay drew a quick and furious response from Dejan Ristic, the acting director of the Serbian Museum of Genocide Victims. It was published in the *Jerusalem Post* just two days after Goldman's original piece. Serbia, of course, has an incentive to promote high numbers of victims, and especially high numbers of Serbs, because it enhances their victimhood status and promotes their nationalist agenda. But more important than high numbers is the overall integrity of the camp as a legitimate Holocaust site and not as a whimsical political ragdoll that has victim numbers ranging over nearly three orders of magnitude, and that is entirely lacking in relevant evidence.

Ristic's rebuttal—"Shame on those who seek to revise history of the Holocaust"—is as poorly argued as it is poorly written.[7] (Though, oddly, the *Post* website still displays this rebuttal, whereas the original essay is long gone.) Ristic expresses "astonishment" at the "pseudo-scientific and revisionist text" by Goldman, which contains, he says, little more than "a series of inaccurate statements and semi-information." Ristic is incensed that Goldman dares to cite the ragged history of victim numbers; the Museum clearly accepts a figure in the mainstream range (80,000 to 90,000), though with the opportunity for higher figures in the future. Ristic writes,

> As the research of the experts of the Museum...continues, it is to be expected that the number of Jasenovac victims will be corrected. ... The estimated total number of victims is, unfortunately, far higher than the one that historical science will ever be able to identify with the precise data.

He is anxious to quell all thoughts of a mere few thousand deaths, and he equally seeks to avoid any suggestion that the figure approaches a million or more; as he well knows, both extremes threaten to undermine all credibility about the camp.

Most amusingly, in his entire lengthy rebuttal, Ristic never once mentions the "bombshell" about the bone-dissolving machines—not once. This is a tacit admission that the point holds, that no evidence was sought or found, and that the whole basis for Jasenovac as a top-tier death camp rests on little more than rumor and innuendo, if not outright falsehood.

The central problem for both Ristic and Goldman, however, is that their back-and-forth arguments promise to expose the far more consequential problems of the main Holocaust camps. In fact, Ristic does the nasty work for us. He writes, "we could ask a question as to whether it is possible

---

[7] *Jerusalem Post* (17 Aug 2021).

to deny, in the same way, the number of 1,200,000 to 1,500,000 killed in Auschwitz since there is no forensic evidence for that claim either?" Touché, Mr. Ristic! The irony is that he is entirely correct, of course. No evidence (or scarcely any) for Auschwitz; none for Treblinka; none for Belzec—the same old story.

Grave Implications

Goldman's main beef is with the ad hoc lie of the bone-dissolving machines, but this echoes the many, far more grievous lies about Auschwitz, Belzec, Treblinka, and indeed all six of the so-called death camps.[8] Of these, Goldman of course is silent. But he does decry the ongoing process of myth-formation surrounding a camp like Jasenovac, "where myths of Serbian and Jewish suffering were interwoven, providing a new series of national myths" (to cite the author David McDonald). Goldman, though, naturally avoids the similar but far greater myth-formation process about Auschwitz, the other camps, and the broader Holocaust. It is this very myth-formation process that has led to numbers like 1 million Jews gassed at Auschwitz, when, on the far more plausible revisionist thesis, perhaps 150,000 Jews died there—and none in gas chambers.

Likewise, Goldman ridicules the notion of human remains "yet to be discovered" at Jasenovac, and he rightly jabs a finger at the Yugoslav government, which, "during its 47-year rule of the site, never bothered once to try and locate these mysterious 'missing' remains." The same, of course, can be said for the current Croatian government and its on-going 30-year rule. (One strongly suspects that there are simply no remains to be found there.) But this again raises the same question for the other camps: Where are the remains of anything approaching 1 million Jewish bodies at Auschwitz? Or 900,000 Jewish bodies at Treblinka? Or 600,000 Jewish bodies at Belzec? Do we have anything? Bodies, bones, ash—anything? Do we even have *the holes in the ground* where the Germans were said to bury the hundreds of thousands of victims, only to later dig them up and burn them "to ash" on open-air fires over wooden logs? Based on my years of research, the answer to all these questions is 'no.'

---

[8] Such lies are vast, both in content and type. They cover all aspects of the Holocaust, and include overt lies, lies of omission, half-truths, dissembling, gross exaggeration, hyperbole, and many more. They were promoted by survivors, "eyewitnesses," coerced and captive Germans, and present-day "experts." I can't begin to elaborate these here; they are the subject of several dedicated books. For starters, one might refer to *Auschwitz Lies* (G. Rudolf and C. Mattogno, 2017, Castle Hill), *Treblinka* (C. Mattogno and J. Graf, 2020, Castle Hill), or *Belzec* (C. Mattogno, 2016, Castle Hill). Or for a good overview of these issues, see my own work *Debating the Holocaust* (2020, 4th ed., Castle Hill).

What about the alleged 1 million Jews killed in the various ghettos? Where are their remains? What about the alleged 1.6 million Jews killed by shootings, mostly along the Eastern front; where are their remains? (Such figures are stated or implied by all our experts, and are absolutely required to get us to the mandatory "6 million" total.) Not all their remains, mind you, or even most of them. We would be satisfied with, say, half, or even a quarter, as long as we had a good explanation for the remainder. But instead we get stories of "600 bodies found here" and "250 bodies found there" and ashes consistent with perhaps "a few thousand bodies" at most. These are so far short of the "6 million" that they constitute an effective refutation of that very figure. Just as the "700,000 to 1 million" at Jasenovac is a farce, so too is the "6 million Jews" for the broader Holocaust.[9]

And yet, our intrepid reporter David Goldman has the gall to write, "Those who have conflated the only [!] wartime concentration camp without any verifiable data, with scientifically proven [!] Holocaust facts, have done immeasurable harm to Jewish history." He is either ignorant of the truth or (more likely) deliberately covering up the reality. The true "immeasurable harm" has been done by his fellow Jews and their intellectual lackeys who, for decades, have promoted an unsustainable myth of Jewish suffering.

The days of the "6 million" are numbered, and I suspect that Goldman, Goldstein, and friends know it. When that crumbles, so too collapses what little remains of Jewish credibility. When the orthodox Holocaust story goes down, the dominoes may well begin to fall. And when that happens, all bets are off.

---

[9] This is not to deny that many thousands of Jews did die during the National Socialist era. By most revisionist accounts, perhaps 500,000 in total died, from all causes. But this is more than a 90% reduction from the claimed 6 million. And it reduces Jewish deaths to a mere footnote in the larger catastrophe that was World War II.

— 15 —
The Holocaust of Six Million Jews —In World War One

I take it that the reader is familiar with the basics of the so-called Holocaust: the alleged deaths of some six million Jews, many in gas chambers, at the hands of the Nazis in World War Two. This was, we are told, a deliberate policy of Hitler and his top men, something of highest priority—even above the war effort itself—and a policy of the utmost secrecy. It was so secret, in fact, that hard documentation and forensic evidence on this catastrophic, world-changing event are almost nonexistent: no 'Hitler order' to kill the Jews, no plans for homicidal gas chambers, no physical remains of gas chambers,[1] no photos of gas chambers or gassed Jews, no autopsies confirming death by gas, no consistent or coherent records of mass shootings that must have totaled over 1.5 million, no evidence of any of the 1 million or so ghetto deaths. Those ingenious devils, the Nazis, managed to destroy all the evidence—including the physical remains of virtually all six million Jewish corpses—in order to conceal their heinous deed. They were truly evil geniuses. Or so we are told.

But this is not my topic for today. (Suffice to say that there are many facts about this notorious event that our friendly 'Holocaust experts' would rather have us not know.) Here, I want to focus on a related but perhaps more surprising event: the Jewish "holocaust" of World War One. (I will use the lower-case 'holocaust' for pre-WW2, reserving the upper-case 'Holocaust' for WW2 itself.)

Wait, you say; *World War One?* But didn't that occur decades before WW2? Yes. Wasn't that years before the Nazi party even existed? True enough. Wasn't Hitler a mere foot soldier in that initial war? Indeed he was. Then who committed the crime? And why? And how many Jews suffered in *that* holocaust?

It is truly a remarkable story, one that is too little known. It has often been said that "history repeats itself." But who would have guessed that a monumentally tragic event like a holocaust could repeat itself, inflicted on the same people, in the same region of the world, and in the same numbers, in just three decades? This amazing occurrence is worth a bit of exploration;

---

[1] Those alleged gas chambers that they show to tourists in Auschwitz Main Camp, Majdanek, and Dachau are postwar reconstructions, and could never have functioned as mass killing sites using poison gas.

the holocaust of WWI has huge implications for the Holocaust of WWII, and by extension, for Jewish-Gentile relations in the world today.

Context for War

The precursors and causes of WWI are vast and complicated, and I cannot delve into those here. But a key factor, and likely decisive, was the action of the global Jewish Lobby of the day, which pushed for war at every possible juncture; I have detailed this aspect in my book *The Jewish Hand in the World Wars* (2019), and I refer interested readers to it. The same Jewish Lobby, it turns out, also had a decisive hand in the holocaust narratives.

For the moment, I will have to restrict myself to the basic facts. The First World War, as we recall, began in July 1914 and ran for a bit more than four years, ending on 11 November 1918. For the majority of this time, the Triple Entente of the UK, France, and Russia faced off against the Triple Alliance of Germany, Austria-Hungary, and (initially) Italy.[2] The US eventually entered the war on the side of the Entente in April 1917. Russia, torn apart by the Judeo-Bolshevik Revolution, withdrew in March 1918. Germany held out for another seven months, but eventually it too was disrupted by internal Jewish agitation, succumbing in November 1918. In the end, the Alliance suffered some 8 million total casualties (military plus civilian), and the Entente around 10 million. Despite the many complicating factors, a defeated Germany was ultimately assigned full blame for the war—completely overlooking the fact that that nation "did not plot a European war, did not want one, and made genuine…efforts to avert one," in the words of historian Sidney Fay.[3] The onerous postwar reparations inflicted on Germany set the stage, in large part, for the later emergence of Hitler and his NSDAP party.

As in all wars, many civilians were caught in the crosshairs; here, the Jews were no exception. Their suffering, however, had already been ongoing for many years prior to the war. Or perhaps we should say, *self-inflicted* suffering. Jewish behavior, attitudes, actions, and beliefs have been a constant source of conflict throughout the centuries—even through millennia.[4] Jewish abrasiveness became particularly pressing by the late 18th century, as was noted by many prominent critics, including Kant, Voltaire, Hegel, Fichte, and Herder. By the mid-19th century, the likes of Schopenhauer and Bruno Bauer were issuing scathing critiques.

---

[2] Later, the Ottoman Empire (Turkey) became the dominant third party.

[3] As quoted in Fay's "classic study" of the war, *The Origins of the World War* (1928), p. 552.

[4] For this story, see my book *Eternal Strangers* (2020).

A particularly disturbing situation, though, was developing in Russia. By the late 1800s, Russia had some 5 million Jews within its borders, nearly all of whom lived in the so-called Pale of Settlement in the far west of the country; this represented about half of the global total of around 10 million Jews. This large Jewish population was a disruptive and agitating force within Russia and hence earned the dislike of Czars Nicholas I (reigned 1825 to 1855) and Alexander II (reigned 1855 to 1881). By 1871, Russian activist Mikhail Bakunin could make this observation about the Jews:

> This whole Jewish world which constitutes a single exploiting sect, a sort of bloodsucker people (*ein Blutegelvolk*), a collective parasite (*einzigen fressenden Parasiten*), voracious, organized in itself, not only across the frontiers of states but even across all the differences of political opinion—this world is presently, at least in great part, at the disposal of Marx on the one hand and of the Rothschilds on the other. ... Jewish solidarity, that powerful solidarity that has maintained itself through all history, united them [both].[5]

In 1881, a gang of anarchists known as Narodnaya Volya, which included a few Jews, succeeded in assassinating Alexander; this unleashed a series of anti-Jewish pogroms that persisted for decades.

By the late 1880s, American media was beginning to take notice of the Jewish situation in Russia—especially the *New York Times*. A brief item from 1889 began with the question "How many Jews are there?" meaning, globally. At a minimum, "the number of the ubiquitous race [is] 6,000,000." It then continues with a reference to Jewish suffering: "With the exception of half a million, they are all in a state of political bondage." Furthermore, "in Russia alone there were 4,000,000 of their race whose every step was dogged by that curse, religious hatred and persecution".[6] Here we find an early reference to (almost) six million suffering Jews.

Another short piece appeared in 1891 entitled "Russia's Christianity: Rabbi Gottheil says a word on the persecution of the Jews." In a public lecture, Gottheil examined a number of facts "in relation to the treatment of Russia's 5,000,000 to 6,000,000 Jews by the Christian population." Notably, the population of Russian Jews, which was just 4 million two year earlier, was now as high as 6 million. Gottheil then proceeds to quote a recent article by one E. B. Lanin, who said, "about six millions [sic] per-

---

[5] Cited in Wheen, *Karl Marx* (1999), p. 340.

[6] 10 February, p. 14.

secuted and miserable wretches remain steadfastly faithful to a religion that causes their life to be changed into a fiery furnace …"[7] Prophetic, indeed.

Nearly a decade later, in June 1900, Rabbis Gottheil and Stephen Wise were the keynote speakers at a "Zionist mass meeting" in New York. They were anxious to highlight Jewish suffering around the world to help make their case for a Jewish homeland in Palestine. Gottheil spoke generically of the "oppressed in Russia," but Wise made the point explicit: "There are 6,000,000 living, bleeding, suffering arguments in favor of Zionism".[8] Within a few years, the pogroms became increasingly intense, eventually leading to small-scale killings. The so-called "Kishineff (or Kishinev) massacre" of 1903, in which all of 49 Jews were killed, became, for the first time, a "holocaust." The NYT quotes from an editorial of the *Jewish Chronicle*:

> We charge the Russian Government with responsibility for the Kishineff massacre. We say it is steeped to the eyes in the guilt of this holocaust. (16 May, p. 1)

The editorial proceeds to speak of how the Russian Jews are being "slowly annihilated" and subject to "the process of extermination." Such words obviously anticipate similar charges that would be leveled against the National Socialists some four decades later.

Two years later, we read that the "holocaust" is still ongoing. A short item of 1905 is headlined "Simon Wolf asks how long the Russian holocaust is to continue".[9] Also that year, the NYT reported, once again, on "our 6,000,000 cringing brothers in Russia".[10] The following year, in 1906, we read of "startling reports of the condition and future of Russia's 6,000,000 Jews"; it is a "horrifying picture" of "renewed massacres" and "systematic and murderous extermination".[11] At this point, one is tempted to ask, What is it about the Jews, such that they are subject to such continual and horrific abuse? And furthermore, why isn't the figure of six million, first reported back in 1890, growing any larger? Is it now, somehow, fixed at six million? If so, why?

In 1910, we find "Russian Jews in sad plight," and we are saddened over "the systematic, relentless, quiet grinding down of a people of more

---

[7] 26 January, p. 8.

[8] 11 June, p. 7. Incidentally, the *New York Times* was, by this time, formally a Jewish newspaper; Adolph Ochs purchased the firm in 1896. It has retained Jewish ownership and management ever since.

[9] 10 November, p. 2.

[10] 23 March, p. 7.

[11] 25 March, p. SM6.

than 6,000,000 souls".[12] In 1911, the NYT reported that "the 6,000,000 Jews of Russia are singled out for systematic oppression and for persecution by due process of law".[13] And yet things got worse still:

> That Russia is pursuing a definite anti-Jewish policy, that the condition of the Jews in Russia is worse now than it ever was before, will be gathered from the following extracts… [T]he restrictive laws now in existence…intensif[y] the oppression of the Jews, and by which it is making the 6,000,000 Jews a people economically exhausted—a people without any rights at all. (10 December, p. SM8)

We need to remind ourselves that the leading Russians had a very low opinion of the Jews, and felt themselves fully justified in any recrimination. Sometimes their words were shocking. Russian prime minister Pyotr Stolypin wrote the following in 1911:

> It is important that racial characteristics have so drastically set the Jewish people apart from the rest of humanity as to make them totally different creatures, who cannot enter into our concept of human nature. We can observe them the way we observe and study animals, we can feel disgust for them or hostility, the way we do for the hyena, the jackal, or the spider, but to speak of hatred for them would raise them to our level. … Only by disseminating in the popular consciousness the concept that the creature of the Jewish race is not the same as other people, but an imitation of a human, with whom there can be no dealings—only that can gradually heal the national organism and weaken the Jewish nation so it will no longer be able to do harm, or will completely die out. History knows of many extinct tribes. Science must put, not the Jewish race, but the character of Jewry into such condition as will make it perish.[14]

Just a few months later, Stolypin was assassinated by a Jewish radical, Dmitri Bogrov.

I emphasize that it was not only the NYT that was reporting on the six million suffering Hebrews. Zionist Jews were repeating the same lines

---

[12] 11 April, p. 18.

[13] 31 October, p. 5.

[14] Cited in Vaksberg, *Stalin Against the Jews* (1994), p. 6.

to their own people. Speaking at the 1911 Zionist Congress, Max Nordau said the following:

> Virtuous governments…lay the groundwork with their own hands for the destruction of six million persons, and no one except the victims themselves raises his voice against this—even though this, of course, is an infinitely greater crime than any war which as yet has never destroyed six million human lives.[15]

Thus we find repeated linkage, over a period of many years, of "six million," "extermination," and "holocaust" with respect to the Jews. History indeed repeats itself.

Into the Great War

It seems, then, that our holocaust journey is even more intriguing than I indicated above. The *first* Jewish holocaust occurred in Russia, running, at a minimum, from the years 1903 through 1911. We don't know how many Jews were killed in that period, but it was unquestionably small, given the over-emphasis on relatively minor events in which, for example, 49 were killed. Based on scattered reports, the total would have been on the order of a few thousand, at most. And yet, the figure of 6 million recurred repeatedly, as a kind of token of mass Jewish suffering. This set the stage for the *second* holocaust, of World War One, as I am about to explain. And this, of course, leaves "the" Holocaust of WW2 as *holocaust number three*. A rather remarkable turn of events, and one not likely to be covered in your local history class.

As I stated above, WW1 began in July 1914. Already in December of that year we were reading accounts of mass suffering of Jews—and we can guess the number. The NYT reported as follows:

> Appeal for aid for Jews: American Committee tells of Suffering Due to War. The American Jewish Relief Committee called a conference…to consider the plight of more than 6,000,000 Jews who live within the war zone. (2 December, p. 12)

The "war zone" in question was the Eastern Front, which ran through parts of present-day Poland, Ukraine, Austria, and Hungary, as well as portions of western Russia. Just a month later, the NYT reported,

---

[15] Cited in *Herzl Year Book*, vol. 2 (1959), p. 156. The chapter author explicitly comments on Nordau's "astonishing accuracy."

> In the world today there are about 13,000,000 Jews, of whom more than 6,000,000 are in the very heart of the war zone; Jews whose lives are at stake and who today are subjected to every manner of sorrow and suffering. (14 January, p. 3)

A year later, we read that the head of a Jewish aid society has declared that "even the wrongs of the Belgians could not be compared to the outrages heaped upon the Polish Jews. 'Nearly six million Jews are ruined, in the greatest moral and material misery… And the world is silent'."[16] And in case we had forgotten, the NYT soon would remind us that, indeed, this horrific situation constituted…a holocaust. In October, a Jewish organization—The Joint Distribution Committee of Funds for Jewish War Sufferers—launched a $10 million appeal with these words:

> The new campaign is the largest ever undertaken by Jews of the United States… Dr. Judah Magnes has been enabled [to ascertain] the present needs of the Jewish people in Europe, who have fallen under the blight of the world holocaust. (29 October, p. E9)

Into 1917, the war evolved into a sort of stalemate, with the infamous trenches defining much of the front. Despite growing fatalities on all sides, the number of suffering Jews stayed remarkably constant: "Six millions [sic] of Jews are living in lands where they are oppressed, exploited, crushed, and robbed of every inalienable human right".[17] By September of that year, the NYT was reporting on an appeal for an aid fund,

> to alleviate the suffering of Jews in the European war zones…[whose] suffering is unparalleled [!] in history. … [W]omen, children, and babies must be saved if the Jewish race is to survive the terrible holocaust… (24 September, p. 20)

Once again, we see the repeated connection between 'holocaust' and 'six million' suffering Jews.

By mid-October of 1918, it was becoming clear—at least to the crew at the *New York Times*—that the war was about to end. Hence they excitedly reported on an astonishing "$1 billion fund to rebuild Jewry" (18 October, p. 12).[18] As it turns out, of those "six millions" of Jews who were suffering, starving, and dying in the "holocaust"—well, miraculously, *all*

---

[16] 28 February, p. 8.

[17] 22 January, p. 6.

[18] In present-day dollars, this would come to almost $20 billion.

of them survived. And they need *cash.* "Six million souls will need help to resume normal life when war is ended," we read. Send your checks now.

Interwar Holocaust?

No sooner had World War One ended than our ever-industrious Jewish Lobby went to work again, conjuring up yet more Jewish suffering. In September 1919—less than one year after the war—the NYT was reporting on renewed mass Jewish suffering, now in Poland and Ukraine. In a story headlined "Ukrainian Jews Aim to Stop Pogroms," we read, with by now little surprise, that "6,000,000 are in peril." Apparently half of these are in Poland, half in Ukraine, but "all of whom are in need of assistance from America." According to the story, President Wilson had recently issued a statement of concern in which he said:

> This fact that the population of 6,000,000 souls in Ukrainia and Poland have received notice through action and by word that they are going to be completely exterminated—this fact stands before the whole world as the paramount issue of the day. (8 September, p. 6)

Assuredly so.

Lest we might forget, this situation was quickly described as, yes, a "holocaust." In one of the most craven and pandering articles ever to be penned by a non-Jewish politician, former New York governor Martin Glynn published an essay for *American Hebrew* in October 1919, titled "The Crucifixion of Jews Must Stop!" It reads, in part:

> From across the sea, six million men and women call to us for help, and eight hundred thousand little children cry for bread. … With them reside the illimitable possibilities for the advancement of the human race as naturally would reside in six million human beings. … In this catastrophe, when six million human beings are being whirled toward the grave by a cruel and relentless fate… Six million men and women are dying from lack of the necessaries of life; eight hundred thousand children cry for bread. … In this threatened *holocaust* of human life, forgotten are the niceties of philosophical distinction… And so in the spirit that turned the poor widow's votive offering of copper into silver…the people of this country are called upon to sanctify their money by giving $35 million in the name of the humanity of Moses to six

> million famished men and women. Six million men and women are dying… [italics added]

A truly appalling bit of servility, if there ever was one. Clearly Glynn owed much to his Hebrew supporters.

The very next month, the NYT reported on prominent Jewish banker Felix Warburg, who had recently traveled to Europe to witness the suffering firsthand:

> The successive blows of contending armies have all but broken the back of European Jewry, and have reduced to tragically unbelievable poverty, starvation, and disease about 6,000,000 souls, or half the Jewish population on the earth. (12 November, p. 7)

The storyline persisted in subsequent years:

- April 1920: "Mr. Louis Marshall declared that typhus menaced 6,000,000 Jews of Europe".[19]
- May 1920: "Hunger, cold rags, desolation, disease, death—six million human beings without food, shelter, clothing…"
- July 1921: "Russia's 6,000,000 Jews are facing extermination by massacre" (again!).
- September 1924: "1,235 Pogroms" in the Soviet Union; "The Jewish population, which number in Russia over 6,000,000, live scattered… [Events] have subjected the Jews to greater suffering than any other section of the Russian population."

And so on. But the point is proven. Through a long series of incredible, unbelievable circumstances, six million Jews were perpetually suffering through various incarnations of a "holocaust" for decades prior to WW2. Such references tapered off through the 1930s, but accelerated again with the approach of the second great war. Several mentions of the "six million" appeared between 1936 and 1939. With the onset of war in September 1939, the predictions became explicit. In June of 1940, leading Zionist Nahum Goldmann was quoted as saying "Six million Jews in Europe are doomed to destruction, if the victory of the Nazis should be final".[20] What

---

[19] Notably, it was typhus that likely produced most Jewish fatalities during WW2.
[20] 25 June, p. 4.

an astonishing prediction! How could Goldmann have known, at that early date, of the final death toll? Jewish foresight never fails to amaze.

Conclusions

The facts here are clear and indisputable. The reader is strongly encouraged to look up a few of the old *New York Times* citations that I mentioned, to confirm that the words are really there. Most any online search engine or a local library research database can find them. They are highly damning. Our friends in the Jewish Lobby have no plausible reply, no reasonable defense, no good explanation; they can only stifle the whole discussion. And this is precisely what they do.

There are clear lessons here for history. If six million Jews suffered, but very few died, in the first holocaust (Russia), and if another six million suffered, but very few died, in the second holocaust (WWI), then we might reasonably infer, by inductive logic, that perhaps the alleged toll in the third Holocaust (WWII) was—let us say—not quite right. Especially so, given the facts that I mentioned at the very start of this essay. We can also plausibly infer that the claimed 'six million' figure of WWII did not come from a body count—it didn't—but rather is a symbolic number, a token, used over many years, to represent mass Jewish suffering. As an actual death toll, it could be far removed from reality.

And if all this is true, then there are profound consequences. First, we must significantly rewrite our history of the mid-20th century; second, we have to hold accountable all those historians and politicians, Jewish or otherwise, who foisted upon us a distorted picture of human suffering; and third, we need to recompensate Germany, Switzerland, Belgium, and all those who were extorted into paying billions in "reparations" to Israel and global Jewry. It is not hard to find the money; American Jews alone own or control some $75 trillion in assets, and this would go a long way toward a restorative justice.[21] We have the means. We need only muster the will to act.

---

[21] See chapter 17, "A Brief Look at Jewish Wealth." But the situation has become even more extreme due to the Covid pandemic, during which Jewish tech billionaires prospered immensely. Just the five wealthiest American Jews—Larry Ellison, Larry Page, Sergey Brin, Steve Ballmer, and Michael Bloomberg—now own nearly half a trillion dollars. We need to contemplate this for a moment: five individual men, five Jews, collectively own almost $500 billion. When we then consider the total wealth of the six million or so American Jews, it is quite easy to reach $75 trillion, or more.

— 16 —
DENYING HOLOCAUST DENIAL

In April 2022, it was announced that Canada would soon be joining an illustrious club: the enlightened nations of the world that have elected to ban so-called Holocaust denial.[1] Depending on how one interprets the law, there are currently 18 nations that either explicitly ban "Holocaust denial" (including Germany, Austria, France, Israel, Italy, Poland, Hungary, and Russia) or generically ban "denial of genocide" (Switzerland and Lichtenstein). Canada would then be the 19th nation in this honor roll of obsequiousness.

Canada's action comes not long after the UN General Assembly approved a related resolution, A/76/L.30, on 22 January 2022, "condemning" such denial. (The resolution was passed "by consensus," meaning that *no actual affirmative votes* were cast. Evidently no country had the courage to demand a rollcall vote.)

The text of Canada's bill is apparently unavailable—it seems that it will be buried in a larger spending bill—but the UN resolution has some interesting remarks. It first defines the Holocaust as an event "which resulted in the murder of nearly 6 million Jews, 1.5 million of whom were children." This is notable because it codifies in international law the infamous '6 million' figure—a number which is doomed to eventual collapse, given the dearth of evidence. Also, I know of no source for the "1.5 million children," but a lack of substantiation has never stopped our intrepid authorities in the past, and it surely won't here.

The resolution goes on to describe what it means by Holocaust denial:

> Holocaust denial refers to discourse and propaganda that deny the historical reality and the extent of the extermination of the Jews by the Nazis and their accomplices during the Second World War… Holocaust denial refers specifically to any attempt to claim that the Holocaust did not take place, and may include publicly denying or calling into doubt the use of principal mechanisms of destruction (such as gas chambers, mass shooting, starvation, and torture) or the intentionality of the genocide of the Jewish people.

---

[1] As reported in the *Toronto Sun*: "Holocaust denial — and downplaying Nazis' murder of Jews — to be outlawed" (8 April 2022).

As usual, such wording is a combination of ambiguity and meaninglessness. First, no revisionist claims that the Holocaust "did not take place"—if by this we are to understand that no one, no Jews, actually died. No revisionist calls into doubt that mass shootings of Jews occurred, nor that many Jews suffered from starvation and "torture." They do, however, specifically challenge the idea that homicidal gas chambers were used to murder masses of people, and they do question the actual intentionality of Hitler and other leading National Socialists to literally kill the Jews.

This requires a bit of elaboration. On the first point, Zyklon-B (cyanide) chambers as instruments of mass murder face a large number of major technical problems, including (a) infeasibility of rapid, mass gassing, (b) personal danger to the alleged gassers, (c) inability to remove gas and Zyklon pellets after gassing, (d) inability to remove gas-soaked corpses, and (e) inability to dispose of masses of corpses in any reasonable time. Worse still are the so-called "diesel exhaust" gas chambers, which are alleged to have killed some 2 million Jews—twice the number of the infamous Zyklon chambers. (If this is news to you, you need to do some research.) These chambers allegedly relied on captured Russian diesel engines to produce fatal carbon monoxide gas. However, (a) diesels actually produce very little CO, far too little to kill masses of people in any reasonable time, (b) diesel engines cannot pump exhaust gas into sealed, "airtight" rooms, and (c) the corpses at those alleged camps showed no sign of CO poisoning—namely, a pink or bright-red coloration of the skin. If the traditional advocates of the Holocaust were serious about defending their view, they would start by addressing these obvious questions. Instead, they ignore them, and retreat to legal remedies.

On the question of intentionality, the actual words of Hitler, Goebbels, and others matter. They often spoke of the *Vernichtung* ('destruction') or *Ausrottung* ('rooting-out') of Jews, but these terms do not require the mass-killing of the people in question. We know this because, first, the Germans used these very terms for years, decades, in public, long before anyone claims that a "Holocaust" had begun; clearly they meant little more than ending Jewish dominance in society and driving most Jews out of the nation. Secondly, the Germans consistently used other language that explicitly called for deportation, evacuation, and mass removal of Jews—ethnic cleansing perhaps, but not mass murder. Thirdly, we have innumerable examples of other Western leaders, from Bush to Obama to Trump, who have similarly spoken publicly of "destroying" or "annihilating" their enemies (usually Arabs or Muslims) without implying mass murder. Tough talk has always played well for politicians, and the Germans were no different.

The UN resolution continues with some specifics on the definition of denial:

> [D]istortion and/or denial of the Holocaust refers, inter alia, to:
>
> (a) Intentional efforts to excuse or minimize the impact of the Holocaust or its principal elements, including collaborators and allies of Nazi Germany,
>
> (b) Gross minimization of the number of the victims of the Holocaust in contradiction to reliable sources,
>
> (c) Attempts to blame the Jews for causing their own genocide,
>
> (d) Statements that cast the Holocaust as a positive historical event,
>
> (e) Attempts to blur the responsibility for the establishment of concentration and death camps devised and operated by Nazi Germany by putting blame on other nations or ethnic groups.

Four of these points—"excuse or minimize impact," "blame the Jews," "cast the Holocaust in positive light," and "attempts to blur responsibility"—are all but irrelevant to serious revisionism. Serious revisionists, including Germar Rudolf, Carlo Mattogno, and Jurgen Graf, among others, virtually never discuss such things. They focus on far more pragmatic matters: the infeasibility of the mass gassing schemes, the lack of corpses or other physical evidence, the absence of photographic or documentary evidence showing mass murder, and the many logical inconsistencies of witnesses and survivors. But our fine Holocaust traditionalists never raise these troublesome issues, because they know that they have no reply.

Of the five points, only (b), "gross minimization of the number of victims," is relevant—in other words, the questioning of the '6 million'. But what counts as "gross minimization"? Does '5 million' count? If so, noted (and deceased) orthodox researcher Raul Hilberg would be quickly tarred with the 'anti-Semite' label; the fact that he hasn't suggests otherwise. What about '4 million'? If so, then early researcher Gerald Reitlinger is in for trouble; he long advocated around 4.2 million Jewish deaths. Does '3 million' count? Or '2 million'? Or will we "know it when we see it"? For the record, serious revisionists today estimate that around 500,000 Jews died in total at the hands of the Nazis—most of these due to typhus contracted in the various camps, many in assorted shootings at the Eastern front, and virtually none in "homicidal gas chambers."

So what, exactly, does the UN want from the world? As we read in the text, the UN

> 1. Rejects and condemns without any reservation any denial of the Holocaust as a historical event, either in full or in part;
>
> 2. Urges all Member States to reject without any reservation any denial or distortion of the Holocaust as a historical event, either in full or in part, or any activities to this end;
>
> 3. Commends those Member States which have actively engaged in preserving those sites that served as Nazi death camps, concentration camps, forced labour camps, killing sites and prisons during the Holocaust…
>
> 4. Urges Member States to develop educational programmes that will inculcate future generations with the lessons of the Holocaust in order to help to prevent future acts of genocide…
>
> 5. Urges Member States and social media companies [!] to take active measures to combat antisemitism and Holocaust denial or distortion by means of information and communications technologies, and to facilitate reporting of such content;
>
> 6. Requests the United Nations outreach programme on the Holocaust as well as all relevant United Nations specialized agencies to continue to develop and implement programmes aimed at countering Holocaust denial and distortion…

Of course, if we wish to designate the loss of some 500,000 Jews as a "holocaust," then we are welcome to do so. But we had best get our facts and arguments straight. To resort to legal prohibitions is tantamount to admitting defeat.

None of these points were lost on a Jewish *Boston Globe* columnist, Jeff Jacoby. He was motivated to write a short op-ed entitled "It's a mistake to ban Holocaust denial" (24 April). He quotes Canada's public safety minister, Marco Mendicino: "There is no place for antisemitism and Holocaust denial in Canada." Despite agreeing with this view, and despite "despising" Holocaust deniers, Jacoby opposes the pending law. And he explains why—though not before displaying an embarrassing ignorance and an appalling shallowness.

He first informs us that Holocaust "deniers" (never defined) are "contemptible antisemites and brazen liars," overflowing with "Jew-hatred" and seeking to "rehabilitate the reputation of Hitler." They attempt to refute "the most comprehensively documented crime in history" by insisting that it "never occurred." Such people deserve "all the obloquy and contempt" that one can muster, he says. To call such claims unjustified and unwarranted is an understatement of the first order; the reliance here on *ad hominem* attacks is a sure sign of an impending vapidity of argumentation.

Still, Jacoby opposes anti-denial laws on two grounds. First, such laws run afoul of the spirit of the First Amendment (free speech and press). More broadly, he rightly notes that "it's dangerous to empower the state to punish ideas." Indeed, "any government that can criminalize Holocaust denial this week can criminalize other opinions next week." Left unspoken, though, is a key point: How is it that, in Canada, a 1% minority of Canadian Jews are able to push through a law that specifically benefits them? One would think that, in Canada, a 1% Jewish minority would have, say, half the clout of the 2% minority of American Jews. But clearly not. Canadian Jews are about to prevail yet again.

Jacoby's second reason for opposing such laws is that, as I noted above, they amount to "intellectual surrender." He quotes Holocaust scion Deborah Lipstadt to the effect that such laws imply that one is unable to construct a rational argument in defense of the traditional view. And this, in fact, is true. Just look at any traditionalist account of the Holocaust, even by the most learned academician. Look at any commentary on Holocaust denial. None will address the basic issues that I cited above. None will mention a single recent revisionist book, or a single active researcher, such as Rudolf, Mattogno, or Graf. None will examine or refute a single relevant revisionist argument. None will provide a breakdown, by cause, of the infamous '6 million' deaths. These are telling facts.

For his part, Jacoby obviously has no answer. All he can do is make flat and baseless assertions: "never was a genocide more meticulously recorded by its perpetrators…or more comprehensively described by scholars and survivors"; "an immense ocean of evidence attests to the horror of the Holocaust." Unwisely, he attempts to use General Eisenhower's "visual evidence…of starvation, cruelty, and bestiality" to defend his point. But this fails; as he likely is unaware, Eisenhower's 550-page postwar memoir, *Crusade in Europe* (1948), has not a single reference to any Holocaust, gas chambers, or Auschwitz. A single paragraph in the book (p. 439) states only that the Jews "had been beaten, starved, and tortured." One finds absolutely no mention of mass murder, extermination, gassing, crematoria, or the like. Eisenhower is hardly a good witness for the defense. (For what it's worth, neither Churchill's nor De Gaulle's postwar memoirs had any mention of Auschwitz, gas chambers, or extermination either. Ike was no anomaly.)

But does all this really matter? What's the big deal about the Holocaust? some may say. In fact, it is hugely important. The Holocaust is the lynchpin of Jewish power. It is the *raison d'etre* of the state of Israel. It is the number one guilt-tool used against Whites everywhere. And it is the embodiment of Jewish narcissism. When that story crumbles, the whole Judeocratic edifice may well fall, too. We should never underestimate the power of Holocaust revisionism; the Jews certainly don't.

A final thought: I'm happy to hear that Jeff Jacoby believes in free speech. It's too bad that he doesn't have equally strong feelings about openness and honesty, about the many problems with the Holocaust story, and about a global Jewish Lobby that is able to pass laws, ban books, and impose a cancel culture on anyone that it doesn't like. Now, that would be an op-ed worth reading.

Part III

Contemporary Issues

— 17 —
A BRIEF LOOK AT JEWISH WEALTH

Throughout history, the power and influence of the Jewish Lobby has been legendary. This power in turn derives neither from political might, nor from popular support, nor from moral rectitude, nor from God. It is, simply, the power of money. The wealthy have always held disproportionate influence in their societies, typically to the benefit of individuals or their families. But when a distinct ethnic minority works more or less collectively, with great wealth behind them, then that minority can exercise massively disproportionate power. This monetary power is amplified by Jewish power deriving from ownership of media, their position as creators of media content, and their influence on elite culture, particularly in the academic world.

Too often, though, one reads fulminations on the "rich Jews" without knowing the history and without any facts or details behind it. My intent in this short essay is to provide some factual data, and to draw some plausible conclusions. The situation is, I think, more extreme than many have assumed.

Some Historical Context

As usual, a bit of history is helpful in order to establish the context for the present day. The earliest connection between Jews, money, and power seems to come from Cicero, around 59 BC. His speech *Pro Flacco* offers a defense of a Roman propraetor in Asia by the name of L. V. Flaccus who was charged with embezzling Jewish gold shipments destined for Jerusalem. (Recall that Rome had just conquered Judea some four years prior.) Cicero begins with a telling statement:

> You know what a big crowd it is, how they stick together, how influential they are in informal assemblies. So I will speak in a low voice so that only the jurors may hear; for those are not wanting who would incite them against me and against every respectable man.

He is clearly mocking the Jews, but their power must have been well-known by that point or else his jab would be pointless. He proceeds to give a rousing defense of his friend, citing Flacco's "act of firmness, to defy the crowd of Jews" and their illicit "attempt to fix odium on him."

A second early allusion to Jewish wealth comes from Emperor Claudius in his Third Edict of 41 AD. Addressing civil unrest in Alexandria, Claudius singles out the Jews, who live "in a city which is not their own." "They possess an abundance of all good things" but abuse their wealth by continuing to oppose local authorities and sowing general discord. In a sense, writes Claudius, the Jews could be blamed "for fomenting a general plague which infests the whole world."

Then in 100 AD we have the well-known critique by Tacitus, in his *Histories*. Amidst a discussion of "the race of men hateful to the gods"—a people who are "base and abominable," as well as "depraved"—he remarks that the Diaspora Jews, "the worst rascals among other people," have worked relentlessly to send "tribute and contributions to Jerusalem, thereby increasing the wealth of the Jews." It's clear that this wealth was used for pernicious ends.

Around the year 220, Cassius Dio wrote his *Roman History* in which he describes the second and third Jewish uprisings of 115 and 132 AD, respectively. Of the latter event, Dio explains that "Jews everywhere were showing signs of hostility to the Romans." And they were evidently able to use their wealth to bribe others into coming to their aid: "many nations, too, were joining them through eagerness for gain." Clearly it must have taken considerable wealth to pay "many nations" to fight at their side. And evidently the Jews succeeded in drawing in a multitude of others: "the whole earth, one might almost say, was being stirred up over the matter."

Though they would lose in that uprising, the Jews managed to regroup and reassert their power—a power that had become legendary by 300 AD. It was at this time that Justin the Historian wrote his lengthy treatise *Historiarum Philippicarum*. Book 36 addresses the ignoble origin of the Jewish people and explains the growth and cohesiveness of this singular tribe. Their pragmatic theology merged religion with politics in a way that proved to be highly successful; as a result, "it is almost incredible how powerful they became."

Powerful, indeed. Around 420, the Roman poet Rutilius Namatianus could write, in his *De redito suo*, of the Jews' ability, despite their being formally defeated by the Romans, to continue to exercise a dominating influence: "'tis their own conquerors that a conquered race keeps down".[1]

Middle Ages to the Present

After the collapse of Rome and during the rise of the early Church, Jews continued to amass wealth and exercise power. We know this because

---

[1] Source information for the above passages, and far more examples, can be found in my book *Eternal Strangers* (2020).

they, as a small minority, still had the power to influence rulers throughout Europe. Charlemagne's son Louis the Pious (778–840 AD), emperor of the Holy Roman Empire, notably catered to the Jews, enacting a charter of privilege for them. This was a pragmatic move because, as Bernard Bachrach explains, Jews of that time were "militant, aggressive, and powerful".[2]

Much of their power and wealth derived from usury—viewed as exorbitant and needlessly-high interest rates on loans—which accelerated during the early Renaissance. By the time of the Fourth Lateran Council of 1215, Pope Innocent III was prepared to enact canons targeting Jewish usury. "The more the Christians are restrained from the practice of usury, the more are they oppressed in this matter by the treachery of the Jews…" (Canon 67). Not being subject to Christian moral restrictions, the Jews dominated finance and lending at interest, profiting immensely. This situation drew a rebuke from Thomas Aquinas: "It would be better for [royalty] to compel Jews to work for a living…than to allow them to live in idleness and grow rich by usury".[3] It was still a problem for the Church 300 years later, as Martin Luther felt compelled to comment critically, calling the Jews "thieves and robbers" who profited "by means of their accursed usury".[4]

The secular world also took note of Jewish wealth and power. As early as 1798, German philosopher Immanuel Kant could make this surprising assessment: "the wealth of the Jews…apparently exceeds per capita that of any other nation at the present time".[5] In 1823, Lord Byron's poem "The Age of Bronze" remarked on the fact that "all states, all things, all sovereigns they control." Indeed: "'Tis gold, not steel, that rears the conqueror's arch." In 1843, Bruno Bauer wrote that "The Jew…determines the fate of the whole [Austrian] Empire by his financial power. The Jew…decides the destiny of Europe".[6] And perhaps more than Europe. In an essay of 1860, Ralph Waldo Emerson remarked on Jewish toughness, brought on by years of persecution and suffering: "The sufferance which is the badge of the Jew, has made him, in these days, the ruler of the rulers of the earth".[7]

In 1880, Laurent Oliphant could write of the Jews' "financial operations of the largest scale." "Owing to the financial, political, and commercial importance to which the Jews have now attained," they have become an indispensable ally in any future conflict.[8] A decade later Goldwin Smith

---

[2] *Early Medieval Jewish Policy and Western Europe* (1977), p. 104.
[3] *De regimine judaeorum*, 81-88.
[4] *On the Jews and Their Lies* (2020; T. Dalton, ed.), p. 153. See also p. 121.
[5] *Anthropology* (1798/1978), p. 102.
[6] Cited in Marx, "On the Jewish Question," *The Marx-Engels Reader* (1978), p. 49.
[7] "Fate", in *Conduct of Life* (1860).
[8] *The Land of Gilead* (1880), p. 503.

confirmed this view: "Judaism is now [in 1894] the great financial power of Europe, that is, it is the greatest power of all".[9]

It was around this time that a French journalist named Edouard Drumont published a large and relatively influential book titled *Jewish France* (1885). Here he made a shocking and frankly unbelievable claim: "Jews possess half of the capital in the world." Commenting specifically on France, he noted that the total wealth of that nation was around 150 billion francs, "of which the Jews possess at least 80 billion"—that is, slightly more than half.[10] One is taken aback at such claims; "Impossible!" we want to say. Obviously Drumont was somehow mistaken.

Naming Names

Or perhaps not. Consider the present-day situation in the United States.[11] Of the 10 richest Americans, five (50%) are Jews:

1) Larry Page ($93 billion)
2) Sergey Brin ($89 billion)
3) Larry Ellison ($88 billion)
4) Steve Ballmer ($86 billion)
5) Michael Bloomberg ($70 billion)

Most of this money comes from the high-tech industry: specifically, Oracle (Ellison), Google (Page and Brin), and Microsoft (Ballmer).[12]

Of the 50 richest Americans, at least 26 (52%) are Jews.[13] In addition to the above five, we have M. Zuckerberg, M. Dell, L. Blavatnik, C. Icahn, D. Bren, J. Simons, L. Lauder, E. Schmidt, S. Cohen, S. Schwarzman, M. Adelson, R. Perelman, D. Newhouse, D. Tepper, S. Bankman-Fried, D. Gilbert, and J. Koum. Technically, this list should also include George

---

[9] *Essays on the Questions of the Day* (1894), p. 260.

[10] In *The Jew in the Modern World* (2011, Mendes-Flohr and Reinharz, eds.), p. 315. Chapter One of Drumont's book is reproduced in *Classic Essays on the Jewish Question* (T. Dalton, ed., 2022).

[11] This is always changing, of course, but the following gives a representative snapshot in time.

[12] All figures are as of late 2022. Some claim that Jeff Bezos of Amazon fame ($142 billion), is either wholly- or part-Jewish, although this is unverified. But Amazon does regularly defend Jewish interests, as in their censorship of books that challenge the Holocaust narrative, and in their illegal blockade of alternate translations of *Mein Kampf*. And he retained Jewish chief editor Martin Baron when he bought the *Washington Post*; it is highly unlikely that the Jewish Graham family, prior owners of the *Post*, would sell to a non-Jew.

[13] Data from Bloomberg Billionaires Index, accessed October 2022.

Soros, whose net worth was around $26 billion until he 'donated' $18 billion to his own personal charity. The combined wealth of just these named individuals comes to roughly $820 billion. Note well: If Jews were proportionately represented among the top 50, there would be *one* individual on this list; instead, there are at least 26.

Or take another measure of wealth, CEO income.[14] Among the 10 highest-paid American CEOs, at least six (60%) are Jews: Jeff Green (Trade Desk), Zig Serafin (Qualtrics), Peter Kern (Expedia), Ari Emanuel (Endeavor), David Zaslav (Warner Bros.), and Andrew Jassy (Amazon).

Thus, whether looking at total assets or income, this cursory look at the data suggests that, in America, Jews in fact own or control about half of the wealth—at least among the wealthiest elite. These people are the movers and shakers of our political process, and if the political situation was perceived by Jews as a crisis, the amount of money that could be poured into the political process is almost beyond comprehension.

We can make a further inference. If Jews control around half of all wealth at the top, it is reasonable to infer that they may hold a similar share throughout the wealth hierarchy[15]—at least among, say, the top 20% of wealth-holders, who collectively own more than 90% of all household wealth in the US. At any rate, the following is an attempt to use that inference to estimate total Jewish wealth in the US.

So, how much money is this? In 2022, the Federal Reserve reported that the total assets of all private households in the US hit $150 trillion. If American Jews own or control half of this, then their share comes to something like $75 trillion.

Now, this demands a moment of reflection. If Drumont's numbers were shocking, this one is absolutely jaw-dropping. Think of it: American Jews possessing $75 trillion—or for those numerically challenged readers, *75,000 billion dollars*. If the true numbers are anything close to this, the implications are astounding. Perform this quick thought experiment: Think of how much power *one man* with *one* billion dollars possesses; now consider the equivalent of 75,000 such individuals, working more or less in unison. That's the financial power of American Jewry.

Take a specific example. Tom Steyer is typical of a middling Jewish billionaire, with net assets of merely some $1.5 billion. But he is exceptionally active in the political scene, as anyone who has been following

---

[14] Data from *New York Times* / Equilar, as of October 2022.

[15] There is some evidence that the Jewish percentage declines as we consider the broader pool of wealth. A few years ago, Steve Sailer estimated that, of the 400 richest Americans, around one-third were Jewish; I am not aware of any more recent assessment. But given the proven increase in wealth accumulation at the top, the Jewish share may well have increased in recent years.

politics knows. Steyer is a top donor for the Democrats. In the 2018 midterm election, it was announced that he would spend $110 million "to redefine the Democrats"—to his liking, of course. This made him "the largest single source of campaign cash on the left," and put him on the road "to create a parallel party structure" of his own. If one minor but motivated billionaire can do this, think of what the equivalent of 75,000 billionaires can do.

Of course, there are nowhere near that many American billionaires. In fact, the total number (Jews and non-Jews combined) was estimated by Forbes in 2022 to be just 735, who own a combined wealth of $4.7 trillion. If the above analysis is roughly correct, as many as 365 of these are Jews. Their total wealth would then be about $2.3 trillion.

We can press a bit further. Depending on how we define them, there are something like 6 million Jewish Americans. These 6 million therefore control, on average, about $12 million per person—$12 million for every Jewish man, woman, and child. A typical Jewish family of four would thus own nearly $50 million. Not a bad life.

And then consider the Jewish top "1%," which comes to about 60,000 individuals. If the same rough distribution holds among them as among the public at large, then this top 1% owns about 35% of total Jewish wealth. Thus, the top 60,000 Jews would own about $25 trillion. The remaining $50 trillion would therefore be divided amongst the other 5,940,000 Jewish Americans, yielding a still mind-boggling more than $8 million per person.

Some Troubling Questions

At this point, a whole series of further questions arise: Apart from the named individuals, who else pulls the strings on all this wealth? As I said, the top 26 'only' account for around $800 trillion. The top 365 richest Jews own around $2.3 trillion. And the top 60,000, around $25 trillion. Who are these people? Apart from the handful at the very top, can we even begin to know who the other leading individuals are?

And what form is this wealth in? Cash? Stocks? Real estate? Precious metals? (Do Jews still hoard gold?) All of the above, no doubt. But where is the cash? Which stocks? Which real estate? Foreign or domestic?

And then the larger questions: What, if anything, can be done about this? Simply on the face of it, it seems grossly unjust for, say, 60,000 Jewish Americans to own around $25 trillion in assets. Especially when the bottom half of Americans—about 160 million people—own a *combined* total of about $0.3 trillion. And when the bottom 25% of Americans—around 80 million people—have a *negative* net worth, i.e., more debt than assets. This is not an accident, and it's not just bad luck. The wealth distribution system in America is designed, by Jews, to achieve this outcome, and Jews earn a hugely disproportionate benefit from it.

What could be done to ensure a more just allocation of national wealth? In the old days, circa 100 AD, Roman authorities instituted a *fiscus Judaicus*, a 'Jew tax,' precisely to offset the extra cost burden placed on society by Jews. Dare we suggest reinstating such a thing?

Or more dramatically, what about confiscation of assets? Surely much of that $75 trillion was ill-gotten, either illegally or by legal-but-unethical means. The federal government seizes assets all the time—bank accounts and real estate owned by domestic and foreign criminals. Why not investigate and seize ill-gotten Jewish wealth? Several trillion dollars, justly redistributed, could go a long way to right the wrongs of modern society.

Unrealistic, you say. Perhaps. But it has to start somewhere. Someone needs to raise these possibilities in print, in public, in order to begin the conversation. Stranger things have happened in the past. Stranger things will surely happen in the future.

— 18 —
A REJOINDER ON 'WHITE GENOCIDE'— AND ITS CURE

Of late, much has been made in the dissident-right press of the idea of "White genocide" as an existential threat posed by mainstream society, aimed at the obliteration of Whites in their formerly dominant homelands in Europe and North America. This movement—conceived and implemented by Jews and their leftist lackeys—is said to portend the virtual or literal end of the White race. It has no standard definition, and goes by various labels; one writer, for example, refers to the "White replacement and destruction movement" (WRDM). It has been expressed concisely (if ambiguously) by another writer who stated that, on this thesis, "the White race will have no future, and the future will be without the White race." It sounds grim.

While it is true that White rule in many nations is under threat, I think it is premature—at least in the coming decades—to decry the physical elimination of Whites anywhere. Exaggeration and hyperbole do not serve White interests. We need to think a bit more carefully about 'White genocide,' and indeed about the concept of genocide itself, lest we get lost in a storm of hype. Real threats to White interests risk getting subsumed by bogus—or at least exaggerated—dangers.

Let us start with a look at the word 'genocide'—a term with thoroughly Jewish origins. We can begin with standard dictionary definitions, but even here, there is a studied ambiguity. My Merriam-Webster has a single definition: "the deliberate and systematic destruction of a racial, political, or cultural group." Dictionary.com is very similar, adding only "or national" group.

The construction of the word is straightforward: *geno+cide*, from the Greek *genos-* (birth, origin, or race), and Latin *-cide* (from *cidere*: death, killing). The word was coined in 1944 by a Polish-Jewish lawyer, Raphael Lemkin, in light of the on-going Nazi attack on Jews. Etymologically, then, the meaning is, or should be, clear: the physical death of an entire race of people—that is, the physical elimination of a genotype.

But upon further examination, we immediately run into problems. First, as anyone knows who studies the issue, the Germans did not seek, nor did they implement, the physical annihilation of the Jews; rather, they wanted something much less ominous: a German Reich cleansed of Jews, by a process of deportation and removal. The deaths—and there were many thousands—were an incidental byproduct, not the objective.[1]

Second, Lemkin himself explicitly decreed that genocide did not entail killing. A passage from his 1944 book is instructive:

> New conceptions require new terms. By 'genocide' we mean the destruction of a nation or of an ethnic group. This new word, coined by the author to denote an old practice in its modern development, is made from the ancient Greek word *genos* (race, tribe) and the Latin *cide* (killing), thus corresponding in its formation to such words as tyrannicide, homicide, infanticide, etc. Generally speaking, genocide does not necessarily mean the immediate destruction of a nation, except when accomplished by mass killings of all members of a nation. It is intended rather to signify a coordinated plan of different actions aiming at the destruction of essential foundations of the life of national groups, with the aim of annihilating the groups themselves.
>
> The objectives of such a plan would be disintegration of the political and social institutions, of culture, language, national feelings, religion, and the economic existence of national groups, and the destruction of the personal security, liberty, health, dignity, and even the lives of the individuals belonging to such groups. Genocide is directed against the national group as an entity, and the actions involved are directed against individuals, not in their individual capacity, but as members of the national group.

Here we see a fine example of Jewish duplicity at work. Genocide means "destruction" of an ethnic group, *except when it doesn't*: "Generally speaking, genocide does not necessarily mean the immediate destruction of a nation, except when accomplished by mass killing." Rather, he says, it is a collection of actions aimed at the "destruction of essential foundations" of national life, i.e. the "disintegration of political and social institutions," of "culture", "language," "national feelings," "economic existence," and so on. In the paragraph that follows the above, Lemkin even implies that something as benign as "confiscation of property" (!) may count as genocide, if targeted at people solely due to their ethnicity.

Much hinges on the meaning of the word 'destruction'—a term used four times in Lemkin's key paragraph. It turns out that this, too, has non-lethal meanings, and in no way demands the killing of the entity in question.

---

[1] See my book *Debating the Holocaust* (2020; 4th ed.) for details.

'Destroy' comes from *de-struere*, meaning to 'de-structure' or 'unbuild' something. The leading definition in my dictionary states: "to ruin the structure, organic existence, or condition of." The word can mean 'kill,' but it also can mean 'neutralize,' 'subject to crushing defeat,' or 'demolish.'

Lemkin, then, uses 'destruction' in its nonlethal sense, allowing a whole variety of nonlethal activities to fall under the genocide umbrella. And all this was based on his contemporaneous experience with the Jews under National Socialist Germany. Hence it seems that he was admitting that the "genocide" of the Jews—that is, the Holocaust—consisted primarily of nonlethal actions designed to eradicate Jewish life, culture, and predominance in the Reich. This, of course, is precisely the stance of present-day Holocaust revisionists, who have argued for a primarily nonlethal reading of German actions. So we have a striking conclusion: As defined by Lemkin, the Holocaust now can be read as a primarily nonlethal set of actions design to reduce or eliminate Jewish cultural and economic dominance in the Reich. This will surely come as news to the vast majority of the Western world.[2]

A third problematic issue is that the UN largely adopted Lemkin's interpretation in 1948. The "Convention on the Prevention and Punishment of the Crime of Genocide" (GA Res 260A-III) states that the "odious scourge" of genocide shall be defined as follows (Article II):

> In the present Convention, *genocide* means any of the following acts committed with intent to destroy, in whole or in part, a national, ethnical, racial, or religious group, as such:
>
> - Killing members of the group;
> - Causing serious bodily or mental harm to members of the group;
> - Deliberately inflicting on the group conditions of life calculated to bring about its physical destruction in whole or in part;
> - Imposing measures intended to prevent births within the group;
> - Forcibly transferring children of the group to another group.

This is an astonishingly broad and vague definition, to the point that it is virtually useless—or perhaps highly useful, for those who wish to use the term as a cudgel. And this is the formal, legal definition under international law!

Let's analyze this for a moment. It declares as genocide "any" of the listed acts, with "intent to destroy" (how shall we judge intention? and

---

[2] And perhaps we will now have to declare Lemkin an evil "Holocaust denier."

what about the many meanings of 'destroy'?), "in whole or in part" (how small a part?), a national, religious, or racial group. The culpable actions include killing, of course, but also "serious harm," both bodily and mental (!). So psychological distress now counts as genocide. And what "conditions of life" could count as imposing "physical destruction, in whole or in part," of a people? Genocide includes sterilizations or enforced abortions (ok), but also the forcible transfer of children—but not adults? Apparently not, otherwise they would not have added this point; they would have simply said "forcible transfer of people of the group…" Strange.

Not content with this impossibly vague definition, the UN proceeded to list all related actions that are punishable. In addition to the act of genocide itself, they include (Article III):

- Conspiracy (to commit genocide),
- Direct and public incitement (to genocide),
- Attempt (to commit genocide),
- Complicity (in genocide).

Again, impossibly vague and sweeping conditions that could plausibly include vast numbers of people.

Thus defined, the Germans did indeed conduct a program of genocide—as did virtually every other government, in virtually every military conflict, before or after WW2. As legally defined, the term is effectively worthless. It retains only rhetorical value. Had the international community stuck to the obvious and direct meaning—the killing of a targeted ethnicity with intent to eliminate—then it might have had some substance. As it is, the term is vaporous and functionally devoid of content. As with so many Jewish concepts, it means whatever they want it to mean.

Whites by the Numbers

Now, back to the topic at hand: *White genocide*. Armed with our impossibly-vague notion of genocide, indeed, governments and organizations everywhere are engaged in White genocide—as they are in black genocide, Hispanic genocide, Christian genocide, and on and on. Again, unless we are prepared to carefully and concisely define the term, it is worthless to rail against genocide of any stripe. Best to drop all such talk, and focus on real, concrete issues.

So, what are the real, actual threats to White interests and White well-being? In the near term, it's not 'genocide'—which has now been revealed as a meaningless, amorphous Jewish concept—but rather declining political power and loss of self-determination. These are serious matters that deserve deeper examination.

First, though, a brief word on who counts as 'White.' Though obviously a color designator, pigmentation alone cannot define an ethnicity. Skin color is too diverse and subjective to serve a truly useful purpose.[3] Almost as useless is 'Caucasian,' which nominally refers to people of the Caucasus region, lying between the Caspian and Black Seas, and including parts of present-day Armenia, Azerbaijan, Georgia, and Russia. Geographical features are likewise not much help, as the 'European' continent is typically said to extend as far east as the Ural Mountains, which are some 1,000 miles into Russia.

In the context of a dissident-right discussion, we can plausibly limit Whiteness to people of indigenous European ancestry, comprising the current EU nations and their immediate neighbors (Switzerland, Sweden, Lithuania, and the former member-states of Yugoslavia). Western portions of the Ukraine and Belarus arguably count as well, and we may plausibly extend our White geography into western Russia. Excluded, though, are all Turks, North Africans, and all indigenous peoples of the Middle East. *Jews are not White.*

As for the status of Whites globally, the vast majority reside in the US, Europe (as defined above), Canada, and Australia. In rough numbers, there are around 750 million in these four areas, along with perhaps 50 million scattered throughout the rest of the world.[4] So let us say, 800 million globally. This represents about 11% of humanity. White numbers are in gradual decline, but non-Whites are proliferating rapidly. Thus by 2050, when the planet reaches some 9.5 billion, Whites will drop to 8%.

In the US as well, the situation is not positive. The present White population of some 195 million (61%) is forecast to gradually *decline* to 185 million by 2050, according to the US Census Bureau.[5] This would put

---

[3] Pale skin is a necessary but not sufficient condition for whiteness. Many Middle-Easterners, Latinos, and Asians have equally pale skin, but they are not White in the requisite sense. The earliest true White people, incidentally, seem to have arisen, unsurprisingly, in the Scandinavian region. Excavations at Motala, Sweden have analyzed the genetics of people there dating to 5700 BC, finding both gene variants for light skin (along with a third variant for blond hair and blue eyes). Whiteness thus existed at this time, but likely not much sooner. Data from southern Europeans circa 6500 BC show a lack of the White genes, and they would likely have appeared to us as Black. It wasn't until around 4000 BC that the White genes spread widely throughout Europe—a surprisingly recent date. (Interestingly, the genes themselves are quite ancient, appearing to have originated in Africa around 1 million years ago. But they were never expressed until people reached northern climates.)

[4] Europe (510 million), US (195 million), Canada (27 million), Australia (20 million).

[5] "Non-Hispanic Whites" in the lingo of the Bureau; these are 'true Whites.'

Whites at around 48% of the US total, and therefore in a minority position before mid-century. Latest estimates put the crossover date around 2045.

Biracial and multiracial Americans, incidentally, are forecast to almost triple, from around 8 million (2.5%) to 22 million by 2050 (5.5%). Hispanic Americans will double, from 55 million (17%) to 110 million (28%). Black Americans will grow from 41 million to 55 million. The 21 million Asian Americans will double, to 43 million.

So, how do we assess the situation, from a White perspective? Negative for sure, potentially dire—though not genocidal. American Whites are declining at around 0.15% per year, and European Whites at around 0.30%.[6] If we assume a global average decline of about 0.25% annually, the total number of Whites will drop from 800 million today to around 655 million in 2100. Into the distant future, this implies something like 510 million in the year 2200, and 400 million in the year 2300. Projections beyond this are largely meaningless. It does imply the continuing existence of millions of Whites on Earth for centuries to come, but they will become increasingly marginalized as non-White population expands.

In the US, Whites could drop below 30% of the population by 2100, if present trends continue, and significantly less than that in several states. This bodes ill for the preservation and assertion of White interests, as we increasingly lose out to demands of non-Whites—who are, as we know, on the whole less intelligent, less industrious, and more antisocial.[7] As non-White numbers grow, society pays a price. I can't recall a single case where increasing non-White population brought demonstrable gains in quality of life. Anyone—any White—who has had firsthand experience of increasing diversity in their city or neighborhood can confirm this fact. In no case do things get better; they always get worse.

Restoring White Majority

What to do? In theory, the solution is clear: the country should be restored to a large White majority. As a nominal target, we can aim for the status of the country at the beginning—say, in 1800. At that time, we had slightly more than 5 million people, of whom around 1 million were Black (slaves), along with a few thousand people of other ethnicities and races. Hence the country was about 80% White.

---

[6] These correspond to fertility rates of about 1.7 and 1.5, respectively (children per woman).

[7] Excepting the 20 million Asian Americans, who are, on average, more intelligent than Whites. But they represent just 15% of non-Whites, and in any case, the many cultural and social differences make large numbers of them undesirable. Still, if there are to be any non-Whites in the US, they should be mostly Asian.

Given that we are today around 60% White, it is not at all unrealistic to aim for a return to 80%. It can't happen overnight, but given a reasonable timeframe—say, 30 years—it is entirely achievable. In fact, we can put some hard numbers on this. Currently we have around 195 million Whites (60%) and 125 million non-Whites (40%). By 2050, we might like to have, say, 220 million Whites (80%) and 55 million non-Whites (20%), for a total of 275 million people. The non-White population thus would have to drop by about 2.3 million per year for the next 30 years.

How, specifically, can this happen? Broadly speaking, it's obvious: get more Whites and have fewer non-Whites. We can increase our White population by (a) increasing White immigration, (b) discouraging White emigration (a nonissue, in reality), and (c) increasing White birthrate. We can decrease our non-White population through the opposite policies: reduced immigration, increased emigration, and reduced birthrate.

Let me take each of these in turn. We can incentivize White immigration, much like we did in the early years of America: financial or other material enticements, and various service benefits. We could offer free (or subsidized) land or housing. Free job placement service. Free tuition at public universities. Free (or subsidized) health care. Again, all this only for true Whites, of wholly indigenous European background.

On the outbound side of the equation, White emigration is so small as to be irrelevant. According to the US State Department, some 9 million Americans are living abroad (non-military), but the annual departures are unknown, as are the number of Whites among these. The most common driver for White emigration is likely retirement, to cheaper foreign locations. We could offer better retirement benefits, to keep Whites in the country.

Increasing the White birthrate can be done by financial incentives (e.g. tax breaks, tuition assistance) and by education—on the need and benefits of an increasing White population. Larger White families could be positively portrayed, rather than, as is often the case today, glorifying the single lifestyle. This would require exerting control over a largely-Jewish mass media that is disinclined to assist Whites—to say the least.

Then let's look at the non-White side of the ledger. This requires firm and decisive action. First, non-White immigration into the US must stop completely. *Zero. Immediately.* No refugees, no asylum-seekers, no family 'chains,' no corporate work visas, no student visas—*nothing.* Non-Whites should enter only as tourists, stay not more than a month, and then be compelled to leave. And this policy should stay in place indefinitely, until attaining the 80% goal.[8]

---

[8] Of course, this is not to say that 80% is the permanent goal. It is an interim target, upon which gains would have to be assessed and future actions evaluated. It

On increasing emigration, this should be done as benignly and humanely as possible—voluntarily at first, but with financial incentives as encouragement. We can selectively raise costs on non-Whites (through taxes and special fees, for example), and we can offer financial payments, such as one-time travel or relocation expenses, to encourage them to leave. Simply by adjusting the amount of the incentives, we could control the rate of departure. If we need to lose around 2 million non-Whites annually, and if we offered an average of, say, $5,000 incentive per person, this would cost only $10 billion per year—a trifle in a nation that allocates over $1,000 billion per year to national security.[9] And the cost would be more than offset by the immediate gains in quality of life.

The question of citizenship remains. Non-White citizens who voluntarily emigrate would renounce their citizenship. Non-White non-citizens have no such issue, though they might receive less assistance. Birthright citizenship for non-Whites is a disaster and must be immediately ended.

Then there is the question of where they will go. Most non-Whites do in fact have a country of origin: Hispanics, Asians, and Jews all have their native homelands. Only the blacks, generally, lack connection to a specific homeland. Of the 125 million non-Whites today, around 85 million (the non-blacks) can identify a nation of origin or a national homeland; they have a clear place of return.[10] For the 40 million blacks, DNA analysis can now, in many cases, pinpoint a nation or African region from which they came. Special assistance may be required to ease a transition back, but this is the extra burden that White Americans must accept for their original sin of slavery.[11]

The third point, reduced non-White birthrate, is perhaps the most contentious of all. Again, all measures would have to be humane and voluntary, but with incentives to comply. Free birth control, free abortion services, and

---

may well turn out that white Americans would prefer a nation that was 90% or 95% white. This would be left to future generations.

[9] Since not all would accept the offer, unused funds could be redistributed to offer more to the ones willing to go. This would effectively create a kind of automatic 'marketplace' that would drive the assistance levels higher and higher, until people took them. Everyone has their price. Wealthy non-Whites, incidentally, would get no such assistance, and their financial penalties would have to be correspondingly increased, to encourage emigration.

[10] Even the (non-black) non-Whites who were "born here" still have, in the vast majority of cases, an identifiable nation of origin. For example, much has recently been made of the fact that Alexandria Ocasio-Cortez was "born here," and thus has nowhere to return. This is nonsense. She is 100% Puerto Rican. Her father was born in New York to Puerto Ricans, and her mother was born in Puerto Rico itself.

[11] Slavery and colonialism are the twin scourges of Western Civilization. Whatever small benefits they brought were outweighed a thousand-fold.

free family planning advice are obvious first steps. Government could also offer free sterilization services for all childless non-White adults, along with a cash incentive. There would be no welfare handouts or subsidies for having children, and no tax breaks. In fact, there would be a tax penalty after, say, the second child. Non-White couples wishing to have large families would be encouraged to emigrate, where they could then have all the children they liked. No one says they can't have kids; they just can't have them here.

Such is my sketch of a plan to respond rationally and humanely to the social and political threats posed to Whites by rising numbers of non-Whites. We may call it the "great restoration": restoring Whites to their traditional majority role, and restoring non-Whites to their native homelands. No one wants to admit it, but a large majority of repatriated non-Whites would flourish, especially with their cash incentives in hand and their American schooling (such as it may be). They return with relative wealth and relative education. They likely have extended family there. Furthermore, their bodies are physiologically well-suited to their native climates—I'm thinking especially of blacks, who suffer from a whole range of health problems when living in non-tropical climates. Repatriated minorities can be leading members of their societies, rather than denizens of a perpetual underclass among White society.

Practically speaking, of course, we are a long way from implementing such a policy. Ideally, the dissident right community would pick up on this idea and make it a central ideological plank. Then we would need the appropriate political system to implement it. Perhaps there even needs to be a new party: *The Great Restoration Party*. Its primary plank would be to restore Whites to a dominant majority, and to return non-Whites to their native homelands.

If progress could be made here, virtually all other political and economic challenges would fall in line. Imagine: an America in which the numbers of blacks, Jews, Hispanics, and Asians were *cut in half*. We can scarcely anticipate the benefits that would flow from such a situation. It would be all but miraculous. We had that once; we could have it again.

And even this could be but Phase One of yet further-reaching objectives. The racial homogenization of America would certainly lead to self-compounding benefits and a positive feedback cycle, one that might drive minority levels to vanishingly small levels.

But we can imagine the outcry. Liberal leftists and mainstream Jewish media, along with most all non-Whites, will naturally scream 'racism!' and 'fascism!' at the mere mention of such a proposal. So be it. Let them scream. The discussion needs to begin, and it needs to begin now. There is no time to waste.

— 19 —
The Impeachment Parade of Jews

Late in 2019, the American people were treated to a highly-revealing political saga: the impeachment of Donald Trump. It was revealing, but not so much due to the various political machinations, which were fairly predictable; rather, what transpired was a strikingly transparent display of Jewish reach, influence, and power. A close look at this situation makes clear, once again, both the dominance and the thorough-going corruption wrought by American Jews and their global network of coreligionists. It is worth taking a moment to document this story, "for the record"—and then to draw a few conclusions.

Let's start at the top. All recent American presidents have been steeped in Jewish entanglements, but few as personally as Trump, given that his daughter Ivanka converted to Judaism upon marriage to orthodox Jew Jared Kushner. The only closer personal connection would have been with our presidents who were, themselves, likely part-Jewish: Teddy and Franklin Delano Roosevelt, and perhaps Lyndon Johnson.[1] Apart from this family connection, we have Trump's cohort of major Jewish donors: Lew Eisenberg, Sheldon and Miriam Adelson, Mel Sembler, Ron Weiser, Steve Wynn, Elliott Brody, Laurie Perlmutter, and Carl Icahn.[2] Then we have his many Jewish personal and professional associates, who include, among others, Bill Barr (half), Avi Berkowitz, Michael Cohen, Gary Cohn, Reed Cordish, Boris Epshteyn, David Friedman, Jason Greenblatt, Larry Kudlow, Stephen Miller, Steven Mnuchin, Jay Sekulow, David Shulkin, and Allen Weisselberg. All those Trump-defenders out there in America should be dismayed at his vast linkages to the people of Israel.

But let me set all these individuals aside for now. The impeachment process was deeply involved with developments in, of all places, Ukraine. Jewish Ukrainians came to play a surprisingly prominent role in the proceedings. That nation has a long and tragic history of Jewish residency, reaching back over 1,000 years. Their numbers grew through the centuries, peaking at around 3,000,000 in the early 20th century. Present-day estimates vary between 200,000 and 400,000 Jews, representing less than

---

[1] For evidence on these three individuals, see my book *The Jewish Hand in the World Wars* (Castle Hill, 2019), 32, 95-99, 162-163. Also, Bill Clinton of course has close personal connections as well, given his daughter Chelsea's marriage to Jew Marc Mezvinsky; but that was in 2010, long after Clinton had left office.

[2] "7 big-buck Jewish donors," *Forward*, 17 Nov 2016.

one percent of the current Ukrainian population of 42 million. And yet, as elsewhere around the world, Jews exercise remarkable and disproportionate influence in that nation—and in ours.

Though the name meant little to Americans at the time, Trump's impeachment was largely triggered by a phone call, in July 2019, with none other than Ukraine's newly-elected president, Volodymyr Zelensky. Zelensky, then 41, was born in the Ukraine "to Jewish parents," as they say, and proceeded to make a name for himself in the entertainment business, as a comedian. Becoming famous for playing president in a Saturday Night Live-like television show, he, on a whim, decided to actually run for the office—and won, in March 2019. Notably, it was reported that "Zelensky has not mentioned his Jewish identity in interviews before or during the campaign, which critics say is purposefully vague".[3] This was certainly a good strategy, given Ukraine's historic problems with Jews; as a modern-day crypto-Jew, Zelensky learned this lesson well.

The key issue at hand began even earlier, with the placement of Joe Biden's son Hunter on the Board of the Ukrainian gas company Burisma in April 2014, a post he held for five years. The leading figure at Burisma, incidentally, is Mykola (Nikolay) Zlochevsky—a man who, with a Jewish surname, is almost certainly a member of the Hebrew tribe. Hunter received upwards of $500,000 a year for his services, and the Ukrainians got indirect access to VP Biden and President Obama. Trump's call was one event in a chain that apparently attempted to expose corruption and abuse of power on the part of the two Bidens, allegedly for Trump's own personal political gain.

The Proceedings

On 24 September 2019, Nancy Pelosi announced the start of the impeachment process with the formation of six House committees, each of which would have a role in the proceedings. Of the six corresponding chairmen, three were Jews: Adam Schiff (Intelligence committee), Jerry Nadler (Judiciary), and Eliot Engel (Foreign Affairs). Closed-door depositions began on October 11, and the public hearings on November 13. At the time, Schiff and his committee garnered all the attention, given that they led the public testimony phase.[4] Nadler's committee drew up the actual articles of impeachment, and Engel's group provided unspecified assistance. The three non-Jewish committees served only perfunctory and ceremonial roles.

---

[3] "Jewish comic who play Ukrainian president on TV lead Ukraine's presidential race," *Times of Israel* (13 Mar 2019).

[4] Among Schiff's fellow committee members was the Jewess Jackie Speier (D-Cal.).

But even before the initial, closed-door phase could begin, Ukrainian Jews made another appearance. On October 9, news broke that two associates of Trump's lawyer Rudi Giuliani were arrested at Dulles airport on their way out of the country—two Jewish Ukrainians (and US citizens) by the names of Lev Parnas and Igor Fruman. They were hit with unspecified charges relating to "a complex web of financial and political interactions linking diplomacy to alleged violations of campaign finance law," according to the *Washington Post*. Their connection to Giuliani went back years; they initially hired him, apparently, as a sort of consultant, and then later the tables turned and they came to work for him, as the pressure grew to investigate the Bidens and Burisma. Parnas and Fruman evidently had the right Ukrainian (and Jewish) connections to get the job done. But the details of their criminal activities have never come to light.

Public testimony began on November 13. As the master of ceremonies and chief wire-puller, Schiff oversaw the entire two-week public process and himself conducted much of the questioning. But much was also directed by the Jewish lead lawyer for the Intelligence committee, Daniel Sachs Goldman. Goldman has family ties to the (Jewish) Levi Strauss corporate empire, providing him with considerable personal wealth.

It was decided that 12 individuals would offer public testimony. Among them were yet two more Jews: Alexander Vindman and Gordon Sondland. In Vindman, the Ukraine makes another appearance. He and his identical twin brother were born there in 1975, came to the US in 1979, and became naturalized US citizens. He rose steadily through the US intelligence community, coming to work for the National Security Council in 2018. Vindman was in on the now-infamous July phone call; he objected to the presumed quid pro quo, and hence was summoned to testify.

Sondland is a 62-year-old Jew from Washington State who made a considerable fortune in the hotel business. Through a handful of privately-run companies, he donated around $1 million to Trump's campaign, and as a result, was appointed US ambassador to the EU in 2018. Sondland thus joined a host of Jewish US ambassadors, including the likes of Philip Goldberg (Columbia), Robin Bernstein (Dominican Republic), Jonathan Cohen (Egypt), David Cornstein (Hungary), David Friedman (Israel), Lewis Eisenberg (Italy), Lawrence Silverman (Kuwait), and Daniel Rosenblum (Uzbekistan).

As those two came to testify, we were treated to quite a spectacle: A Jew (Schiff) presiding over the questioning of a Jew (Vindman/Sondland) by another Jew (Goldman). It was truly a remarkable scene; one could have been excused for mistaking events as some random hearing in the Knesset rather than in the US Congress.

As things proceeded with the other witnesses, numerous references were made not only to Zelensky but also to a mysterious and nebulous group of people, the so-called "Ukrainian oligarchs." It turned out that this elite group, like their counterparts in Russia, were mostly Jewish. Of the five richest and most influential Ukrainian billionaires at that time, four were Jews: Rinat Akhmetov, Viktor Pinchuk, Ihor Kolomoysky, and Gennadiy Bogolyubov. Right behind them in the hierarchy were such Jewish-Ukrainian multi-millionaires as Oleksandr Feldman and Hennadiy Korban. These individuals exercised considerable power in the Ukraine, often outstripping official governmental agencies; they were effectively a government unto themselves.[5] Their status changed dramatically, of course, with the coming of the war with Russia in early 2022; like most wealthy Ukrainian Jews, they apparently fled the country early on.

In pre-war Ukraine, though, the new Jewish president Zelensky had very close ties to one of the Jewish oligarchs, Kolomoysky. Uncoincidentally, Kolomoysky owns the TV station "1+1" that was responsible for Zelensky's rise to nationwide fame. It was also reported that "Kolomoysky's media outlet provided security and logistical backup for the comedian's campaign".[6] The same article mentioned that Zelensky traveled 14 times in two years to Kolomoysky's two foreign homes in Geneva and Tel Aviv.

As might be expected, Kolomoysky himself was caught up in a variety of corruption allegations and lawsuits. He had been the owner of Ukraine's largest bank, Privatbank, until its forced nationalization in 2016. During his ownership, it was reported that "97% of its corporate loans had gone to 'related parties' of Kolomoysky and [his Jewish partner and fellow oligarch] Bogolyubov".[7] An independent audit found that Privatbank had been subjected to "a large-scale and coordinated fraud over at least a 10-year period ending in December 2016." Kolomoysky was also charged with embezzling more than $5 billion from the bank. And he and his "right-hand man," the above-mentioned Korban, have been implicated in numerous other crimes, including murder, kidnapping, arson, and bribery. A fine bunch indeed.

And then there's George Soros. The Jewish-Hungarian billionaire (and US citizen) has been indirectly linked to the impeachment scandal, with roots going back years; much of this derives from his longstanding penchant for influencing governments of Eastern Europe. He has long had an interest in Ukraine, and apparently had regular meetings with the former

---

[5] The complaint about a Jewish "state within the state" goes back many years, at least to Johann Fichte in the late 18th century: "Do you not remember the state within the State? Does the thought not occur to you that if you give to the Jews, who are citizens of a state more solid and more powerful than any of yours, civil rights in your states, they will utterly crush the remainder of your citizens?"

[6] "The comedian and the oligarch," Politico.com (14 Apr 2019).

[7] "A bank scandal, an oligarch, and the IMF," CNBC.com (20 Sep 2019).

Ukrainian prime minister—and Jew—Volodymyr Groysman. Soros is also a key investor in the *Anti-Corruption Action Centre* (AntAC), a group founded in 2012 in Ukraine, ostensibly to "fight corruption" but almost certainly acting to manipulate governmental policy. Most recently, it has emerged that Soros' "Open Society Foundation" had spent years in contact with key people at the State Department relating to Ukraine policy, most notably including (Jewess) Victoria Nuland. Other alleged connections are hard to assess. Alex Jones and others accused impeachment testifier Fiona Hill of being a "Soros mole," which she, naturally, vehemently rejected in her private testimony. The exact nature of that connection remains unknown.

Media Coverage, Media Bias

With this remarkable convergence of diverse members of single small ethnicity, one might expect an objective and independent media to highlight and examine this fact. Unless of course your media were *also* dominated by that single small ethnicity—in which case, you would expect no discussion at all. And in fact that's exactly what we have: no discussion at all. Yes, there was passing mention of Sondland as the "son of Holocaust survivors"—leaving viewers to make the identification with his Jewishness—and passing references to anti-Semitism regarding critics of, say, Vindman. But that's it. Certainly nothing on Schiff, Nadler, Goldman, Zelensky, et al. Even Joe DiGenova's attack on Soros as "running the State Department" included no mention of Soros' Jewishness—that would be a bridge too far.

But we cannot simply charge our mass media with a pro-Jewish bias unless we provide the facts—in this case, the names. So, consider the following list of media journalists and program hosts. Let's focus for the moment on the three main 'opinion-news' channels: CNN, MSNBC, and Fox. Start with MSNBC—a network owned and operated by NBC Universal, which in turn is owned by Comcast. Both parent companies have a notable Jewish presence in upper management: Brian Roberts and David Cohen at Comcast, and Robert Greenblatt, Bonnie Hammer, Noah Oppenheim, Andrew Lack, Mark Lazarus, and Ron Meyer at NBC Universal. As for the more visible, on-air personalities, we see on MSNBC such individuals as Rachel Maddow, Chuck Todd, Katy Tur, Andrea Mitchell, and Ari Melber—all Jewish.[8]

Trump's beloved Fox News has its own Jewish presence, in the figures of Howard Kurtz, Mark Levin, Geraldo Rivera, and (previously) Chris Wallace. But perhaps more indicative is Fox's perennial pro-Israel stance,

[8] For purposes of expediency, I include here individuals who are half-Jewish.

voiced by the likes of (non-Jew) Sean Hannity—and driven, presumably, by Fox's rabidly Zionist corporate owners, the Murdoch family.

Most striking of all, though, is CNN, whose on-air staff is remarkably slanted in the Jewish direction. For one quick indication, we can check the Wikipedia entry "List of CNN personnel," where we find a section on "Political and legal analysts." Of 26 names listed, at least 16 (61%) are Jews: Dana Bash, Richard Ben-Veniste, Rebecca Buck, Carl Bernstein, Wolf Blitzer, Gloria Borger, Harry Enten, Jamie Gangel, David Gergen, David Gregory, Maggie Haberman, John King (converted), Josh Rogin, Jake Tapper, Jeff Toobin, and Samantha Vinograd. The following two sections reveal additional Jewish names, such as David Axelrod, David Frum, Peter Beinart, Steve Israel, Jason Kander, Sally Kohn, Catherine Rampell, Hilary Rosen, Aaron Miller, Tony Blinken, and Michael Weiss. And this is not to mention others like anchor John Berman; frequent guests like Bianna Golodryga, Max Boot, or Alan Dershowitz; converts like Kate Bolduan; and non-Jews with Jewish spouses, like Christiane Amanpour. All of this was undoubtedly supported by CNN chief Jeff Zucker (until his resignation in early 2022, amidst sexual misconduct charges), who in turn answered to his corporate bosses at Warner Media—namely, Richard Pepler and David Levy.

Given this situation, it is unsurprising that the Jewish parade during the impeachment process received little or no attention. In fact, it was to be expected. Anything less would have been astonishing.

A Few Conclusions

This rare insight into the American Judeocracy affords us the opportunity to draw a few plausible conclusions. First is the power of money. Jews attain positions of influence and power, not because they are so talented, smart, noble, or well-liked, but rather because they effectively buy their way into power. They are adept at using cash donations, personal connections, intimidation, and 'sharp elbows' to maneuver themselves into key positions in government and media, and then to use those positions to further enhance their wealth and personal network.

It is a self-reinforcing cycle of the most malicious sort: of using wealth to create wealth, of using power to grow more powerful. And they do this in what, for most persons, would be considered highly unethical (when not outright illegal) ways. Everyone accepts that 'money corrupts politics,' but they never acknowledge that the bulk of the political money—roughly 25% to 50%, depending on race and party—comes from one source: the Jewish Lobby.[9] Once in their pocket, politicians then readily

---

[9] See "The Jewish Vote: Political Power and Identity in US Elections" by Gil Troy. In this report, he states that "In a political system addicted to funds and fundraising,

write or alter laws to further enhance Jewish power. Again, it's a self-serving process of the highest order. The ultimate goal of all action is, simply put, Jewish wealth and power; not justice, not fairness, not equity, not efficiency, not compassion. Hence all such things are fundamentally lacking from our government.

Second, we see how Jews have come to control both major political parties. There is no opposing view, no real third alternative. Even the microscopic threat posed by such groups as the Green Party must be controlled—such as through the Jewess Jill Stein. Our two dominant parties, who fight to the death on nearly every issue, and agree on virtually nothing, find common cause in just one thing: Jewish/Israeli interests. Jewish judicial and cabinet nominees get immediate bipartisan approval. So too does aid to Israel, amounting to some $6 billion a year, every year. Hate speech laws are passed, and 'white supremacy,' 'white nationalism,' 'anti-Semitism,' and 'racism,' are routinely and mindlessly denounced by both sides. Reasonable and nonviolent protests against Israeli crimes, such as actions related to boycotts, divestment, and sanctions (BDS), are automatically condemned and even outlawed. Even otherwise-sacred First Amendment rights of free expression are trampled and abused whenever such things threaten Jewish interests.

Third, we see the time-honored Jewish strategy of distraction from the real underlying issues. Fake, superficial political battles mask a subterranean congruence of interests. Jews will fight among themselves for degrees of power, but when threatened as a group, they circle the wagons. Against perceived enemies, they employ the most brutal pack-hunting techniques. Only the toughest and most principled opponents survive.

Fourth is the astonishing compliance and subservience of non-Jews, who act in evident contrast to their own long-term interests. We cannot believe that they do this blindly, and hence we must assume that they are fully aware of their actions and their consequences. Media goyim like Sean Hannity, Anderson Cooper, Chris Cuomo, David Muir, Lester Holt, and others, are guilty of the most appalling and treacherous of crimes: of selling out one's nation and one's race for personal gain. The same holds for the traitors in corporate leadership and government. Political leaders like Mike Pence, Nancy Pelosi, Devin Nunes, Chuck Grassley, Mitch McConnell, Kevin McCarthy, etc are criminal traitors to this nation; they cover for and defend the hidden ruling power—the true 'deep state'—and thus subject us all, and the whole planet, to uncounted miseries. In a truly just world, they would all be called to account, and pay for their sins.

Jews donate as much as 50 percent of the funds raised by Democrats and 25 percent of the funds raised by Republicans." Other sources argue for even higher figures than these.

The gravest betrayal is that of Donald Trump. Due to his erratic and infantile behavior while president, it is hard to assess his thinking. But some things are relatively clear. By any reasonable accounting, Trump is little more than an unprincipled, semi-literate, egomaniac. But owing to his extremely thin margin of public support, he was compelled—indeed, forced—to appeal to true conservatives, the working class, and the dissident-right. Clearly he had no intrinsic desire to help such groups, and he had no sympathy for their plight. Trump is the epitome of a privileged, wealthy, out-of-touch elite. But to stay in power, or to return to power, he must occasionally throw us a bone. We on the dissident-right can take it and make some hay with it; but we mustn't expect much more. Trump's actual policies and decisions will certainly favor his wealthy compatriots and the Jewish power-brokers he works with.

But it's worse than this. Trump is such a fool, degenerate, and race-traitor that he would auction off his own beautiful daughter to the Judeocracy, presumably simply for the money and power that it would bring. (It obviously says little about her judgement that she would comply.) The Clintons did the same with their (much homelier) daughter Chelsea—and at nearly the same time, in 2009-2010. It is perhaps no coincidence that once Hillary and Trump cemented their respective family ties to the Tribe, they both later rose to the height of influence in their corresponding political parties. If the Jewish Lobby can't have a Jew directly in power, a family-connected Gentile is the next best thing. Hence every presidential election battle is best seen as a struggle between the two wings of the Lobby; each has their favored candidate, and the Lobby is guaranteed to win, no matter the outcome. President Biden and his largely Jewish cabinet are a prime case in point. Nothing like stacking the deck.

A fifth conclusion is that things are unlikely to get any better in the near future. The 2020 presidential election was a heavily Jewish affair. Biden and the Democrats—the nominal winners—were even more saturated by Jewish money and influence than the Republicans. At one point in the Democratic primary race, there were 18 active contestants, among whom were *five Jews*: Bernie Sanders, Tom Steyer, Marianne Williamson, Michael Bennett, and Michael Bloomberg. Imagine: a *presidential* field with 30% Jews, in a nation where they number around 2%. But it almost didn't matter because the remaining non-Jews were nearly as bad: pro-Israel, anti-White, anti-'racist', pro-military, etc—with the sole exception of Tulsi Gabbard, whose presence in the race was something of a minor miracle. She alone was willing and able to confront the Jewish power structure behind the Democrats. But Gabbard had no chance of winning the nomination.

Sixth and finally, the dominance of the Judeocracy is so overarching that all other causes fade into insignificance. Nothing happens without the explicit or implicit approval of the Lobby. If they oppose some given governmental action, it will not happen. If there is an outcome that they desire, there is a very good chance it will happen, in one form or another. Of course, the Lobby doesn't always get what it wants, but the main reason for this is due to internal Jewish squabbling; liberal Jews are occasionally at odds with conservative Jews, and this can lead to a stalemate. But there is enough unanimity among Jews of all stripes that, more often than not, they get their way. And more often than not, "their way" works to the detriment of non-Jews in the US and abroad.

This has an immediate consequence for every American who has any causes or policies that they support. No matter your area of concern, no matter what cause motivates you—if it doesn't align with Jewish interests, it will fail. Environmentalism, Medicare-for-all, anti-abortion, anti-war, smaller government, tax reduction, election transparency, free speech, reduced wealth disparity…none of these have Jewish support, and thus they are doomed to failure. This affects everyone—liberals, conservatives, socialists, libertarians, anarchists, you name it. *Therefore, everyone's top cause should be reigning in the Jewish Lobby.* Without that, nothing else will be done.

The Lobby effectively subjugates every other political priority to its own needs, and therefore everyone should, above all, combat that power directly, if we are to have any hope of resolving our many grievances. It's as simple—and as challenging—as that.

— 20 —
THE ABCs OF THE DISSIDENT RIGHT

Preamble: As a long-time professor who has taught at a number of American campuses, I have seen how universities work from the inside. And for years before that, as an undergrad and then graduate student, I have seen how student life develops and evolves, and how important it can be for shaping future views and attitudes. Now is a good time to bring together these diverse sets of experiences and offer some insight and advice for current university students who seek to get more out of college than merely a degree.

Let me start with the politics of Right and Left. There has long been a "liberal bias" on campus, but for many years it was relatively benign; it consisted primarily of an openness to new ideas, an escape from dogmatic religion, a willingness to challenge traditional power structures, and an ethical idealism—all good things. A liberal was a forward-thinking individual, selfless and civic-minded, and a participant in the global community. In short: an enlightened person.

But then sometime in the 1980s, things began to change. Campuses stayed liberal while national politics went 'conservative'—but it was a conservatism with a twist. With the presidency of Ronald Reagan, which started in 1981, American conservatives made some significant shifts in policy, as compared to their traditional views: (a) they became more militarily activist around the world, anxious to project American power and to "bring democracy" to others; (b) religion—in the form of fundamentalist Christianity—became more important to civic and social life; (c) complex ideological issues got reduced to simplistic black-and-white, "us or them" terminology; and (d) conservative Jews became increasingly prominent and influential. These new tenets came to compose a new brand of conservatism: "neo-conservatism," or neo-con, for short.

Liberal college professors and administrators were generally appalled at these developments, and reacted accordingly. They became *more* liberal, and more *militantly* liberal. They grew determined to tackle the problem at its roots: at the level of college-educated youth, who would henceforth become increasingly indoctrinated in the key concepts of liberalism: intrinsic human equality, intrinsic equal rights, over-socialization, radical feminism, excessive pity for the underprivileged, and the corresponding determination to impose such values on all Americans, and indeed on the world. Such ideas took certain concrete forms: anti-racism; advocacy for minority and immigrant rights; an inordinate celebration of multiculturalism and multiracialism; denigration of White culture, 'White privilege,' and White

European civilization; functionally anti-male policies; attacks on the nuclear family; gay rights; and defense of gender and sexual-orientation 'flexibility.' But for all their differences, the militant liberals had one thing in common with the hated neo-cons: a prominent Jewish presence. Hence anti-Semitism stood as the one, universally agreed-upon policy of the right and the left.

Meanwhile, caught in the vice between neo-conservatism and radical liberalism, traditional "old" ("paleo") conservativism struggled for its very existence. The most prominent advocate was probably Pat Buchanan, a former candidate for president who opposed much of the neo-con agenda. Buchanan and other paleo-cons argued for a strong form of nationalism, and generally opposed much of the globalist agenda of the neo-cons and liberals. They also opposed military intervention around the world; argued for protectionist economic policies; defended core concepts of classic Western civilization; advocated for "states' rights" policies (i.e. that individual states should have much authority to establish their own laws); supported traditional but not fundamentalist religion; and generally opposed gay and minority rights. As a consequence, they also frequently came into conflict with Jews on both the neo-con right and the liberal left; as such, they have often been slandered as anti-Semitic.

Through the 1990s and 2000s, up to the present, militant liberalism has only increased on college campuses—dramatically so, with the election of Donald Trump in late 2016. In that election, radical liberals were convinced that "their man"—Hillary Clinton—would win. Bill Clinton was good, Obama was better, but Hillary was going to be the best. Feminists were elated that they were finally getting a woman president: one who was ultra-liberal, pro-Israel, pro-Jewish, pro-immigration, anti-racist, pro-big-government, and more than willing to project US military power around the world to enforce these "enlightened" values. They could scarcely contain their champagne corks.

But of course, it didn't turn out that way. With Trump's upset victory, many academic liberals 'snapped.' They were in shock and denial. They simply couldn't believe that a "misogynistic racist" could have won the presidency, especially over their beloved Hillary.

So they redoubled their efforts. They vowed to drive out all remnants of conservative thinking; to harass any faculty that failed to demonstrate fealty to radical leftism; to hire only the most militant—preferably female, preferably of color—faculty; and to punish right-leaning students. They created "safe spaces" for fragile egos. They condemned "hate speech" and instituted "speech codes." They hired yet more "diversity officers" and promised to step up efforts to cater to any offended minorities or protected classes of individuals. Everyone, it now seems, had their protectors and defenders—everyone except White males.

Enter the alt-right, otherwise known as the dissident right. In one sense, it is the natural outgrowth of paleo-conservatism: a kind of return to classical ideas of nationalism and political self-sufficiency. But it adds new angles as well: an emphasis on biological realism, in which evolution and genetics are seen as strongly determinative of human characteristics; an explicit defense of White interests and White European civilization; and an explicit and active critique of Jews and Judeocentric policies. And indeed, these can be seen as the three main pillars of the dissident-right:

(1) biology is destiny,
(2) Whites and White culture deserve to be protected and defended, and
(3) Jews pose an overriding threat to White interests.

(Jews, incidentally, like all Latinos, are not White—not in any relevant sense.) Among the wide-ranging dissident right, we see additional points of concern and variations on these themes, but in general, we can roughly define the dissident-right movement as centered on these three concepts.

The first, on biology, is proven more and more true by the day; new studies repeatedly show that, to a very large degree, biology and genetics determine what we loosely call 'human nature,' and that these things have a corresponding effect on society and culture. The second is straightforward and obvious: if blacks, Hispanics, Asians, Muslims, and so on each have a right to their cultures and ethnic integrity, so do Whites. The third becomes clear whenever one takes a look at the objective data regarding Jewish presence and Jewish influence in academia, government, media, Hollywood, and high tech. Jews are massively over-represented in all these fields, and constitute a force in themselves; with their highly-effective in-group strategy, they manage to reinforce their own wealth and power. In fact, this becomes their overriding priority: an increase in Jewish wealth and power.

A Brief Manifesto. The dissident right, then, advocates for White culture and White interests, and does so in a way that is aligned with science, history, and rationality. When it veers into the realm of politics, it effectively becomes a form of *White nationalism*: the idea that Whites should be self-governing and self-determining, and that, like all ethnicities, they have a fundamental right to do so. As with 'dissident-right,' there are varying definitions in the literature. But there seems to be a broad consensus that White nationalism accords with the following ideas:

1) The White race is of inherent value to humanity, has created the lion's share of Western civilization, and as such deserves protection and defense.

2) Whites globally are under threat, due to (a) declining numbers, (b) declining physical, mental, and moral health, and (c) loss of political autonomy and self-government.

3) Some of the threats are sociological, economic, or environmental in nature, but others arise from deliberate and intentional actions by anti-White parties.

4) The global Jewish lobby has an intrinsic interest in seeing a general decline in White well-being and a loss in White political power. They and their non-Jewish supporters pose the primary direct threat.

5) Racial and cultural diversity has a net negative effect on human society.

6) All humans are, by nature, best suited to live in social and environmental settings from which they evolved—societies that are broadly uni-racial and monocultural. Humans have little or no evolutionary experience living with diverse races or ethnicities, and doing so causes inevitable problems.

7) From the early Industrial Revolution, modern society has enabled the mass movement of people from indigenous to foreign lands. Left to their own initiative, people will always attempt to move from 'worse' to 'better' societies, but if this happens *en masse*, it will contribute to the decay of the very societies that they seek out. Such movement must therefore be stopped.

8) The only long-term solution for many present-day problems is to restore human society to its natural and original conditions—uni-racial and monocultural, broadly speaking. This entails political separation and/or repatriation of minority peoples to their native lands.

9) The above goal can only be achieved, in the present world, by confronting and undermining Jewish power.

These are eminently practical and realistic issues. Nothing here entails violence, hatred, misogyny, or other such evils. These are simple statements of fact; and they lay out a roadmap for any White society that hopes to survive and flourish in the long run.

How to Organize. I now shift my focus to you, the student reader, and your efforts to make a positive impact on this troubled world. So much of college life is pointless or trivial, but you now have an opportunity to create a truly transformative college experience. In a very real sense, the future of our society lies in your hands. You can act now, to make a real difference.

Here are some key points to keep mind, and some specific suggestions on how to move forward. Readings cited here are included in the list at the end of this essay.

- *You have more power than you think.* In a university, you are the paying customer. Your tuition money pays a large share of your professors' and administrators' salaries. Let them know that. You are the future, they are the status quo. You have ethics and high principles; they are just trying to keep their jobs. Even a very small group, intelligently run, can have a huge impact.

- *Know your rights.* You have the right to speak up and make yourself heard. As long as you stay within the broad rules of the university, they can't punish you. Don't let faculty or staff intimidate you. It's like dealing with a spider or mouse: they are more afraid of you than you should be of them. Be assertive but not obnoxious.

- *Organize.* Create a student group or club that explicitly advocates for dissident-right views. Pick a good name. It can be relatively innocuous, like "Campus Republicans" or "Campus Conservatives," or it can be more confrontational: "The New Right," "Dissident Conservatives," "White and Right," and so on. Be creative.

- *Have concrete goals.* Your group should, at a minimum, hold regular meetings. Simply talking through things among yourselves and sharing ideas has value. But you will likely want to do more: bring in speakers; hold debates; organize panel discussions; "table" your group in a visible spot on campus; do fundraisers; write for your student newspaper. Visibility and success breed more success.

- *Don't let egos get in the way.* This is not about who is president, or who has key roles. It's about the ideas and the mission: to develop and communicate dissident-right ideas on campus. Leaders need to be self-confident, but if it becomes more about self-glorification, time to get another leader.

- *Plan for the future.* There is constant turnover in student groups; some people lose interest, some graduate, some have personal issues, others just get too busy. To sustain and build membership, you need to be constantly planning ahead. Get to the younger students and recruit them. They're not "just freshman"; your group needs them, and every new class presents new opportunities. Also, plan for post-graduation. You need to sustain activity after you move on to your career. This again presents new opportunities for action. Stay in touch with fellow grads—and not just on-line. Meet face-to-face.

• *Don't make it a "guy's club."* Dissident-right groups tend to be heavily male. Acknowledge this, accept it, but be open to female participation. As long as they buy into the main principles cited above, there is no reason not to welcome women. You want members—and they represent half (actually, more than half) of your student population. Be respectful, and allow them full participation. Listen to their ideas; they know better how to reach other women than you males do. They are smart and motivated. They have as much equity in the future as you do. Women are also good networkers, and may make connections that the guys tend to overlook. And besides, most all of us want partners in life, and this is a great chance for both genders to meet like-minded friends.

• *Have high standards.* Try to avoid crude polemics, name-calling, and dirty tricks. Be mature. You are a role model; try to act like one. Intelligent commentary and well-organized events are much more effective than some graffiti sprayed on a dorm wall.

• *Be knowledgeable, be smart.* There is much to learn about dissident-right and dissident ideas. Take the time to study, like a serious and intelligent person. And not only on-line blogs, and not just Youtube videos. Get actual books and read them. The list below offers several good sources to start with. And then be a good detective: follow up on interesting leads, hunt for clues. Learn how to sift out the bullshitters and the nonsense. There is a lot of bogus information out there, especially on the Internet; some of it is there to deliberately mislead you. Be skeptical, and do background research.

• *Stay agnostic on religion.* Conservatives tend to be more religious than average, and so you may well attract religious people. Accept them, but don't let theology rule the discussion. Keep religious ideas safely to the side. Be particularly wary of fundamentalists, who tend to be too irrational to be much good. The same holds for so-called Christian Zionists. Beyond this, there are good reasons to believe that Jesus, for example, is a Jewish construction, and serves Jewish purposes (read Nietzsche). And in truth, all Christians (and all Muslims) worship the Jewish God, albeit with a different name. In sum, best to let that dog lie.

• *Get political (1).* Yours' is a movement of major political importance. You need to acknowledge this, and engage in political debates. There are many local, regional, and national policy implications for the dissident right. Engage at every level. Make well-reasoned recommendations, and defend them against critics.

- *Get political (2).* There are good reasons to think that the situation may be hopeless at the national level; the corruption may simply be too deep to be redeemed. Rather than 'fixing' Washington, we may need to abandon it. Consider a strong "states' rights" position, even to the point of secession. In a practical sense, White nationalism may only be realized in smaller political units than that of the monstrous, multiracial mish-mash of an American nation. Start by reading Leopold Kohr's *Breakdown of Nations.*

- *Know your opponents.* As a dissident-righter, your main opponents are non-Whites, Jews, and liberal Whites (among both students and faculty). Even some mainstream Republicans may oppose you. Learn how they think, and what their 'hot button' issues are. A calculated incitement of your opponent can be very useful. Non-Whites, for example, typically get excited by talk of limiting immigration or of mass deportations of illegal aliens. Jews get excited by talk of boycotts, divestment, and sanctions (BDS) against the state of Israel. They also hate when prominent Jews are outed. And they hate when someone questions the highly-dubious Holocaust story—see sources below. Don't be afraid to use these issues to your advantage.

- *Name names (1).* In other words, be specific and detailed in your critiques. Use facts, and check your facts. Instead of saying "the Jews in the Sociology department are complaining about us…" say "Jewish faculty like Bob Greenberg and Joel Baumgarten in Sociology are complaining…" Instead of railing against "media Jews," rail against "Jewish media execs like Noah Oppenheim and Andrew Lack at NBC." Specificity shows that you know what you are talking about.

- *Name names (2).* Here's an interesting project: Conduct your own 'faculty diversity survey,' to determine rough numbers of Whites, non-Whites, and Jews. They are certainly pro-diversity, so they can hardly object. Note: you are looking for Jews as an ethnicity, not a religion (recall that 'Jew' can be either). Print up a simple survey with a few specific categories: White (non-Hispanic, non-Jewish), black, Asian, Jewish, Hispanic/Latino, mixed/other. Responses will be very instructive.

- *Watch out for moles.* Any moderately visible or successful group will very quickly attract attention, from both friends and enemies. A well-worn tactic of the other side is to infiltrate successful groups and manipulate them from within—ideally, even take on leadership roles. It is amazing how many Jews, for example, have taken positions of influence within nominally dissident-right or dissident right groups; think of Andrew Breitbart, Larry Solov, Milo Yiannopolous, Alex Marlow, Ben Shapiro, and Joel Pollack, all associated with Breitbart News; or Stephen Miller, the alleged "White nationalist" in the former Trump administration; or Michael Savage; or Matt Drudge. Know your members, and look for signs of less-than-honest opinions.

- *Watch out for spies.* In line with above, successful groups often attract quiet members who are just "taking notes"—and perhaps reporting out. There's not much you can do about this, but be aware that someone in your group may be looking for dirt. Keep things above-board, and don't give them anything to report.

- *Don't demonize the masses.* In general, it's not good strategy to refer to your fellow students as idiots, morons, dupes, etc. For the most part, you need them. You are trying to win them over—even if they are idiots or dupes. Educate them. Be patient. Be tolerant. Figure out what is stopping them from accepting the truth, and slowly bring them around.

- *Insults are a badge of honor.* Don't take it personally when your enemies start calling you names. In fact, welcome it; it's a sign that you are succeeding. And have no doubt, they will call you every name in the book: Nazi, racist, bigot, fascist, anti-Semite, Klansman, White supremacist, and so on. Show poise; just let it roll off your back. Point out that they don't really know what they are talking about; most of them cannot even define 'Nazi', or 'bigot,' or 'fascism,' etc. Be smarter than them, and use your knowledge to upstage them. Show them to be the fools that they are.

- *Learn about the real Nazis.* Since it's inevitable that you will be called this, you might as well learn something. 'Nazi' is short for National Socialist, and there is nothing inherently evil about either nationalism or socialism. Adolf Hitler was arguably the first major dissident-righter of the 20th century. He spent his youth in a social environment not so different from our own. As a young man, he faced many of the same problems that we do. His story is instructive; see the list below for some good sources.

- *Stay healthy in body and mind.* Again, be a role model. Be better than the average slacker. Watch your weight, and stay in shape. Work out. Get strong. Cut down on meat, sugar, and junk food. Avoid recreational drugs and heavy drinking—these things can destroy your focus and motivation. Avoid mindless Internet surfing, and stupid TV reruns, and moronic Hollywood trash. Get the airpods out of your ears, shut off the insidious black rap "music," cut down on texting and Instagramming. You have a mission in life, and you need all your faculties to succeed. Jews and liberals would like nothing more than for you to spend nights smoking pot and binge-watching their garbage on your laptop or phone. Don't give in to them.

• *Don't get sucked into the technology.* Along the same line as above, be very cautious about getting sucked into technology day and night. Excessive gaming, Internet addiction, on-line porn, too much social media...these things pose real psychological and physical risks to your well-being—seriously. Keep them all to a bare minimum. And then get informed on the many risks of high-tech (read Ted Kaczynski, for starters).

• *Be visible.* Take some time to get organized, but once you are up and running, get the word out. Put articles or ads in the school newspaper. Post flyers around campus, or leave them loose on desks in random classrooms. Scribble messages on blackboards/whiteboards. Go on the school radio. Talk to local media.

• *Don't get too stuck on ideological labels.* 'Right' and 'left,' like 'liberal' and 'conservative,' are vague terms, and arguably are more harmful than helpful. In reality, they don't allow for much subtlety of definition. Yes, you are dissident-right, but don't hang everything on this one label. Many liberals have some conservative opinions, and many dissident-righters hold some traditionally liberal views. This is not a major problem, and don't be pushing ideological purity tests on anyone. Views shift over time, especially for college students. Any student who thinks he has it all figured out has a lot to learn. It's not a weakness to change your opinions—it's a sign of growth.

• *Avoid the "woke."* 'Woke' is one of those truly stupid labels that you should avoid at all costs. It comes from black slang (appropriately), and refers to a heighted sensitivity to racism, black interests, oppressed minorities—in other words, all those traditional leftist views. It represents political-correctness run amok. What you *do* want is people to "awake"—wake up to the false and distorted reality they have been living in. But that's something entirely different.

• *Be persistent, take notes, follow up.* This is just good organizational technique. Write things down, because everyone forgets. Get people to commit to tasks, and hold them accountable. Acknowledge and reward those who follow through and get results. It's a long war, and nothing of value is won overnight. Pace yourselves. Don't burn out. Be in it for the long haul.

- *Use publicity to your advantage.* Universities hate two things: money problems and bad press. Your group is a constant threat for the latter. This is one of your few pieces of leverage over them. Use it appropriately. If you are succeeding, get the word out, not only on campus but among the public at large. If you are under attack, publicize the implicit assault on your rights of free speech and association.

- *If they disband your group, go underground.* An effective group will get attention, and a really effective group will get a lot of attention. At some point, they—the university bureaucracy—may well concoct some reason to shut you down, even if you've broken no rules. If they do this, publicize how unjustified they are. Let your fellow students know that free speech and free expression are not welcome on your campus. Then go underground. Most universities are public institutions, and they cannot forbid your group from meeting—they can only withhold funding and institutional support. If that happens, so be it. Meet in the library, in the student union, or at a local café. They can't stop you from posting flyers, doing stuff on-line, renting small spaces, organizing events. This can even have its advantages; underground groups have a lot more freedom than ones reliant on university funding. Put this to good use.

- *Stay in touch, and network.* Work with other student groups and other campuses, where possible. Build alliances where you can.

- *Document your work.* Write, publish blogs or hard-copy essays. If you're up to it, publish a small book (renegade publishers like Clemens & Blair can help you). Keep track of successes and failures. We all can learn from each other, and we should try to avoid repeating each others' mistakes. You are working not just for the present, but for the future. Those to come will benefit from your hard work.

- *Speak the truth.* Sometimes these days, just saying the truth out loud is a revolutionary act, one that calls for real courage. The truth is on your side. Be strong, be confident, and speak the truth.

This last point bears repeating: You have justice and truth on your side. Your cause is just. You have the weight of history behind you. Many great thinkers of the past and present stand at your side, ready to help. Don't give up, don't apologize, don't surrender. There are people around who can help with questions, problems, or advice. Don't hesitate to reach out. Good luck; we're counting on you.

Suggested readings:

Dalton, T. 2020. *Debating the Holocaust* (4th ed.). Castle Hill.
Dalton, T. 2016. *The Holocaust: An Introduction*. Castle Hill.
Dalton, T. 2019. *The Jewish Hand in the World Wars*. Castle Hill.
Dalton, T. 2020. *Eternal Strangers: Critical Views of Jews and Judaism through the Ages*. Castle Hill.
Dalton, T., ed. 2022. *Classic Essays on the Jewish Question*. Clemens & Blair.
Duke, D. 1998. *My Awakening*. Free Speech Press.
Goebbels, J. 2019. *Goebbels on the Jews*. Castle Hill.
Hitler, A. 2019. *The Essential Mein Kampf*. Clemens & Blair.
Hitler, A. 2019. *Hitler on the Jews*. Castle Hill.
Hitler, A. 2022. *Mein Kampf* (2 volumes; T. Dalton, ed.). Clemens & Blair.
Johnson, G. 2018. *The White Nationalist Manifesto*. Counter-Currents.
Kaczynski, T. 2019. *Technological Slavery* (vol. 1). Fitch and Madison.
Kohr, L. 1955. *Breakdown of Nations*. Dutton.
MacDonald, K. 1994. *A People That Shall Dwell Alone*. Praeger.
MacDonald, K. 1998. *Separation and its Discontents*. Praeger.
MacDonald, K. 1998. *The Culture of Critique*. Praeger.
Nietzsche, F. 1887. *On the Genealogy of Morals*. Vintage.
Nietzsche, F. 1888. "Antichrist." In *The Portable Nietzsche*. Penguin.
Plato. 1997. "Republic." In *Plato: Complete Works*. Hackett.
Shaw, G. (ed.). 2018. *A Fair Hearing: The Alt-Right in the Words of its Members and Leaders*. Arktos.

Suggested websites:

www.theoccidentalobserver.com
www.thomasdaltonphd.com
www.clemensandblair.com
www.davidduke.com
www.unz.com
www.holocausthandbooks.com
www.codoh.com
www.vdare.com

— 21 —
STUDENT LIFE AND THE DISSIDENT RIGHT: REPLY TO GRIFFIN

As a relatively new movement—some 10 years old now—the dissident-right, like any such movement, must be open to continual refinement and articulation. Thus it is both to be expected, and welcome, that we get a range of opinions from diverse perspectives. People have different experiences and different knowledge bases, and they naturally approach such a topic from different angles. This is especially true here, given that we are dealing with a serious and potent social theory, one that furthermore comes into direct conflict with the prevailing power structures in the West. In such a case, we need to hear the pros and cons of our various ideas, especially from thoughtful and knowledgeable colleagues.

Along this line, I published an essay entitled "The ABCs of the Alt-Right" in late 2019.[1] It drew many compliments but also a few critiques. Of special interest was a piece by Dr. Robert Griffin: "A Rejoinder to 'The ABC's of the Alt-Right: A Guide for Students' by Thomas Dalton, Ph.D".[2] Griffin shares a common background with me, and has a similar interest in campus life in particular. I can't match Dr. Griffin's 47 years of teaching, but I have been teaching at universities on and off (mostly on) since the early 1980s, which gives me well over 30 years' experience. I have taught at three different American universities, and two foreign, in that time.

Perhaps more to the point, throughout much of that period I have been actively involved with student groups and student activists, often serving as an official or unofficial faculty advisor; this experience helped to inform my previous essay. Though he does not say so explicitly, I get the impression that Dr. Griffin has perhaps less direct experience in working with student groups. Be that as it may, I will take a look at his many helpful remarks, to see if I can offer a response or rebuttal. After all, we share many of the same goals, and so it is certainly worthwhile to examine our different thoughts on how to arrive at them.

To begin with, Dr. Griffin jumps directly to my final section, "How to Organize." I take this to mean that he is in broad agreement with the first two sections. My initial "Preamble" laid out some history and context of

---

[1] Reprinted, with modifications (including revising 'alt-right' to 'dissident right') as chapter 15 in the present volume.

[2] Griffin's essay was published, like my original, on the Occidental Observer website (www.theoccidentalobserver.net).

the dissident right, and identified the three pillars of dissident-right philosophy: 1) biology is destiny, 2) Whites and White culture deserve defense, and 3) Jews pose an overriding threat to White interests. My short middle section offered a "brief manifesto" of White nationalism, summarizing its nine key points, and emphasizing the scientific, non-violent, and 'non-hatred' nature of such a view. The three pillars seem to be widely recognized, whereas the nine points of White nationalism are my interpretation of this worldview. Given that he offers no comment at all on these issues, I have to assume that Griffin accepts the general outline that I presented.

The disagreements come in my final section, where I offer thoughts on how to promote and advance a dissident-right view on college campuses. It goes without saying that there is no one "right way" to do this, and the wide variability in campus cultures, student bodies, local social attitudes, and individual student beliefs necessarily requires much flexibility in how to implement such a program. My original essay was, indeed, a "guide" in every sense of the word: guidelines and recommendations, thought-starters and practical advice. It was never intended to lay down the law on student dissident-right activism.

In that section, I gave 31 bullet-point items of brief discussion. Griffin offers critical commentary on 13 of these; hence I presume that he has little or no objection to the remaining 18 (it's always good to note points of agreement). Thus we will focus on the points of contention.

(1) *Students have more power than they think.*[3] Griffin emphasizes the difference between individual and collective power. Yes, of course, any one student has only a microscopic impact on university finances, as does any one taxpayer with respect to his state or federal government. My main point was that students are, in large part, funders of the university; they (or yes, their parents) are the paying customers; and as such, they have all the rights of any paying customer. They have the right to be treated fairly and with respect. They have the right to complain. They have the right to point out abuses or incompetence on the part of their "employees." And they have no particular obligation to their fellow paying customers, provided that they follow the broad rules of behavior that apply equally to all. That said, I see no real point of disagreement here. Yes, it's more complicated than taking your money elsewhere, but the principle is the same. You pay (a lot!), and you have rights. Don't let your "employees" tell you otherwise.

(2) *Stay within the rules of the university, and they can't punish you.* Here, we begin to get into more substantive disagreements. Dr. Griffin seems inordinately sensitive to negative opinions of others. Or at least, he is

[3] For sake of brevity, I am summarizing the 13 points from my original wording.

imputing such sensitivity to many (most?) students. I guess it goes without saying that if you are a sensitive flower, don't become a dissident-right activist. Anyone bothered by "verbal disconfirmation," "looks of disdain," or not being called on in class is probably too immature to engage in contentious politics. Same with anyone affected by "put-downs, smirks, snubs, exclusion" or social media bashing. The movement needs young people with a thick skin and a strong backbone.

And I don't know how things work at Vermont, but in my experience, a professor cannot simply dish out "bad grades" to students he doesn't like. Sure, some things are subjective, but much is not. A biased professor is likely to get called out and have to explain himself. I have had many students whom I found distasteful, but I always gave them fair grades and never considered using grades as a weapon. Any such individual professor who might do that can usually be safely avoided.

Or is Griffin implying that masses of faculty—all Jewish professors, say, or all liberals—would recognize and collectively retaliate against a specific student? That's highly unlikely, in my experience. But if the whole college is indeed out to get you, then you really are making a mark!

(3) *Create an explicitly dissident-right student group or club.* Though I wouldn't call it "centrist," I agree that a pro-White movement is not intrinsically left or right on the political spectrum. As I noted, many liberals hold some conservative views, and many conservatives (even dissident-righters) have some traditionally liberal opinions. If it's true that many academics avoid self-labeling these days as liberal or left, that doesn't mean that they are centrists; rather, they are crypto-leftists, which is worse. Griffin seems to want students to be crypto-rightists. In fact, he says as much later on, with his recommendation to be like the French underground in WW2, and his call for "secret meetings," "pseudonyms," "codes," and so on. Certainly this is always an option, but it probably is not the preferred approach. Dissident right students should be free—*are* free—to self-identify as such. And without penalty.

(4) *Don't make it a guy's club.* Dr. Griffin suggests that my brief manifesto would alienate young women. Sorry about that, but that's the reality of the situation. I'm not generally in the business of reworking my philosophical views to please a particular gender or age-group. I try to tell the truth, straight-up, and I would hope that every thinking person, of all ages and both genders, would accept it as such. MLK's ideas and values are not much help for us; nor are the Jewish-inspired techniques of emotional manipulation and pity-mongering. But here again, Griffin's sensitivity training comes to the fore; his endorsement of "tugging at our heartstrings," "making us feel sad," and "getting us to emphasize" (*sic erat scriptum*—I

presume he means 'empathize') are to no avail for the dissident-right. But I agree with his other points here: yes, be patient about getting out your message; yes, focus on that which is unfair and hurtful to Whites.

(5) *Stay agnostic on religion.* Now we're getting down to brass tacks. Based on a quick survey of his writing, I'm guessing that Griffin is a committed Christian. Unsurprisingly, he objects to my sidelining, and mild disparagement, of his religion. One might speculate that this, in fact, is at the root of his entire critique of my essay. This is unfortunate—but serves to prove my point.

I'll say more about Christianity in a moment, but first I want to address two points he raises here. He suggests that the anti-Christian crowd is also the anti-White crowd, thereby implying that we Whites can't trust—and certainly shouldn't side with—any anti-Christians. The truth is this: Part of the anti-Christian crowd are Jews, of both orthodox and secular persuasion. There's a lot to unpack here, but in short, the orthodox Jews oppose Christians on a theological basis, and the secular Jews on the basis of scientific materialism and rationalism. Both mock Christianity, but both can find some use in it as well, especially in its Zionist form. The other main group of anti-Christians are the secular, rationalist, and naturalistic Whites. These people, I would suggest, are among the toughest and most resolute White nationalists. Griffin's ploy to link 'anti-Christian' and 'anti-White' fails to hold.

His second point is that dissident-right students should use Christianity to their advantage. But he offers no concrete suggestions at all (Hey students, "see what you can come up with"). What, indeed, could one even plausibly "come up with," in a dissident-right sense, from a Christian point of view?

Let me take a minute to examine this matter a bit more closely. Consider this question: What in God's name (so to speak) is even remotely pro-White about the Bible? I'll tell you: *nothing*. The Old Testament was written by Jews, about Jews, and for Jews. It is resolutely anti-goyim. It is nothing more than a war manual for the defense of the Jewish race, along with some moronic theological cover. The New Testament was also written by and about Jews: Jesus, Mary, Joseph, 12 Apostles, Paul, 'Mark,' 'Luke,' 'Matthew,' 'John'—all ethnic Jews. The chronology of events, furthermore, strongly suggests that Paul invented his demi-god Jesus, primarily, it seems, as a stunt to undermine Roman paganism and to draw in the gullible masses, to persuade them to worship the Jewish God and his "son." With its emphasis on the presumed afterlife, Paul's constructed theology was profoundly anti-life, anti-world, and anti-corporeality. He never believed in it—that artful liar—nor did any of his fellow Hebrews. Present-day Jews are laughing up their sleeve over the foolish Christians and their "love thy neighbor" and "turn the other cheek"; and of course, they are right there, first in line, ready to exploit that love.

There is no sense, then, in which the Bible is pro-White. In fact, the New Testament, rightly understood as an anti-Roman manifesto, is profoundly *anti*-White. At best, we might say that the Bible is pro-humanity. But even here, it is cloaked with an insidious Jewish leveling of all peoples, all "equal before God"—all except the Jews, who are first among equals.

The bottom line: Can anyone who worships a long-dead ethnic Jew as his god and personal savior really be dissident-right? Really?[4]

(6) *Name names, be specific in your critiques.* Again, I don't know the faculty culture at Vermont, but to suggest that aggrieved Jewish professors might have you "worked over" because of your dissident-right views is rather shocking! (If so, stay away from Vermont.) And are they really going to haunt you after graduation? How in the world will they know which jobs you are applying for, unless they work for the Mossad? This comes across as little more than scare tactics—ones that the Jewish Lobby would certainly view with favor.

(7) *Insults are a badge of honor.* See my reply to (2) above. Again, if you are a delicate soul, one who is deeply wounded by name-calling, then by all means, don't become a dissident-right activist.

(8) *Learn something about the real Nazis.* Griffin overstates my point. I never said, "Cozy up to Hitler." I said, learn something about him, his situation, and his movement. There is much of value to learn from history.

(9) *Be visible.* For starters, I am puzzled by my alleged "last sentence" of this item ("And be prepared to take shots for it"). Where did that come from? I didn't write it, and it's not in my essay now. In any case, yes, I agree, intentional visibility is optional. Word will get around soon enough, no matter what you do. Griffin, though, recommends the opposite—be invisible. Perhaps this is good advice. I leave it to each student, and each group, to choose the most appropriate strategy. I would prefer to see a confident group working fully above-board, but that may not always be prudent.

(10) *An effective group may get shut down.* Same reply as #9.

---

[4] It's clear that simply being a Christian does not exclude one from being anti-Jewish—Martin Luther being a prime example. See my newly edited version of his important book, *On the Jews and Their Lies* (2020).

(11) *Don't get stuck on ideological labels.* Griffin seems to generally agree with me here, and so no need to reply. Labels are vague and discretionary.

(12) *Don't be 'woke.'* Griffin apparently views Black culture, and in fact all racial minorities, favorably. Of course, every ethnicity has a right to its own culture and values—but not here, not in this country. I certainly want Blacks, Hispanics, Muslims and so on to be happy, but in their nations of origin. Neither they nor we can be truly happy in a multiracial, multicultural mish-mash of a nation. Research data, evolutionary theory, and common sense all support this view.

(13) *Speak the truth.* …unless it starts to hurt, says Griffin, and then knuckle under. Just stay quiet, keep your head down, hold it in, "get along – go along," grin and bear it, "cover your ass." Or maybe, "Turn the other cheek," as a Jew once said. Sorry, but I can't do that. Millions do it, on a daily basis, but some of us have to lead. My original piece was not intended for the masses; it was meant for those few who are the future leaders of their generation. A medium-sized college campus may only have five or 10 such individuals. We need to reach them, and help them become strong, confident leaders.

In sum, Griffin offers as much commentary and elaboration as real criticism of my essay. In contrast to my piece, his scattered suggestions seem to boil down to (a) stay low key, (b) welcome and even use Christianity, and (c) don't ruffle too many feathers, either with Jews or other minorities. So be it. Perhaps some will follow his advice, and others will take the more assertive approach that I recommend. God knows (so to speak), we need all the help we can get.

— 22 —
TAX THE RICH!

Everybody loves to hate taxes. As the old saying implies, taxes are right up there with death among humanity's least favorite things. Yet they are as old as civilization itself; tax records have been found from as far back as the Ur III dynasty of 2,000 BC, and possibly older. And we can be sure that its residents paid them grudgingly.

Tax resistance is thus another perennial theme in history, dating back to Jesus, at least, and his alleged "forbidding us to pay taxes to Caesar" (Luke 23:2). Lady Godiva's mythic ride through Coventry was allegedly on behalf of excessive taxes. Dozens of wars, revolts, and uprisings in the 16th, 17th, and 18th centuries occurred over taxation. We all know of the infamous "no taxation without representation" and Boston Tea Party, leading to the American Revolution. Thoreau was briefly jailed in 1846 over a failure to pay taxes, in an act of civil disobedience against the Mexican-American War. Among the American public, there was significant resistance to tax increases during both World Wars and the Vietnam War. Even today, scarcely a month goes by without some anti-tax action making the news somewhere in the world.

And yet, everyone except pure anarchists wants some level of service from their government, and thus we all more or less accept the inevitable. Everyone has their favorite governmental program that they want funded; but they always want someone else to pay for it. We all would love to get something for nothing from the feds. But most of us realize that government cannot function without revenue, and that it cannot simply create money out of thin air—at least, not indefinitely. And so we pay.

Most galling of all, I suppose, is *income tax*: government "tribute" taken directly from our paychecks, before we see a single penny. Long hard hours put in at the daily grind, dealing with obnoxious bosses and coworkers, moronic customers, deadlines, 60-hour weeks...and then the government steps in and takes its "fair share." We can sometimes get tricky and defer payment until Tax Day, but eventually the bill comes due; and we pay. In the US, the average worker pays between 20 and 25% of income to the federal government, and another 5% to state or local governments: upwards of a third of our income, gone, lost, squandered.

But what if we—most of us, anyway—didn't have to pay any income tax? What if we could have all the same governmental services that we do today, but surrender nothing from our hard-earned paychecks? It may surprise the reader to know that, for most of the history of the USA, citizens paid no income tax at all. And for decades more, only a very small percentage paid them. For 150 years, it worked. What if we could have that again? And what if the lost funds could be covered, in large part, by that most prosperous of ethnic minorities, the Jews? There would be a sort of sublime justice in that, would there not?

A Short History of Taxation in America

Born out of tax revolt, the early United States government was uniquely sensitive to the question of taxation. Much of the debate centered on the role and size of a federal government. The so-called federalists, like Madison and Hamilton, argued for a strong central government and hence significant taxation, whereas others like Jefferson defended a small, decentralized, states-rights model that necessarily required lesser federal taxes. But neither side wanted to tax the nation's farmers and small businessmen, and so it was agreed that import taxes—tariffs—would be employed to fund the government. These were easy to collect at ports of entry, and they had the added benefit of protecting nascent American industries. Tariffs, along with a few selected excise taxes on specific commodities, funded the entire federal government.

Correspondingly, the early government was relatively small. At no time in those early years did federal spending exceed 5% of the nation's GDP; whereas today, the figure is around 21%.[1] Jefferson's argument evidently held sway, for well into the 19th century. The US continued to rely almost exclusively on tariffs and minor excise taxes, right up to the Civil War. Thus, for the first 85 years of its existence, the United States had precisely zero income tax.

With the advent of the Civil War in 1860, things changed, at least temporarily. The Revenue Act of 1861 imposed a 3% tax on income over $800 (equivalent to about $25,000 today). The income threshold was lowered the following year to $600, thus bringing in additional revenue. In 1864, the rate increased to 5% for most wage-earners, and up to 10% for the highest incomes. In any case, it was all justified only by the urgencies of war. With Union victory in 1865, the on-going need vanished and the income tax was rightly abolished a few years later.

For the next two decades, the nation again relied on tariffs for the vast majority of its funding. But in the meantime, pressure to reduce them steadily grew, in part to allow for lower prices for businesses and consumers on imported items. Congressmen realized, however, that another tax would be needed to offset the lost revenue. Hence came the Wilson-

---

[1] Federal spending is now about $4.1 trillion, which is roughly 21% of our current GDP of $21 trillion. More on this below.

Gorman Tariff Act of 1894, which reintroduced income taxes, now of 2% on earnings over $4,000—equivalent to about $120,000 today. It was truly a tax for the well-off.

Unfortunately for the government, it was also unconstitutional. When a New York company, Farmer's Loan and Trust, attempted to enforce the law, a wealthy stockholder, Charles Pollock, objected, sued the company, and won in the Supreme Court. It seems that, at the time, the US Constitution had no provision for a "direct" tax on income without a complex system of apportionment, i.e. payment back to the states. In effect, by the court's ruling, the income tax was functionally abolished. For the next 20 years, the feds again had to rely on import tariffs.

This little dilemma was resolved in 1913 with the passage of the 16th Amendment to the Constitution. It reads, in full:

> The Congress shall have power to lay and collect taxes on incomes, from whatever source derived, without apportionment among the several States, and without regard to any census or enumeration.

There were some oddities connected with both the wording of the amendment and the ratification process, but I won't go into those here.[2] In any case, Congress wasted no time, and the Revenue Act of 1913[3] reduced tariffs but imposed a 1% tax on income over $3,000, rising to a rate of 6% on incomes over $500,000. The income threshold of $3,000—about $78,000 today—effectively applied only to the top three percent of earners; a full 97% of Americans were unaffected. The vast majority of people continued to pay no income tax.

Enter "The Chosen"

It is perhaps coincidental, but it was just around this time that the American Jewish Lobby emerged on the scene and began to exert considerable influence on the federal government. The story is enlightening, and worth a bit of a detour.

From the late 1800s on, American Jews took an increasing interest in events overseas, and one area of particular concern for them was the treatment of their coreligionists in Russia. Things first turned ugly in 1881 when a gang of anarchists, one or two of whom were Jewish, succeeded in killing Czar Alexander II. This unleashed a multi-decade series of periodic

---

[2] See, for example, the work of Bill Benson and his book *The Law That Never Was* (www.thelawthatneverwas.com).

[3] Also known as the 'Underwood Tariff' or the 'Underwood-Simmons Act.'

pogroms, most minor but some killing multiple hundreds of Jews. The increased Russian crackdown caused many belligerent Jews to flee the country; many eventually came to the US. Russia was more than happy to see them go, upon which it effectively closed the door to all Jewish immigration. As Russian foreign minister Sergey Sazonov explained, "Many agitators, revolutionaries, and anarchists who were adherents of the Hebrew religion had emigrated to America during the recent troubles, and it was not to be expected that Russia should encourage the return of these elements".[4] Of course: the Russians were no fools, after all.

For the American Zionists, though, it was intolerable that their coreligionists should be excluded from that country. Thus, as an act of punishment, the Zionists took it upon themselves to initiate the abrogation of a longstanding agreement, the Russo-American Treaty of 1832.

In January 1911, a leading Zionist, Louis Marshall, "officially opened the public campaign for abrogation." He immediately appealed not to Jewish interest—though that was the sole motive—but rather to allegedly American interests. "It is not the Jew who is insulted; it is the American people," he said. As Robert Shogan put it, "a key to the [Jewish] strategy was to frame its demand as a plea to protect American interests in general, not just the rights of Jews".[5] The AJC then embarked on a massive propaganda effort. They made the case "in popular emotional terms," organized petitions and letter-writing programs, and held dedicated, pro-abrogation rallies. Everything was designed to put maximum pressure on Congress.

By November of 1911, just 11 months after launching their public campaign, the Jews were confident of victory. That same month an "unofficial delegation" of Jews met with President Taft, convincing him that Congressional action was inevitable, and veto-proof. Taft relented, agreeing to sign the resolution when it reached his desk. On December 13 the House approved the measure—by the astounding tally of 301 to 1. A slightly modified version came up for Senate vote on December 19, which passed *unanimously*. A reconciled bill was approved the next day, and Taft signed it. So it came to be that, on 20 December 1911, the US government sold its soul to the Jewish Lobby. It has yet to win it back.[6]

The Russians, incidentally, were stunned at this action. They knew of the Jewish hand at work, but could hardly believe that it had the power to carry through on its threat. The NYT again gives a useful report:

---

[4] In S. Singer, "President Taft and the Jews" (*The Jewish Press*, 23 Dec 2015). Sazonov served from 1910 to 1916.

[5] *Prelude to Catastrophe* (2010), p. 22.

[6] For a fuller treatment of this incident and its implications, see my book *The Jewish Hand in the World Wars* (2019).

> In parliamentary circles here [in Russia] the prevailing comment is characterized by astonishment that the American government has responded so readily to the Jewish outcry. The opinion is expressed by members of the Duma that in all probability the Jews will now attempt to force matters further. (20 Dec 1911; p. 2)

Such was the state of affairs in America and globally at that time. International Jewry had sufficient wealth and influence to steer events at the highest levels, and American Jews had come to permeate the government—and American culture generally. The situation so impressed German economist Werner Sombart that he made this observation in 1911: "For what we call Americanism is nothing else than the Jewish spirit distilled".[7] From the perspective of a century hence, this would seem truer than ever.

Hence it is likely that American Jews had a hand in both the reduction of the tariffs—something which would facilitate global trade—and in the initiation of an income tax that would land hardest on wealthy Gentiles like Andrew Carnegie, J. P. Morgan, Andrew Mellon, and John Rockefeller. For the Jews, it was a double-win.

In any case, the Revenue Act of 1913 was happily signed into law on October 3rd of that year, by first-term president Woodrow Wilson. For his part, Wilson seems to have been the first president elected with the full blessing of the Jewish Lobby. As Henry Ford saw it, "Mr. Wilson, while President, was very close to the Jews. His administration, as everyone knows, was predominantly Jewish".[8] His major political donors were Jews, including the likes of Henry Morgenthau, Jacob Schiff, Samuel Untermyer, Paul Warburg, Bernard Baruch, and Louis Brandeis. Wilson was also the first president to fully reward their support; Morgenthau was named ambassador to the Ottoman Empire and Warburg was appointed as the first chairman of the newly-formed Federal Reserve. Later, Baruch would assume vast powers in his War Industries Board, and Brandeis would become the first Jew on the Supreme Court.

Onset of War

Meanwhile, trouble was brewing in Europe. A complex series of treaties and alliances, combined with the untimely assassination of Archduke Ferdinand on 28 June 1914, inaugurated the First World War. For a full two years, the US avoided entanglement. Wilson ran for his second term in late

[7] *The Jews and Modern Capitalism* (1911/1982), p. 44.

[8] *Dearborn Independent*, 11 June 1921.

1916 with the slogan "He kept us out of war." But to no avail; soon after winning, he declared war on Germany, in April 1917.

With the US now involved, revenues would need to be drastically increased, and one obvious means was via the income tax. Hence the War Revenue Act of 1917: a quadrupled rate of 4% (still with a $3,000 per year income threshold), along with incremental marginal rates ranging from 1% to 50%.

Into the last year of the war, 1918, rates again increased: combined rates ranged from 6% to 77%. Also, the income threshold was lowered to $1,000 per year (for individuals), drawing in many more taxpayers—though still amounting to just the *top five percent* of all taxpayers.

Postwar, the US experienced both the Roaring '20s and the Depressing '30s, all while retaining the same basic tax structure. As Benjamin Ginsberg explains,

> Prior to the New Deal [of the 1930s]…a high tax threshold and numerous exemptions meant that only about 3 percent of American adults were subject to [income] tax. … The system depended on more or less voluntary compliance by a small number of well-to-do individuals. This meant that income taxation was not at first a major source of federal revenue.[9]

Thus, right up until the eve of World War Two, and excepting for a few years during the Civil War, the vast majority of Americans paid no income tax at all—in over 150 years. But that was about to change, thanks to a prominent Hebraic influence in the US Treasury.

Onset of War (again)

Just as Henry Morgenthau, Sr.'s political patronage of Wilson earned him a prime governmental post, so too his son, Henry Jr, earned the favors of the next wartime president, Franklin Roosevelt. Henry Jr and FDR went back many years, well before the latter's stint as governor of New York in the late 1920s. As FDR prepared for his run for president, Henry and other Jews were there, happy to donate. As Myron Scholnick explains, "A number of wealthy Jewish friends contributed to Roosevelt's pre-nomination campaign fund: Henry Morgenthau Jr., Lt. Gov. Lehman, Jessie Straus, [and] Laurence Steinhardt." Once the primaries were out of the way, "Roosevelt's campaign was heavily underwritten by Bernard Baruch".[10]

---

[9] *How the Jews Defeated Hitler* (2013), p. 57.
[10] *The New Deal and Antisemitism in America* (1990), p. 193.

As with Wilson, FDR did not fail to reward his donors; Morgenthau, for example, was named Secretary of Treasury in early 1934.

But it wasn't only Morgenthau, of course. In time-honored tradition, Henry brought in a host of fellow Jews to help direct American economic policy:

> Among those working for Morgenthau at Treasury were large numbers of Jewish economists and statisticians, including such contemporary and future luminaries as Jacob Viner, Walter Salant, Herbert Stein, and Milton Friedman, who helped to fundamentally change America's tax system…[11]

And change it they did.

War came again to Europe in September 1939, and by late 1940 it was becoming increasingly apparent that the US would get drawn in, one way or another.[12] Total federal spending in 1939 was about $8 billion, of which around $1 billion (12%) came from personal income taxes. But with war looming, Morgenthau and friends knew that spending, and thus revenue, would need to dramatically increase. They had three options: personal income tax, corporate income tax, and war bonds. So they set to work; "in the realms of both taxation and bond sales, Jews played major roles," writes Ginsberg.[13]

Special emphasis was placed on increasing personal income taxes, both by lowering the threshold for paying, and by increasing the tax rates. The effect was dramatic. The number of taxpaying adults increased from a very modest 1 million in 1939, to 5 million in 1941, to 40 million in 1942—at the time, constituting virtually all non-farm wage-earning adults. Corresponding revenues soared from $1 billion to $40 billion by the last years of the war. Revenue increases matched spending increases, as federal expenditures rose from $8 billion in 1940 to over $100 billion by 1945.

At the start of the war, however, the Treasury Jews knew that enforcement of new tax laws would be difficult. Millions of Americans who had never even considered the possibility of paying an income tax were suddenly asked to contribute thousands of dollars. What to do? Morgenthau's boys devised a clever plan:

> A number of Jewish economists [including Milton Friedman and Morgenthau himself] championed the introduction of

---

[11] Ginsberg, p. 56.

[12] Again, as with WWI, there was a prominent Jewish role in our entry into the war; see Dalton (2019)—supra note 6.

[13] Ginsberg, p. 56.

> *payroll withholding*, or 'collection at the source,' which to this day ensures a smooth, regular flow of billions of dollars into the federal government's coffers.[14]

That is, the government would work with employers to extract the worker's share of taxes prior to paying their wages. Corporations were much easier to coerce than unruly citizens, and rates could be arbitrarily raised in the future with little fuss. This tactic was a "central feature" of the 1943 Revenue Act, and would remain in effect for all future years. Thanks to payroll withholding, income tax evolved "from a minor tax levied on wealthy Americans into a major tax levied on all Americans".[15]

With this glorious new cash cow in place, the Treasury Jews never looked back.[16] As a result, Americans today pay an astonishing $2.1 trillion in income and "payroll" (FICA, or social security plus Medicare) taxes, accounting for roughly 68% of all federal revenue. In other words, over two-thirds of the entire funding of our federal government comes directly out of citizens' paychecks. This monumental burden is carried by 84% of all households, who pay either income tax, or payroll tax or, most likely, both. Most of the remaining 16% of households—representing about 50 million people—are impoverished and earn too little to pay any income tax at all.

And yet even this is not enough for our voracious feds. The $2.1 trillion is supplemented by some $760 billion in corporate taxes (income tax plus their share of payroll), and another $260 billion in excise and estate taxes. In sum, the government currently takes in about $3.3 trillion. But it spends around $4.1 trillion annually, mostly on defense and military-related costs, which approach a breath-taking $1.25 trillion per year.[17] The difference—an annual deficit of about $800 billion—is pushed onto future

---

[14] Ginsberg, p. 57.

[15] Ginsberg, p. 59.

[16] And indeed they are "Treasury Jews," even through the present day. Witness current Treasury Secretary Janet Yellen—who succeeded another Jew, Steven Mnuchin—who succeeded yet another Jew, Jack Lew.

[17] Total annual military-related spending includes several categories, far beyond simply the Dept of Defense. In 2019, it was reported that total military-related spending exceeded $1 trillion. This includes: base DOD budget ($550 billion), "war" budget, aka OCO ($174 billion), DOE and nuclear spending ($25 billion), FBI defense-related ($9 billion), Veterans Affairs ($216 billion), Homeland Security ($69 billion), international affairs and foreign military aid (mostly to Israel) ($51 billion), military intelligence, CIA, and NSA ($80 billion), and lastly, defense-related share of the national debt ($156 billion)—*for a total cost of $1.25 trillion.* For details, see "America's defense budget is bigger than you think," *The Nation* (7 May 2019).

taxpayers, in the form of additions to the federal debt, which currently stands at nearly $22 trillion. We may be excused for holding the Treasury Jews in contempt.

Return of the "3 Percent" Plan

So: What to do? Here's one idea: Let's return to the old "3 percent" rule—that is, that the entire income tax burden should again be borne by the richest 3% of households. It worked for the decades leading up to WW2, and it could work again. After all, we're not at war, at least, officially (I'll discount our current 'proxy war' with Russia in the Ukraine). In a nominal peacetime economy, the wealthiest Americans should rightly bear the full cost of income taxation.

There are several ways to make this happen. Here is one proposal. Data exists to make a reasonably accurate set of calculations. Let's consider the numbers:

At present, we have about 160 million tax households in the US, representing our 325 million people. The top one percent—that is, the richest 1.6 million households—earn an average of about $880,000 per year.[18] The 2nd-richest one percent earn around $400,000 on average, and the 3rd one-percent about $325,000. Altogether, our top 3% are paid about $2.6 trillion every year.

The problem, however, is that we need to raise $2.1 trillion in taxes from these folks. The simplest way would be to tax them at a flat rate of 80%. Imagine: you earn a hefty $1 million per year from your vulture capitalist hedge fund, and you have to pay $800,000 to the feds. What a shame; hard to make those yacht payments on just $200,000 a year.

Cruel, you say? Perhaps. Fortunately, we have an alternative. It turns out, unsurprisingly, that most of our top 3-percenters (in terms of income) are also millionaires or billionaires (in terms of assets). They have *real assets*—assets that can be taxed. Each household in the top one-percent, in fact, owns an average of $22 million in assets—mostly in property, stocks and bonds, and corporate equity. The 2nd percentile household owns some $7.5 million, on average; the 3rd percentile, $5 million. In total, this group of individuals owns or controls *about $56 trillion in assets*—an utterly incredible sum, to say the least.

Here then is my proposal: tax the upper 3-percenters income at a flat rate of 60%; this will raise about $1.5 trillion annually. Then let's also impose a mere 1% wealth tax on their assets, which will raise another $560 billon. In sum, we get nearly exactly the desired total of $2.1 trillion. Our

---

[18] Howard Gold, "Never mind the 1 percent, let's talk about the 0.01 percent", 2017 (www.review.chicagobooth.edu).

richest people have fully funded the federal government. And the remaining 97% of us—around 315 million people—get to keep *all* of our hard-earned income. Imagine that.

And who, exactly, are these poor buggers who are about to personally fund the federal government? We know the big names: Elon Musk, Bill Gates, Warren Buffett, Mark Zuckerberg, Jeff Bezos, the Koch brothers. But they are just the tip of the iceberg. When we run down the list of leading names, we find a striking fact: *around half of them are Jews*. Among the top ten, we find five Jews: Larry Page, Sergey Brin, Larry Ellison, Steve Ballmer, and Michael Bloomberg. Of the top 50, at least 26 are Jews, including Mark Zuckerberg, Michael Dell, Carl Icahn, David Newhouse, Micki Arison, Mariam Adelson, Len Blavatnik, and Stephen Ross.[19] More broadly, we can cite once again Benjamin Ginsberg, who wrote, "Today, though barely 2% of the nation's population is Jewish, close to half its billionaires are Jews".[20]

Based on such data, we can infer that up to half of the top 3-percenters are Jews.[21] As a whole, they therefore own or control up to $28 trillion in assets. On my proposal, they will correspondingly pay half of the annual $2.1 trillion to keep our government afloat, and to fight foreign wars on their behalf. As the prime beneficiaries of American economic policy, this is only fair.

At a minimum, some such proposal deserves wider discussion, given that it offers massive financial benefit to fully 97% of the nation. By rights, something like this should be discussed in every political debate and on every nighttime news program. The closest thing we had was Senator Elizabeth Warren's wealth tax proposal of 2020: 2% on assets between $50 million and $1 billion, and 3% on assets over $1 billion. By my estimates, this would apply only to the top 0.1% of households (versus my 3%), and would only bring in, she says, around $275 billion annually (versus my $560 billion). It's weak, but at least a step in the right direction. And yet her proposal got almost no discussion, and virtually no endorsement.

This is unsurprising, given that our media bosses include multi-millionaire Jews like Alan Horn, Peter Rice, and Bob Chapek at Disney/ABC; David Levy, Doug Shapiro, and Ann Sarnoff at Warner/CNN; Noah Oppenheim, Robert Greenblatt, and Ron Meyer at Universal/NBC; and Shari Redstone, David Nevins, and Susan Zirinsky at Paramount/CBS. They certainly have no interest in any wealth tax, as it would hit them directly in the pocketbook. By definition, if it's bad for them, it's bad, period.

---

[19] Bloomberg Billionaires Index (2018).

[20] *The Fatal Embrace* (1993), p. 1.

[21] For details, see chapter 12.

Still, such a tax system, disproportionately falling on American Jews, would have vast implications. Think of it: A $1 trillion annual contribution from the American Jewish community, in order to provide for the health and security of all Americans. It would go a long way toward burnishing the Jews' long-besmirched image, and lessening anti-Jewish hostility. By draining away some of their excessive wealth, it would reduce their ability to meddle in government and the corporate world. It would be a boon to the US economy, lifting millions out of poverty and allowing millions more to get out from under crushing debt. It would serve as a measure of true economic justice. And it would allow for an honest, transparent, fair, and just system of taxation.

But don't hold your breath.

— 23 —

DISMANTLING JEWISH SUPREMACY

On 2 June 2020, Ben Cohen and Jerry Greenfield—the two notorious Jews of "Ben & Jerry's Ice Cream"—released a formal corporate statement entitled "*We must dismantle White supremacy*".[1] This appalling, duplicitous, and hypocritical bit of anti-White propaganda expresses their "outrage" at the deaths of George Floyd and other blacks, as a result of the "toxic seeds planted on the shores of our country in Jamestown in 1619," when the first (Jewish-traded) slaves arrived in North America. Such deaths, they claim, are "perpetuated by a culture of White supremacy." Floyd's demise "was the predictable consequence of a racist and prejudiced [American] system and culture."

Now they urge Americans "to take concrete steps to dismantle White supremacy in all its forms," calling for four specific actions: 1) Trump must "disavow White supremacists and nationalist groups" and must "commit our nation to a formal process of healing and reconciliation"; 2) Congress must formally create an anti-discrimination commission to study the situation and recommend actions; 3) a "national task force" must be created to pass laws "ending racial violence and increasing police accountability"; and 4) the Dept of Justice must "reinvigorate" its Civil Rights Division.

The horror of White supremacy will only end, they conclude, when "White America is willing to collectively acknowledge its privilege, take responsibility…and commit to creating a future steeped in justice." So, the moral here is that Floyd's death, and the deaths of virtually any black for virtually any reason over the past 400 years, is a result of White supremacy and White racism, for which all (White) Americans must make amends. The fact that many of these blacks died at the hands of non-Whites is apparently irrelevant, as are the facts behind the unique circumstances of every individual death. Rather than simply state that any criminal action, by anyone of any color, should be treated fairly under the law, the Ice Cream Jews use the present situation to slander and threaten the entire race of White Americans.

There are specific reasons why they do this. First, it is well-known that Jews are more comfortable and more effective at controlling and manipulating diverse, multiracial, and multicultural societies, than ones which are largely homogenous—and especially which are largely White. Jews succeed much more easily where they are one of many ethnic minorities.

---

[1] Published on www.benjerry.com.

In such cases, they can work hard for "minority justice," all while accruing the lion's share of benefit for themselves.

Second, Jews fear White societies more than any other—because Whites are their most formidable opponents in the struggle for social control. Thus, any actions to protect, defend, and increase the numbers of non-Whites work to their benefit. More non-Whites mean more exploitable social crises, more interracial dating and mating, and the consequent miscegenation, more crime, and therefore more decay of the hated White civilization.

Third, as a propaganda effort, such "calls" warp and confuse the public mind, causing many weak-minded people—and unfortunately many weak-minded Whites—to assume that anti-racism and an anti-White stance are the morally superior positions. Jews thereby both draw in other non-Whites to their cause and they encourage Whites *to work against their own interests* and *against their own well-being*. And with the full force of media, government, and academia behind them, they frequently succeed. We need only watch the evening news these days to see the result.

Supremacy and Corruption

Apart from the duplicitous and self-serving nature of such a statement, there is a vast truth here that is covered over and safely stashed away, never to be discussed. This is the reality of the American situation, which is a condition of *Jewish supremacy*. This Jewish supremacy, furthermore, is the root cause of many social ills in this country, and is the cause of uncounted suffering here and around the world. It is this very Jewish supremacy which must be addressed, exposed, and destroyed, if we are to get to a better state of affairs in this country.

I haven't the space here to provide an elaboration, but a few words are necessary to demonstrate the extent of this problem, and to outline a solution. First, let there be no doubt: From its beginning, the United States was a White nation. From the start, every Founding Father, and every citizen, were White. Some 1 million blacks lived here, but they were of course slaves with no civil standing. And the few thousand Jews here—most of whom were petty shopkeepers, bankers, or slave-traders—exercised little direct influence. There were no Hispanics and no Asians to speak of. Under such conditions, America flourished.

Our nation began to unravel in the mid-1800s, first with giving civil rights and then citizenship to all blacks—and indeed, to anyone born on US soil. This "birthright citizenship" of the 14th Amendment (1868) was a catastrophic development in our history; we have been paying the price ever since. Suddenly, some 6 million blacks, representing around 18% of the nation, became citizens. It was a burden, to be sure, but with no other substantial minorities, America could still progress.

Things further decayed from the late 1800s onward, as the Jewish population in the US boomed: from 250,000 in 1880, to 1.5 million in 1900, to 3.5 million in 1920. Already by 1910, Jews were able to exert considerable influence on Congress—witness the 1911 abrogation of the US-Russia Trade Treaty, which served only to promote Jewish interests.[2] From that point on, Jewish "supremacy" in American society accelerated. Jews had a prominent hand in US involvement in both World Wars[3]—drawing in our nation when we had no compelling interest in the conflicts. Jews—led by New York congressman Emanuel Celler—pushed the Johnson administration to pass the Civil Rights Act of 1964, which was another milestone in American decay. At the same time, they drove American involvement in the Vietnam War, ensuring that many White Americans would die. After the 1967 War in the Middle East, the American Jewish Lobby assumed a dominant role in society and government that it has never relinquished.

When naïve Whites or other non-Jews are first confronted with the concept of Jewish supremacism, their first instinct is to deny it. They will deny that Jews "run the media" or "control the government." And yet, a few facts easily dispel those mistaken notions. Take the media. There are currently five major media conglomerates, and each one is owned or run by Jews: *ABC/Disney* (Alan Horn, Ben Sherwood, Alan Braverman, Lowell Singer, Alan Bergman), *Warner/CNN* (John Stankey, David Levy, Jeff Zucker, Doug Shapiro, Ann Sarnoff), *NBC/Universal* (Robert Greenblatt, Bonnie Hammer, Noah Oppenheim, Ron Meyer), *21st Century Fox* (Murdoch family), and *CBS/Viacom* (Shari Redstone, David Nevins, Susan Zirinsky, David Stapf). American entertainment and American news programming are unquestionably Jewish-oriented, and serve Jewish interests.

Or consider politics. The main Jewish Lobby, AIPAC, is the dominant lobby in Washington, rivalling even the NRA and the AARP. Jewish donors give between 25% (Republicans) and 60% (Democrats) of all political funds, and thus can virtually dictate policy of their choosing. Recent US presidents—including Obama, Trump, and Biden—were all badly entangled with Jews, through family connections, political appointments, major donors, and political allies.

Other areas of society are likewise dominated, such as the high-tech sector. Jews run Facebook (Zuckerberg and Sandberg), Google (Page and Brin), Oracle (Ellison and Catz), and Dell Computer (Dell). And they play a critical role in the vast system of technological surveillance.[4]

---

[2] For a concise discussion of this abrogation, see chapter 17.

[3] See my book *The Jewish Hand in the World Wars* (2019).

[4] See, for example, Whitney Webb's article "How the CIA, Mossad, and 'the Epstein Network' are Exploiting Mass Shootings" (www.mintpressnews.com).

Once we have established the facts of Jewish supremacy, the next typical response is: "So what?" The reply to this is simple: Americans are virtual slaves to Jewish interests, and are allowing themselves to be brainwashed, degraded, and deceived in the process. Literally trillions of dollars are being diverted to Jews and their institutions, primarily from the pockets of hard-working Whites. And primarily White soldiers are fighting and dying in the American military, simply in order to make the world safe for Israel and Jews globally. The costs to society could scarcely be higher. Jewish supremacy must end, now.

Taking a cue from the Ice Cream Jews, I hereby offer my own declaration:

WE MUST DISMANTLE JEWISH SUPREMACY
Silence is Not an Option

The Black Lives Matter chaos among American cities, and throughout American society at large, is neither surprising nor unexpected. In fact, it was absolutely predictable and inevitable. In the history of humanity, there has never been a stable and successful multiracial, multicultural nation. In fact, such things were always the precursors of social decay, decline, and collapse. This was true for ancient Babylon, it was true for the Roman Empire, it was true for Austria-Hungary, it was true for the Soviet Union. And it will be true for America. Disease, economic upheaval, political corruption, social unrest, crime, moral decay—all these are inevitable in the present-day United States.

The recent fuss over George Floyd is a smokescreen. Floyd was a petty criminal caught passing fake bills; he was also apparently drunk or stoned, and was likely driving that way. Through an unfortunate series of events, he ended up dead, but there are far worse tragedies happening in this nation on a daily basis. And top of the list is *Jewish supremacy*—that unspoken scourge upon civilized humanity.

Virtually every major social, political, and economic problem faced by this nation is driven, at root, by Jewish supremacy—by the policies and dictates of wealthy and influential American Jews in government, media, commerce, and academia. Jews dominate or control every major American media corporation. They give 25% to 50% of all political donation funds, and hence are able to buy politicians; the Jewish Lobby, headed by AIPAC, dictates much of federal legislation, and has the power to destroy any politician who fails to bow down. And their wealth is astonishing; Jews constitute over half of the richest 50 Americans, and between a third and a half of the top 500. The 6 million American Jews own or control, in total, around $75 trillion. The facts of Jewish supremacy cannot be denied.

As such, Jews must assume primary responsibility for the many failings of American society—the economic exploitation of workers, the rampant drug abuse and addiction, the moral corruption of TV and cinema, the wanton manipulation and distortion of news media, the trillions of dollars spent on foreign wars for Jewish and Israeli benefit, and the large and growing presence of non-Whites in our nation. Such things are the poisonous fruit of the toxic seeds of Judaism that were planted on our shores over 400 years ago. We—White Americans—must tackle these many problems, but we also must embark upon the more complicated work of delivering justice to all those harmed by Jewish supremacy in America, especially in the past 100 years.

Today, there is an urgent need to take concrete steps to dismantle Jewish supremacy in all its forms. To this end, I call for six actions:

> First, *educate*: There is vast public ignorance on Jewish supremacy. Likewise, there is vast ignorance on the thousand-year history of Jewish malfeasance and misanthropy, of Jewish contempt and hatred for all non-Jews.[5] The facts are undeniable; they need to be widely disseminated.
>
> Second, *identify*: Prominent Jews often escape public notice because they are not obvious, and they are not outed. Religious (orthodox) Jews are relatively easy to spot, but the many secular Jews are not. Jews in media, government, business, and academia need to be called out; as the black apologists like to exclaim, we must *say their names*. Jews, half-Jews, those with Jewish spouses or children must be named and outed. It is intolerable that they circulate largely unnoticed.
>
> Third, *isolate*: We need to sanction and boycott all Jewish-dominated institutions. We must stop patronizing their corporations, their media, their technology, their universities. This action is consistent with the Boycott, Divestment, and Sanction (BDS) policy against Israel; similar actions need to be taken against all Jewish-owned or -controlled entities. Simultaneously, we need to create and support local, White-owned and operated organizations.
>
> Fourth, *quota*: Jewish overrepresentation in all fields must be circumscribed by specific quotas. At least initially, we must

---

[5] See my book *Eternal Strangers* (2020).

> limit Jewish representation to that which they exist in the US; currently, the figure is around two percent. Thus, Jews must immediately be restricted to 2% of Congressmen, 2% of tech executives, 2% of Hollywood producers and directors, 2% of university instructors. And most vitally, Jews must be restricted to just 2% of the total private wealth in the US; this will entail a massive confiscation and redistribution of Jewish wealth—much of it ill-gotten in the first place. This is only fair, and any claims to the contrary can only be deemed 'racist.'
>
> Fifth, *penalize*: American Jews must pay, literally, for their many crimes against humanity. As noted above, asset confiscation is a start. If American Jews own or control $75 trillion, but their 'fair share' is, say, $2 trillion, then we need immediate confiscation of some $73 trillion in Jewish assets.[6] Additionally, we need to reestablish the ancient idea of a "Jew tax," something implemented by the Romans after the Jewish rebellion in Jerusalem in the year 70 AD. Jewish income must be subject to a considerable tax—perhaps a flat rate of 50% on all incomes—in order to restrict their ability to regain wealth.
>
> Sixth, *evacuate*: The ultimate goal, as many prominent thinkers have realized over the centuries, is to rid the nation of its Jews. The pernicious and endemic character of Jewish corruption can truly be solved in no other way. History has proven that wherever Jews accumulate in more than a fraction of a percent of a populace, they begin to exert a corrupting influence. They cannot be restrained, they cannot be civilized, and they cannot be taught. This is a sad but eternal fact of the Jewish people. Therefore, any nation that hopes to prosper and thrive must banish them. Voluntarily or forcefully, slowly or quickly—out they must go. Away to Israel, to their native homeland.

Once Jewish supremacy and Jewish power have been destroyed in America, other problems—with blacks, with Hispanics, with Asians—can begin to be addressed. Here too, we will need a process of education, of isolation, of penalty, and ultimately of repatriation. Multiracial America will cease being multiracial, or else it will cease to exist.

---

[6] We can only imagine the economic benefits that such a windfall would bring.

Unless and until White America is willing to collectively acknowledge its responsibility for its own well-being, and to acknowledge the fundamental role of Jewish supremacy in the many crises of our nation, our problems will never end. We must use this moment to turn the tide against the Jews, to reclaim our country, and to secure, for the first time in many decades, a vastly brighter future.

— 24 —
A Thousand Points of White

In June of 2020, dissident-right writer Giles Corey published a compelling and thought-provoking essay, "American Roulette: Imagining a Dark Future and How to Deal with It".[1] Corey's piece is passionate, clear, and well-written, if a bit loosely-argued at points. Still, he makes a powerful and inspirational case, in a short space. My intent here is to build on his ideas and add some needed details. In the spirit of Corey's piece, I will be concise and blunt; the time for niceties is fast coming to an end.

Herewith is a brief outline of an argument and a strategy for establishing a functional form of White Nationalism. For sake of clarity, I will express it in a series of numbered paragraphs. Let's start with the big picture:

1) *The United States is irredeemably corrupt.* It cannot be salvaged and it cannot be saved. The entire political and economic infrastructure is lost. We have neither a democracy nor an oligarchy, but rather a Judeocracy: rule by Jewish power and Jewish money. Jews are assisted at all levels by Whites (and others) who act as their willing front-men, and who thus disguise the deeper workings of the system. Republicans, Democrats, Greens, Libertarians—they're all the same. No party has the guts to confront the Jewish power structure. The media, of course, is also hopelessly corrupted by Jewish influence; witness the battle between CNN, MSNBC, and even Fox News, to see who can display greater fealty to the Hebrews.[2] Thus we can expect nothing but biased and malicious reporting from any of them. The American system cannot be reformed; we should not even try.[3]

2) *American corruption can work to our advantage.* As the US continues on its path of decay and decline, more and more opportunities will emerge for White nationalists. The American Judeocracy will inevitably destroy itself; it's only a question of time. Jewish misanthropy and kleptomania will consume itself and the whole

---

[1] Published on www.theoccidentalobserver.net (15 June 2020).
[2] Sean Hannity of Fox is particularly pathetic in this regard. His repeated and unconditional defense of Israeli and Jewish interests is utterly appalling.
[3] Throughout the South, they have signs saying "Pray for America." What they should say is "Pray for America's destruction—and soon."

federal infrastructure in the process. However, the American system will likely not collapse in a sudden, catastrophic paroxysm. Rather, it will be a slow and steady loss of integrity, of stability, of coherence, and of credibility. This is what has happened in the latter stages of most all imperial-like political entities in history. Eventually, the political system and the ruling authorities simply lose the willpower and ability to intervene against rebels or invaders. This works massively to our benefit.

3) *White Nationalists should assist the process of decline.* The more ethnic diversity, more economic disruption, more political division, and more crime that we experience, the faster will be the process of decline. Recent events are making clear to millions of Whites that a multiracial, Jewish-run America will be a catastrophe in the future. And they can't be too happy about it.

   So, let's help the process along: More Latino and Asian immigration! More Blacks in corporate America! More Jews in Washington! More aid for Israel! More affirmative action! More street marches! Defund the police! More looting! More arson! We can use the liberal Zeitgeist against itself—use its own logic to drive it into the ground.

4) *Washington is rapidly losing the moral and political basis for effective action.* Biden's (and before him, Trump's) various stupid proclamations and (in)actions, and the paralysis in Congress, are all good signs. We are seeing federal dysfunction at all levels: in the response to the coronavirus, in various military conflicts around the globe, and in international relations. The US is being pushed around by hostile nations, and our allies—even the Jewish-dominated ones in Europe—are increasingly ignoring us. Again, this is all good news.

5) *Whites deserve, and have the right, to self-rule.* There is no good reason why Whites anywhere should submit to rule by Jews, Blacks, Hispanics, Asians, or any combination of these. This is not because such people are "inferior"; rather, every race and every ethnicity has its own values and its own culture, rooted in genetics, and these should not be imposed on unwilling Whites. Whites have the right to be proud of their values and their cultural achievements, which comprise the highest and greatest achievements in human history. Let the other races build their own nations

and their own cultures, in their own lands.[4] And let them live with the consequences.

6) *White self-governance cannot be achieved at a national level in the US—not for a century, at least.* We need to give up on Washington. The federal system needs to end, and governance rebuilt at the local level. A nation of 330 million is ungovernable, even of a single ethnicity; a multiracial nation of this size is utterly unsustainable. Perhaps someday, many decades down the road, a kind of White American coalition or confederation will be possible; but not in our lifetimes. Again, this is not bad news.

7) *Start local, start small.* Given that there will not be a federal White nationalist movement or party, we need to look for local or state-level groups advocating White self-rule—or at first, White identity and White self-interest. Here's one suggestion: Start a local "White Lives Matter" group. This process can be very small and very simple. *One person* can reserve a room in a library, school, or church basement. *One person* can reach out to friends, spread the word on social media, or print up flyers to post around town. Pick a day and time, book a room, advertise—and see who comes. Even a small turnout is a start. We ought not forget that, in Germany many years ago, National Socialism began with weekly meetings of just seven or so men ("the same old seven," lamented Hitler)[5]. If you get seven at first, consider it a victory.

8) *"It's just a club."* At first, any such "WLM" group will likely be a mere discussion group: politics, news, local developments. Think of it as a social club: like-minded Whites getting together, on a regular basis, to discuss issues of common interest. This alone, as innocuous as it might seem, is a radical step in today's climate. The sheer existence of a WLM group will likely draw negative attention; be prepared, stay cool, stay calm, stay rational. *You have a right to your own self-interest.* Use negative publicity to your advantage. Remember: Anyone who accepts BLM but rejects WLM is an evil "racist."

9) *Become politically active.* As the group grows, establish some structure: take attendance, collect modest annual dues, have offic-

---

[4] CNN reported on the nation of Ghana, which is inviting Black Americans to "come home" and resettle there. An excellent plan, for all concerned!

[5] *Mein Kampf*, volume one, section 12.11.

ers. Watch out for spies and moles; they are inevitable, but can be managed. Once the group is stable, then you are in a position to engage in local politics. Write op-eds or post things on a local blog. Make yourselves known; be open, be public.

10) *Have definable and clear local objectives, moving toward a White society.* It doesn't matter if you live in a city, suburb, or rural area: establish a group, meet regularly, and get engaged. If your area is already mostly or all White, there should be little resistance. If it is majority-minority, consider moving. If your area, like mine, is a mostly-White suburb but with encroaching non-whites, *put up resistance.* The larger objective is for White self-determination and self-rule, and this starts by making non-whites realize that *they are no longer welcome here.* Pick a local geographic region—neighborhood, city, or county—and *declare it White.* Don't hold a vote, don't look for a majority—*just declare it.* How outrageous!—a dozen (say) local folks declare their neighborhood or city to be White! And then they have the nerve to say, publicly, that non-whites are not welcome, and should leave! Revolutionary! But that's what it takes. No ugliness, no violence, no cross-burnings. Just a polite and civil statement: *This is now a White area, and non-whites are no longer welcome.*

11) *Develop a local identity.* This will likely mean creating your own distinctive logo or slogan. Put them on stickers, letterhead, flyers, T-shirts, flags, yard signs. Spread them around. You want to see these things on cars, houses, neighborhood kiosks, etc. Even people who won't attend a meeting might be sympathetic and put a sign in their window. Public visibility has a tremendous effect.

Let me pause here a moment. By the above simple and elementary acts, Whites everywhere can take concrete steps to reassert their right to self-governance. Groups need not adhere to any specific ideology, nor align with any particular White movement. To be counted under the broad heading of "White nationalist," groups need only endorse something like the follow general precepts:

- The White race is of inherent value to humanity, and as such deserves protection and defense.
- Whites have an intrinsic right to self-rule and self-governance.
- Whites everywhere are under threat, due to (a) declining numbers, (b) declining physical, mental, and moral health, and (c) loss of

political autonomy and self-government. These threats are various and complex, and require action on several fronts to address.
- The chief threat to White well-being comes from the global Jewish lobby, which has an inherent interest in seeing a general decline in White prosperity and a loss in White political power. Jews must therefore be confronted and challenged at all levels of society.
- All humans are, by nature, best suited to live in social and environmental settings from which they evolved—societies that are broadly uni-racial and monocultural. Humans have little or no evolutionary experience living with diverse races or ethnicities, and doing so causes inevitable problems. Therefore, racial and cultural diversity have profound negative effects on society.
- The only long-term solution for many present-day problems is to restore human society to its natural and original conditions—uni-racial and monocultural, broadly speaking. This entails political separation and/or expatriation of minority peoples.
- As a rough provisional goal, White regions of self-governance ought to aim for a minimum of 95% White populations, with all non-White minorities numbering, collectively, less than 5%. Jewish numbers ought to be *severely limited*; perhaps 0.1% or less.
- Only Whites will be fully enfranchised—that is, possess the right to vote, and to hold public office. All others will have minimal civil rights, perhaps on par with a foreign tourist today—basic legal protections, but little more.

Most any sane White person who wishes to live in a stable, secure, and prosperous community ought to accept these points. Those who do not are likely either (a) paid to oppose them, or (b) brainwashed by our present Judeo-centric culture and academia. The brainwashed can be educated, but the sell-outs, especially the White ones, are utterly contemptible; they deserve the harshest punishment we can muster.

Additionally, we need not worry excessively about who "counts" as White. In the vast majority of cases, it is obvious: those whose ancestry derives from indigenous European peoples and nations. There are ambiguous cases, such as Ukraine, Belarus, and Russia, that deserve more discussion. More important, though, is who is *not* White: Jews are not White, despite their own frequent proclamations to the contrary. Arabs or other Middle Easterners are not White. Hispanics and Latinos are not White. 'White' is not simply a matter of skin color; it is also a question of heritage, of worldview, of culture, and of values. Don't be fooled by light skin or blond hair.[6]

This said, we can console ourselves in the fact that America is still a predominantly White nation, and will be so for many years to come. White Americans currently number about 195 million, in a nation of nearly 330 million. And even though our numbers are projected to decline slightly in the coming decades, we will still long be the numerically-dominant ethnicity. Hispanics here could top 100 million by 2050, but that is roughly half of White numbers; Blacks will not number more than 55 million or so, and Asians not more than 45 million. And we mustn't forget that American Jews number only some 6 million. One of our strengths is our numbers, and we must always bear this in mind. Jews and other non-Whites certainly know it, and they fear it. Large numbers of active Whites spell doom for them.

Still, based on combined effects, America will be a 'majority-minority' nation by 2045, and coalitions of non-Whites, led by Jews, could soon exercise even more power than they do at present. And the trends for the end of this century are even more dire. This is unacceptable, hence the urgent need for White action on many fronts.

Let me conclude with a few final points, in our drive for White nationalism.

12) *Gradually assume more power, quietly and nonviolently.* As local White or WLM movements grow, and as intimidated non-Whites move out, White groups will be able to assume a greater civic role, just by default. Volunteer groups can provide social services, self-police, and participate in local schools. White nationalists will then naturally come to gain power in local politics, exercising yet more autonomy. All the while, the autonomous zones should continue to grow, by declaration.

13) *The biggest threat will come from local and state police, and potentially state National Guards.* Small, decentralized White autonomous zones generally need not fear the feds. Yes, we all remember Waco and Ruby Ridge, but those were anomalies of the past. With a degraded federal justice system, and with (hopefully) dozens of White zones popping up around the country, the feds will be in no position to confront them. The larger threat, I think, is from local and state authorities. Fortunately, these groups are now being alien-

[6] Mixed-race individuals are also problematic, but again, they are a small minority. Roughly speaking, we can say that anyone with three-quarters or more of White heritage counts as White, presuming that they do not adhere to non-White values or culture.

ated on a large scale. As current policemen resign in disgrace, less and less qualified people will take their places, resulting in growing inefficiency and incompetence. Eventually they will be unable to, or chose not to, take action against peaceful civilian groups who only seek self-governance. Remember, the goal here, at least initially, is to create White autonomous zones which are self-governing and relatively independent from state or federal authorities. The central tactic is to 'walk away slowly,' rather like you might do when confronted by a maniac with a large knife. Don't antagonize, don't threaten—just walk away.

14) *Undermine Jewish financial power*. Jewish power derives almost exclusively from their vast wealth; 6 million American Jews control some $75 trillion in assets. But this is denominated in corrupt, inflated, debt-ridden, and intrinsically valueless US dollars. Therefore, we need to declare the US dollar *worthless*, and move our financial assets into new, local currencies—perhaps something we might whimsically call 'Aryan Bucks.' AB's could, by law, be held and spent only by Whites. They would be declared worthless and illegal in the hands of Jews or other non-Whites. At first, both currencies would have to circulate in parallel, but as quickly as possible, Whites would want to migrate to their own financial system. The political and economic benefits from this step alone would be enormous.[7]

15) *Accelerate growth of autonomous zones*. As White zones grow, and as disaffected Whites move into the newly-declared regions, the remaining areas will grow darker in complexion. This will only accelerate the decline of multiracial America. Ideally, a positive feedback situation will emerge in which Whites rapidly move into local safe-zones as the other regions collapse. This makes expansion all the easier.

    Numerous local White zones, incidentally—meaning, several in each state or large city—make for a much more practical strategy than, say, picking a few large rural areas. There aren't many White Montanans or Californians ready to move to rural Arkansas, but they might be willing to move an hour or two away to a local zone in a familiar area.

[7] The idea of local currency is well-established in the US. Wikipedia lists over 100 active local currencies.

16) *Be prepared to fight, as a last resort.* If we are smart, we can achieve nearly everything we want non-violently. But sadly, that may not always be the case. Therefore, as Corey states, we will need to be armed. At present, something like 35 million White households own at least one gun; presumably, most by the man in the family. So let's say we have 35 million armed White males in this country—an awesome force, indeed. If there is one thing Jews and Blacks fear more than White men, it's White men with guns. I wouldn't hesitate to state that armed White American civilians constitute the most formidable fighting power on Earth. No one—not even the Jewish-run American military—could defeat them. If the US military can't subdue a few thousand low-IQ Muslims in Iraq and Afghanistan, they haven't a prayer against millions of pissed-off Whites. This is our ace-up-the-sleeve. But we need to use it judiciously.

Ideally, White autonomous zones would pop up like mushrooms around the country: a few in each major city, several in the rural areas of each state. Under good circumstances, they might grow and join together, combining their collective power. These "thousand points of White," as I like to think of them, would pose an insurmountable problem for federal and local authorities, especially if they were peaceful, and especially at the early "club" phase. Being decentralized, there is no single pressure point for the feds to squeeze; they would have to address multiple, simultaneous local issues at once. And if there were still on-going riots, or economic chaos, or some new pandemic…well, the authorities will quickly reach the end of their rope.

And then we win.

— 25 —
Christianity: The Great Jewish Hoax

At 2.1 billion people, Christianity is the largest religion on Earth. And yet, not a fraction of a percent of these people understand even the basic facts of their own so-called religion. If they did, they would be utterly appalled. Their entire religion is a fraud; it is based upon Jewish lies and Jewish duplicity to an extent that is astonishing. My objective here, in this short essay, is to highlight the basics of the Judeo-Christian hoax in an effort to awaken the more open-minded Christians out there, and hopefully to raise their awareness of ongoing harm caused by this corrupt and soul-destroying theology.

Though we obviously can't know for sure, there are very strong reasons for thinking that Jesus' birth, his life story, and in fact the entire Christian project are Jewish constructions. I will argue here that most or all the Christian story is mythology, fabrication, and yes, a lie. It was a kind of fraud perpetrated, originally, on the superstitious pagan masses. And they bought it—hook, line, and sinker. And millions continue to buy it, to this day, two millennia later. How this could have happened is one of the most important and least known stories in Western civilization.

Origins and Miracles

Let's start by thinking about what we know, and what we don't know, about the origins of the Christian story. Unsurprisingly, it turns out that the latter is much larger than the former.

We are told that Jesus was born around the year 3 BC. The star of Bethlehem—so central to the Christmas story—was the first Christian miracle. It appeared "in the East," moved through the sky, and hovered over the manger so that the three Magi could find it. Various attempts have been made to explain this "star," including a rare planetary alignment, an unusually bright Jupiter, a comet, or a supernova. This is almost certainly nonsense. We have no independent confirmation of any unusual celestial events around that time, and even if we did, it doesn't help the story. In no case could anyone use a light in the sky to "find" a particular village like Bethlehem, let alone a specific manger.

Jesus allegedly began his ministry when he was "about 30" (Luke 3:23), and it continued for three years, until he was crucified around the year 30 AD. During these three years, he preached to "great throngs" of people. He allegedly performed some 36 miracles, depending on the details, which included exorcisms (around 7), resurrections of the dead (3), manipulations of nature (9), and healings (18). Two of these miracles—the two separate 'fishes and loaves' episodes (Mark 6:30 and 8:1)—were performed in front of at least 4,000 and 5,000 people, respectively: hence a total of more than 9,000 witnesses. And he had 12 apostles following his every move.

But the main problem with all these miracles is this: *We have no independent confirmation.* How could it be that 9,000 people witnessed the fishes-and-loaves miracle, for example, and yet not one of them wrote anything? (Or at least, nothing that survived.) Nor reported it to someone who could write? Why did the 12 apostles—who were more convinced of Jesus' divinity than anyone else—never write anything? Why, in fact, do they disappear from history as soon as Jesus dies? It does no good to cite Paul; he was *not* one of the 12 apostles, and never knew Jesus personally. And it does no good to cite Acts, which allegedly provides facts on a few of the apostles; this document was written by the same anonymous author of the Gospel of Luke, and thus provides no independent confirmation.

What about the Romans? They were the ruling power in Palestine, arriving six decades before the alleged birth of Christ. They were acknowledged experts at documentation. We have records of military battles, taxes, foreign trade, political events, and other such things, all from the early first century. We have coins; we have papyrus fragments; we have stone engravings. We have the "Pilate Stone" that confirms the existence of Roman governor Pontius Pilate, during the years 26 to 36 AD. And yet we have *not one piece* of Roman documentation mentioning Jesus, his miracles, or his following, from the time in which Jesus lived. This is clearly absurd. As governor, Pilate would surely have heard many of the Jesus stories, and would surely have written many times to Rome, asking for advice, more troops, etc. Yet we have nothing at all from Pilate nor any Roman authorities.

What about the Roman writers? There were many who lived at that time, or shortly thereafter, and thus had an opportunity to comment on Jesus. They were major figures in the Roman world, among the brightest and most perceptive men of the age: Apion, Seneca, Petronius, Quintilian, and Plutarch, among others. But we find not one word from any of them. In fact, the earliest Roman reference to Jesus is from the historian Tacitus, in his work *Annals*—written in the year 115. And then, only a mere two sentences.

How could it be that the ruling authorities and experts—Pilate and the Roman writers—failed completely to document the coming of the Son of God? All of them? "Perhaps they did, and all such records are lost to history," says the Christian apologist. But this would have been incredibly bad luck: The greatest event in history, and every shred of contemporary documentation is lost to us? Impossible.

Jesus the Jew

The lack of contemporaneous evidence is so striking that we could legitimately conclude that any such "Jesus" never existed at all—that he was an outright literary construction from whole cloth. But for reasons that I explain below, I suspect that there was a kernel of truth in the Jesus story. I think it was most likely that an ordinary man, a "Jesus of Nazareth," most likely did live at that time. He likely was a Jewish rabbi, a defender of the impoverished Jews, and likely a rebel against Roman rule. And he likely did get crucified. But beyond that, we know literally nothing reliable about his life or thinking.

If Jesus the man—not the 'son of God'—did exist, then it is unquestionable that he was a Jew. There is much evidence for this in the New Testament, which I take to contain, as well, a kernel of truth underneath the vast fraud. (Frauds with a kernel of truth are always more convincing, after all.)

Consider what the Bible tells us about Jesus. His mother, Mary, was a Jewess: she was a woman "born under the law [of Judaism]" (Gal 4:4). And she was a blood relative of Elizabeth, of the tribe of Levi (Luke 1:5, 1:36). Jesus' father, Joseph, was of the "House of David" (Luke 1:27). Both parents "performed everything according to the [Jewish] law of the Lord" (Luke 2:39).

Jesus himself is repeatedly called 'Rabbi' (Mark 9:5, 11:21, 14:45; Matt 26:25; John 1:38, 1:49; 3:2). He celebrated Passover (John 2:13). The Gospel of Matthew opens with these words: "The book of the genealogy of Jesus Christ, son of David, son of Abraham." We read in Hebrews that "it is evident that our Lord was descended from Judah" (7:14). He regularly attended the local synagogue (Luke 4:16). Jesus himself told the people that he came "to fulfill the [Jewish] law and the [Jewish] prophets" (Matt 5:17). And of course everyone thought of him as "king of the Jews" (Matt 2:2; John 19:3).

This much, then, is clear: Jesus, Joseph, Mary, along with all Jesus' friends, acquaintances, and disciples, were Jews. This is precisely why Nietzsche, commenting on this situation, said, "The first thing to be remembered [about Christianity], if we do not wish to lose the scent here, is that we are among Jews" (*Antichrist*, sec. 44). Indeed.

This being the case, we would expect that, at the very least, that Jewish scholars of the time would comment extensively on this miracle-man who emerged in their own community. But no. As it happens, not a single Jewish scholar of Jesus' time, nor for decades afterward, makes even a single documented remark on this new Christian movement. For example, Philo of Alexandria was a famous Jewish philosopher who lived from 25 BC to 50 AD. He wrote extensively, volumes of which have survived, but never mentioned a Jesus of Nazareth, son of God.

As it happens, one Jewish writer did eventually mention him: Josephus (37-100 AD). His work, *Antiquities of the Jews*, briefly refers twice to Jesus and the Christians; but it wasn't written until the year 95—some 60 years after the crucifixion. His earlier work, *The Jewish War*, circa 75 AD, has no mention at all of the "son of God." Something is clearly not right with the traditional story.

The Plot Thickens

If we temporarily disregard the writings of Paul (circa 50 to 70 AD) and the four Gospels, we see that the few lines by Josephus, in the year 95, are the very first non-Christian references to Jesus. And we have to go all the way to Tacitus, in the year 115, to get the first Roman mention of the Christian movement. Such a thing is absolutely impossible, if Jesus, miracle-working son of God, actually existed. Either "Jesus of Nazareth" was so inconsequential that no one of his day, or even decades after his death, bothered to mention him. Or else he never existed. There is no other reasonable conclusion.

Given the utter lack of independent confirmation of *all* major aspects of the Christian story—the star of Bethlehem, the miracles, the crucifixion, the resurrection, the apostles—we can conclude only one thing: *the story was made up*. It was a deliberate and willful fabrication. And yet, *it was presented as the truth*. The conclusion is clear: *somebody lied.*

This raises some important questions: Who lied? When did they do it? And why? We have some clues that may provide answers. Our first main suspect is Paul (aka Saul) of Tarsus, the Jewish Pharisee, whose letters are the earliest known documentation on Christianity. Good Saint Paul—first liar of Christianity. I will return to his story shortly.

The most egregious lies, though, occur in the four Gospels. Consider this question: When, reasonably speaking, would someone have documented in writing the life and sayings of Jesus? Probably during his adult life—that is, roughly 25 to 30 AD—or at least, immediately upon his death and resurrection. Surely not more than a few years later. But this is not what happened. The earliest Christian writings, the letters of Paul, weren't written until 50 AD. The first of the four Gospels, Mark, wasn't written until 70 AD. Matthew and Luke, not until 85 AD. And the Gospel of John, around 95 AD.[1] These are *decades* after Jesus' death—40 years, at a

[1] Dates based on standard expert consensus.

minimum. Why wait so long? And how accurate could they have been, with so much time having gone by?

We have no good answers. Unfortunately, the liars who wrote the Gospels are unknown to us. Whoever they were, they were not apostles, and they certainly did not know Jesus personally. They were, however, almost certainly *Jews*. They had extensive knowledge of Judaism, Jewish tradition, and the Jewish Old Testament. Their label as 'Christian' was strictly a name; by birth, ethnicity, and blood, Paul and the Gospel writers were unquestionably Jewish. And they constructed the Christian story that we know today.

The final question then is: Why did they lie? What was their motive?

"They never would have lied," interrupts the Christian apologist. "Christians were persecuted by the Romans, and it would have been madness, if not fatal, to promote Christianity." But of course, *all* the Jews were *already* persecuted. The Jews of Palestine were in constant conflict with their Roman governors. They developed a deep-seated and visceral hatred of the White Aryan Romans. The elite Jews hoped, ultimately, to drive them out and regain power over the region—a power they held prior to the Roman invasion of 63 BC. Both the (few) 'Christian' Jews and (many) 'Judaic' Jews were in constant opposition to Rome, and were thus constantly oppressed. It was neither better nor worse to be a Christian.

But this situation, in fact, gives us a clue to the possible motive. The local Jewish tribes would have been hugely overwhelmed by the invading Romans. Jews were vicious fighters—recall the Biblical extermination of the Canaanites in the 1200s BC—but they were no match for the Roman Empire. They would have bitterly resented Roman rule, and sought all possible means to undermine it. Military force was not really a viable option, but various guerilla operations could cause some damage. And there is evidence that Jewish factions fought back, at least from the first decade BC.[2] But one can imagine that such actions would have had little lasting effect. Better options were needed.

Recall that the Jews were a minority in Palestine at that time—as, of course, were the Romans. The majority consisted of the indigenous Palestinian masses, along with any incidental Egyptians, Syrians, Phoenicians, Persians, Greeks, and so on, who lived in the region. The masses were neither Roman nor Jewish. And of course, they weren't yet Muslim; that religion would not exist for some 600 years. They would have been a grab-bag of pagan traditions: Zoroastrian, cults of Adonis and Mithras, Sibylline cults, and various sun-worshippers. These sects were generally ill-defined, superstitious, and highly mythological in nature.

---

[2] The so-called *sicarii* were basically Jewish assassins who attacked Roman soldiers and government officials.

The Jews knew this. And they also knew that, in order to make an impact on Roman rule, they would have to get the superstitious masses on their side. But this was a big problem. The masses were not intrinsically anti-Roman. In fact, more likely the contrary. From their viewpoint, when the Romans moved in, it was more or less a change in government. And for the good: the masses generally disliked the Jews anyway, and the Romans brought with them many advancements in civilization. So the Jews had a big problem: How to win the masses over to their side, and turn them against Rome?

Clearly they could not make them 'Jewish.' Judaism wouldn't permit it, the ethnic and racial exclusivity of the Jews wouldn't allow it, and the masses would never go for it, even if they could. All of Judaic tradition from the Torah onward was geared towards manipulating and exploiting the inferior Gentiles. The Jews would never have dreamt of mass conversion.

Therefore, something else was required: a new way, a new outlook, a new worldview—something to subtly and perhaps subconsciously bring the masses into opposition with the Romans, and on the side of the Jews. Not Judaism, but something *Jewish in essence*. A new story, a new moral system, and yes, a new religion: Christianity.

A New Religion

This was likely the thinking of Paul and his small band of followers, which may have included Peter, Luke, and Mark.[3] To win over the masses, they would need to construct a new mythology, one that would both entice and frighten—a carrot and a stick, as it were. To be successful, it would have to be both anti-Roman, in some sense, and yet rooted in Jewish values. Ideally it would also draw on pagan traditions and concepts, to make for easy assimilation. And finally, it must ultimately weaken, not strengthen, the masses; there certainly was no wish to create some Frankensteinian monster. All in all, a challenging task, to say the least.

Paul would start with God—not the Roman or Greek conception, not the pagan gods, but the Jewish God, Jehovah. The masses would have to worship the Jewish God. But this deity was distant and abstract; indeed, according to the Jews' own rule, no graven image was permitted. Such a god would not work for the masses. They needed something tangible, something concrete, something they could touch, feel, and love. They needed *a man*: God incarnate, one who loved them as much as they should love him. This man would prove his love by giving his life—for them, for their eternal life, for their "salvation" from this world of woe. It was the

[3] Again, these are just names of otherwise anonymous writers. We know almost nothing of their true identity.

ultimate sacrifice. Who could fail to revere such a man? And all the better, if he was a Jew.

This man, this son of God, this God himself, would need a name—a *common* name: Jesus. He would have to have lived in a small provincial town: Nazareth. (Harder to verify things this way.) He would have to be born in an even smaller and more obscure place: Bethlehem. Befitting a god, he would need a miraculous, virgin birth—to a Jewish woman, of course. He would have to play the role of "savior." This was a clever double entendre: saving the masses from eternal damnation, and saving the Jews from the Romans. To ensure no mortal remains, the story would have to end with a vanishing of the body. To boost credibility, it would be interwoven with factual people and places—just enough truth to make it seem believable. This suggests that maybe Paul took a real Jew, Jesus, who really got himself crucified, and turned him, years later, into the Messiah and son of God.

The final step would be to place the whole story at least 20 years in the past: near enough to be current and yet far enough to be hard to verify. This would explain why the earliest of Paul's letters—Galatians and 1 Thessalonians—date to around the year 50. And it is consistent with the fact that we have absolutely no evidence at all of Jesus or the Christian story prior to that date, from any source whatsoever.

God, Jesus, eternal life in heaven—these were the carrots. What about the stick? What is the fate of those who refuse to believe in the Jesus story? We know the answer: *hell*. Hell—defined as a place of permanent torment for the wicked sinners and unbelievers—seems to have been a Jewish innovation. The Old Testament, surprisingly, contains nothing like this. It does have a related term, 'Sheol,' but this is simply the afterlife and not a dedicated place of punishment, in contrast to a heaven. Greek and Roman mythology, on the other hand, had Tartarus: a hell-like place in the underworld, reserved for those deserving punishment. It seems that the New Testament writers borrowed the idea but renamed it 'Gehenna' or 'Hades'—both translated as 'hell.' For Paul and friends, dying wasn't frightful enough. It had to be hell-fire, eternal flames, lake of fire, and eternal torment for the non-believers (Mark 9:43; Matt 5:22; Luke 16:23). Only this could scare the superstitious and unthinking masses into their welcoming arms.

Finally and most importantly, there was the moral component. This "Jesus" had to proclaim values that would turn the masses away from Rome and toward the Jews, all while weakening them. "Salvation is of the Jews," after all (John 4:22). Great and powerful Rome would be represented as evil, sin, corrupting power, sensuality, worldliness—the devil. Jesus, the Jewish rabbi, is peace-loving, blessed, humble, holy—innocence itself. The good Christian is an innocent lamb, just as Jesus himself is "the lamb of God" (John 1:29). The Christian should "love thy neighbor"—that is, the Jew, neighbor for centuries, and not the Roman intruder. Meek, mild, and timid, he will "inherit the Earth"—someday. Eyes thus fixed on the glorious afterlife, following herd-like after their Jewish shepherd Jesus, the Christian masses turn away from Rome. The Romans become sinful heathens, non-believers, devil worshippers. At this point, the moral victory is complete. Political victory is not far behind.

Victory—Three Centuries Later

And victory was indeed achieved, though it took a few centuries. Paul died sometime during the first Jewish rebellion of 66-70 AD, and so never lived to see the fruit of his efforts. The so-called 12 apostles and the anonymous Gospel writers were gone by the early 100s. By that time, however, the doctrine—"cult," actually, as the Romans put it—had spread to the masses. Very quickly, Christianity ceased to be a Jewish movement, and became dominated by non-Jews. The most prominent early Christians—Clement of Rome, Ignatius of Antioch, Polycarp, Quadratus, Papias, Marcion—all seem to have been Gentiles. Not understanding the origins of the story, and not comprehending the Jewish penchant for revenge against Rome, the naïve Gentiles accepted it as literal truth. A new religion was born.

Being now dominated by non-Jews, Christianity quickly developed a self-conception as a religion that was 'different' from Judaism. A tension emerged: yes, Jesus, Mary, Paul, Peter, and so on were Jews; yes, Jehovah was God; yes, Jews were "the chosen people"; but still…Jews never did accept Jesus as their savior. They didn't believe in hell. They never came to church. And in any case, their racial exclusivity and obnoxious customs and social mores made them as detested as ever. Thus we find the classic love-hate relationship emerging early in Christian history. Already with Melito of Sardis, circa 160 AD, we find anti-Jewish comments. They appear again in Tertullian (ca. 200) and Hippolytus (ca. 220). And they become explicit and harsh in Gregory of Nyssa, Chrysostom, and Jerome, around 375.[4]

All the while, the Christian "cult" spread throughout the Empire. By the late 200s it reached into the upper echelons of Roman society. In 313, Emperor Constantine himself converted. And in 380, Theodosius made Christianity the official state religion. Victory was assured. Having been eaten away from the insides, the great Roman Empire was now on its last legs. And indeed, it fractured and collapsed just 15 years later, in 395. With that, the hated Romans disappeared from Palestine. The goal was achieved. Paul won in the end. And he continues to win to this day.

---

[4] For details, see my book *Eternal Strangers* (2020).

An Old Story, Still Unknown

This, then, is the likely origins of Christianity. Obviously we can't know for certain, but such an account does accord with the facts, and does so better than any alternative. Something happened in those early decades of the first century, but it certainly was not the coming of the Son of God and his miraculous story—all of which are completely unsubstantiated. The Christian story was a first-century construction, a fable, a hoax, one that eventually gained traction as literal truth. The known origins of the fable lie in the Jewish community, and they furthermore had every motive to concoct such a thing. In the end, it served them well.

As radical and shocking as this alternate account may seem, it has been around, in various forms, for many years. Already by 1769, Baron d'Holbach's *Ecce Homo* argued for the fictional nature of Christianity. Another early writer to deconstruct the traditional story was German theologian David Strauss, whose work *Das Leben Jesu* ('The Life of Jesus,' 1835) challenged the divinity of Christ. The arguments came to a head in the work of Nietzsche (*On the Genealogy of Morals* and *Antichrist*, both circa 1888) and Albert Schweitzer (*Quest of the Historical Jesus*, 1906).

Nietzsche's critique is particularly incisive. For him, the victory of Christian values over the far superior Greco-Roman values was an utter tragedy for Western civilization. In a sense, we have yet to recover. Paul and his band of "little ultra-Jews" (*Antichrist*, sec. 44) were ultimately able to defeat the Romans, and to bring their servile Judeo-Christian moral system to power in Rome itself. This is proven by the fact that Rome, the former center of the civilized world, became the global head of this new religion—a religion steeped in Jews. Nietzsche is brutally explicit:

> Just think of who it is that people bow down to today in Rome itself, as the personification of all the highest values—and not only in Rome, but in almost half the earth, everywhere people have become merely tame or want to become tame—in front of three Jews, as we know, and one Jewess (Jesus of Nazareth, the fisherman Peter, the carpet-maker Paul, and the mother of the aforementioned Jesus, named Mary). This is very remarkable: without doubt, Rome has been conquered. (*Genealogy*, I.16)

In worshipping the Jew, and in accepting the Jewish lie, the Christian becomes a virtual Jew; in fact, he becomes *more Jewish than the Jews themselves*:

> In Christianity, all of Judaism, a several-century-old Jewish preparatory training and technique of the most serious kind,

> attains its ultimate mastery as the art of lying in a holy manner. The Christian, the *ultima ratio* of the lie, is the Jew once more—even three times a Jew. (*Antichrist*, sec. 44)

"I don't care about all that," says the apologist, now grasping for straws. "No one can really know what happened back then. And in any case, Jesus' life and teachings give us a wonderful guide for an ethical life. His story just makes me feel good." Really? Does it really not matter that we have, not 'a little' evidence for Jesus, not 'conflicting' evidence, but rather *no evidence at all?* Does the obvious plausibility of a Jewish lie not matter? Can it really lead to good outcomes and a noble life, if you live according to a lie? Is the factual truth or falsehood of the Christian story really irrelevant?

"And anyway, how could it be that millions of people were fooled into believing a lie, for so many years?" But of course, humanity has been fooled on many occasions. For centuries, we believed that the material world was composed of just four elements: fire, air, water, and earth. For centuries, we believed that the stars were attached to a gigantic celestial sphere that rotated around the Earth. For centuries, we believed in, and burned, witches. We believed in all manner of ghosts, goblins, spirits, fairies, and demons. Mythology is very powerful, especially one like Christianity with such a potent carrot and stick. But if all those other beliefs are now accepted as false, why not the Christian myth?

Finally: "If this alternate account is so plausible, how come we don't read about it in school, or hear it discussed in the media?" This is hardly surprising. It's no wonder that we don't hear much about this version of events. Christians are obviously too embarrassed to examine such inconvenient facts, and in any case are, in recent years, all too anxious to appease their Jewish brethren. Jews certainly aren't going to bring it up; as "artful liars" (Hitler) and "great masters of the lie" (Schopenhauer), it makes them look mighty bad. Academia is too Jewish and too politically-correct to mess with such a touchy subject. And the corporate world sees no profit in it. Better to let sleeping Christians lie.

Any rational and objective person must come to just one conclusion: that Christianity is a Jewish hoax, conceived to demoralize and cripple the hated Gentile masses, as a way of getting even with Aryan Rome. It has no basis in fact, and no contemporaneous evidence; it is illogical and indeed idiotic ("God sent *himself* down here, and then *killed himself*, because he loves us"[!]); and it keeps White and Gentile masses absorbed in a fairy-tale world until the day they die.

Christians! Your lives are a fraud. Paul and his fellow Jews pulled a colossal hoax on you, and present-day Jews are only too happy to perpetuate this fraud. And you pay the price, every single day.

— 26 —
DISSECTING TUCKER CARLSON

For many on the dissident right, Fox News' primetime anchor Tucker Carlson is a kind of hero. He's pro-Trump and anti-liberal. He comes off as a true ("paleo") conservative, and rails against the neo-con agendas of the dominant Right. He calls out attacks on Whites, both physical and ideological. He exposes lies and hypocrisy in the liberal mainstream media, especially at CNN and MSNBC. He is blunt, funny, and smart. What more could a White alt-righter hope for?

Lots, it turns out.

Night after night, Carlson manages to pull off a remarkable feat: He manages to criticize the self-serving lies and hypocrisy of the Left with an opposing but, in its own way, misleading and deficient presentation. This is no small task. He and his crew of scriptwriters must put in hours of work each day, to prepare for his nightly one-hour performances. And surely they have their own in-house censors and ideological gatekeepers who must approve all final topics, themes, wording, and guest-lists. All these things impose limitations on what can be said.

But they succeed. Carlson's Fox team is to be congratulated on achieving their goals. Much of what they produce is enlightening and important. But unfortunately, they are to be equally condemned for all their implicit biases, shallow analysis, and vital omissions. In what follows, I will attempt to dissect Carlson and his crew, in order to lay bare both the insights and the deceptions that he offers up each evening.

Let me start with his upbringing and family background. Now, in general, I try to avoid assigning blame for an individual's faults to his past or his family. People are, for the most part, responsible adults, and must be held personally responsible for their own actions. But in this case, Carlson's family history reveals a fairly lengthy tale of woe, malfeasance, and assorted immoralities; surely this has some bearing on his beliefs and actions as an adult. At a minimum, it helps us to better understand the man and his motivations.

Tucker Swanson McNear Carlson was born in 1969 in San Francisco to Dick Carlson and Lisa McNear Lombardi. Both parents led troubled lives. Dick Carlson was born in Boston in 1941, to a 21-year-old male and a 15-year-old girl—a situation that today would qualify as statutory rape. Ashamed of her pregnancy, the girl gave baby Dick up for adoption. At the age of two, he was adopted by the Carlson family and took their name. Moving to California in his 20s, Dick became a freelance journalist, eventually becoming involved in a libelous story against the mayor of San Francisco. In the 1970s, Dick tried his hand at banking, but was soon involved in a political patronage scandal and accusations of dubious lending practices.[1] In the 1980s, after a failed run for mayor of San Diego, he was appointed chief propagandist (though of course they didn't call it that) at the Voice of America radio station, under Reagan. In 1991, George H. W. Bush appointed him ambassador to Seychelles. Today, at age 79, he has settled into a comfortable retirement.

As for Tucker's mother, Lisa, she was evidently a very—shall we say—flaky person. She married Dick in 1967, gave birth to Tucker in 1969 and then another boy in 1973, and then simply abandoned the family in 1975, when Tucker was six. Only a very disturbed woman would up and leave her husband and two young children for no apparent reason. Lisa's whereabouts since that time remain a mystery.

Dick would eventually marry another troubled woman, Patricia Swanson, in 1979, when Tucker was 10 years old. Fortuitously, Patricia was an heiress to the Swanson Foods fortune, built up in the 1930s and 1940s by her grandfather, Carl Swanson. Her marriage to Dick was her third; at 18, she married a Jew, Howard Feldman, only to divorce a year later, and a second marriage ended in 1975. At any rate, Dick at least "married into money," attaining by current standards a modest fortune. As they approach 80, both will soon be passing along a fair amount of money to Tucker.

In any case, Tucker led a privileged life from birth, despite his parental troubles. He grew up in the wealthy community of La Jolla, California, and was schooled in Switzerland and at the prestigious Trinity College in Connecticut, eventually earning a degree in history. Drawing on his father's connections, he held various reporting and journalistic positions, eventually gaining his first television stint with CNN in 2000. Tucker jumped to MSNBC in 2005, and finally to Fox in 2009. In 2016, he was given his own program at that station.

Thus, by all accounts, Tucker is doing quite well for himself these days. His show on Fox has earned the highest ratings *ever* for a cable news show. His salary is in the neighborhood of $6 million per year,[2] and his net worth is variously estimated at $20 million to $30 million. At least his critiques of the wealthy corrupt of our country are well-sourced, given that he himself is a member of the very club that he loves to lambast.

---

[1] Dick Carlson was eventually interviewed by Mike Wallace for *60 Minutes*, as part of the larger scandal.

[2] Which is significantly less than his main competitor, Anderson Cooper at CNN, who earns around $12 million per year.

The Tucker Model

Carlson seems to have been a life-long conservative, even during his tenures at CNN and MSNBC, where he played the conservative foil to the dominant liberal voices. So we need not doubt his sincerity on that matter, at least. But like all TV figures, he quickly learned how to "play the game" in order to get his share of airtime. The primary rule: never question, challenge, or 'out' your bosses; always stick to the party line. This of course is true pretty much everywhere, but in the news media, when your very job is to be an honest, diligent, and brave presenter of the truth, it seems particularly appalling to have to sacrifice basic morals—both personal and professional—simply to keep your job. Yes, much of the blame goes to the corporate bosses, who demand ideological conformity from their news teams, but blame also goes to the individual TV figures who allow themselves to be used and corrupted for the money and fame. Sadly, this is an old story.

This is particularly troublesome for the dissident right because there are many who view Carlson as a real voice for their concerns and as a courageous defender of the truth. But all too often, his real concern seems to be for himself and his fellow members of the wealthy elite, and his version of "the truth" leaves much to be desired.

Let me start with what Carlson gets right. Yes, the Democrats are appalling hypocrites and liars. In the whole Covid crisis, Carlson has made much hay by exposing their double standards on things like mask-wearing, quarantine, haircuts, and salon visits. Yes, they will say and do nearly anything to keep Trump out of the White House. Yes, Joe Biden is a near brain-dead dupe of party operatives, lacking in anything like personal principles or convictions. Yes, "Sandy" Cortez (AOC) carries an outsized liberal influence and indeed has many "radical" policies she wants to implement. Yes, Democrats feign being environmentalists of the highest sort, and yet when in power they do little or nothing—witness the eight years of Clinton-Gore in the 1990s, or the eight Obama years. Democrats also claim to "support our troops" but find it impossible to end our hopeless foreign wars and bring the troops home, or to dismantle our global network of imperial military outposts that costs taxpayers upwards of $500 billion a year.

It's a similar story on the media side: Yes, Tucker's competing news celebrities at CNN and MSNBC are appalling hypocrites and liars. He rightly calls out the blatant stupidity and ethical lapses of people like Chris Cuomo (now at NewsNation) and Don Lemon. CNN and MSNBC both are utterly predictable in which stories they present and which they *don't* present, and Carlson has a field day with this. These are the kinds of things that rightly earn him praise from the dissident right.

But let's look a bit more closely at Tucker's universe. In his world, things are relatively black-and-white. There are *good* things, and there are *bad* things. The Tucker 'goods' include: America, the American way of life, God (of the Judeo-Christian persuasion, of course), a second Trump presidency, capitalism, free trade, personal wealth, and unrestricted freedom of choice. These things are standard goods for conservatives, both paleo and neo-con, *but not necessarily for the dissident right.* Many in the right see America as a failed state, as a disaster—at least in practice, if not also in theory. Many would like to see our present corrupt nation vanish into oblivion. Few in the dissident right are rich. Many see Trump as an embarrassment or worse, hardly worth defending. And many are at least skeptical, if not downright contemptuous, of the Judeo-Christian hoax and its ridiculous sky-god Jehovah.[3]

More troubling are the Tucker 'bads,' which include: racism, anti-Semitism, White nationalism, Black Lives Matter, Antifa,[4] riots and anarchy in the streets, unwinnable foreign wars like Afghanistan, the 9/11 attacks (when involving "the Saudis"), Chinese global aggression (especially vis a vis Russian aggression), and climate change "alarmism." Clearly and obviously for those in the dissident right, many of these things are in fact not bad, and some are unconditional goods. Let's go down the list in a bit of detail:

- Racism, Tucker loves to repeat, is a great evil. "All men are created equal," after all, according to his beloved Declaration. Both of these assertions are, of course, utter nonsense. The proper, positive reading of 'racism' is (a) to think in racial terms about all aspects of human society, and (b) to have an appropriate self-pride in one's own race. Any sane and rational person would likely agree with this definition. Science, genetics, anthropology, and sociology all testify to the overriding importance of race or ethnicity in accounting for human values and behavior. And to not be proud of one's own race is akin to hating one's own family; normal, well-adjusted people have a positive self-image, and this applies to themselves, to their extended family, and to all those of their kind.

  Consequently, there is no meaningful sense in which all humans are equal—not in interests, abilities, values, predispositions, inclinations…nothing. If anything, humans are radically *unequal.* "Equal before the law" is trivial, relatively meaningless, and functionally-speaking not even true. "Equal under God" is sheer absurdity. Human

[3] See chapters 4 and 25 in the present volume.

[4] Both the term 'antifa' and its ideology have long roots, having been founded in Germany in the early 1930s. Only in the past four or five years has the concept assumed prominence in the US.

equality is a fiction. Thus, any thinking, intelligent, and morally-intact person ought to be a 'racist.'

- Likewise, any thinking White is necessarily anti-Semitic, meaning, they recognize Jews as the primary threat to their collective well-being and indeed to the well-being of all humanity. To be openly and proudly anti-Semitic is to take a stand against the gang of criminals—the "planetary master criminals," in the words of Heidegger—that have been plundering Western civilization for some two millennia.[5]

- White nationalism and White interests are of course the *raison d'être* of White activism. Whenever the topic crosses Carlson's lips, however, it morphs into 'white supremacy' or 'neo-Nazism' and is explicitly or implicitly condemned. Whites never have valid interests as Whites, in his mind.

- Antifa and BLM are motley collections of confused, self-hating, opportunistic, vicious, and mindless individuals, of all races (including Jews[6]). They are loosely organized, if at all. Isolated hit-squads, perhaps assembled for pay, leap into action under their banners and make a big splash; but for the vast majority of Whites and the vast majority of American cities, they pose no real threat at all. Yes, they are contemptible, as Carlson says. Yes, they should be jailed, or worse. But no, they pose no existential threat to the dissident right. (Carlson's main concern with them seems to be that they often target the wealthy, which hits too close to home for his comfort.)

- Likewise, Tucker hates riots and anarchy because they threaten the comfortable order of the economic elites. But let's get this straight: *There are plenty of good reasons to be rioting in the streets*—but George Floyd is not one of them. If we're going to have riots, let's do it, for example, over the American Judeocracy that has destroyed any semblance of fairness and justice in our society. Or over the $1 trillion spent every year in this country to maintain a global military hegemony, much of it on behalf of Jews and Israel. Or over the obscene accumulation of wealth by American Jews, amounting to as much as $75 trillion. It's not the rioting *per se* that is wrong; it's the motivation behind it that matters. But Carlson will have none of this.

---

[5] For more on Heidegger, see my book *Eternal Strangers* (2020).

[6] See "Are These Antifa/BLM Riots a Jewish Coup?", by Kevin MacDonald.

- Both Iraq wars (1991 and 2003) and the war in Afghanistan were Jewish-instigated neo-con wars on behalf of Israel—period. They had nothing to do with American security. To this day, there are still some 5,000 troops in Iraq and an unknown number in Syria, fighting "terrorists" who might someday threaten Jews in Israel. This is an utter disgrace, and even a crime against humanity. It must end now, as Tucker says—though he will never speak the truth about these conflicts.

- As for the 9/11 attacks, suffice to say that, once again, they seem to have been conducted on behalf Jewish and Israeli interests. To demonize the Saudis, as Carlson does, is to distract from the real issues at hand.

- Distraction, too, seems to be his motivation for a focus on Chinese aggression rather than Russian. As a widely-detested global hegemon, the US naturally faces continual threats on many fronts. To pick out one or the other of these threats is to distract from the deeper issues involved. The short solution here is: stop being a hegemon, and you will have far fewer enemies.

- Carlson claims to be an environmentalist, but it's clear that he qualifies only as one of the shallow and instrumentalist types. By contrast, many in the dissident right have legitimate concerns about climate change and would like see this nation move toward less fossil fuels, while expanding protections for wilderness and undeveloped rural areas. Dare I add that the original dissident right, the National Socialists, placed great value on nature. Once again, Carlson seems primarily concerned with the potential hit to his bottom line, and that of his fellow elites.

Tucker and the Jews

Finally we come to the black hole at the center of Carlson's galaxy. And a supermassive one it is, too. Of that most influential, most wealthy, most corrupt, and most destructive of minorities, he offers us precisely nothing. Jews are all but invisible on the Tucker Carlson Show.

Correction: Jews *qua Jews* are invisible. He has plenty of them on his show, but they are almost never identified as such (of course not—because that would be RACIST!). Carlson's regular Jews include Dr. Marc Siegel, Rick Leventhal, Mark Steyn (part-Jewish), and Dave Portnoy. Several other Jews make occasional appearances, including Glenn Greenwald, Alex Berenson, Seth Barron, Lester Friedman, and Dov Hikind. He did an entire hour-long interview with the contemptuous Jew Curtis Yarvin. As on every news outlet—left, right, or center—Jews are massively over-represented.

This is not an accident. For his part, Tucker seems more than happy to give the Jewish voice yet more airtime.

Yes, he condemns the likes of Harvey Weinstein and Jeffrey Epstein, and of Jeff Zucker and Michael Cohen, but again, never as Jews. Their Jewishness is, for him, utterly irrelevant. Those of us who know better can see consistent patterns of behavior, clannish in-group defense, masterful lying, and an absolute lack of morality in these individuals. This is not a coincidence. We are dealing here with genetic, in-born traits that reach their highest and most ruthless fulfillment in such men. Wherever Jews number more than a fraction of a percent of the population, there will be Weinsteins and Epsteins, Zuckers and Cohens.

A typical Carlson viewer, however, could be excused for thinking that such people as Jews didn't even exist—unless it involves calling attention to anti-Semitism and Jewish victimhood. Apart from that, the word 'Jew' is virtually never uttered. Not even when it is most relevant; *and not even when it involves the very people he loves to criticize the most.* Consider the highly relevant and surely uncoincidental relationships between Biden, Kamala Harris, and the Jews. Take Biden, who has long had a cozy relationship with Jews, dating back at least to his fond memories of meeting Golda Meir in 1973. In early 2007, he famously stated that "I am a Zionist," adding "You don't have to be a Jew to be a Zionist" (true enough). This certainly helped his political future, considering that the Judeophile and *Judenknecht* Obama soon thereafter chose him as his running mate.

But what secured Biden's support among the American Judeocracy was surely his family connections.[7] Joe had three children by his first wife: Beau, Hunter, and Naomi. The wife and one-year-old Naomi were killed in a car crash in 1972, but the two boys lived to adulthood (Beau died of brain cancer in 2015). Joe then had a fourth child, Ashley, by his second and current wife, Jill. Ashley married a Jewish doctor, Howard Krein, in 2012. Beau married a Jewish dry-cleaning scion, Hallie Olivere, in 2002; they had two children before he died in 2015. After his death, Olivere (now Hallie Biden) shamelessly began an affair with the alcoholic and married younger son, Hunter—he of the Ukrainian Burisma and FBI laptop scandal fame. Hunter then divorced his first wife (Kathleen) to take up fulltime with the Jewess Hallie, but that relationship fell apart in 2018. After getting a stripper pregnant, Hunter then took up with another Jewess, "filmmaker" Melissa Cohen. They married in 2019 and had a boy in 2020.

Bottom line: All three of Biden's adult children married Jews, and he has at least three Jewish grandchildren. This is remarkable, and surely not

---

[7] See "Everything you need to know about Joe Biden's Jewish relatives" (*Forward*, 7 Nov 2020).

accidental. Jews flock to power, and those in power, at least the most depraved and corrupt ones, are only too happy to cement their Jewish family connections. The same holds, as we know, for the Clintons, Trump, and Nancy Pelosi, among many others.[8]

For her part, Kamala Harris married the Jew Douglas Emhoff in 2014. As the offspring of an Indian mother and a Black Jamaican father, and now married to a Jew, Harris is a poster child for the degenerate racial mixing that passes for normality in liberal-Democratic circles these days. We can see why they praised her selection for VP.

But rest assured, you won't be confronted with any of these ugly facts on the Tucker Carlson Show. No sir! Because that would be RACIST!

Perhaps the biggest Jewish problem, from Carlson's standpoint, is the possible (likely?) Jewishness of his Fox corporate owners, the Murdoch family. The family patriarch, Rupert, now 89, has managed to obscure details of his family background. His mother, the former Elisabeth Greene (1909-2012), is claimed by some to have been Jewish. Journalist Richard Curtiss stated as much in 2003.[9] There is a weird, possibly-doctored photo showing her looking quite chummy with an Australian rabbi. And Rupert's sister, Anne, apparently married a Jew named Kantor. Suggestive, but far from definitive.

But what is not in dispute is that the Murdoch empire has been relentlessly pro-Israel, pro-Jewish, and pro-Zionist for decades. Whether for personal, religious, or commercial reasons, the Murdochs have found it in their interest to sidle up to the Jews. This stance unquestionably works its way down the entire Fox media network, and thus we are unsurprised that the anchors avoid the whole topic whenever possible. The Jewish Question is, as always, That Which Shall Not Be Spoken.[10]

It is particularly frustrating, though, when folks like Carlson actually provide cover and defense for the Jews. On many occasions, for example, he has stated or implied that Jews are White—that they benefit from "White privilege" or that they are targeted "because they are White." Let me make this as clear as possible: *Jews are not White*—not in any relevant sense. Jews are White like Jessica Krug and Rachel Dolezal are Black; that is, only to the extent that it serves their interests to deceive. Yes, Jews' skin tone matches ours, but that is merely an unfortunate and superficial fact of

---

[8] One wonders what the children of these power-elites are thinking. What sane person would willingly marry into the lowest and most despicable minority on Earth? And then have children with them? Were they bribed? Coerced? Brainwashed? The topic is surely worthy of a book-length treatment in itself.

[9] See "Fanatical Zionist Rupert Murdoch: Jewish or Not?" (*National Vanguard*, 19 Jun 2017).

[10] I'm tempted to call it "the elephant in the room," but that would be an insult to elephants, so I won't.

biology. To further obscure the issue, they use plastic surgery to hide the nose and to minimize the uniquely repulsive effects of Jewish aging. This allows them to circulate in White society unnoticed. But they are not White. Neither are Lebanese, Syrians, Iranians, nor any other light-skinned Arabs or Middle Easterners. 'White' refers only to the indigenous people of Europe, Ukraine, and Western Russia. *Jews are not White.*

But Carlson seems unable to comprehend this fact, and thus he continues to perpetuate the "Jews are White" myth. Apparently he is unwilling or unable to grasp the alternative, namely, that Jews are a distinct ethnicity with distinct genetics, and therefore with distinct skills, abilities, values, and group interests—many of which directly conflict with those of Whites.

His sins against Whites are compounded by the fact that he himself is White. This situation is particularly galling to me and many in the right. We can at least understand the patent self-interest when Jewish anchors like Wolf Blitzer, Jake Tapper, Rachel Maddow (half), Chuck Todd, Ari Melber, Mark Levin, and John Berman offer us biased reporting or lies of omission that benefit Jews. But for Whites and other non-Jews to do the same is disgraceful. Carlson, at least, manages to salvage some dignity in his willingness to openly criticize Jews, even if without naming them as such. But for left-leaning White broadcasters like Anderson Cooper, Chris Cuomo, and Chris Hayes to provide active cover and defense for Jews is utterly appalling. They are among the leading and most damaging race-traitors in the mainstream media. For them, no punishment can be too severe.

Despite all this, Carlson has a path to salvation. Tucker, here it is: Pick a random night in the not too distant future, and go off script, live, and tell the truth about the Jews. Ye (Kanye West) has made a good start; now follow his lead. You're smart, you know the truth, just say it. When the inevitable firing comes, take it like a man. With $30 million in the bank, you've got more than enough for yourself, your kids, and your grandkids. Then use your money and fame to become a *real* advocate for the truth. Speak out against the Jewish monopolization of our power structure, and against Jewish malfeasance at all levels of society.

They say you might even run for president in 2024. Imagine the commitment and support you would gain by speaking the truth. But do it now. There isn't a moment to lose. We'll be waiting.

— 27 —
TRUE Q: ELEMENTS OF TRUTH IN Q-ANON

Sympnoia panta ("All things conspire").
Hippocrates[1]

"I know nothing about QAnon."
Donald J. Trump[2]

What can be more fun than a conspiracy? Conspiracies are sneaky, salacious, cryptographic, lurid, and enticing. They promise secret knowledge of the inner workings of society—knowledge that only a relative few possess, thus empowering the knower. They claim to identify and expose evil wrongdoers, thus holding out hope for retribution, true justice, and a better world. And they bring a kind of order and coherence to an otherwise incoherent time. If, in the end, they turn out to be incomplete, or partially wrong, so what? No harm in investigating the machinations of society, and in any case, some elements of truth are certain to be flushed out in the process. Much to gain, little to lose.

Conspiracy theories have been around for thousands of years—at least. Claims of secretive and malevolent Jewish schemes, for example, go back to 300 BC.[3] Anti-Christian conspiracy theories date to the early second century, as found in the writings of Tacitus and Pliny the Younger. In the Middle Ages, stories about the Inquisition, the Knights Templar, Freemasons, and the papacy all gave rise to a variety of conspiracy claims. For centuries, it was a "conspiracy theory" to believe that the Donation of Constantine—a document granting ruling authority to the Catholic Church—was fraudulent; but this conspiracy was proven true by Lorenzo Valla in 1440, when he exposed the charade. Catholic conspiracies continue to serve as grist for popular exposés, both fictional and nonfiction, to the present day.

But what, exactly, is a conspiracy? In the most general terms, it is a secretive, hidden effort by a relatively small group of people to steer events in a chosen direction. Literally, it is a group of people who "breathe together" (*con+spirare*, 'to breathe'), but it also has a connotation of the

---

[1] Circa 400 BC, as quoted by Leibniz in his *Monadology* (sec. 61).
[2] Town Hall meeting hosted by NBC, 15 October 2020.
[3] See the writings of Hecateus of Abdera, in my book *Eternal Strangers*.

Latin *spiritus* ('spirit'), meaning 'those of a shared spirit.' A conspiracy is thus a group of people with a shared spirit, a common outlook, who, at least in part, work closely together—"breathe together"—to achieve their hidden ends.

Thus understood, it is clear that there are countless conspiracies at work in the world today, as there have been throughout history. Every governmental office that works behind closed doors to enact policy, every corporate boardroom that crafts strategy and action, every leadership group of virtually any organization that coordinates any action whatsoever, is technically a conspiracy. Each of these act, at least in part, "secretly," and does so on behalf of certain beneficiaries—such as the citizens, the stockholders, or the members of the organization. Of course, in most cases, we don't call such actions 'conspiracies'; in common usage, we restrict the term to a deliberately secretive, conniving, scheming group of individuals, usually a handful in number, who work illegally or immorally to gain wealth or power. In this restricted sense, virtually any criminal effort, if it involves more than one person, is a conspiracy. But it applies as well to countless corporate and governmental actions, many of which are illegal or immoral or both. Suffice to say that conspiracies of all stripes are alive and well in the modern world. To believe in conspiracies—that is, to be a "conspiracy theorist"—is simply to acknowledge reality.

But this is not good enough for our global elite. They want to restrict the term even further. Media, government, and academia would have us believe that a conspiracy—*any* conspiracy—is by definition a false, baseless, and sophomoric notion that only a fool or an idiot would believe. They want us to think that simply by labeling something as "a conspiracy theory" that we will see it as both ludicrous and grossly untrue, and that therefore any believer of such a thing must be an ignorant, deluded, or hopelessly confused person. Thus the term adds to a long line of similar slanders, insults, and *ad hominem* fallacies; a 'conspiracy theorist' is akin to a 'racist,' a 'bigot,' a 'far right-winger,' a 'Holocaust denier,' an 'anti-Semite,' and a 'White supremacist.' These favored elite catch-phrases offer shorthand dismissal and vilification of inconvenient ideas or individuals.

That said, what can we meaningfully say about the QAnon conspiracy theory? Here is one summary published in August 2019 by Salon.com, based on an interview with a *Washington Post* reporter:

> QAnon is based upon the idea that there is a worldwide cabal of Satan-worshiping pedophiles who rule the world, essentially, and they control everything. They control politicians, and they control the media. They control Hollywood, and they cover up their existence, essentially. And they would have continued ruling the world, were it not for the election

> of President Donald Trump. Now, Trump in this conspiracy theory knows all about this evil cabal's wrongdoing. But one of the reasons that Trump was elected was to put an end to them, basically. And now we would be ignorant of this behind-the-scenes battle of Trump and the US military—that everyone backs him and the evil cabal—were it not for 'Q'.[4]

Q, of course, is the secret governmental source who has special inside knowledge of such things, and who leaks them out regularly and often on web-based imageboards like 4chan, (the now-defunct) 8chan, and (currently) 8kun.[5] The letter 'Q' allegedly refers to the highest level of security clearance—"Q clearance"—at the US Department of Energy. Q first appeared in late 2017, with a post on an alleged forthcoming arrest of Hillary Clinton ("HRC"):

> HRC extradition already in motion effective yesterday with several countries in case of cross border run. Passport approved to be flagged effective 10/30 @ 12:01am. Expect massive riots organized in defiance and others fleeing the US to occur. …

This was followed soon thereafter by a related claim that John Podesta would be arrested, again with subsequent riots. Needless to say, no such arrests or extraditions have yet occurred. But these were only the first of many predictions to come.

As of late 2022, Q has amassed a large body of posts, or "drops," numbering around 5,000. They vary in length and subject matter; some are clear and straightforward, but many are cryptic—involving vague allusions, mysterious acronyms and abbreviations, and tantalizing implications. Members of QAnon spend countless hours deciphering and interpreting Q's many clues. They further repost all Q drops at various Internet sites; qalerts.app, www.qanon.pub, and qposts.online are three good sources.[6] Technically, these posts from Q himself are the only "legitimate"

---

[4] "QAnon is the conspiracy theory that won't die: Here's what they believe, and why they're wrong" (17 Aug 2020).

[5] The full domain name is www.8kun.top. An imageboard is an online forum based on short postings of images and accompanying text. Most of the posters are anonymous.

[6] There are technical questions about the identity of Q over time—in other words, it is an open question if the Q posting today is the same man (or woman, or group) who posted back in 2017. Imageboard posters have a unique identifier code—a "tripcode"—that proves that the poster is the same source over time. But Q's tripcode (currently it is this string: !!Hs1Jq13jV6) has changed at least three times over

sources of conspiracy information. Anything else has been grafted on by followers (or opponents, as the case may be).

Following the 2020 presidential election, in which Trump narrowly lost to Biden, Q went nearly silent for many months. There was a short post to a Youtube video on 8 Dec 2020, and then nothing for a year and a half. Q reappeared on 24 Jun 2022 ("Shall we play a game once more?"), followed by a few scattered posts, followed by a half-dozen more, before and after the 2022 midterm election. For example, this was posted on the day of the election:

> Endless lies. Endless wars. Endless inflation. Endless 'printing.' Endless oppression. Endless subjugation. Endless surveillance. Who will put an end to the endless? Taking control. Q

As before, stream-of-consciousness ideas without much coherence or clarity.

Evolution of a Conspiracy

The QAnon phenomenon emerged in late 2017, most notably with the Twitter-backing of (Jewish) celebrity Rosanne Barr. But the story didn't get real media coverage until early 2018. *The Daily Beast*, for example, wrote in March of that year that "[Q] claims to be a high-ranking government official with inside knowledge of the White House where, he claims, Trump is planning mass arrests of top Democrats for allegedly being involved in a satanic child-sex-trafficking ring." The mass arrests constitute an event referred to as "the Storm," which is yet to materialize. But Q-spiracists have faith that it is coming, and soon.

Before long, Q signs and slogans began showing up in Trump rallies around the country. Web journal Mashable.com wrote about the movement in August 2018, using a boatload of pejoratives, including "mountain of bullshit," "insane," "batshit crazy," "irrational," and so on.[7] Mashable argued that QAnon was a kind of right-wing diversion from actual pedophilia and sexual abuse/harassment cases against prominent Republicans, including Dennis Hastert, Roy Moore, and Jim Jordan. They then blamed execs at Facebook, Twitter, and Google for allowing this "batshit-crazy" conspiracy to gain traction—as was the case, they claimed, with so-called Holocaust denialism.

---

the past three years. It is strictly an article of faith that it was the same person all along. For sake of simplicity, I will assume that Q is the same individual, an unidentified male, who has been posting from the start. But nothing much turns on this assumption. I furthermore note that, of the many online articles I have reviewed, none has given the details of where to find the Q drops—almost as if they didn't really want the reader to find out for himself. This in itself is revealing.

[7] "QAnon conspiracy blew up because of a bigger internet problem."

Around March 2019, the Q-stories got weirder. Vox.com reported on QAnon as "based on the idea that special counsel Robert Mueller and President Donald Trump are working together to expose thousands of cannibalistic pedophiles hidden in plain sight (including Hillary Clinton and actor Tom Hanks) and then send them to Guantanamo Bay." QAnon-ers also believe, they claimed, that Hillary Clinton "was executed by lethal injection," and that "John F. Kennedy Jr. is still alive"—neither of which were asserted by Q himself.[8] Such claims came from outside sources, quite possibly to discredit the nascent movement.

By August of that year, as reported in Salon (article cited above), the story turned ominous. The original "satanic" had now morphed into "Satan-worshipping," and worse, the "pedophiles" were now "a worldwide cabal" who "rule the world"; as cited above, "they control politicians, they control the media, they control Hollywood, and they cover up their existence." There is, of course, only one such group that fits that description: Jews. More on them below.

Also by this time, mainstream journalist-critics began emphasizing the putative "religious" nature of Q's ideology. Salon.com reported on the "apocalyptic" quality of the conspiracy, on the group's vision of a coming battle "between absolute good and absolute evil," and Q himself was depicted "like [a] religious millennialist." There is some truth to this. Q refers to God on countless occasions, and frequently cites the Bible. He is particularly fond of Ephesians 6:10, especially the passage calling for us to "put on the full armor of God," in preparation for the coming struggle. References to Jesus, by contrast, are almost nonexistent; this suggests that Q is an ardent Catholic, perhaps of a fundamentalist bent. He is certainly a typical conservative: pro-God, patriotic, pro-Trump, anti-Democrat, anti-liberal, etc. But the religious language has caught fire with American Christians in particular, and seems to be a driving force behind Q's rise to prominence.

The religious angle thus attained top priority. In June 2020, *Atlantic* was writing of "The Prophecies of Q." "The language of evangelical Christianity has come to define the Q movement," they wrote (disregarding the utter lack of references to Jesus). "Among the people of QAnon, faith remains absolute." One true believer is quoted as saying "I feel God led me to Q." One of the supposed "best-known QAnon evangelists," according to *Atlantic*, is David Hayes, aka PrayingMedic. *Atlantic*'s view is summarized thusly:

---

[8] "The Mueller investigation is over. QAnon, the conspiracy theory that grew around it, is not" (29 Mar 2019). Also, there seem to be only a handful of drops referring to John Jr., and just one old post mentioning Tom Hanks.

> It is a movement united in mass rejection of reason, objectivity, and other Enlightenment values. And we are likely closer to the beginning of its story than the end. The group harnesses paranoia to fervent hope and a deep sense of belonging. The way it breathes life into an ancient preoccupation with end-times is also radically new. To look at QAnon is to see not just a conspiracy theory but the birth of a new religion.

Mainstream media's view is clear: QAnon-ers are irrational, unhinged, quasi-religious lunatics who are detached from reality. For their part, *Atlantic* simply can't make heads or tails of such people; "QAnon is complex and confusing." We will see why they say this momentarily.

QAnon and Jew-Anon

It was also at this time that our intrepid journalists began to reveal perhaps their greatest fear: the connection between QAnon and anti-Semitism. *Atlantic* wrote that "the most prominent QAnon figures have a presence beyond the biggest social-media platforms and imageboards. The Q universe encompasses … alternative social-media platforms such as Gab, the site known for anti-Semitism and white nationalism." Indeed, they say, Q-like conspiracy theories "have helped sustain consequential [social] eruptions, such as … anti-Semitism" at all points in time.

Here, finally, we seem to be getting to the root of media hysteria over QAnon. Backing Trump was bad enough, but once Q-ers started turning anti-Semitic, well…time to crush that bug. The issue went bigtime in July of this year, in such pieces as *Wired*'s "The dark virality of a Hollywood blood-harvesting conspiracy." As the Jewish writer Brian Friedberg explains in his subtitle, "A centuries-old anti-Semitic myth is spreading freely on far-right corners of social media—suggesting a new digital Dark Age has arrived." Now we get to the rub. As Friedberg sees it, QAnon-ers are resurrecting and modernizing the ancient "blood libel" charge against Jews, which was traditionally based on the idea that Jews would kidnap and kill Christians—typically children—in order to use their blood for various religious rites, for its alleged healing powers, and to consume in various food products.

For Friedberg and others, the charge of blood libel is nothing more than "an anti-Semitic myth that pervaded Europe throughout the Middle Ages." Wikipedia calls it "an anti-Semitic canard." Unfortunately for Friedberg and other Jews, this "myth" has a large basis in fact. The earliest reports of Jewish human sacrifice date to 300 BC, and the use of body parts was cited in the first century BC by Apollonius Molon and Posidonius, and mentioned again circa 0 AD by figures such as Damocritus and

Apion. More specifically, the blood libel charge, which emerged in popular form in the twelfth century in Europe, has an extensive factual basis, as documented in the now-infamous 2007 book by Israeli scholar Ariel Toaff, *Passovers of Blood.*[9] Jews have in fact historically valued and used human blood, preferably of children, for its alleged magical healing powers. The killing of Christians actually served a double benefit, also acting as a kind of revenge against the Gentiles for the prior killing of Jews throughout history. As Toaff demonstrates, trafficking in human blood was undoubtedly true in the Middle Ages, and given its grounding in basic Jewish theology and psychology, may well still be the case today. There may in fact be certain present-day groups of orthodox Jews who still find ways to capture and kill Gentile children, perhaps even by crucifixion, to attain both symbolic vengeance and the "potent" youthful blood. Needless to say, this situation, if proven, would have huge implications for current Jewish-Gentile relations.

In its latest QAnon form, the historically-grounded blood trafficking by Jews has turned into a bizarre variant based on a substance called 'adrenochrome.' This compound, with chemical formula $C_9H_9NO_3$, results from an oxidation reaction of the hormone adrenaline—according to that indubitable source, Wikipedia. For a period of time in the past, adrenochrome was studied in connection with schizophrenia, either as a cause or treatment, but no clear outcomes resulted. According to some researchers, in concentration it is both cardiotoxic and neurotoxic. But in the mass media version of QAnon, it is now an essential part of the conspiracy. The Satan-worshipping elites now not only kidnap children and youth to have sex with them, they then kill them for the adrenochrome in their blood; this is the "cannibalistic" aspect of the conspiracy. The adrenochrome is said to be the key element of the blood, something that provides either a chemical 'high,' youth-restoration, or both.

In fact, there does seem to be something of a medical basis for the rejuvenating properties of youthful blood. The phenomenon is called *parabiosis*. In several animal studies, it has shown beneficial results; but the extrapolation to human beings is still apparently unclear.[10] And the specific value of adenochrome is less clear yet. From a medical standpoint, blood transfusions are quite common, but they carry significant risks. Transfusions are useful for anyone who has lost a lot of blood through accident, surgery, or other illness. They can help people with specific diseases, like

---

[9] Now available in a new edition, edited by myself: *Passovers of Blood* (2020; Clemens & Blair).

[10] See, for example, "Young Blood Rejuvenates Old Bodies: A Call for Reflection when Moving from Mice to Men" (B. Hofmann, 2018, *Transfus Med Hemother* 45(1): 67-71).

anemia, hemophilia, sickle cell, and certain cancers. Still, there is some medical basis for the benefits of youthful blood; if so, we can be sure that blood-trafficking Jews will be there to exploit it.

But consider this: If you wanted to discredit both the "anti-Semitic" QAnon and the (true) blood libel charges against Jews, you could do little better than to inject an entirely bogus element into that discussion. First, under a fake name, you portray yourself as a Q-fanatic, and then you make up some bizarre talk about a real blood-based substance like adrenochrome. And then, under a different name—perhaps your real name—you attack the very forums that you just posted on, as being "insane," "irrational," "batshit crazy," and so on. It's a nifty trolling trick, surely indispensable to many Jewish journalists and Internet activists.

Furthermore, it would seem to be significant that Q himself has never, in some 5,000 drops, explicitly mentioned adrenochrome, blood libel, or anything of the sort.[11] The whole topic, to the extent that it is real, was introduced by outsiders, likely as a discrediting tactic.

Not only is it not mentioned by Q, but as Friedberg points out, "adrenochrome harvesting isn't outwardly blamed on Jews" at all. In fact, the word 'Jew' virtually *never* appears in any Q drops. So how can Q, and by extension the QAnon followers, be considered anti-Semitic?

It seems that Q, being an unrepentant cypher, prefers to list specific Jews by name, and then leave it to the "anti-Semitic" reader to make the obvious generalization. Or at least, that's what our faithful journalists would have us believe. Among the many Q drops, one finds several references to such Jews as George Soros (approx. 36), Jeffrey Epstein (54), Anthony Weiner (18), and "the Rothschilds" (21). This may seem like a lot, but it represents a small fraction—less than 2%--of the total drops. Furthermore, references to these individuals are typically situation-specific, without any obvious extension to other or all Jews. Other potentially suggestive references seem largely absent. Such words as 'cabal' appeared a few times in 2018, but not since then. Words like 'ruling' and 'elite' are almost nonexistent in the relevant contexts. Q's alleged anti-Semitism consists of little more than criticizing a few Jews by name, but without even identifying them as such.

Still, it begs certain questions about the Jewish role in sexual abuse and child molestation, and in their dominant standing in elite Western society. It is truly remarkable to consider, for example, the number of prominent Jews who, in the past few years, were caught up various sexual assault or harass-

---

[11] It is always difficult to say for certain, however, what exactly Q means by his various hints and clues. References to "human trafficking / sacrifices" (drop #586, 22 Jan 2018) and "ability to harvest" (#2319, 3 Oct 2018) are occasionally cited as references to adrenochrome, but these are too obscure to be meaningful.

ment scandals. In addition to above-mentioned Epstein and Weiner, we have Epstein's co-conspirator Ghislaine Maxwell, Harvey Weinstein, Les Moonves, Andrew Lack, Matt Lauer, Al Franken, Woody Allen, Alan Dershowitz, Dominique Strauss-Kahn, Ari Shavit, and Steven M. Cohen, to name but a few. As disproportionate as they are in elite circles, Jews are also disproportionate in the realm of reprehensible crimes against women and youth.

And what about the "world-ruling elite" that QAnon-ers are supposedly so obsessed about? Again, we find little from Q himself. Words like 'elite' and 'rulers' appear rarely in the drops, and when they do, it is typically as part of a biblical passage. Surely Q knows, however, that Jews hold massively disproportionate power throughout the West, and therefore throughout the world. This sad story is widely known by now, but a short recap is in order. Jewish control over Hollywood is so banal as to be a trivial observation.[12] Jewish money dominates American government, to the point that at least 25% of conservative money and 50% of liberal money comes from Jews.[13] American Jews own or control up to half of the private wealth in the US, potentially amounting to some $75 trillion. This is why they exercise such considerable influence in American government and media. A similar situation holds in the UK, France, Canada, Australia, and in Russia's oligarchy.[14]

Here, then, is another bit of truth behind the QAnon hysteria. Prominent Jews, in the guise of "Soros" and "the Rothschilds," really do run the show, to an astonishingly large degree. If innocent Q readers start to search on these and other Jewish names, they will surely come across some rather nasty factual data that our Jewish elite would rather not have them know. Since they can no longer stifle or censor the movement, the elite's second-best strategy is to slander it like mad. Thus we see headlines like the recent "QAnon is a Nazi cult, rebranded." Here is the leading paragraph of that story:

> A secret cabal is taking over the world. They kidnap children, slaughter, and eat them to gain power from their blood. They control high positions in government, banks, interna-

---

[12] "Vulture Capitalism, Jews — and Hollywood" (E. Connolly, *Occidental Observer*, 9 Feb 2020).

[13] "US Jews contribute 50% of all donations to the Democratic Party and 25% to the Republican Party" (*Jewish Business News*, 27 Sep 2016).

[14] See: "Unexamined, Unquestioned, Unchallenged: Jewish Power in Brave New Britain," "Jewish Influence and Ethnic Networking in France," and "The Jewish War on White Australia," all at *Occidental Observer*; "The Jewish Takeover of Canada" (RealJewNews.com), and "Know Your Oligarch: A Guide to the Jewish Billionaires in the Trump-Russia Probe" (*Ha'aretz*).

> tional finance, the news media, and the church. They want to disarm the police. They promote homosexuality and pedophilia. They plan to mongrelize the white race so it will lose its essential power.

Elements of truth: Yes, there is a "cabal" of wealthy Jews who have obscene levels of power in the West, and via the American superpower, functionally have "taken over the world." They certainly have in the past, and may well continue to, kidnap Gentile youths, exploit and abuse them sexually, and in certain cases, kill them and extract their blood for psychotic Judaic religious ceremonies, for purposes of anti-Gentile hatred and revenge, or for utterly unscientific health reasons. They do in fact control high positions throughout America and much of the West. Liberal Jews are in fact leading the charge to "defund the police," to promote LGBTQ rights, and to provide so-called "open door" immigration policies in the US and Europe—with a net effect, if not intent, of racially diluting and debasing every traditionally White nation on Earth.[15]

QAnon Meets the Holocaust

The article cited above also informs us of the growing global nature of the movement. QAnon, we read, "has now spread to neo-Nazis in Germany." Of particular concern to our media elite is a small, decades-old, right-wing group known as *Reichsbürger* ("Reich citizens"), who have joined in the Q party and adopted some of its themes. In a recent report from CNN, we read that "Reichsburger followers deny the Holocaust happened" and traffic in other "anti-Semitic tropes." More generally, online journal Venturebeat.com writes that "QAnon attaches itself to a variety of issues, such as anti-mask protests, child trafficking conspiracies, and Holocaust denial…"

Unfortunately for our all-knowing media, we find here another element of truth: It turns out that the evil "Holocaust deniers" are on to something, that the traditional Holocaust story is riddled with holes, falsehoods, and logical inconsistencies, and that all reasonable arguments point to a Jewish death toll substantially less than 6 million. Should our intrepid QAnon-ers stumble upon this truth, they are in for another eye-opener, one of monumental importance.

---

[15] See "Jewish News Outlet Exposes Jewish Role in LGBT Civil Rights Movement" (*The Realist Report*, 2 Jun 2019); and "Jewish Involvement in Contemporary Refugee and Migrant Organizations" (*Occidental Observer*, 28 Dec 2018).

Trump, the Savior

But not to worry, because Trump will save the day! This was the final piece of the picture. As it happens, Q rarely mentioned Trump by name, much preferring that silly but long-established acronym "POTUS" ("president of the US") instead. It is clear that Q was always on Trump's side, and supported him against the "Democratic party corruption" embodied in Obama, Clinton, and now Biden. A typical (and typically cryptic) drop is this one:

> Why was POTUS framed re: Russia collusion? Protect truth re: Hillary/DNC Russia collusion? Why was POTUS impeached re: Ukraine? Protect truth re: Biden/[CLAS 1-99] Ukraine collusion? Blame 'opponent' for what they themselves are guilty of? [DNC media push echo submitted 'talking points' generate false narrative]. Q (drop #4872, 15 Oct 2020)

But the "mass arrests" story—the Storm—is almost nonexistent in the past two years. One has to go back to late 2018 to find such suggestive posts as this: "Are you ready to see arrests? Are you ready to see PAIN? Are you ready to be part of history? Q" (drop #2344, 4 Oct 2018). But again, here we are, years later, and no mass arrests of anyone.

So this begs another important question: What did Trump actually do against the cabal that is behind Democratic corruption, sexual abuse, and human trafficking? The answer is: *almost nothing*. During his time in office, Trump showed little appetite for confronting and dismantling the Judeocracy that runs our country; and worse, he has positively supported it. We all know about his daughter Ivanka, who married the orthodox Jew Jared Kushner, converted to Judaism, and had three children with him.[16] Trump has always had a large number of Jewish friends, colleagues, and confidantes. As I have written previously, these include such prominent donors as:

> Lew Eisenberg, Sheldon and Miriam Adelson, Mel Sembler, Ron Weiser, Steve Wynn, Elliott Brody, Laurie Perlmutter, and Carl Icahn, not to mention Bernie Marcus. Then we have

---

[16] Ivanka seems to really have a "thing" for Jews. According to Wikipedia, she dated at least two Jews prior to Kushner: investment banker Greg Hersch, and "documentary producer and playboy" James ("Bingo") Gubelmann. For someone allegedly raised Presbyterian, this is remarkable. It suggests some natural affinity to Jews, perhaps through Jewish family connection, such as her mother.

> his many Jewish personal and professional associates, who include, among others, Bill Barr, Avi Berkowitz, Michael Cohen, Gary Cohn, Reed Cordish, Boris Epshteyn, David Friedman, Jason Greenblatt, Larry Kudlow, Stephen Miller, Steven Mnuchin, Jay Sekulow, David Shulkin, and Allen Weisselberg. All those Trump-defenders out there in America should be dismayed at his vast linkage to the people of Israel.

In terms of policy, Trump placated hardline Jews by withdrawing from the Iran nuclear deal and moving the US Embassy to Jerusalem in 2018. He also recognized Israel's claim of sovereignty over the Golan Heights, and his "peace process" has been consistently on the side of Israel. He has defended Israel in the UN, and has done nothing to cut foreign aid—some $5 billion to $6 billion per year—to that country.

Where, then, is the Storm? It's certainly not against the real power structure, the real "swamp," the one that is pulling the strings in Washington. Against them, he did nothing. Worse, he seemingly pandered to them at nearly every occasion. Trump occasionally threw a small bone to White nationalists and the dissident right, but he quickly retracted or denied his statements. It's just a tease. Trump is fully in bed with the Hebrew wire-pullers, and he knows it. He has no intention of doing otherwise. It's simply too much in his own personal interest to continue pandering to them.

Q likes to make predictions. Here's one of mine: No Storm, no mass arrests, no reining in of the Jewish Lobby—with or without Trump. And until this happens, no meaningful change in Washington, period.

Meanwhile...

Media bashing of QAnon in the final weeks prior to the 2020 election was relentless. The group constitutes the "ultimate conspiracy theory," according to *Foreign Policy*.[17] QAnon-ers have "attempted political violence," and are linked to "apparent acts of domestic terrorism," they state with due qualifications. The group is the ideological successor to "dark ideas like *The Protocols of the Elders of Zion*," again bringing in the anti-Semitic angle.[18] Indeed, "apocalyptic vibes radiate through all of Q's messages" they say, without the slightest bit of exaggeration. In sum, Q's many drops comprise "a constellation of bullshit."

For its part, CNN repeated the emphasis on the *Protocols*, attributed to the group the idea that "the coronavirus is a hoax," and associated Q-ers

---

[17] "QAnon's Creator Made the Ultimate Conspiracy Theory" (6 Oct 2020).

[18] "Notably, QAnon builds heavily on *The Protocols of the Elders of Zion*, one of the world's most enduring conspiracy theories."

in Germany with the neo-Nazis.[19] Perhaps most surprising, this nominal news organization took unilateral, proactive measures to stifle QAnon. As they admitted, "CNN recently sent Facebook details of dozens of groups and pages that embraced QAnon conspiracy theories. Facebook said it would investigate them and had begun removing some pages." This is a remarkable admission; the Jews at CNN collaborated with Mark Zuckerberg at Facebook to suppress a global free-speech movement that they jointly dislike. The global elite strike again.

Biden, of course, would go on to win a highly contested election in 2020, and many, to this day, still believe in mass election fraud. Be that as it may, truth took one small step forward. And more people than ever now understand exactly how the US, and the world, truly operate.

---

[19] "How the 'parasite' QAnon conspiracy cult went global" (7 Oct 2020).

— 28 —
THE CASE FOR SECESSION

> "Perhaps law-abiding states should bond together and form a Union of states that will abide by the Constitution."
>
> Allen West, Chair
> Texas GOP
> 11 December 2020

Now that we are well into the Joe Biden-Kamala Harris regime, it's time to consider next steps. As bad as things are for White America today, they are about to get a lot worse. Physical, psychological, moral, and political threats hang over all our heads. We are being dispossessed in our own nation. The situation is grim but not hopeless. We have options.

In the continental US, 24 states voted majority for Trump in 2020, including some of our most populous ones: Texas, Florida, Ohio, and North Carolina, among them. The 10 largest Trump states comprise over 100 million people, and all 24 combined are pushing 150 million. This is a considerable block of people, with a considerable amount of power—political and otherwise. If these people wish to retain a modicum of self-determination—not to mention self-respect—they will have to consider the strongest possible actions. These actions include the possibility of literal secession from the United States. It's time to examine that option with all seriousness.

Biden's Jewish-Diversity Retinue

First, let's be clear about the threat posed by the Biden administration. It is clear that they hold an antipathy toward Whites, especially White males, and that they intend to either do as little as possible to support and represent White interests, or worse, to actively impede and harm those interests.

One good clue comes from Biden's Cabinet. Of his 16 major selections, we find the following: four White males (Brian Deese, Denis McDonough, Tom Vilsack, and Jake Sullivan); five Blacks, of whom four are women (Lloyd Austin, Marcia Fudge, Susan Rice, Cecilia Rouse, and Linda Thomas-Greenfield); one Indian woman (Neera Tander); one Hispanic man (Xavier Becerra)—and five Jews (Tony Blinken, Avril Haines, Ron Klain, Alejandro Mayorkas, and Janet Yellen).

Here we see a few points of interest. First, there are no White women at all—given that Jews are not White, not in the relevant sense. Second, Blacks and Jews *each* have more representation than Whites among the top 16, which is amazing in itself, given that Blacks (12.8%) and Jews (circa 2%) are distinct minorities in this country. Third, at least one of the White men, Jake Sullivan, has proven himself to be remarkably philo-Semitic; his appointment "drew broad praise from Jewish leaders," and his wife, Maggie Goodlander, worked extensively with influential Jews like Joe Lieberman, Stephen Breyer, and Merrick Garland.[1] Fourth, we have an interesting "double-banger" in Mayorkas, who manages to be both Cuban and Jewish, thus checking two important boxes. Fifth, by placing Yellen in charge of the US Treasury, Biden continues a long, nearly-unbroken line of Jews in charge of the top US financial institution.[2]

Furthermore, Biden has placed yet more Jews in important positions among his second tier. These include the half-Jewish John Kerry (environmental advisor), Jared Bernstein (council of economic advisors), Rochelle Walensky (head of CDC), and Jeff Zients (Covid czar and "counsellor to the president").

And then, of course, we have the infamous "family ties" among both Biden and Harris. Biden's three adult children all managed to acquire Jewish spouses: Hunter married "filmmaker" Melissa Cohen in 2019, daughter Ashley married Howard Krein in 2012, and (the now-deceased) Beau married the Jewish dry-cleaning heiress Hallie Olivere in 2002. For her part, Kamala Harris married the Jewish lawyer Douglas Emhoff in 2014, so we can be sure where her sympathies lie—as if there was any doubt. Bottom line: Look for lots of policies favoring Jews and Israelis, and little in the way of support for the 61% of Americans who are White. Look for so-called open borders (i.e. very generous immigration and amnesty policies), for promotion of all kinds of 'racial sensitivity' awareness and training, and for increased attacks on "hate speech," that is, on anything that the minority-laden Judeocracy decides that it doesn't like.

What To Do: Independence!

Given all this, it is difficult to find a path forward for concerned Whites. Their quality of life, their financial security, and their physical and mental health are all more or less guaranteed to decline over the coming four years. As more Democratic-leaning minorities enter the country or are granted amnesty, and thus acquire voting rights, liberal-left anti-White

---

[1] See "A closer look at Biden's foreign policy team" (*Jewish Insider*, 24 Nov 2020).
[2] Previously, Trump appointed the Jew Steven Mnuchin. For a brief further discussion, see my book *Jewish Hand in the World Wars* (2019: 140-142).

policies will become more entrenched and more extreme. This process will then accelerate over the next 25 years, as Whites become a numerical minority in the US—currently projected for around the year 2042. Jewish influence will increase proportionately, given that they are by far the leading donors, and thus the leading wire-pullers, among the Democrats.

It is clear, then, that ordinary political means—the ballot box—will no longer suffice to promote White interests. The political system is irrevocably slanted against Whites, and it will not change in our lifetimes; at least, not in the nation as it now exists. Unless we consider radical structural change, anything like a present-day America is virtually certain to increasingly pander to Jewish and non-White interests, and therefore to suffer irrecoverable decline—socially, economically, culturally, intellectually, and morally. Anything like the America that we knew in the 1950s and 1960s is done, over, finished. The three seeds of its demise were planted, in fact, many years ago: in a Jewish-dominated African slave trade that made Blacks an astonishing 20% minority already in the 1770s; in the "all men are created equal" clause of the Declaration; and in the flood of Jewish immigrants circa 1900. At that point, our fate was sealed. It was only a matter of time. Victory in WWII deferred our collapse for a few decades, but the inevitable outcome presses forward inexorably. Our end is now clearer than ever. And it will not be a happy one for Whites.

As the South recognized long ago, the only hope for long-term salvation lies in political separation. Had the Confederacy prevailed in the 1860s, the status of Southerners (and Northerners!) would be vastly higher than it is today. It is one of the great tragedies of history that a power-mad Abraham Lincoln—a man who disliked Blacks and who actually, and correctly, sought to ship them back home to Africa[3]—decided to sacrifice thousands of his fellow countrymen simply to save "the nation." In the end, some 650,000 American soldiers on both sides died; this is more than the death toll from WWI, WWII, and the Vietnam War *combined.* And this is not counting thousands of innocent civilians and slaves who also died, nor the many thousands left with crippling and debilitating injuries. Lincoln was, without doubt, the biggest war criminal in American history. We continue to pay the price to this day.

GOP-Texas leader Allen West was correct, then, in his 2020 pronouncement that the anti-Biden (I hesitate to call them pro-Trump) states ought to separate from the corrupt morass of Washington DC's America, and to form a new, better union. West considers them to be the Constitution-loving states, which is perhaps correct—although he should be careful there. The core US Constitution is a fairly useful document, but it is notably vague on who can vote. And the Amendments are highly problematic

---

[3] See "The Great Emancipator and the Issue of Race" (www.IHR.org).

in themselves, and should mostly be scrapped. But at that time, in the 1780s, the vast majority of voters were White male landholders—which, tragically, allowed Jewish men to vote. This problem must be fixed in the new nation that West envisions. Also at first, as we know, women and Blacks could not vote. As a new, White-friendly, anti-minority nation, this "new America" must certainly allow White women to vote, but it has no obligation to any minorities of any kind. In fact, any clear-thinking and brave-hearted new nation would deny citizenship to all non-Whites: all Blacks, all Hispanics, all Asians, and all Jews. It would end, and revoke existing, birthright citizenship. All this is essential, if we want to get down to fundamental issues and to address the root causes of our present decay. A properly-conceived and executed secession movement can address all these issues in a single stroke.

Some Open Questions

But there are many logistical problems here, obviously. One is the matter of which states, precisely, would compose this new America. As I mentioned at the outset, there are around 24 Red states, comprising some 150 million people. Further, they happen to be geographically contiguous, meaning that, in theory, they could unify and create a connected, single nation—one that would chop the remaining US into three or four separate blocks; but that's their problem. Additionally, we can well imagine that portions—perhaps the rural areas—of several nearby states would also like to join this newly-emergent nation. Parts of Colorado, New Mexico, Illinois, Michigan, Pennsylvania, Georgia, and Virginia, among others, may well choose to secede from their own state and join the "constitution-lovers." We can easily imagine the combined numbers approaching 200 million people in all.

Then there are further issues. Given that Jews of all types will be violently opposed to this idea, we have to take into consideration the size of the Jewish population in each of these states. Among the 24, Florida is the outlier; it has a large Jewish population, comprising around 4% of the total. Of the remaining 23, only two (Ohio and Missouri) are over 1%, and of the rest, many are under 0.5%. Consequently, Florida is unlikely to go along with a new, constitution-loving, pro-White nation. Perhaps they will have to go it alone.

Along the same lines, large Hispanic populations, especially in Texas and Florida, will pose problems for a pro-White nation. But with significantly less clout than Jews, and without a Jewish lobby actively defending them, Hispanics will be out of luck. Perhaps they will find it in their own best interests to return to Mexico or Latin America—places that would welcome their relatively advanced education, skills, and comparative wealth.

There is a third problematic group, and that is Christian Zionists. If it's true that up to 25% of American adults consider themselves "evangelical Christians" and that up to 80% of these are some version of Zionist—meaning broadly that they support Jews and Israel, for Biblical reasons—then this poses a potentially large issue, especially in the southern states.[4] But this is a regional issue, one requiring regional solutions. Secessionists will have to play up the benefits of religion, freedom, and independence, and argue that this outweighs any sanctions against local Jews.

All these issues come to a head in a larger concern: *the problem of size*. It has long been recognized, since ancient times, that overly-large states are in for trouble. Biologically-speaking, this makes sense. Humans evolved over 2 million years in small hunter-gatherer bands of perhaps 50 to 100 people; for millennia, this was the size of our 'state.' Our emotional and rational psyches evolved to deal with groups of this size, and no more. Larger groups are both unnatural and unhealthy; in larger societies, systemic corruption inevitably creeps in.

The ancient Greeks understood this intrinsically. Plato said that the maximum, ideal society would consist of 5,040 households, or around 25,000 people—for the entire city-state.[5] Hippodamus argued for an even smaller state of 10,000 citizens.[6] Aristotle broadly concurred, saying that the ideal state must be "one and self-sufficing." In Book 7 of *Politics*, he elaborates:

> [A] *great polis* is not to be confounded with a *populous* one. Moreover, experience shows that a *very populous state can rarely, if ever, be well-governed*; since all states that have a reputation for good government have a limit of population. ... *To the size of states there is a limit*, as there is to other things, plants, animals, implements. For none of these retain their natural power when they are too large or too small, but they either wholly lose their nature, or are spoiled. ... In like manner, a state when composed of too few is not, as a state ought to be, self-sufficing; when of too many, though self-sufficing in all mere necessaries, as a nation may be, *it is not a state*, being almost incapable of constitutional government. For who can be the general of such a vast multitude, or who the herald, unless he has the booming voice of a Stentor?

---

[4] See "Countering Christian Zionism in the Age of Trump" (www.merip.org, 8 Aug 2019).

[5] See *Laws*, Book 5 (737c-744e).

[6] As mentioned by Aristotle, in *Politics* II.8 (1267b).

> A state, then, only begins to exist when it has attained a population sufficient for a good life in the political community: it may indeed, if it somewhat exceeds this number, be a greater state. But, as I was saying, there must be a limit. What should be the limit will be easily ascertained by experience. For both governors and governed have duties to perform; the special functions of a governor to command and to judge. But if the citizens of a state are to judge and to distribute offices according to merit, then *they must know each other's characters*; where they do not possess this knowledge, both the election to offices and the decision of lawsuits will go wrong. When the population is very large, they are manifestly settled at haphazard, which clearly ought not to be. Besides, in an over-populous state, foreigners and aliens will readily acquire the rights of citizens, for who will find them out? *Clearly then the best limit of the population of a state is the largest number which suffices for the purposes of life, and can be taken in at a single view.* (Book 7.4; italics added)

Remarkable insight, and utterly appropriate for the present day.

More recently, social theorists like Leopold Kohr, Ivan Illich, and E. F. Schumacher have also persuasively argued for smaller states. Kohr suggests that, under modern, technological conditions, the maximum size for a well-governed and rational state is perhaps 10 million people.[7] Say what you will about the small European nations today, but if nothing else, they are, for the most part, rationally governed; generally speaking, they "work". And their smallness and relative ethnic homogeneity play a large part in their success.

This all helps to explain, first, the insanity of trying to manage a present-day America of 330 million people. Three hundred million Gandhis would be ungovernable, let alone the present American mish-mash. Second, it suggests that Allen West's "new America" of perhaps 150 million is likewise far too big. Texas alone is 30 million people; it really ought to become its own nation-state. Florida, Ohio, and North Carolina, all over 10 million, could easily be their own nation-states. The smaller US states might fruitfully band together. Ultimately, the Red states could form five or ten independent nations, which might then organize a local American confederation of some sort, to advance their collective interests—but without surrendering local sovereignty. Five or ten small, independent, pro-White nations would further allow for a fair amount of social and political experimentation, yielding successes that could be transferred to the others.

---

[7] See his fascinating book *The Breakdown of Nations* (1957/2012).

And diverse states would be harder to undermine by any potentially-resurgent Jewish Lobby—just as a unified European Union is much easier to corrupt than 27 independent nations.

So This Means War!

"Yes," says the critic, "all fine and good. But the mighty US military will come in and crush any budding secession movement. You haven't a prayer against them." Yes and no. A single movement by a single state might be squelched, but simultaneous movements across the nation would be much harder to address. We have to understand that our federal government is actually much weaker than it appears, at least when it comes to internal disruption. We can bomb the hell out of Afghanistan, but a "CHAZ" microstate in downtown Portland carries on for months, run by nothing more than a handful of degenerate anarchists. Black Lives Matter lunatics managed weeks of looting and burning because they were a diversified, incorrigible, lawless band, working in several locations simultaneously. "Oh, but BLM and CHAZ had the implicit support of the Democratic power elite." Fine—but a multi-state secession effort would have the implicit support of many in the Republican power elite. For them, there is much to be gained. Lots of new states mean lots of new presidents, new governments, and new institutions (imagine: new universities not dominated by a Jewish intellectual class!). Plenty of new opportunities for business, charities, religious groups, academia—the possibilities are immense.

Still, we have to be honest. It could come down to war, at least in some form. We need not worry about cruise missiles raining down on Dallas or Columbus, or tanks rolling through the Indiana plains, but we can imagine federal troops being compelled to take some sort of action. Well, then—*defend yourself*. Thus it has always been. As I've argued in the past, if a few thousand low-IQ Afghans can hold the US military at bay for 20 years, then a few million motivated Whites can do much more. After all, those unwilling to fight are those undeserving to win anything. We would do well to recall what Nietzsche said about liberalism and the struggle for freedom; I quote him at length:

> *My conception of freedom*. The value of a thing sometimes does not lie in that which one attains by it, but in what one *pays* for it—what it *costs* us. I shall give an example. Liberal institutions cease to be liberal as soon as they are attained: later on, there are no worse and no more thorough injurers of freedom than liberal institutions. Their effects are known well enough: they undermine the will to power; they level mountain and valley, and call that morality; they make men

> small, cowardly, and hedonistic—every time it is the herd animal that triumphs with them. Liberalism: in other words, *herd-animalization*. …
>
> For what is freedom? That one has the will to assume responsibility for oneself. That one maintains the distance which separates us. That one becomes more indifferent to difficulties, hardships, privation, even to life itself. That one is prepared to sacrifice human beings for one's cause, not excluding oneself. Freedom means that the manly instincts that delight in war and victory dominate over other instincts, for example, over those of "pleasure." The human being who has become free—and how much more the *spirit* who has become free—spits on the contemptible type of well-being, that dreamt of by shopkeepers, Christians, cows, Englishmen, and other democrats. The free man is a *warrior.*
>
> How is freedom measured in individuals and peoples? According to the *resistance which must be overcome*, according to the *exertion required*, to remain on top. The highest type of free men should be sought where the highest resistance is constantly overcome: five steps from tyranny, close to the threshold of the danger of servitude. This is true psychologically if, by "tyrants," are meant inexorable and fearful instincts that provoke the maximum of authority and discipline against themselves; most beautiful type: Julius Caesar. This is true politically too; one need only go through history. The peoples who had some value, attained some value, never attained it under liberal institutions: it was *great danger* that made something of them that merits respect. Danger alone acquaints us with our own resources, our virtues, our armor and weapons, our spirit, and forces us to be strong. First principle: one must *need to be strong*—otherwise one will never become strong.
>
> Those large hothouses for the strong—for the strongest kind of human being that has so far been known, the aristocratic commonwealths of the type of Rome or Venice—understood freedom exactly in the sense in which I understand it: as something one has or does *not* have, something one *wants*, something one *conquers*.[8]

Do we really *want* to be free? Do we *want* to be strong? Do we have the *courage* to be strong? I believe we do. I believe that White Americans—at

---

[8] *Twilight of the Idols*, chap. 11, sec. 38.

least, some core segment of this group—will find it in themselves to take the reins, to fight, and consequently "to force the will of millennia upon new tracks" (to quote Nietzsche once again). We need to hit them where it hurts. Now is the time to act.

And I can promise you, the American Judeocracy fears nothing more than a widespread, pro-White secession movement; it is their greatest nightmare. Let's work to make it come true.

— 29 —
NATIONAL SOCIALISM TODAY

Background

The moral, social, and philosophical bankruptcy of our modern political/economic ideologies is becoming more apparent by the day. Free-market capitalism, conventional socialism, democracy, and communism are all demonstrable failures. All fail to sustain and uplift humanity; they fail to acknowledge racial realities; and they fail to establish a balanced and sustainable relationship with nature. Political corruption, widespread fraud, unprincipled spinelessness, moral and spiritual decay, and blatant self-enrichment mark the current systems of nearly all developed nations on Earth. All seemingly compete in a race to the bottom, to see which can achieve the most undignified and degrading form of social existence in the shortest period of time.

In the past 100 years, only one system has proven able to defy this trend: Adolf Hitler's National Socialism (1933-1945). NS Germany was able to achieve, in a period of less than 10 years, unprecedented and remarkable gains in economics, military power, social and cultural advancement, and national morale—and all amidst a global depression that was utterly crushing other advanced nations. Hitler's system proved such a threat to the other world powers, and especially to the Jewish oligarchy that ruled in Europe and America, that they became determined to destroy it. And destroy it they did.

The threat from Hitler was never military—he never sought war with the West, and always only wanted to move to the East in order to acquire badly-needed living space for his people, and to counter the looming Judeo-Bolshevist threat in the Soviet Union. Rather, the threat was Germany's *success*: that Hitler might prove to the world that by driving out the Jewish element, by refocusing economies inward, and by promoting a non-materialistic worldview that extolled human character and spirit, that he would expose the many failings of Western Jewish-capitalist-materialistic society. This positive counter-example was something that the Western powers simply could not countenance, and so they conspired to destroy Hitler and his nascent society. In May of 1945, after five long years of fighting, with the entire industrial world arrayed against one nation, they prevailed.

The Allies defeated NS Germany, but not its ideas. Ideas, as they say, are bulletproof. They are eternal and immortal. Hitler's vision still lives, and it has the power and potential to restore the world to a semblance of sanity, sustainability, and justice. This essay briefly outlines what National Socialism is, what a NS nation might look like today, and offers a few preliminary steps toward achieving such a vision.

What is National Socialism?

National Socialism is, of course, a conjunction of nationalism and socialism. *Nationalism* is any tendency to favor one's own nation or nationality, as opposed to outsiders, foreigners, or those of other ethnicities or races. It typically involves national independence, self-reliance, strong self-determination, and a robust sense of patriotism. A nationalist is usually concerned to have a military capable of self-defense (but not empire-building), to have an economy and a currency that operates independently of other nations, and to emphasize traditional culture and social norms. A 'nation,' in turn, is literally a breed, stock, or race of people. The word derives from the Latin *nasci* or *natus*, 'to be born.' A nation, then, is a group of people who are genetically related, of common ancestry, and who comprise a unified ethnicity. Nationalism works for the sole interest of the dominant ethnicity.

The opposite of nationalism is 'internationalism'—that is, globalism. Internationalists, such as those who predominate in the West today, promote global trade, global treaties and business pacts, currency unification, and active involvement in foreign affairs. In the old days, they pushed for colonialism. Today they promote international business practices (such as low-cost labor in third-world countries), and they like to project military power around the world and to engage in so-called 'nation building.' Being unconcerned with ethnic unity or national homogeneity, globalists advocate for mass immigration, interracial marriage, racial equality, and multiculturalism—none of which are historically or biologically natural, and all of which are proven detriments to the national majority.

Socialism—loosely defined as any system in which the government owns or controls large sectors of the economy—is widely practiced around the world, often in a kind of partnership with capitalist activities. Socialism is not a single entity but rather a spectrum of political and economic positions that can range from relatively unobtrusive to highly active and controlling. Socialism tends to benefit society as a whole, especially the middle and lower classes, whereas capitalism tends to benefit capital—i.e. the wealthy, and in practice, wealthy Jews disproportionately.

Hitler found virtue in both nationalism and socialism. He decided that it was necessary, early in his career, to take the small existing German Workers' Party (DAP) and make it both nationalist and socialist—hence, the NSDAP, or 'Nazi' party. This was neither radical nor evil; it was simply common sense, for someone who was concerned about the well-being of his fellow Germanic people.

As a movement, Hitler's National Socialism was remarkably progressive and benign. It was codified in the famous 25 Points that he established 100 years ago, in 1920. Even today, they are highly relevant. They call for equal rights for German people (Points 2 and 9). They give citizens the right to select the laws and governmental structure (6). They abolish war-profiteering (12). They call for corporate profit-sharing with employees (14). They support retirement pensions, a strong middle class, free higher education, public health, maternity welfare, and religious freedom (15, 16, 20, 21, 24). And they explicitly endorse the principle of "Common good before individual good" (24).

On the other hand, only a relatively few points appear threatening or aggressive. They grant citizenship only to ethnic Germans, explicitly denying it to Jews (4). They block further immigration, and compel recent immigrants to leave (8). They seek to prohibit all financial speculation in land (17). More harshly, the plan calls for the death penalty against "traitors, usurers, and profiteers" (18). It demands that the German-language press be controlled only by ethnic Germans—but doesn't restrict press in other languages (23). And it calls for "a strong central authority in the State" (25), thus being opposed to anything like parliamentarian democracy.

Despite Hitler's well-known and openly admitted anti-Semitism, Jews are only mentioned in passing in the 25 Points. They are banned from citizenship, and therefore from any role in government or the German-language press. Recent (since August 1914) Jewish immigrants, like all immigrants, must leave. And the National Socialist view of religious freedom "fights against the Jewish materialist spirit" (24). But apart from these two references, there is no explicit mention of Jews or any other minorities. There are no threats to imprison or kill Jews. Longtime Jewish residents can stay in the country. There is no confiscation of Jewish wealth, with the stated exceptions. There is no repression of Gypsies or gays. And there is certainly nothing that sounds like a looming 'Holocaust.'

In sum, Hitler's National Socialism was essentially the product of German nationalism and progressive socialism, combined with a mild form of anti-Semitism. It is hardly the evil that is portrayed. In fact, quite the contrary: It proved itself to be a recipe for astonishing success.

A Modern Vision of National Socialism

Hitler's Germany—the Third Reich—was a unique product of the people and the time. Formally speaking, it cannot be duplicated today. However, certain core elements of this ideology can be reproduced and implemented in the present day. In what follows, I offer one vision of a modern NS program, and then suggest some proposed steps on how to achieve that vision.

Hitler's National Socialism was explicitly and exclusively German—by and for the Germanic people. But we know that he extolled the virtues of the Aryan people generally, that is, of indigenous European Whites. Any modern form of NS should therefore be generalized to address all White people globally. 'White' may be loosely defined as people of predominantly European ethnicity, which extends to Ukraine and the western portions of Russia. 'White' is not a matter of skin color but of national ethnic origin; as such, neither Jews nor any Middle Easterners, neither Arabs nor Asians nor North Africans, qualify as White, no matter how pale they appear.

As a first step, we may update, generalize, condense, and reissue the famous 25 Points. I hereby present a new program:

20 Points of Contemporary National Socialism

1. We demand that all White people everywhere have the right to live in a White nation, with White governance, on the basis of the universal principle of self-determination of all peoples.

2. We demand that Whites have the right to self-governance in all those nations and regions that have been historically colonized and developed by Whites—that is, Europe (including the United Kingdom), Ukraine, western Russia, the United States, Canada, Australia, and New Zealand. Whites need not form a single, global nation; rather, individual regions and groupings of Whites must be free to create their own regional nations, ones that are best able to respond to their local conditions.

3. Only Whites can become citizens of White nations. Only those who have a predominantly White ancestry can be fellow countrymen. Therefore, neither Jews, Middle Easterners, Arabs, nor North Africans can be citizens of a White nation.

4. Those who are not citizens must live in White nations as foreigners and must be subject to the law of aliens. Non-citizens are entitled to none of the rights of White citizens.

5. The right to choose the government and determine the laws of the state shall belong only to citizens. We therefore demand that no public office, of whatever nature, whether in the central government, the province, or the municipality, shall be held by anyone who is not a citizen. We strongly oppose the widespread present-day practice of parliamentarian and representative democracies in which people are appointed to government posts by favor of the party, individual leaders, or financial donors, without regard to character and ability.

6. We demand that the state shall above all undertake to ensure that every citizen shall have the possibility of living decently and earning a livelihood. If this ever becomes difficult to achieve, then aliens (non-citizens) may be expelled to free up space and resources for citizens.

7. Any immigration of non-Whites into White nations must be prevented. All non-Whites who were foreign-born shall be compelled to leave immediately. All native-born non-Whites, who are automatically non-citizens, shall be encouraged to leave by all possible means.

8. All citizens, including women, must possess equal rights and duties. This does not, however, imply any sort of human equality.

9. The first duty of every citizen must be to work, physically or intellectually. No individual shall do any work that offends against the interest of the White community to the benefit of all.

Therefore we demand:

10. That all unearned income—that is, purely financial income derived from speculation and loan-interest—be abolished. In practice, such income will be taxed at 100%. This will prevent people, especially the poor and the middle class, from falling into a condition of interest slavery.

11. We demand profit-sharing with employees for all large industries.

12. We demand a generous increase in old-age pensions.

13. We demand the creation and maintenance of a large and sound middle-class.

14. We demand agrarian reform in accordance with our national requirements. We demand the prohibition of all land speculation. We demand respect for nature—for animals, plants, and the land—and we demand the designation and protection of vast areas of wilderness in each bioregion.

15. We demand the harshest punishment for those who work to the detriment of the common welfare. Traitors, usurers, profiteers, etc., are to be punished to the maximum extent of the law, regardless of creed or race.

16. In order to make it possible for every capable and industrious White citizen to obtain higher education, and thus the opportunity to reach into positions of leadership, the state must assume the responsibility of thoroughly organizing the entire public cultural system. The conception of the state idea (civics) must be taught in the schools from the very beginning. We demand that exceptionally-talented children of poor parents, whatever their station or occupation, be fully educated at the state's expense.

17. The state has the duty to help raise the standard of national health by providing maternity welfare centers, by prohibiting child labor, by increasing physical fitness through the introduction of compulsory games and gymnastics, and by the greatest possible encouragement of associations concerned with the physical education of the young. Special emphasis shall be placed on healthy diet and nutrition.

18. We demand the firmest opposition to those who propagate deliberate political lies and disseminate them through the press or media. In order to make possible the creation of a true and unbiased press, we demand that all press and media outlets be under the full control of White citizens, with no non-White or foreign influence. Regarding the media and entertainment content, we demand the firmest opposition to all those tendencies in art, television, cinema, and literature that have a disruptive or degrading influence upon the life of our people; any organizations that offend on this basis shall be dissolved.

19. We demand freedom of thought for all rational and morally-uplifting worldviews and philosophies, insofar as they do not endanger the state or offend the moral and ethical sense of the White race. White nations everywhere shall fight against the Jewish materialist spirit within and without, including its Marxist and capitalist forms. The prosperity of White people can only come about from the principle: *Common Good before Individual Good.*

20. In order to carry out this program, we demand the creation of a strong central authority in the state.

These principles form the core of what may be called a contemporary, 21st-century National Socialism. They can apply to all White people anywhere in the world.

Steps Toward Implementation

Whites globally are under threat due to declining health, declining relative numbers, and declining influence in their own nations. All these trends must be reversed, and will be reversed, under a new National Socialism. The above 20 Points lay out a vision of national life that is far from the current situation: one in which Whites are dominated by a small Jewish elite and their collaborating non-Jews, are subject to degrading and humiliating Jewish cultural values, and are compelled to share national space and national resources with large (and growing) numbers of non-Whites.

How to begin? Like Hitler in 1920, we must start small. The precursor to the NSDAP party was a small group of just seven men who met weekly—"the same old seven," as Hitler put it. But they were steady and consistent. They had a number of tasks to fulfil, and they set themselves to work, slowing growing a true social movement.

Education is undoubtedly the first task—education of oneself and of others. Today, we must learn from history, and learn the facts of the contemporary world. Anyone moving forward with a program of contemporary National Socialism must be intellectually well-armed. *Know the facts: know the history, know the enemy.* Here, then, are the basic facts:

- *Race matters.* Whites, like all races and ethnicities, have unique qualities and capabilities. But as history has shown, Whites are exceptional in their ability to build culture and civilization. Blacks and Latinos have generally proven unable to construct complex and elevated societies. Jews participate in Western civilization, but in a parasitic and ultimately destructive manner. Asians have some ability for culture-building, but on terms quite different from the West.

- *Multiculturalism is destructive.* Throughout history, as nations and civilizations became more diverse, they declined. The greatest civilizations in history were always mono-cultural and mono-racial. Multiculturalism and racial mixing are recipes for decay and collapse. This is an iron law of history.

- *Jews are uniquely dangerous.* As Hitler, Goebbels, and others understood, Jews pose unique and deadly risks to White society. Because Jews appear White, they can move throughout White society largely undetected. Yet they virtually always retain their racial tribal identity as Jews, and they work collectively (and sometimes subconsciously) for Jewish interests, despite any appearances to the contrary. Jews promote the lowest social and cultural values, by which they simultaneously degrade and profit from gullible Whites. Jewish emphasis on money and power reflects the age-old Jewish fixation on material things, and a consequent rejection of higher aims and goals. Jews will stoop to the basest and cruelest actions if it furthers their interests; war, mass-murder, large-scale sickness and disease, environmental destruction, mass impoverishment—all these are ready weapons for the Jewish elite.

- *Whites are highly vulnerable.* Whites are generally open, honest, and trusting people. They are selfless, altruistic, and idealistic. Such values have given the world the heights of artistic, cultural, and intellectual achievement. These values should be honored and protected. But unfortunately they also make Whites uniquely vulnerable to control and manipulation by ruthless, parasitic, and immoral non-Whites—Jews among all. In a cruel irony, Whites' best qualities are turned against them. Hence, they must all be made more sensitive to the nature of the danger. There is nothing worse for White well-being than a gullible and naïve liberalism.

- *White society is right and just.* The Jewish media and Jewish-funded political elites are relentless in their condemnation of "white supremacy" and "white nationalism." Anything remotely along these lines is labeled as "Nazi" or "neo-Nazi," with the obvious implication that they are something evil. And yet, "Black lives matter," and illegal immigrants and fleeing refugees are "owed" protection and civil rights. The hypocrisy and illogic are appalling.

- *White societies have been the greatest in history.* From the early civilizations of ancient Greece and Rome to the heights of the Renaissance and the Enlightenment, to the British Empire and the early American experiment, Whites have achieved astonishing and unmatchable feats. Art, literature, science, philosophy, music—the greatest achievements in all these fields occurred in White nations. Our present degraded world does not allow for White greatness; but with focus and effort, it can be restored.

- *Perhaps no society in modern history has achieved more, in less time, than Hitler's Germany.* Hitler took power in 1933, and within just three years he had conquered runaway inflation, driven down unemployment, and put industry back to work. After six years, Germany was once again a world power. And within eight years, only the combined militaries of all other industrial nations could stop them. To understand the context of German greatness, read *Mein Kampf.*

- *The Holocaust was, in large part, a fiction.* This supposed ultimate evil of the Third Reich is largely a composite of rumor, hyperbole, and outright fraud. The gas chambers could never have operated in the manner claimed, and most were certainly life-saving delousing chambers. Many of the Jews killed during WW2 were partisan fighters, especially in Russia, and thus were 'fair game' for German soldiers. Many Jewish camp deaths were a result of typhus and other diseases that were exacerbated by Allied attacks. Hitler's plan was always and only to expel the Jews and ship them to captured Soviet territories, never to mass-murder them. Actual total Jewish fatalities amounted to some 500,000, not six million. Read the best sources on this event, such as *Dissecting the Holocaust* (Rudolf), *Holocaust: Introduction* (Dalton), or *Debating the Holocaust* (Dalton).

- *The so-called virtues of modern society, such as democracy, equality, and freedom, are in fact vices.* Democracy is, in effect, rule by the masses, and the moral and intellectual level of the masses is so low as to be disastrous, if they hold the power to choose leaders. The typical parliamentarian "representative of the people" is an unprincipled, amoral dupe of political lobbies, utterly unworthy of positions of authority. All this explains why the current political discourse, and the words of our politicians, are so crude and simplistic. Democracy is based on human equality, but unfortunately human equality is a myth that has its roots in the Judeo-Christian Bible; in reality, there is no meaningful sense in which people are equal. And modern freedoms—like freedom of the press—are either illusions or nonsensical concepts. Present-day libertinism, liberalism, and excessive freedom lead to social decay, as even Plato recognized. The solution to these problems is a folk-oriented yet strong central government with rulers of vision and character who are of the same ethnicity as their citizens.

- *Traditional Judeo-Christianity is an ideological death-trap.* Traditional Christianity is a wholly Jewish construct, and a fraudulent one at that. The Jesus-story is a pile of absurdities that cannot possibly be true, and in any case relies on blind faith in an itinerant Jewish rabbi, "Jesus of Nazareth." The entire New Testament is an *ex post facto* construction by the Jew Paul of Tarsus, simply to delude and debase the gullible Gentile masses and to turn them against the stronger and nobler Roman values. To believe in the Jewish God (Jehovah) and in a fairytale afterlife is to lead a life of supreme stupidity. Hitler and the National Socialists understood this, which is why they emphasized the value, for the masses, of a "positive Christianity"—meaning, an ennobling and transcendent worldview appropriate for Aryan humanity.

But this has almost no connection to the Jewish-inspired gutter-bin Christianity of Catholicism or Protestantism.

- *White National Socialism is neither 'hatred' nor 'supremacy.'* There is nothing hateful in the above 20 Points, or in these various elaborations. The only true hate to be found is in the Jewish and ultra-liberal hatred of these ideas, and in their hatred of Whites who wish to lead their own lives, out from under the Jewish thumb. By seeking to live in a White society, Whites obviously have neither desire nor need to be 'supreme' over anyone. Blacks, Hispanics, Jews, Asians and other such ethnicities are encouraged to live their own lives according to their own values—*in their own countries*. A White National Socialism would encourage and assist this process to the greatest possible extent.

- *'America' is finished.* The largest White nation on Earth is the United States, with around 200 million Whites. Unfortunately, the US is also the most corrupted and debased nation on Earth. Nowhere else are Jewish values and Jewish wealth more dominant. The seeds of American decay were planted many years ago, in the importation of millions of Black African slaves (with the considerable aid of Jewish slave traders), in the "all men are created equal" clause of the Declaration, and in the mass immigration of Jews at the turn of the 20th century. At that point, we were doomed. It was only a matter of time. Today, we are seeing the fruit of these tragic errors. 'America' is finished. So put away your American flags and your banners, ditch your MAGA hats, and set yourself to the hard work of building a new White nation under National Socialist principles.

Education, then, is the overriding task at the moment. But let me close this essay with a few short thoughts on additional actions that Whites can take in self-defense. If education is the first task, *small-scale organizing* is the second. Initiate local groups, with actual face-to-face meetings. Call them "alt-right," "dissident right," "White lives matter," or some related name. Advertise locally, and expect resistance. Discuss local issues, discuss history, discuss global politics. Develop local strategies appropriate for each local region. There is no substitute for face-to-face interaction.

Task three: *Reach out to the public*. Establish websites or social media. Do local flyering or advertising. Let people know who you are, and don't be shy about defending National Socialism. When they call you a Nazi, say "Thank you!"

Task four: *Claim authority*. Stake out a local territory and declare it liberated from Jewish control. Establish a "Jew-free autonomous zone." Declare it White-only, and encourage any non-Whites to leave. Declare local rule by National Socialist principles. Explain to the local populace that you no pose no risk, are not violent, and are only working in their own best interests. Do good local works: charity, volunteer, environmental. Uphold the highest standards of character and morality. Set a good example, and prove yourselves worthy of respect and self-rule.

Task five: *Network*. Reach out to other nearby groups, and establish working links. Learn from each other's successes and failures. Build alliances, but do not sacrifice your basic National Socialist principles.

Task six: *Bide your time, and be prepared.* All current social trends are negative, and things could get much worse very quickly. In America, the Biden regime and its attendant Jewish entourage will surely accelerate the decay. In the coming social chaos, opportunities will arise. Be ready. Be prepared to take a more active role in local governance.

Amidst the coming widespread strife and decay, the best will emerge. Be that vanguard. Strive not for perfection but for greatness. The future awaits.

— 30 —
THE EMPEROR'S NEW MASK

In March of 2021, Texas eliminated all restrictions related to the Covid pandemic. After one full year, the shutdown ended, restaurant capacities were restored to 100%, and perhaps most significantly for everyday life, mask mandates were lifted. Masks were the most visible, and the most individually obtrusive, aspect of the pandemic. At the time, 34 states had some form of mask mandate; the 16 states without mandates included Texas plus Alaska, Arizona, Florida, Georgia, Idaho, Iowa, Mississippi, Missouri, Montana, Nebraska, North Dakota, Oklahoma, South Dakota, and Tennessee. This meant that around 100 million Americans were free to go maskless, whereas over 200 million were still under mandates.

Among all states taking action against the virus, six are generally recognized as having been the harshest: California, Illinois, Michigan, New York, Vermont, and Washington.[1] Of these, Michigan seems to have suffered the most, economically; 32% of its private sector businesses were closed due to the lockdown mandated by Gov. Gretchen Whitmer, the highest in the nation.[2] This fact alone put her in strong contention for Worst Governor in America, surpassing even such luminaries as Gavin ("The French Laundry") Newsom and Andrew ("Strip Poker") Cuomo. At least Michiganders did not have to worry about her sexually harassing any female staffers—though we can't quite say the same for Whitmer's Jewish-lesbian AG, Dana Nessel.

Along with the Michigan business lockdown, of course, came stringent mask mandates, which were initiated in July 2020. The mask mandates in themselves warrant some investigation.

At the time, a correspondent of mine in Michigan contacted his local state representative, a Democrat, regarding the status of lifting the mask mandate. He received a terribly snarky reply from a staffer, along the lines of, "the Representative has no interest in rescinding mask mandates anytime soon." Furthermore, added the staffer, "it is extremely unlikely that you will see any push to repeal mask mandates (by Republicans or Democrats) until the majority of our people are vaccinated and the virus is under

---

[1] "Six pack of states that remain tough on COVID-19," *HBS Dealer* (22 May 2020).
[2] "Michigan Businesses Nation's Hardest Hit By Government Lockdowns," *Michigan Capitol Confidential* (7 Dec 2020).

control"—meaning, of course, little hope of people breathing freely again in Michigan.

To his credit, though, the staffer included a link to an actual scientific study, along with the claim that "masks have been scientifically proven to reduce the transmission of COVID and other airborne illnesses." The report, "An evidence review of face masks against COVID-19," makes for an excellent case study in the whole mask debate.[3] As the one and only piece of evidence offered, it surely must be the most important. Evidently Democrats around the nation were instructed to point to this very study in defense of masks. It is therefore worthy of some critical examination, especially given that the entire mask saga is bound to recur in the near future.

A Few Preliminaries

Before looking at the study itself, let me make one initial point: It is largely irrelevant to claim that "masks have been proven to reduce transmission"—this much is obvious. Any mask, of almost any type, will, to some degree, "reduce transmission" of virus-laden droplets or aerosols. The relevant questions are

1) *To what extent does the reduction in transmission translate into reduced human suffering* (sickness and death), and,
2) *Does this reduction offset the disadvantages and costs of mandating masks.*

If we don't ask the right questions up front, we won't reach any useful conclusions. But it is a nifty trick, to pose a false or trivial question and then easily "prove" it to be correct—something like a Straw Man fallacy in reverse. Nice try.

Let me turn, then, to this most-important of mask studies. We see that the report was published in the prestigious PNAS on 11 January 2021. However, we note also that the paper was submitted on 13 July 2020. There is of course always some lag time, but amidst a global crisis, six months seems unduly excessive. (Also strange is the fact that the paper was accepted for publication on 5 December 2020; there is no obvious reason to wait for almost two months to publish, on-line, a study of such urgency.) Given a July 2020 submission date, all developments between that date and January 2021 were of necessity unexamined. This is significant; as we will see, there was one study that certainly should have been included in any mask discussion.

---

[3] PNAS (11 Jan 2021).

Next there is the question of authorship. The study itself has fully 19 named authors—more names make it more impressive, of course. The lead author (always the main person of the group) is one Jeremy Howard. If we look for Howard's affiliations, we find two: "fast.ai, San Francisco," and "The Data Institute, University of San Francisco." Take the latter first. USF is a small, private university in central San Francisco, which indeed has a Data Institute, dedicated to "creating a new partnership between industry and academia." And this is perfect for Mr. (not Dr.) Howard, because "industry" is what he does best. His other affiliation, fast.ai, is a small high-tech startup run only by himself and a partner, Rachel Thomas. A review of his bio ("About the team") and his Wikipedia entry demonstrate clearly that Howard ("entrepreneur") is in no sense a scientist or researcher; his forte is business and marketing, nothing more. Indeed, Wikipedia only indicates that he "studied philosophy" at his Australian university, *apparently not even graduating with a bachelor's degree.* And this man is the lead author in a vital national, even international, study. Both PNAS and USF seem to have very low standards these days for their "scientific" researchers.

The Study That Wasn't

Turning to the study itself, we read in the Abstract that "the preponderance of evidence indicates that mask-wearing reduces transmissibility per contact"—but again, as I said, this much is obvious. From this fact, they recommend "the adoption of public cloth mask wearing…in conjunction with existing hygiene strategies." The Abstract closes with this: "We recommend that public officials and government strongly encourage the use of widespread face masks in public, including the use of appropriate regulation"—implying, but not explicitly calling for, mask mandates.

The study can be functionally divided into two parts. The first part covers some background and history, and then addresses the important issue of "direct evidence" for mask efficacy. Part two is an elaboration of six questions relating to mask use and impact. Let's examine each part separately.

In part one, the authors rightly note that the best and only truly compelling scientific evidence comes from *randomized controlled trials*, or RCTs (or equivalently, a metanalysis of several RCTs). In an RCT, one group of random subjects is assigned to the intervention method (here, wearing a mask), and another random group is assigned as the control (here, not wearing a mask). The two groups are studied over time, and the effects are then compared. Here, we would like to know, for example, the Covid infection rates for mask-wearers versus non-mask-wearers. This would tell us if masks provide any protection to the user, and if so, how much. (In the best of all worlds, RCTs would be "double-blind," meaning that neither researcher nor subject would be aware of who was in the test group and who was in the control. This works well for pills, because some subjects can be given a placebo. But with face masks, it is obviously impossible to run a blind test.)

Unfortunately for us all, the researchers inform us that "for population health measures, we should not generally expect to be able to find controlled trials [RCTs], due to logistical and ethical reasons." Therefore, they add, "we should instead seek a wider evidence base." "There is no RCT for the impact of masks on community transmission of any respiratory infection in a pandemic." In other words, the gold standard for scientifically valid research—an RCT—is *not possible* for Covid, they say. Therefore, we are stuck with a poor second-best, namely, *observational* studies—studies, which are, by nature, anecdotal, suffer from recall bias, and can point only to correlation, not causation.

But more to the point, the authors are simply *wrong*: we in fact can have RCTs for this (or any) pandemic, and researchers in Denmark reported on just such a study—with very interesting results. But I defer that discussion for the moment.

Howard and colleagues then note that, even with the second-best observational studies, we have *only one*: "Only one observational study has directly analyzed the impact of mask use in the community on COVID transmission." This study, of Beijing households, found masks to be effective, but only if *all* members wore them, and only if use was implemented *before anyone* displayed any symptoms. This study thus has no relevance to broader public use of masks. A few other small studies have been done on SARS and influenza, but the applicability of these to Covid is unknown, and in any case, "none of the studies looked specifically at cloth masks," which is the explicit recommendation of Howard and colleagues.

They continue: A 2011 study of 67 studies, both RCT and observational, on ordinary, non-pandemic occurrences of the flu and other respiratory diseases, showed that "there was *insufficient* evidence to provide recommendation on the use of facial barriers without other measures." Hence, masks alone seemed to offer no protection. If they only work in conjunction with other measures, then it is more likely that the other measures were providing the bulk of the protection.

Most importantly, the authors then briefly mention an April 2020 study on masks and respiratory viruses that examined both RCTs and observational cases (pre-pandemic).[4] Using only the stronger RCT data, Brainard and colleagues concluded that "there was only weak evidence for

---

[4] "Facemasks and similar barriers to prevent respiratory illness such as COVID-19: A rapid systematic review," J. Brainard et al, *MedRxiv*.

a small effect." This, in fact, is what anti-maskers had been saying—of the actual, reliable evidence, we have, at best, "weak evidence of a small effect." And on this basis, we inflicted mandatory masks on hundreds of millions of people, including millions of children.

Summing up part one, Howard and friends did their best to make lemonade: "Overall, direct evidence of the efficacy of mask use is supportive, but inconclusive. Since there are no RCTs [on Covid], only one observational trial [Beijing households], and unclear evidence from other respiratory illnesses, we will need to look at a wider body of evidence." In other words, since real, solid evidence was lacking, they had to hunt around for indirect, anecdotal, and other dubious means of reaching the conclusion that they sought.

Six Questions

Part two opens with an ethical question: Can we conduct true Covid RCTs, which necessarily require that we expose unmasked people to potential infection? Howard badly wants to say 'no.' But of course, medical scientists do this all the time; they always strive to have a test group and a control group, the latter of which is unprotected, given a placebo, or otherwise placed at risk. This is the only scientific way to establish efficacy of medical treatments, and thus it is standard practice. There are only rare exceptions, such as treating children or pregnant women, in which the ethical concerns indeed usually outweigh the benefits of controlled testing. But for adults, we take our risks, knowing that many more will be benefitted than harmed. Despite all this, Howard is adamant: "ethical issues prevent the availability of an unmasked control arm." Again, this is his lame attempt to excuse the utter absence of RCTs, and to force the argument to rest upon much weaker bases.

We see his desperation immediately thereafter, where Howard offers us a fine example of Orwellian doublespeak. Lacking firm RCT data, "we need to consider first principles, alongside observational data, … natural experiments, and policy considerations"—a conglomeration that he wonderfully summarizes as "a discursive synthesis of interdisciplinary lines of evidence which are disparate by necessity." George O himself could not have concocted a better phrase.

He then moves to his six main questions: 1) What are the population effects of mask-wearing? 2) What is required for mask efficacy? 3) Do masks prevent infected wearers from spreading the disease? 4) Do masks protect uninfected wearers? 5) Do masks have unintended drawbacks? and 6) How might we implement mask mandates? I will restrict myself to a few key comments on each question.

First: On population impact, Howard compares both mask and non-mask *nations*, and then mask and non-mask *states* in the US. At the national level, one study found overall transmission rates to be 7.5 times higher in non-mask nations, but there are so many variables at work in different nations that the effect of any one action, like masks, is impossible to isolate (lacking an RCT). Among the various states, another study claims 2% lower daily growth rate in mask states, versus non-mask. But again, multiple and diverse measures were taken in the 50 states, over various periods of time, making it impossible to isolate the mask-alone effect. This is precisely why we need RCT data.

Howard then cites—of all things—a Goldman Sachs study of July 2020 ("Face masks and GDP"), arguing that a nationwide mask mandate could save up to 5% of the US GDP (by avoiding harsh lockdowns), which translates to about $1 trillion. Think of it: compel 330 million people to wear masks, and save $1 trillion! Who could turn that down? Not Jeremy Howard. One trillion dollars is too much for him to pass up: "mask-wearing could be a low-risk measure with a potentially large positive impact." Of course, on the other hand, Congress passed a *$2 trillion* package for "Covid relief"—thus for just *half* that price, everyone could have lived mask-free. What a deal that would have been.

Given the dearth of empirical data, researchers typically turn to computer models, and this is precisely what has happened with Covid. Howard cites a study by Stutt,[5] explaining that "it is impossible to get accurate experimental evidence for potential control interventions, but that this problem can be approached by using mathematical modelling." But math models can easily lead to absurd and unrealistic results. As Howard explains, "the effect is greatest when 100% of the public wear face masks. [Stutt] found that, with a policy that *all* individuals must wear a mask *all* of the time," that viral spread could be eliminated. Right—and if everyone donned spacesuits for the next six months straight, that would do it too. In the end, as Howard admits, "models presented…are only as accurate as their assumptions and parameters"—but 'unrealistic accuracy' is worthless. "Simulations and similar models are simplifications of the real world, and cannot fully model all of the interactions and drivers of results in practice." Of course.

Second: On efficacy and transmission characteristics, Howard offers little of value. He cites the widely-used statistic that asymptomatic individuals account for 40 to 45% of all infections, and then concludes, with no justification, that "everyone, adults and children, should wear masks."

---

[5] "A modelling framework to assess the likely effectiveness of facemasks in combination with 'lock-down' in managing the COVID-19 pandemic," *Proc Royal Soc A* (10 Jun 2020).

Third: Regarding the importance of "source control"—that is, of masks blocking infected individuals from spreading the virus—Howard admits that "there are currently no studies that measure the impact of any kind of mask on the amount of infectious [Covid] particles from human actions." More bad news for the pro-mask lobby. Howard is reduced to discussing old studies on other, non-Covid viruses. In the end, he even cites the infamous "hamster study" that was used in 2020 to justify masks: infected hamsters were separated in a cage from healthy ones by a "mask curtain," and the curtain was found to reduce infections.[6] Nice—if you happen to be a hamster, or live in a cage.

Fourth: As to the question of protection of the user, Howard admits at the start that "it is much harder to directly test mask efficacy for PPE using a human subject, so simulations must be used instead"—with all the shortcomings cited above. He then refers to three observational studies, in "health care environments" (e.g. in a hospital), showing some improvement with masks. In discussing another study, Howard again laments the absence of a real RCT study, noting that "there was not a 'no mask' control group because it was deemed 'unethical'." Most existing data on wearer protection was done with the flu virus, but "it is not yet known to what extent findings from influenza apply to COVID-19 filtration." In the end, Howard offers a pile of qualifications: "Overall, it *appears* that cloth face covers *can provide* good fit and filtration for PPE in *some* community contexts, *but results will vary* depending on material and design, the way they are used, and the setting in which they are used" (emphasis added). It inspires little confidence.

Fifth: Of the sociological considerations, Howard and colleagues provide little of relevance. They are concerned that mask-wearers may become over-confident and thus adopt risky behaviors. They are concerned that mandating masks only for the sick—as has always been done in the past—risks "stigmatizing" them. The same holds for blacks and other minorities, who (rightly) fear being seen as criminal threats if they alone are masked. Howard concludes, unsurprisingly, that mask-wearing as "universal policy" is the best solution.

Best of all, says Howard, masks can create a "new symbolism." Mask-wearing "can provide feelings of empowerment and self-efficacy," which can in turn "make masks symbols of altruism and solidarity." Talk about virtue-signaling! Prove your moral worth!—wear a mask!

---

[6] "Surgical Mask Partition Reduces the Risk of Noncontact Transmission in a Golden Syrian Hamster Model for Coronavirus Disease 2019 (COVID-19)," *Clin Infec Diseases* (30 May 2020).

Six: Howard's "implementation considerations" are devoid of useful content. Mask mandates can be "challenging" and "polarizing" (really?), but with sufficient scare-mongering, governments can drive up rates.

In his short concluding section, Howard ends with another highly-qualified statement: "The *available* evidence *suggests* that near-universal adoption of nonmedical masks when out in public, *in combination* with complementary public health measures, *could* successfully reduce…community spread, *if* such measures are sustained" (again, with emphasis added). He then again cites the Goldman-Sachs figure of $1 trillion savings with a national mandate. In the end, Howard and friends have almost nothing to stand on; they have no valuable RCT study data, they have only weak "observational" results, and they must draw from older studies on non-Covid viruses that are of dubious value. And yet, they can recommend that governments "strongly encourage" the "widespread" use of masks, in conjunction with the "appropriate regulation."

Behold: Real Data!

Had poor Mr. Howard been a bit more perceptive during the writing of his study, he would have encountered an astonishing situation: a team of researchers had started, already in April 2020, to conduct an actual RCT test of Covid infections, in real people, living in real-life situations. This is the very situation that Howard called 'impossible,' and something that was rife with 'ethical problems.' And yet there it was: a team of Danish researchers had recruited 6,000 average Danes to test the efficacy of mask-wearing—specifically, whether masks protected the wearer, and if so, by how much.

A research team led by Henning Bundgaard—an actual doctor with an actual PhD, and a professor at the top medical university in Denmark—gave high-quality surgical-grade masks to 3,000 random healthy people, and simply tracked another 3,000 random healthy people as their non-mask control group. In Denmark at that time, mask-wearing was optional. They followed people in both groups for one month, and then administered a standard Covid test to see how many in each group got infected. The results were striking. The masked group had 42 infections (1.8%), and the non-mask control group had 53 infections (2.1%). So yes, the mask group had a slightly lower infection rate, but given the numbers, it is not statistically significant. For all practical purposes, the two groups were the same; hence, the masks provided no effective benefit. This was precisely their conclusion: "The recommendation to wear surgical masks to supplement other public health measures did not reduce the SARS-CoV-2 infection rate among wearers…"

There were the usual qualifications, as exist with any such study. Due to low relative numbers of infections and other methodological limitations, the Bundgaard study had a confidence interval (CI) of 95%, less than the preferred 98 or 99%. Thus, the data are compatible with a relatively wide variation of possible results; that is, there could actually be a significant reduction from the masks, or even a significant *detriment* from them, statistically speaking. Hence, the study technically provides "inconclusive results," as Bundgaard readily admits. Only more research can answer this question more definitively. Be that as it may, it was still a true randomized control test, and still provides useful and statistically significant results.

Needless to say, these results were not what the dominant pro-maskers wanted to see. Consequently, 'cancel culture' swung into gear against Dr. Bundgaard and team. Or rather, '*pre*-cancel culture': major medical journals refused to publish his study.[7] It was simply not welcome news. This resulted in at least a 3-month delay, which is very unfortunate, given the urgency of the situation. Finally, in late November, the prestigious *Annals of Internal Medicine* published the report: "Effectiveness of Adding a Mask Recommendation to Other Public Health Measures."

The reaction was predictable. The media almost entirely ignored it, as did all those in government and other positions of authority; evidently they felt it was inappropriate to "muddy the water" with such contradictory information. Response from the UK medical profession was more extensive, more honest, and generally positive, though not without its critics.[8] On the negative side, doctors suggested that the low infection rates skewed the results toward 'no difference'; some suggested that better results would have been seen in higher-infection Asian nations, and others pointed out that the sample size (6,000) was simply not high enough to resolve the difference. A few critics argued that a one-month study could not catch all cases, given a 14-day incubation period. But others were very positive about the study. Dr. Simon Clarke wrote:

> This is a well-designed and carefully presented study. It provides very good evidence confirming what many people suspected: that wearing a facemask in public, while others around you don't wear masks, does little or nothing to reduce your risk of being infected by the coronavirus. In fact, it might even slightly increase your risk of being infected. … Taken together, all the evidence shows that it is important for health authorities not to over-stress the effectiveness of

---

[7] See "Medical Journals Refuse To Publish Landmark Danish Mask Study," *The Daily Skeptic* (23 Oct 2020).

[8] "Expert reaction to paper using an RCT to assess mask use as a public health measure to help control SARS-CoV-2 spread (DANMASK-19)," *Science Media Centre* (19 Nov 2020).

> facemasks as a way to protect wearers. If people think that wearing a mask means they are reducing their risk of being infected, they are very much mistaken.

Dr. Paul Hunter added this:

> The results of the DANMASK-19 randomised controlled trial on face mask use is a good study of the potential value of wearing a face mask to protect the wearer. … The DANMASK-19 study was a well-designed community study. … Swabbing and blood tests at one month would pick up most but not all infections, but this is unlikely to have biased the results and they are less likely to be biased than self-reported symptoms without a diagnosis confirmation. … This finding is in line with our own systematic review published in March, where we estimated the value of wearing masks as primary prevention was about 6% but in the range 20% to -19%. Adding this study to our own review would not materially affect our conclusions.

Another researcher, Dr. Julii Brainard, had this to say:

> This is a well-run trial with enough participants to have high confidence in the results—therefore the statistical analysis was adequately powered and inherently adjusted for possible confounders, unlike most studies that try to make conclusions about mask-wearing and catching respiratory disease. … The findings are very similar to what emerged when we assessed earlier research on mask wearing to prevent influenza-like illness: that mask wearing appears to have [only] a small protective effect to the wearers. The magnitude of the protective effect and its statistical significance are *not* at the thresholds that would normally be required to make a recommendation in favour of mask-wearing.

The situation was encapsulated by Professor Ashley Woodcock: "This is a very valuable community study. The paper is very clear, the analysis correct, and the interpretation appropriate." And a short but widely circulated article in the *Spectator* (UK) by two prominent Oxford professors was simply titled, "Landmark Danish study finds no significant effect for facemasks."

Subtler Arguments Against Masks

The primary argument against masks, then, is this: 1) *They do not protect the wearer*. Based on data so far, this seems to be true. Of course, we still want to know if they protect others, meaning, *others who are not wearing masks*—because we already know that others wearing masks are unprotected.

But if we think about it, we realize that there is a certain symmetry at work here. The problem of transmission is one of *output* and *input*: an infected person expels the virus, and a healthy person inhales the virus. But if the masks don't block the inflow (as proven above), then they don't block the outflow. Masks are not a one-way valve. The same airflow patterns 'in' are reflected in airflow patterns 'out.' Yes, these patterns are *different* in masked people versus unmasked, but evidently they do not halt the ingestion of viral particles; hence, they do not halt the expulsion. I suspect that future research will bear this out.

Granted, this seems to conflict with common sense. It would seem that masks, by blocking at least some our expelled droplets, must be helping, at least a little bit. And of course, they do block *some* of the germs. But the evidence suggests that this does not prevent infection. As long as the expelled air is not rigorously scrubbed of droplets—such as in a filtered respirator or full body suit—they still escape, and are still passed on to people, masked or otherwise, at roughly the same rate. This is the moral of the Danish study.

But there are other reasons to reject mask mandates. I set aside here trivial concerns such as cost and inconvenience. Yes, it's a bit of a hassle to 'mask up,' but I don't put much weight on that. Same with cost, given that one can cut up an old T-shirt to make a reusable mask. Bulk paper masks costs perhaps 15 or 20 cents each. I will also bypass the concern that masks cause us to breathe in our own carbon dioxide; this is true to a small extent, but I've seen no evidence that this is detrimental in any significant way. So let me set all these aside.

Consider, then, the following issues, rarely or never discussed:

2) *The mask policy is irrational*. Here's proof: No one yet has been able to answer a very basic question: "What are the objective criteria by which we decide when to stop requiring masks?" When anyone in a position of authority was asked this, they inevitably gave nonsensical answers: "When it seems right," "when infections come down," "when most of the people have vaccines," "when we are confident…," and so on. But these are irrational. A scientific, medical emergency should have quantifiable, objective criteria by which actions are taken. This is not an unreasonable request. But our authorities did not seem to care. Their basic stance was, "We will maintain our mask policy as long as humanly possible, until the political

pressure grows so high that we are forced to backtrack." And for Covid, this is exactly what happened.

3) *Masks are dehumanizing.* The most personal, most intimate aspect of our public person is our face. It is extremely difficult to interact with others, especially strangers, in a mask. The mouth and lower face convey so much unspoken information about who we are, what we are thinking, and how we are feeling. Lacking this input, we are left with the eyes, bodily movements, and the voice. Obviously we can get by, but it is very unnerving for many, and undignifying for all.

4) *Masks for children are a form of abuse.* It's bad enough for adults, but think about the effect on youth and children, who are still learning how to interact with others and how to make sense of all interpersonal clues. It is a horrible abuse of children to make them wear masks, especially given data suggesting that they are at extremely low risk, both for illness and for transmission. During the pandemic, we had 5- and 6-year-olds wearing masks for the entire school day, for a year or more. This is a substantial portion of his or her young life; it cannot but have a detrimental effect.

5) *Masks are ugly.* Say what you like, people in general are concerned about appearance. And masks—all masks—are downright ugly. No one, not even the most beautiful supermodel, looks good in a mask. In fact, the better-looking the person, the uglier the effect. (Believe me, no one cares if a Chuck Schumer or a Deborah Lipstadt wear a mask.) That's why, throughout history, masks have been used by performers, clowns, actors, and criminals; they warp and distort that most-personal of human features, the face.

6) *Masks represent mindless compliance with authority.* Present-day governmental figures, at all levels, are virtually devoid of credibility. Thus, when they order us to wear masks, they had better have some truly compelling and transparent reason to do so. During Covid, they had almost nothing at all—nothing but an appeal to history ("they used masks during the Spanish flu!") and to so-called common sense. But scientifically, neither of these hold up. Lacking a compelling reason, it becomes strictly an obedience test, and a highly visible one at that. It's like a reverse scarlet letter: it is physical, concrete virtue-signaling. "I'm an uncritical rule-follower, I trust the authorities, I automatically yield to their directives"—this is what a mask conveys.

7) *Masks represent a kind of unquenchable sin.* Early in the pandemic, we were told that lockdowns, masks, self-quarantine, etc would only be neces-

sary for two weeks. In 14 days, the virus would cease to be transmitted so virulently, and we could all transition back to our normal lives. But of course, that did not happen. "People are violating the quarantine!" we were told. "Not everyone is wearing masks!" And so two weeks became a month, became six months, became a year. Then, as the original Covid faded away, the dreaded 'variants' appeared, prompting a new round of masking. And who knows what will come next. The bottom line is this: *The sin of coronavirus can never be absolved.* Even fully vaccinated people are not allowed to go mask-free![9] ("You can still harbor the virus," we are told.) This idea of eternal sin is extremely detrimental to human well-being; and there is something deeply Hebraic about it all.

8) *Mandates are a policy of enforced victimhood.* A mask mandate compels you to wear a mask, even when you are feeling fine. Why is this? Because you can be an "asymptomatic spreader." You can be sick and not even know it. In fact, it's worse than this: We *presume* you are sick, and therefore we compel you to wear a mask. The policy is: *Assume you are sick*, and then act accordingly. This is pathological.

9) *Mandates are cowardice.* Many low-level mandates—at gyms, restaurants, libraries, malls—exist because those responsible for the local mandate are simply cowards. They are afraid to buck the trend, or to be the first to drop the mandate. Everyone operates on the mythical "abundance of caution" principle, which means that, in practice, nothing changes. "I'll drop my mandate if you do," "No, you first." On and on, round and round.

10) *Mask-wearing has become cultish.* It is irrational, or at least hyper-paranoid, to demand that everyone wear masks. We are not allowed to ask for evidence, not allowed to question authorities on this matter (lest we be called 'racists' or 'White supremacists'), not allowed to press back on Biden, Anthony Fauci, or the Jewess in charge of the CDC, Rochelle Walensky. It is functionally a cult—*obey, don't question, don't challenge, don't think for yourself.*

So, why do they do it? Granted that there may be some, small rationale for encouraging mass usage of masks, why do the powers-that-be go to the extreme and issue mandates? Are they really that concerned about our well-being? Or are there ulterior motives at work? It would seem that they relish the opportunity to enforce conformity in the population, to frighten

---

[9] See "Here's Why Vaccinated People Still Need to Wear a Mask," *New York Times* (8 Dec 2020).

them into subservience, and to effectively suppress individual thought, individual identity, and individual personality.

Masks, indeed, have a *homogenizing effect*: People lose their individuality in masks. They become, just a bit more, the mindless citizen, the anonymous consumer, the faceless cog. Somehow our leaders relish this idea; individual free-thinkers, after all, are nothing more than trouble-makers for those who would impose uniformity of thought and action. They are the "domestic terrorists"; they are the "White supremacists"; they are the "insurrectionists." In a mask, people look just a bit more alike, and therefore they can be treated just a bit more alike.

Who Is Really at Risk?

The final question to ask is the larger one, beyond mask mandates: Who is really at risk in this entire pandemic? We have long known that children, youth, and the middle-aged are less vulnerable than the elderly; 59% of all Covid deaths occurred in those 75 and up, and 80% in those 65 and up.[10] We have also known that Whites are generally less at risk than non-Whites, specifically, than blacks and Hispanics. Data from mid-2022 show that, in the US, the White morality rate was 268 per 100,000, whereas the black and Hispanic rates were 442 and 446, respectively.[11]

Recent studies have also confirmed what was long suspected, namely, that obesity is a prime driving factor in severe Covid illness. The CDC reported that 51% of all hospitalizations occurred in those who were obese, and another 28% in those overweight. In other words, only 21% of hospitalizations occurred in people who were of normal weight or underweight.

One other group at notable risk is Jews, especially of the Orthodox variety. A report from October 2020 noted that Jews "from Jerusalem to New York" are being decimated by Covid. In the UK, Orthodox Jews have an infection rate approaching 75%, versus 7% for the British public at large.[12] The same article states that "Jewish men are twice as likely to die from Covid-19 than Christian men in the UK, even after adjusting for socio-economic factors." A death rate *double* that of Gentiles suggests some genetic factors at work.

Putting it bluntly, the dominant Covid risk factors for severe illness or death seem to be: *old, fat, Black, Hispanic, or Jew*. These are the people most at risk, and these are the people dying from it. Perhaps there is a sort

[10] "95 Percent of Americans Killed by COVID-19 Were 50 or Older," AARP (1 Apr 2021).

[11] "COVID-19 Cases and Deaths by Race/Ethnicity," www.kff.org (22 Aug 2022).

[12] "Covid: London's Orthodox Jews have one of highest rates in the world," BBC (2 Feb 2021).

of cosmic justice at work; perhaps Nature never intended such people to exist in numbers like those at present; perhaps she is correcting her error. Correspondingly, there is some good news here: if you are White, reasonably fit, and under 80, your risks are minimal, to say the least. But with our Jew- and minority-obsessed government and media in the US, perhaps we can now understand why there is a "coronavirus crisis" in the first place, and why we must wear a mask. It's not for us; it's for them.

In the end, we get something like a distorted version of the Emperor's New Clothes. In the traditional fable, the mad emperor walks around naked and yet his cowed subjects all claim to love his new clothes. Only one virtuous youth is willing to speak the truth. In the real world of today, the mad emperor Biden walks around wearing *something*—his mask—and his cowed subjects all claim to love it, and yet in reality he wears *nothing*—that is, nothing that works, or that works very well. We need to be like the virtuous youth, and show it to be what it is.

— 31 —
CONFRONTING THE JUDEOCRACY: SIX STAGES OF ENLIGHTENMENT

Anyone who has spent even a short time battling against the Judeocracy has surely experienced the frustration of attempting to persuade a trusted friend or colleague of the gravity of the situation—only to fail. This is undoubtedly one of the most discouraging and troubling aspects of those who take up the mission for truth and justice. We repeatedly encounter intelligent and well-read individuals who, we believe, surely must share our sense of concern and outrage. If they do not, it can only be from lack of knowledge; therefore, a short chat or a targeted reading or two, we think, will do the trick. The facts are indisputable, and hence it is merely a matter of information. Once our friends have the requisite facts, they will surely—*surely*—see things our way. And yet, time after time, they do not.

Why is this? What are they thinking? What is their logic? How is it that they can fail to be fully convinced of the severity of the Jewish Question? Or even just be sympathetic to our stance? Why is it that they occasionally even become outright hostile—not to them, but to *us?* How can they be in denial of what is, from a rational and objective standpoint, surely one of the major problems facing civilized humanity? Undoubtedly this could be the topic of a book-length treatment, and I can only outline a few basic ideas here. But I think there is some merit in examining the basic categories of response and denial by those confronted, perhaps for the first time in a serious manner, with the Jewish Question and with the many problems of living under functional Jewish rule.

At its most basic level, the situation is one in which the relative novice is confronted with a difficult, troubling, and potentially catastrophic scenario: profound social corruption by wealthy and powerful Jews. (I stress the 'relative' here; everyone, even the functionally illiterate, has heard *something* negative about the Jews, likely many negative things.) It is a 'bad news' story of the highest magnitude. And the last thing many people want in their lives these days is another bad news story. God knows we've had enough troubles in recent years: political upheaval, riots in the streets, a global pandemic, economic gyrations, unrestrained immigration, environmental decline, opioid crises, surging crime, falling lifespans. Who needs yet one more disaster heaped upon their plates? The Jews? Really? Are you serious? And I suppose the Holocaust never happened! (Hint: it didn't—not in the way described. See my *Debating the Holocaust* for an explanation.) What are you, some kind of Nazi? A white supremacist? On and on.

Despite all this, many of us persevere. We realize that public education is one of our primary weapons in the Great Struggle, and we are bound and determined to press ahead and inform as many as possible of the nature of the problem. Therefore, it is of some use to understand more precisely how people typically respond to our overtures, in order to be more effective in our communication. After all, we are pursuing a noble cause, and we sincerely want people to be well-informed and, ideally, to join us in our mission. Apart from our opponents, we genuinely want people to like and appreciate us. You don't get very far coming off like a fanatic or a jerk. I'm quite confident that virtually none of us relish making enemies for the sake of making enemies. We have no driving urge to be antagonistic or rabble-rousing. Generally speaking, what we have are facts, experiences, and informed opinions on the Jews; these, combined with a general sense of concern for social welfare, justice, and the state of the world, incline us to undertake unusual, unpopular, but highly valuable actions to educate others, and to articulate possible solutions. It is the prototypical 'thankless task,' and yet we do it all the same.

That said, it is helpful to have a model of how people react to the Jewish Question. The approach I will outline here derives from another famous model describing how people react to a different crisis situation: death. In the 1950s and 60s, Swiss (later, American) psychiatrist Elisabeth Kübler-Ross developed a well-known scheme that came to be known as "the five stages of grief." When confronted with imminent death, she said, people typically progress through five relatively distinct mental phases: denial, anger, bargaining, depression, and acceptance. *Denial*: "No, this isn't true, it can't be happening. There must be some mistake." *Anger*: "How could this happen to me? It's just not fair! Someone is to blame. God, how could you let this happen!" *Bargaining*: "Please, God, get me through this and I promise to do x, y, z. Or, doc, you have to help me; I'll do whatever it takes." *Depression*: "There's no use, nothing will work. I'm doomed. What's the use of even trying?" And finally, *Acceptance*: "Everyone dies, and I guess my time is up. So be it. Time to meet my Maker." This schema was first described in her 1969 book, *On Death and Dying*.

I'll not debate the merits or demerits of Kübler-Ross' theory here. Some have found it helpful, and others dismiss it as largely irrelevant or at least unsubstantiated. Still, based only on common sense, I think we can see that there is some insight here, and that many people—perhaps some we have known personally—indeed experience such stages in varying degrees. Obviously not everyone passes through all five stages, and not necessarily in the prescribed order, but nonetheless, these stages do describe some essential aspects of human response to the looming tragedy of ones' own demise.

Inspired by this model, let me then propose something analogous: *The Six Stages of Enlightenment on the Jewish Question.* I claim no real scientific grounding here, and I have done no exhaustive surveys or interviews. This is based simply on my own personal experience, over several years, of confronting people—students, family, friends, strangers—on the dangers of the Judeocracy. My six stages are as follows:

1. Denial
2. Irrelevance
3. Impotence
4. Misplaced Anger
5. Acceptance
6. Righteous Anger and Action

As with Kübler-Ross's theory, I do not claim that all people experience all these stages, nor that they necessarily progress through them in order. But I do think that many people, when confronted with the data, do experience some or most of these stages. Let me briefly describe each in turn, and then outline some of the relevant facts that make the case for enlightenment.

DENIAL. Upon first hearing a serious claim that Jews have outsized and detrimental influence in society, or dominate the ranks of the wealthy, or run the media, or control politics, the usual initial response is denial: "No they don't. That's ridiculous. There are no more Jews in power than anyone else. That's just an anti-Semitic canard." This, even from highly-educated people. Fortunately, this is an empirical question; an overwhelming Jewish presence can be easily proven, given the relevant data. Below I offer a concise version of this argument.

IRRELEVANCE. Once it is shown that Jews are massively overrepresented in key sectors of society, the standard reply is that this fact does not matter. "Ok, there are lots of Jews in media, finance, and politics, but this doesn't really matter. People are just people. There are good ones and there are bad ones. If Jews hold lots of influential positions, that only means that they worked hard and succeeded. And anyway, they're just doing their jobs. If they didn't do them, someone else would."

This seems like a common-sense view, but to make such a claim is to hold an extremely naïve and ill-informed view of the world. It's true that most decent people, and especially most Whites, tend to view others as individuals; there are likely evolutionary reasons for this, which I won't elaborate here, but see Kevin MacDonald's book *Individualism and the*

Western Liberal Tradition for a good recent account. If we judge everyone as basically well-intentioned individuals, then of course, it doesn't really matter if Jews or any other minority dominates society. If Jews are disproportionate, then it can only mean that they are that much smarter or industrious than others, and thus they deserve their standing. And if some Jews commit crimes or other unethical actions, we have to judge and punish them individually, on a case-by-case basis. Or so they say.

The Jewish critic must then respond to this stance with a demonstration that it *does* matter, that Jewish over-representation has a long-standing and deep-rooted grounding in anti-White and even anti-human actions, and that it is remarkably detrimental to social and human well-being. This is a longer and more difficult argument to make, but it can be done; again, I outline this case below.

IMPOTENCE. Once we have shown the deleterious effect of Jewish dominance, the next reply is typically something like this: "Ok, if Jews have so much power and influence, then you can't possibly win. They are just too strong. So why fight them? It can only hurt yourself and your family. Better to just ignore the whole situation and live your life as best you can."

Certainly this is a pragmatic view, and many otherwise well-intentioned critics adopt this line. But ultimately it means surrender: a moral capitulation to a malevolent ruling power. To yield to evil is itself a great evil. It is to condemn ones' own future, and that of your children and grandchildren, to a life of increasing brutality and coarseness, of deprivation and suffering, of conflict and war. No truly concerned person can accept this. We must confront the situation head-on. To fight against evil, even in the face of likely defeat, is noble; it actually makes life worth living. Even if victory is a long way off—and ultimate victory for our side is *inevitable*, once we understand the history—it is still a fight worth pursuing. Living in a Judeocracy means that every major aspect of society is affected. If you have any concerns or causes in this world that you think are worth fighting for—the environment, social justice, education, human rights, health, democracy—then you need to engage in the fight against Jewish rule because it has a negative impact on virtually every other social issue. To paraphrase Spengler, impotence is cowardice.

MISPLACED ANGER. At this point, your friend is likely to start getting irritated—with you. As a typical semi-thoughtful but uncritical television viewer, he has likely absorbed and internalized the conventional pro-Jewish mantra: Jews are a beleaguered and innocent people who have been unjustly attacked over the centuries, most notably during the Holocaust, and thus we owe them vast amends. Furthermore, being a typically decent person, he thinks that anyone attacking Jews, or any minorities, is a morally-deficient racist or neo-Nazi—and now, this is you! For God's sake, everybody hates a racist! Even Tucker Carlson hates racists!—as he informs us every night, in his unthinking, dim-witted, and duplicitous manner. Since you clearly hate Jews, you are now officially a 'hater.' And everyone hates a hater—don't they?

Sensing that he has lost the argument, your friend then launches into either subtle or overt *ad hominem* attacks against you. Rational discussion is out the window, and emotion rules the day. You are now simply a 'bad person'; no further need to debate with you. Having demonstrated your incivility and cruel-heartedness, you are either pitied or detested. Critically, the focus has shifted to *you*; Jews are suddenly nowhere in sight, even though this was the sole issue at hand. They are suddenly off the hook. How convenient; the Jews themselves couldn't have scripted a better outcome.

Sadly, many people remain stuck in this mode for a long time, perhaps for their entire lives. They never address the real issue, but continue only to think negatively of you and you alone. This is a relatively good outcome for them; the social problem is not millions of wealthy, powerful, and corrupt Jews, but little ol' you, and perhaps a few of your like-minded hater friends. It's much easier, and much less threatening, to deal with you and your "ilk," rather than a potent, dispersed, malevolent force like world Jewry.

Sometimes, though, and often in surprising ways, there is a shift in attitude. Your friend becomes curious. He investigates, he reads, he asks questions. Slowly, slowly, he comes around to your side. "You know, I've been thinking, and I think you're on to something. Those Jews are everywhere, once you learn how to spot them. No one criticizes them. No one questions the Holocaust. No one is even willing to simply name the Jews. They get away with everything." Thus we arrive, with luck, at…

ACCEPTANCE. Yes, Jews in fact dominate key sectors of society. Yes, Jews in fact are the major wire-pullers in politics and business. Yes, Jews couldn't care less about human well-being, and they would just as soon cause mass suffering and even death, if it profited them in any way. The denialism has been overcome.

Once at this phase, it is only a short step to the final stage:

RIGHTEOUS ANGER—now against the real enemy—and corresponding ACTION. Anyone with a conscience, with a sense of moral outrage, and with a larger sense of justice, will be utterly appalled at the situation. They will now become activist, speaking out, writing, informing others. They will develop the moral backbone to confront Jewish power and its proxies directly. Being truly knowledgeable and well-informed, they will make a formidable opponent. The movement will have taken one more small step forward. And victory will be one day closer.

Constructing the Case

Given that nearly everyone begins at some level of the 'denial' stage, it is worthwhile to offer some specific facts that can help build the case against it. The goal, again, is to show that Jews are massively disproportionate amongst the wealthy and powerful in society. This is the core truth from which all the rest proceeds. Fortunately, as I said, this is an entirely empirical matter. Basic research will reveal the truth. Of course, the names vary from nation to nation, and they change constantly over time. A specific case must be made at a given point in time, and in a specific nation of interest. Since I am an American, and the data here is extensive, let me briefly review the case in the present-day USA. Even a cursory overview demonstrates the failure of denial.

We can separately examine four sectors of American society: politics, academia, finance, and media. In politics, we have a strong Jewish presence in both Congress and the White House, and on the Supreme Court. Regarding the latter, we currently have two Jews among the nine justices: Elena Kagan and Stephen Breyer. Until the recent death of Ruth Bader-Ginsburg, the figure was three of nine, and if President Obama had had his way late in his final term, it would have been an astonishing four of nine, with Merrick Garland. But even two of nine, or 22%, is *10 times* overrepresentation. By rights, we should have one or no Jews on the Court.

The 2022 US Congress had 38 Jews among its combined 535 members, with 10 in the Senate and 28 in the House. This constitutes around 7% of the Congressional total, versus an American Jewish population of some 6 million, or just under 2% of the nation. Hence Jews are overrepresented in Congress by a factor of 3.5, and in the Senate by a factor of 5. The record high for Jewish representation, incidentally, occurred in the aftermath of the 2008 federal election, when fully 48 Jews held seats in Congress (15 Senate, 33 House).

The Biden administration, like that of Trump, Obama, Bush, and Clinton, has an extensive Jewish presence. Start with the families of Biden and Kamala Harris. Remarkably, all three of Biden's adult children married Jews: daughter Ashley married Howard Krein, son Hunter married "filmmaker" Melissa Cohen, and now-deceased son Beau married Hallie Olivere. Correspondingly, three of Biden's six grandchildren are half-Jews. Biracial VP Kamala Harris married a Jewish lawyer, Douglas Emhoff, back in 2014; thankfully, they have no children.

Biden's sympathies to the Jews extend, of course, to his highest-level administrative positions. Of 25 cabinet or cabinet-level positions, eight (32%) are held by Jews: Tony Blinken, Alejandro Mayorkas, Janet Yellen, Merrick Garland (yes, that Merrick Garland), Ron Klain, Avril Haines (half), Isabel Guzman (half), and Eric Lander. Other high-ranking Biden

Jews include John Kerry (half), Rochelle Walensky of the CDC, Jeff Zients, Wendy Sherman, Gary Gensler of the SEC, David Cohen, "Rachel" Levine, Anne Neuberger, Andy Slavitt, Victoria Nuland, and Roberta Jacobson. And this is not to mention Judeophilic Gentiles like Jake Sullivan, or Gentiles with Jewish spouses, like Samantha Power. Below I offer some thoughts about why, exactly, this situation came to be.

What about academia? Here is one remarkable indication: Of the eight Ivy League schools—Harvard, Yale, Princeton, Columbia, Penn, Brown, Cornell, and Dartmouth—fully seven have Jewish presidents. In other words, 88% of these elite schools are run by Jews. We can be sure that this Jewish orientation then extends down into provosts and deans who are disproportionately Jewish, into faculty members who are disproportionately Jewish, and into the very curriculum itself, which undoubtedly caters to liberal-Jewish interests.

Then consider university faculty more broadly. According to Schuster and Finkelstein,[1] "25% of research university faculty are Jewish, compared to 10% of all faculty." An older study by Steinberg[2] found that 17.2% of faculty at "high ranking" universities were Jewish. By a different assessment, Harriett Zuckerman[3] examined just the "elite" scientific and research faculty. She found the following, by major discipline:

Law	36% Jewish
Sociology	34% Jewish
Economics	28% Jewish
Physics	26% Jewish
Poli Sci	24% Jewish

What about students? Experience shows that when Jews constitute more than just a few percent of the student body, they begin to dominate campus life. As it happens, there are nine major American universities with over 20% Jewish undergrads (in descending order: Brandeis, Tulane, CUNY-Brooklyn, Binghamton, Queens College, George Washington University, Columbia, Boston University, and Washington University-St. Louis). And there are another 23 major schools with more than 10% Jews (Maryland, American University, Brown, University of Miami, Rutgers, University of Florida, Cornell, Penn, Syracuse, Michigan, New York University, Northwestern, University of Hartford, Wisconsin, Yale, Indiana, UC-Santa Barbara, Duke, University at Albany, Harvard, Cal State-Northridge, Florida State, and USC). Hence we have 32 major American universities, represent-

[1] J. Schuster and M. Finkelstein, *The American Faculty* (2006), p. 66.
[2] S. Steinberg, *The Academic Melting Pot* (1974), p. 103.
[3] H. Zuckerman, *Scientific Elite* (1977).

ing the intellectual elite of the nation, with a hugely disproportionate Jewish presence, top to bottom. Again, this in a nation of scarcely 2% Jews.

Consider, next, the realm of finance and wealth. When we run down the list of wealthiest Americans, we find a striking fact: around half of them are Jews. Among the top ten, we find five Jews: Steve Ballmer, Larry Page, Sergey Brin, Larry Ellison, and Michael Bloomberg. We likely should also include the single richest man, Jeff Bezos, with a current personal wealth of about $180 billion. It has long been an open question if he is Jewish, but recent events seem to confirm this; he recently turned over leadership of Amazon to an overt Jew, Andy Jassy. It is a long-standing tradition in major American corporations to keep leadership within the Tribe.

Of the top 50 richest men, at least 27 are Jews, including Mark Zuckerberg, Michael Dell, Carl Icahn, David Newhouse, Micki Arison, and Stephen Ross.[4] The combined wealth of these 27 individuals comes to roughly $600 billion (or over $800 billion, counting Bezos). Note: If Jews were proportionately represented among the top 50, there would be *one* individual; instead, there are *27*.

More broadly, we can infer that this "50% rule" holds throughout much of the wealth hierarchy. In support, we may cite Benjamin Ginsberg, who wrote, "Today, though barely 2% of the [American] nation's population is Jewish, close to half its billionaires are Jews".[5] At present, there are something like 615 American billionaires, which implies around 300 Jewish billionaires.

Or perhaps the figures are even worse than we suspect. A recent study of the most malicious "vulture" capitalists showed a heavy preponderance of Jewish names, far more than half.[6] And one ranking from a few years ago of the richest hedge fund managers in the US listed 32 individuals by name; of these, at least 24 (75%) are Jews. It seems that the more we look, the worse it gets.

Even more impressively, consider total private wealth. In 2018, the total assets of all private households in the US hit $100 trillion for the first time ever. By 2021, that figure had reached $150 trillion. The 50% rule suggests that the 6 million or so American Jews own or control, in total, some $75 trillion. This works out to an average of $12 million for every Jewish man, woman, and child—a truly astonishing figure.

So much for Jewish wealth. More importantly, these various sectors are deeply interconnected. Jewish wealth is directly related to Jewish political influence. Take, for example, Joe Biden's top political donors. It turns out, unsurprisingly, that the vast majority of Biden's political donations

---

[4] Bloomberg Billionaires Index (2018).

[5] *The Fatal Embrace* (1993), p. 1.

[6] "Vulture Capitalism Is Jewish Capitalism," *Occidental Observer* (18 Dec 2019).

came from Jewish billionaires. As Andrew Joyce writes, "of [his] top 22 donors, at least 18 are Jews," followed by the list of names.[7] This is perhaps extreme but not surprising, given that Jews overall provide at least 50% of Democratic political funding, and at least 25% of Republican funds.[8] These are truly disturbing numbers for anyone who cares about political corruption. Note that there are literally hundreds of lobby groups, all donating to their favored candidates. And yet one lobby—the Jewish Lobby—provides 25 to 50%, or more, of major candidate funding. Imagine if, say, half of your income came from one person, and the other half came from a mix of 200 other individuals; who would you listen to? The answer is obvious.

Finally, take the media. Hollywood, as we all know, has long been a Jewish domain—reaching back to its origins in the 1910s and 1920s. It was constructed by the likes of Carl Laemmle (Universal Pictures), Adolph Zukor, Jesse Lasky, Daniel and Charles Frohman, and Samuel Goldwyn (Paramount), William Fox (Fox Films, later 20th Century Fox), and the four "Warner" Brothers—in reality, the Wonskolaser clan: Jack, Harry, Albert, and Sam. They were soon followed by Marcus Loew (MGM), William Paley (CBS), and Harry and Jack Cohn (Columbia), establishing nearly complete Jewish control over the film business.

Today the situation is little changed—and is neither disputed nor even controversial. A notable story published in the *LA Times* in 2008 openly proclaimed that "Jews totally run Hollywood".[9] It investigated every major studio and found nothing but Jewish bosses. Today the names have changed, but not the ethnicities. A recent survey of major executives or owners reveals the following:

20th Century Studios (S. Asbell)
Paramount (S. Redstone)
Disney Studies (A. Bergman, A. Horn)
Warner Bros Studios (T. Emmerich, A. Sarnoff, R. Kavanaugh)
MGM (M. De Luca)
Sony Pictures (T. Rothman, S. Panitch, J. Greenstein)
Lionsgate (M. Rachesky, J. Feltheimer)
Relativity Media (D. Robbins)
Millennium Media (A. Lerner)
The Chernin Group (P. Chernin)
Amblin Partners (S. Spielberg)

---

[7] "Four more years of…" *Occidental Observer* (14 Nov 2020).
[8] "The Jewish Vote: Political Power and Identity in US Elections," Gil Troy, *The Ruderman Foundation.*
[9] "How Jewish is Hollywood?" (19 Dec 2008).

Participant (J. Skoll, D. Linde)
Sister (S. Snider, E. Murdoch)
Spyglass (G. Barber)
Glickmania (J. Glickman)

As before, all these individuals are Jews.[10] With such dominance, we should scarcely be surprised to find pro-Jewish themes repeatedly appear in film: from the Holocaust and the 'evil Nazis,' to the Arab and Muslim 'terrorists,' to the ignorant and corrupt Whites, to support for various socially- and ethically-degrading behavior such as casual sex, homosexuality, interracial couples and families, recreational drug use, crude materialism, and rampant multiculturalism. All these themes serve Jewish interests.

The overall media situation is even more telling. The five largest media conglomerates in the US are: 1) Disney, 2) Warner Media, 3) NBC Universal, 4) Viacom CBS, and 5) Fox Corporation. A look at their owners, largest shareholders, and top officers is revealing:

Disney: *Robert Iger*, executive chairman; *Alan Horn*, Chair, Disney Studios; *Alan Braverman*, exec VP; *Peter Rice*, chair, Content; *Dana Walden*, chair, ABC; *Lowell Singer*, senior VP.

Warner: *Jason Kilar*, CEO; *David Levy*, Pres, Turner Broadcasting; *Jeff Zucker*, Pres, CNN; *Ann Sarnoff*, CEO, Warner Pictures; *Michael Lynton*, chair, Warner Music (Parent company: AT&T: *John Stankey*, CEO).

NBC Universal: *Jeff Shell*, CEO; *Robert Greenblatt*, Chair, NBC Entertainment; *Bonnie Hammer*, Chair, Cable Entertainment; *Noah Oppenheim*, president, NBC News; *Mark Lazarus*, Chair, Sports; *Ron Meyer*, Vice Chair, NBCUniversal (Parent company: Comcast: *Brian Roberts*, CEO).

Viacom CBS: An unusual situation: Viacom is a "public" company but voting stock is 100% owned by *Shari Redstone* and the heirs of *Sumner Redstone*. Leading individuals include *David Nevins*, CCO; *Susan Zirinsky*, president, CBS News; *David Stapf*, president, CBS TV.

Fox Corporation: Similar to Viacom, a public company but 39% of voting stock is owned by *Rupert Murdoch* and *Lachlan Murdoch*.

---

[10] Until 2018, we could have included the Weinstein Company (aka Lantern Entertainment), but the sex scandal surrounding Harvey Weinstein drove the corporation into bankruptcy.

All these individuals are Jewish, with the possible exception of the Murdochs—although it seems certain that they are at least part-Jewish.[11] And given the difficulty in ascertaining ethnicity, Jewish influence is certainly greater than shown here. Hence the above is undoubtedly a conservative estimate. It furthermore says nothing about the many Jewish underlings who implement day-to-day decisions. Once again, it's difficult to convey the degree of dominance here. These five corporations produce the vast majority of all media consumed in the US, which includes all of the major news outlets and most of the major Hollywood studios. In fact, Jewish leadership or ownership at the top translates all throughout the organization, to middle-managers, staffers, reporters, television personalities, and editors. It has a very concrete effect on how the media is produced, what is presented, and what is *not* presented. It affects who we see, and who we *don't* see.

And it's not only the so-called liberal media outlets. The conservative venues also are dominated by Jewish interests—typically, via right-wing or neo-conservative Jews. Fox News, and its parent corporation Fox, owned and operated by the Murdoch family, is every bit as pro-Jewish and pro-Israel as the liberal outlets. Fox News anchors disagree vehemently with just about every liberal position, and yet, remarkably, they are fully onboard with all Jewish issues. They struggle to outdo their peers at CNN and MSNBC in their obeisance to Jewish and Israeli interests.[12] This, again, is no coincidence. It is evidence of Jewish domination of American media, across the political spectrum and across all venues.

In addition to the above, various other media are also well-represented by American Jews. Among newspapers, the *New York Times* has been Jewish-owned and -managed since Adolph Ochs bought the paper in 1896; the current owner, publisher, and chairman is Arthur G. Sulzberger. The *Washington Post* has been Jewish-owned and -operated since it was purchased by Eugene Meyer in 1933; current owner is the likely-Jewish Jeff Bezos. *US News and World Report* is owned by Mort Zuckerman. *Time* magazine is owned by Warner Media, and its current chief editor is Edward Felsenthal. Advance Publications is a mini media conglomerate entirely owned and operated by the Jewish Newhouse family; it manages a wide array of venues including Conde Nast (*Vogue*, *The New Yorker*, *GQ*, *Glamour*, *Architectural Digest*, *Vanity Fair*, *Pitchfork*, *Wired*, and *Bon Appetit*), Discovery Channel, Lycos, and Redditt. And in broadcast

[11] Rupert's mother, Elisabeth Joy Greene, appears to have been Jewish. We could also cite Rupert Murdoch's award from the heavily-Jewish group ADL in 2010, and his son James' $1 million donation to the same group in 2017. If the Murdochs are not Jewish, they are in very good graces with them.

[12] Sean Hannity is particularly egregious in this respect.

media, we have National Public Radio (NPR), which has long been a Jewish preserve; its on-air staff is unquestionably more than half Jewish.[13]

I think we can put to rest all thoughts of denialism here.

Is Jewish Dominance Irrelevant?

If we then proceed to stage two, Irrelevance, we must counter the view that Jewish dominance is inconsequential. Again, from the naïve standpoint, Jews predominating in government, academia, finance, and media seems not to matter. These Jews are largely invisible *as Jews*, and their Jewishness is rarely displayed explicitly. As before, the influence is generally manifest in myriad subtle ways—in which voices and views are presented (and which *not* presented), which individuals are allowed to speak (and which *not* allowed), which values are projected as good and positive, which causes are worthy of attention, and so on.

The central issues here are (a) that Jews tend to work collectively, in their own bests interests, and (b) that they tend to have little regard for all non-Jews, and they tend to hold particular contempt for White Europeans, who have, historically speaking, proven to be their most formidable opponents. Jews work tribally, as a pack; they assist each other in attacking and undermining all perceived enemies. Finance Jews and academic Jews can count on media Jews to give them positive coverage and to down-play or bury any negative stories. Media Jews will slander an enemy even as finance Jews put the squeeze to that person's employer. It can be very effective when multiple actors in a trillion-dollar cabal are arrayed against you.

On occasion, these dominant Jews will indeed fight with each other, as when conservative right-wing Jews spar with their liberal left-wing brethren—such as the 2021 rift between the right-wing Murdoch Jews and the left-wing ADL Jews, especially Jonathan Greenblatt, over comments by Tucker Carlson. But this is only an internal dispute about the best way to promote Jewish interests, nothing more. Much of current political confrontation is mere show; Democratic-Republican squabbles are meaningless when both sides are backed by wealthy Jews. And Jews across the

[13] Current and recent individuals include, at a minimum: N. Adams, H. Berkes, M. Block, D. Brooks, A. Cheuse, A. Codrescu, K. Coleman, O. Eisenberg, D. Elliott, D. Estrin, S. Fatsis, P. Fessler, C. Flintoff, D. Folkenflik, R. Garfield, T. Gjelten, B. Gladstone, I. Glass, T. Goldman, J. Goldstein, J. Goldstein, R. Goldstein, D. Greene, N. Greenfieldboyce, T. Gross, M. Hirsh, S. Inskeep, I. Jaffe, A. Kahn, C. Kahn, M. Kaste, A. Katz, M. Keleman, D. Kestenbaum, N. King, B. Klein, T. Koppel, A. Kuhn, B. Littlefield, N. King, N. Pearl, P. Sagal, M. Schaub, A. Shapiro, J. Shapiro, W. Shortz, R. Siegel, A. Silverman, S. Simon, A. Spiegel, S. Stamberg, R. Stein, L. Sydell, D. Temple-Raston, N. Totenberg, G. Warner, D. Welna, L. Wertheimer, D. Wessel, E. Westervelt, B. Wolf, and D. Zwerdling.

political spectrum love to use Gentile lackeys like Anderson Cooper, Chris Cuomo, Chris Hayes, Sean Hannity, and yes, Tucker Carlson, to cover for them. This again serves to obscure the real power structure.

But the fact that powerful Jews work with each other, against all others, is a well-established historical fact that has been well-attested, over the centuries, by some of the West's most brilliant thinkers. This topic literally requires a book-length treatment—see my book *Eternal Strangers: Critical Views of Jews and Judaism through the Ages* (2020), which is the first to fully document the historical record. It dates back over 2,000 years, at least to remarks by Hecateus of Abdera and Theophrastus circa 300 BC, proceeding to the likes of Cicero, Seneca, Tacitus, Porphyry, Thomas Aquinas, Martin Luther, Voltaire, Rousseau, Fichte, Kant, Hegel, Schopenhauer, Bakunin, Nietzsche, Mark Twain, H. G. Wells, Heidegger, and chess genius (and half-Jew) Bobby Fischer, among many others. It is an impressive list.

The criticisms are uniformly blunt and damning. Jews are "misanthropic and hostile to foreigners," "the very vilest of mankind," "look upon all other men as their enemies," "an accursed race," "the basest of peoples." They are profoundly and deeply different—in a bad way—from the rest of humanity. Medieval theologians condemned the Jews for their usury and their abuse of Christians and Christianity. Luther called them "a heavy burden, a plague, a pestilence, a sheer misfortune," adding that "we are at fault in not slaying them." For Voltaire, they "display an irreconcilable hatred against all nations"; for Rousseau, the Jewish race was "always a foreigner amongst other men." German philosopher Johann Herder called them "a widely diffused republic of cunning usurers." Kant saw them as "a nation of deceivers." Schopenhauer was especially blunt: "scum of humanity—but great master of lies." Heidegger captured the situation well in just three words: "planetary master criminals".[14]

This 2,000-year history of hatred and contempt for the rest of humanity is played out in the present day, though with much stealth and deception. Jews often work in the background, hidden, out of the limelight; they are, as Hitler said, the "wire-pullers" (*Drahtzieher*) of contemporary society, using money and power to steer events in their favor. History tells us that Jews will stoop to anything—the most heinous, the most egregious, the most unethical—to promote their ends. Even *war*: there is an equally long and damning history of Jewish involvement in wars, from the Jewish-Roman wars circa 100 AD to the present-day "war on terror".[15] This is not speculation; all these facts are well-attested and well-documented. We need only do a basic bit of reading, from reputable sources.

---

[14] For an enlightening list of some 50 such quotations, see the website of Clemens and Blair, LLC publishing (www.clemensandblair.com).

[15] See my book *The Jewish Hand in the World Wars* (2019).

The bottom line, of course, is that Jewish over-representation in major sectors of society *does* matter—it matters very much. Arguably it is the root cause of virtually all our present-day social problems, all of which have been created or exacerbated by powerful Jews. We can scarcely imagine what life could be like without their manipulating and malevolent presence.

This brief account of pernicious Jewish influence should help lay to rest the "irrelevance" stage. But impotence need not be the consequence. Accept the realty, and turn your anger onto the real targets. And then act. Bear in mind: Every Jewish victory in past centuries has been ephemeral, and has instead been transformed into concrete action against the Hebrews—isolation, ghettoization, incarceration, expulsion, or worse. And so it will be this time. Either the Jews themselves will recognize that they are on the brink, and voluntarily retreat to their "homeland" in Palestine, or else native peoples around the world will, once again, take action.

The path to enlightenment is hard. And yet it must be pursued, if humanity is to flourish and prosper.

— 32 —
On the True Meaning of Hate Speech

"A law against Jew-hatred is usually the beginning of the end for the Jews."

— Joseph Goebbels, diary (19 Apr 1943)[1]

'Hate' is such an ugly word. And such a juvenile word. It calls to mind the stereotypical eight-year-old girl who screams "I hate you!" to her mother when she is not allowed to join the local sleep-over. The word is most often used half-jokingly—"I hate the Yankees!", "I hate broccoli!", etc.—or to describe some detested task ("I hate cleaning the bathroom"). Or it can be used for rhetorical effect. But the use of the term in the context of 'hate speech' is silly, juvenile, and formally meaningless. We may dislike someone or some group, or be repulsed by them, or wish to dissociate from them. But to hate them? Seriously—what mature individual today is willing to openly and earnestly say "I hate you" to anyone? Only a highly insecure or severely distressed person would do such a thing. It's a sign of weakness.

And yet today, hate seems to be the ethos of the moment. More specifically, we seem to be surrounded by talk of 'hate speech' in the mass media. To judge by various headlines and liberal pundits, hate speech would appear to be among the greatest dangers of modern existence—on par with racism and "White supremacy," and greater than political corruption, international terrorism, global pandemics, financial instability, environmental decline, overpopulation, or uncontrollable industrial technology. Most European countries have legal prohibitions against various forms of hate speech, however ill-defined, as do Canada and Australia. Even in the US there is increasing pressure to create legal sanction for some such concept, the First Amendment notwithstanding.

I take this whole topic very personally. It's no secret that I've written harshly against Jews and other minorities. It's no secret that I prefer living in a White community and a White nation. I have no need to apologize for any of this. And yet, for these very reasons, some people find it appropriate to call me a 'hater': "Dalton hates the Jews"; "he hates Blacks," "he hates Latinos," etc, etc. But I state here, for the record, that nothing is further

[1] Reprinted in *Goebbels on the Jews* (2019; T. Dalton, ed.), p. 199.

from the truth. *I hate no one*. I may dislike certain people, I may find them malevolent and malicious, I may want them punished, and I may want to separate myself from them; but this does not mean that I hate them. In this era of "hate crimes" and "hate speech laws," this requires some explanation.

As usual, we should start by knowing what we are talking about. What, exactly, is it to 'hate'? The word has ancient origins, deriving from the Indo-European *kədes* and Greek *kedos*. Originally, and surprisingly, it meant simply 'strong feelings' in a neutral sense, rather than something negative. In fact, the Old Irish word *caiss* includes both love and hate. But the negative connotation emerged with the Germanic *khatis* (later, *hass*), the Dutch *haat*, and eventually became ingrained in the English 'hate.'

The standard dictionary definition typically runs something like this: "intense or extreme dislike, aversion, or hostility" toward someone or something. As such, the word is fairly innocuous; I can hate my job, hate broccoli, and even hate my boss. But this is not at issue. We are more concerned about hate as a *mindset*, and specifically as oriented toward classes of people, or increasingly, toward certain privileged ideologies.

But we immediately confront a major problem here: Hate is a *feeling*, and feelings are indelibly subjective. And anything that is completely subjective cannot be quantified in objective terms. No one can say with certainty that "Dalton hates X." Only *I* can say, "I hate X," precisely because it is my own feeling. If there is one thing that I insist upon, it is complete sovereignty over my own feelings. No one else will ever dictate how I feel about anything.

And even if I say "I hate X," how does anyone else know that I really feel the hatred? They don't. Maybe I'm being sarcastic. Maybe I'm joking. Maybe I'm just trying to cause a stir. No one will ever know my actual feelings except me—precisely because they are *my own*. No one will ever know if I am expressing "real" hatred, or just pretending. (Does that even matter?)

The point here is that hatred, because it vanishes into a subjective void that is utterly inaccessible to others, can never be quantified or objectified, and thus can never be the basis for legal enforcement—at least, not in any rational sense. Therefore, the corresponding concept of 'hate speech,' viewed as the *expression* of hatred, likewise melts into thin air. It is, technically, an incoherent concept when put forth as a basis for law. This fact, of course, does not stop corrupt lawmakers around the globe from trying to enforce it, though for very different reasons, as I will explain.

So, let me take a look at how some attempt to define the indefinable. Here is one interesting definition from the Cambridge Dictionary: hate speech is

> public speech that expresses hate or encourages violence toward a person or group based on something such as race, religion, sex, or sexual orientation (= the fact of being gay, etc.)

This is a hugely problematic definition, on several grounds. First, how public is 'public'? If I tell my neighbor, is that public? If I publish something in a private chat room, is that public? What if I mumble something aloud to a friend while in a shopping mall? Am I responsible if a private email to a colleague gets reposted online? And so on.

Second: it involves the "expression of hate," *or* "encouragement of violence." These are two vastly different things. 'Expression of hate' is, as I said, functionally meaningless. What, exactly, does it take for something to qualify as an "expression of hate"? Presumably if I say "I hate X," that counts. But what else? Does "I really, really, really dislike X" count? Does "I'd like to see X die" count? What about "I'd like to see X get very ill"? Does "X is a total scumbag" count? We can see the problems. Incitement to violence is somewhat less ambiguous, but still problematic. Who, for example, is to judge 'encouragement'? This is another highly subjective term. And how much violence is necessary to qualify? Is a good shove violent? A pie in the face? Tripping someone? Is 'emotional distress' violence? What about financial loss?

Third, we notice that it's not violence per se, but rather violence "based on something such as race, religion, sex, or sexual orientation." This is very odd. What does the phrase "something such as" mean here? The qualifiers mentioned are usually assumed to be intrinsic to the person or group (race, gender)—except that religion, and even sexual orientation, can be changed at the drop of a hat. Therefore, the qualities need not be intrinsic. So what, exactly, is this mysterious criteria, this "something such as," that is so crucial for the whole concept?

The point here is that the whole notion of 'hate speech,' like hate itself, dissolves into a subjective void. In objective terms, it is virtually meaningless. How, then, can be it be subject to the force of law?

The UN Takes a Shot

As if they don't have enough on their plate already, the United Nations is now highly distressed by the spread of hate speech around the world. In May 2019, they issued a short statement called "Strategy and Plan of Action on Hate Speech." It included this observation:

> There is no international legal definition of hate speech, and the characterization of what is 'hateful' is controversial and disputed. In the context of this document, the term 'hate

> speech' is understood as any kind of communication in speech, writing or behaviour, that attacks or uses pejorative or discriminatory language with reference to a person or a group on the basis of who they are—in other words, based on their religion, ethnicity, nationality, race, colour, descent, gender or other identity factor. This is often rooted in, and generates, intolerance and hatred and, in certain contexts, can be demeaning and divisive.

The key phrases here: "controversial and disputed" (obviously), "any kind of communication" (very broad), "pejorative or discriminatory language" (highly subjective and undefined), and "on the basis of who they are" (mostly intrinsic factors, except for nationality and religion, and possibly "other identity factors"). And then we read the subsequent explanatory paragraph:

> Rather than prohibiting hate speech as such, international law prohibits the incitement to discrimination, hostility and violence (referred to here as 'incitement'). Incitement is a very dangerous form of speech, because it explicitly and deliberately aims at triggering discrimination, hostility and violence, which may also lead to or include terrorism or atrocity crimes. Hate speech that does not reach the threshold of incitement is not something that international law requires States to prohibit.

So, hate speech per se is not to be prohibited, but rather only a special kind of hate speech—"inciteful (to violence) hate speech." In other words, only the worst of the worst, apparently. Clarification and elaboration would soon follow.

Also, the Foreword to the statement reveals something of the deeper motives at work here. We find, in the opening paragraph, references to "anti-Semitism," "neo-Nazis," and the dreaded "White supremacy." Strange how we inevitably find such terms in any discussion of hate speech; more on this below.

Evidently dissatisfied with this short statement, the UN issued a 52-page "Detailed Guidance" report, under the same name, in September 2020. Here they establish three levels of hate speech: 1) the worst kind: "direct and public incitement to violence" (including to genocide), 2) a grey zone of hate speech to be prohibited based on "legitimate aims" and only as "necessary and proportionate", and 3) an unrestricted and lawful form that may still be "offensive, shocking, or disturbing." Level One ("Incitement") hate speech in turn is based on, and determined by, six conditions:

1) social and political context
2) status of the speaker (!)
3) intention of the speaker (!)
4) form and content of the speech
5) extent of dissemination
6) likelihood of harm

Level One Hate must satisfy all six criteria, meaning (presumably): a sensitive time or social context, an influential or important speaker, bad intent, provocative style, widely disseminated, *and* with reasonable probability of harm. Again, *all six* are required, for Level One status. Levels Two and Three may meet some, or none, of these. The six criteria are elaborated on pages 17 and 18 of the report.

Later in the document we find an interesting admission: "The terms 'hatred' and 'hostility' should be understood to refer to intense and irrational emotions of opprobrium, enmity, and detestation towards the target group" (p. 13). This is actually quite a relief; any opposition to Jews or other minorities, if *rational* and *non-emotional* (e.g. fact-based) cannot count as hate speech! Therefore, writings by scholars, academics, or other serious researchers, who build a case based on facts, history, and plausible inference, are under no circumstances engaging in hate speech. This is a huge loophole that somehow slipped past the ideological censors, one which we should be able to use to our advantage.

We—some of us, at least—get further relief on the following page, where we read that Level Three (allowable) Hate includes not only "expression that is offensive, shocking, or disturbing" but also covers "denial of historical events, including crimes of genocide or crimes against humanity." As the UN sees it, so-called Holocaust denial is permissible, or at least non-punishable, hate speech.[2] And in Figure 4 they go further still, stating that Level Three hate "must be PROTECTED" as a form of free expression. This is a remarkable concession.

Ah, but there's a catch: "*unless* such forms of expression *also* constitute incitement to hostility, discrimination, or violence under article 20 (2) of the International Covenant on Civil and Political Rights." This document, written in 1966 and made effective in 1976, includes these words under article 20: "Any advocacy of national, racial or religious hatred that

[2] For the record, I am no denier. I believe that there was a Holocaust of the mid-20th century: it was called World War Two, and some 60 million people died as a result of Jewish-instigated actions both here and in Europe. Jewish fatalities seem to have numbered around 500,000, according to the major revisionists. For more on these issues, see my books *The Jewish Hand in the World Wars* (2019) and *Debating the Holocaust* (4th ed, 2020).

constitutes incitement to discrimination, hostility or violence shall be prohibited by law." So it would seem that, for example, Holocaust "denial" (whatever that means) is not prohibited as long as it avoids any connection to "incitement" of any kind. Presumably discussing it as a historical subject is fine; just don't implicate anyone today who promotes, exploits, or profits from the conventional Holocaust story.

"It's Always About the Jews!"

So, let's get down to the rub. I have a tentative hypothesis that I am willing to put forward: *Hate speech is by, for, and about Jews*. (Oops—is that hate speech?) That is, that hate speech laws have been invented and promoted by Jews, primarily for their benefit. I further hold that Jews are the master-class haters in world history, and that they understand the power of hatred better than any other people. They have furthermore learned how to project their hatred onto others in service of their own ends, including by trickery and deception. Let me marshal whatever evidence I can, mostly implicit, to build a case for this hypothesis.

Start with a little history of Jews and hatred. Perhaps the first explicit connection came way back in 300 BC, in a short writing by Hecateus of Abdera titled "On the Jews." Only two fragments remain, one of which is relevant: As a result of the Exodus, "Moses introduced a way of life which was, to a certain extent, misanthropic (*apanthropon*) and hostile to foreigners".[3] It is striking that, even at that early date, the Jews had a reputation for misanthropy—a hatred of humanity. The same theme recurs in 134 BC, when King Antiochus VII was advised "to destroy the Jews, for they alone among all peoples refused all relations with other races, and saw everyone as their enemy." The king's counselor cited "the Jews' hatred of all mankind, sanctioned by their very laws".[4] Not only was their hatred notable, so too was the fact that it was "they alone, among all peoples"; the Jews were exceptional haters, it seems.

It is worth further expanding on the idea that Jewish hatred is "sanctioned by their very laws"—by which they mean, the Old Testament. We know, of course, that the Jews viewed themselves as "chosen" by the creator of the universe: "For you are a people holy to the Lord your God. The Lord your God has chosen you to be a people for his own possession, out of all the peoples that are on the face of the earth" (Deut 7:6). Clearly, then, everyone else is second-best. We also know that God supposedly gave the Jews a kind of dominion over the other nations of the Earth. The

---

[3] *Eternal Strangers* (2020; T. Dalton, ed), p. 16.

[4] Emilio Gabba, "The growth of anti-Judaism," in *The Cambridge History of Judaism* (vol. 2, 1984), p. 645.

Book of Exodus states, "we [Jews] are distinct...from all other people that are upon the face of the earth" (33:16). Similarly, the Hebrew tribe is "a people dwelling alone, and not reckoning itself among the nations" (Num 23:9). In Deuteronomy (15:6), Moses tells the Jews "you shall rule over many nations"; "they shall be afraid of you" (28:10). There is Genesis: "Let peoples serve you, and nations bow down to you" (27:29); or Deuteronomy, where God promises Jews "houses full of all good things, which [they] did not fill, and cisterns hewn out, which [they] did not hew, and vineyards and olive trees, which [they] did not plant" (6:11). And outside the Pentateuch, we can read in Isaiah: "Foreigners shall build up your walls, and their kings shall minister to you...that men may bring you the wealth of the nations" (60:10-11); or again, "aliens shall stand and feed your flocks, foreigners shall be your plowmen and vinedressers...you shall eat the wealth of the nations" (61:5-6). What is this but explicit misanthropy, sanctioned by God, and sustained "by their very laws"?

Around 50 BC, Diodorus Siculus wrote *Historical Library* where, in the course of discussing the Exodus, he observes that "the nation of Jews had made their hatred of mankind into a tradition" (34,1). A few decades later, Lysimachus remarked that the Hebrew tribe was instructed by Moses "to show good will to no man" and to offer only "the worse advice" to others. And in the early years of the Christian era, the writer Apion commented on the Jewish tendency "to show no goodwill to a single alien, above all to Greeks".[5] Again, repeated observations of Jewish hatred toward Gentile humanity.

The most insightful ancient critique, though, comes from Roman historian Tacitus. His works *Histories* (100 AD) and *Annals* (115 AD) both record highly damning observations on the Hebrew tribe. In the former, the Jews are described as "a race of men hateful to the gods" (*genus hominum invisium deis*, V.3). Somewhat later, he remarks that "the Jews are extremely loyal toward one another, and always ready to show compassion, but toward every other people they feel only hate and enmity" (*hostile odium*, V.5). But his most famous line comes from his later work, *Annals.* There he examines the Great Fire of Rome in 64 AD, and Nero's reaction to it. Nero, says Tacitus, pinned the blame in part on the Christians and Jews—"a class of men loathed for their vices." The Jews "were convicted, not so much on the count of arson as for hatred of the human race" (*odio humani generis*, XV.44). Clearly this was the decisive factor, certainly in Tacitus' eyes and perhaps in all of Rome: that the Jewish *odio humani generis*, hatred of humanity, was a sufficient crime to banish and even slay them.

I could go on, but the message is clear: The ancient world viewed the Jews as exceptional haters. I could also cite, for example, Philostratus circa 230 AD ("The Jews have long been in revolt not only against the Romans,

[5] *Eternal Strangers*, pp. 19, 21, and 25, respectively.

but against all humanity") or Porphyry circa 280 AD (The Jews are "the impious enemies of all nations")—but the point is made.

Importantly, this impression carried on for centuries in Europe, into the Renaissance, the Reformation, and even through the present day. Martin Luther's monumental work *On the Jews and Their Lies* (1543) includes this passage: "Now you can see what fine children of Abraham the Jews really, are, how well they take after their father [the Devil], yes, what a fine people of God they are. They boast before God of their physical birth and of the noble blood inherited from their fathers, despising all other people".[6] Two centuries later, circa 1745, Jean-Baptiste de Mirabaud wrote that "The Jews…were hated because they were known to hate other men".[7] And then we have Voltaire's entry on "Jews" in his famous *Philosophical Dictionary*, which reads as follows:

> It is certain that the Jewish nation is the most singular that the world has ever seen, and…in a political view, the most contemptible of all… It is commonly said that the abhorrence in which the Jews held other nations proceeded from their horror of idolatry; but it is much more likely that the manner in which they, at the first, exterminated some of the tribes of Canaan, and the hatred which the neighboring nations conceived for them, were the cause of this invincible aversion. As they knew no nations but their neighbors, they thought that, in abhorring them, they detested the whole earth, and thus accustomed themselves to be the enemies of all men. … In short, we find in them only an ignorant and barbarous people, who have long united the most sordid avarice with the most detestable superstition and the most invincible hatred for every people by whom they are tolerated and enriched.[8]

British historian Edward Gibbon stated the following in his classic work of 1788, *The History of the Decline and Fall of the Roman Empire*:

> The Jews…emerged from obscurity…and multiplied to a surprising degree… The sullen obstinacy with which they maintained their peculiar rites and unsocial manners seemed to mark them out a distinct species of men, who boldly pro-

[6] *On the Jews and Their Lies* (2020, T. Dalton, ed.), p. 53.
[7] *Eternal Strangers*, p. 68.
[8] *Eternal Strangers*, pp. 70-71.

> fessed, or who faintly disguised, their implacable hatred to the rest of human-kind.[9]

A similar observation came from the pen of German philosopher Johann Fichte in 1793:

> Throughout almost all the countries of Europe, a mighty hostile state is spreading that is at perpetual war with all other states, and in many of them imposes fearful burdens on the citizens: it is the Jews. I don't think, as I hope to show subsequently, that this state is fearful—not because it forms a separate and solidly united state but because this state is founded on the hatred of the whole human race...[10]

Who, then, are the master haters in all of history?

Particularly striking are the words of Nietzsche. A long series of negative comments on the Jews began in 1881 with his book *Daybreak*, where he observes in passing (sec. 377) that "The command 'love your enemies' had to be invented by the Jews, the best haters there have ever been." So it would seem that the Jews are truly best at something after all: hatred. Then in *The Gay Science* (1882), Nietzsche sarcastically notes that the Jews are indeed 'chosen' people, precisely because "they had a *more profound contempt* for the human being in themselves than any other people" (sec. 136).

But the most stunning discourse appears in Nietzsche's work of 1887, *On the Genealogy of Morals*, where he offers a detailed analysis of hatred from the Judeo-Christian perspective. In short, Jewish hatred is manifested most visibly in their rabbis, religious men, and their priests. Sanctioned by God, priestly hate is the deepest and most profound; it is the hatred of those without tangible power. Jewish hatred then metastasized in Christianity, taking form as its nominal opposite, namely, love. The First Essay is a masterpiece of literature and philosophy; I quote it at length:

> As is well known, priests are the *most evil of enemies*—but why? Because they are the most powerless. From their powerlessness, their hate grows among them into something huge and terrifying, to the most spiritual and most poisonous manifestations. The really great haters in world history and the most spiritual haters have always been priests—in com-

[9] *The History of the Decline and Fall of the Roman Empire* (1788/1974, vol. 2), p. 3. See also *Eternal Strangers*, p. 59.

[10] *Eternal Strangers*, p. 78.

parison with the spirit of priestly revenge, all the remaining spirits are generally hardly worth considering.

Let us quickly consider the greatest example. Everything on earth which has been done against "the noble," "the powerful," "the masters," "the rulers" is not worth mentioning in comparison with what *the Jews* have done against them: the Jews, that priestly people, who knew how to get final satisfaction from their enemies and conquerors through a radical transformation of their values, that is, through an act of the *most spiritual revenge*. This was appropriate only to a priestly people with the most deeply repressed priestly desire for revenge. In opposition to the aristocratic value equations (*good = noble = powerful = beautiful = fortunate = loved by god*), the Jews, with an awe-inspiring consistency, dared to reverse things and to hang on to that with the teeth of the most profound hatred (the hatred of the powerless)… (sec. 7)

But you fail to understand that? You have no eye for something that needed two millennia to emerge victorious? … That's nothing to wonder at: all *lengthy* things are hard to see, to assess. However, *that's* what took place: out of the trunk of that tree of vengeance and hatred, Jewish hatred—the deepest and most sublime hatred, that is, a hatred which creates ideals and transforms values, something whose like has never existed on earth—from that grew something just as incomparable, a *new love*, the deepest and most sublime of all the forms of love: —from what other trunk could it have grown?

However, one should not assume that this love arose essentially as the denial of that thirst for vengeance, as the opposite of Jewish hatred! No: the reverse is the truth! This love grew out of that hatred, as its crown, as the victorious crown unfolding itself wider and wider in the purest brightness and sunshine, which, so to speak, was seeking for the kingdom of light and height, the goal of that hate, aiming for victory, trophies, seduction, with the same urgency with which the roots of that hatred were sinking down ever deeper and more greedily into everything that was evil and possessed depth. This Jesus of Nazareth, the living evangelist of love, the "Saviour" bringing holiness and victory to the poor, to the sick, to the sinners—was he not that very seduction in its most terrible and most irresistible form, the seduction and detour to exactly those *Jewish* values and innovations in ideals? (sec. 8)

On this view, Christian 'love' grows out of Jewish 'hate,' like the crown of the tree from its roots. The Jews (and Paul specifically), the master haters, purveyors of the "deepest and most sublime hatred" that has ever existed, created the idea of a saviour who loves everyone. They did so as cover for their hatred of humanity, and as an enticement into their Jewish-inspired worldview—one of a Jewish man-god (Jesus), of Jehovah the Almighty, of heaven and hell. These destructive and nihilistic "values and innovations" could only be foisted upon a humanity that was detested. Christianity was thus the greatest manifestation of Jewish hatred ever conceived.

Nietzsche summarizes his thesis concisely in section 16:

> In Rome the Jew was considered "*guilty* of hatred against the entire human race." And that view was *correct*, to the extent that we are right to link the health and the future of the human race to the unconditional rule of aristocratic values, the Roman values.

The nihilistic Christian values—based on a mythical God and an unknowable and perhaps nonexistent future life—managed to undermine and ultimately displace the superior Greco-Roman values that had flourished for 800 years and created the foundation of all of Western civilization. Only an overthrow of Judeo-Christianity and a return to classic, aristocratic values can save humanity at this point. The quoted passage refers, of course, to Tacitus.

We can't leave the *Genealogy* without brief mention of a fascinating and humorous allegory on hatred that Nietzsche offers in section 13. There he compares the situation between lowly (Judeo-Christian) haters and the strong and noble (Roman) aristocrats to the opposition that might exist between baby lambs and some nasty predator (*Raubvogel*), like an eagle. The lambs are innocently and peacefully munching grass in a field, but live in constant fear of a predator who may, at any time, swoop in and snatch them up. The weak lambs are *haters*; they hate those birds of prey. But the noble eagles don't hate at all. Nietzsche explains:

> But let's come back: the problem with the *other* origin of the "good," of the good man, as the person of ressentiment has imagined it for himself, demands its own conclusion. —That the lambs are upset about the great predatory birds is not a strange thing, and the fact that they snatch away small lambs provides no reason for holding anything against these large birds of prey. And if the lambs say among themselves, "These predatory birds are evil, and whoever is least like a predatory bird, especially anyone who is like its opposite, a

> lamb—shouldn't that animal be good?" there is nothing to find fault with in this setting-up of an ideal, except for the fact that the birds of prey might look down on them with a little mockery and perhaps say to themselves, "*We* are not at all annoyed with these good lambs. We even love them. Nothing is tastier than a tender lamb."

The noble don't hate; they rule and dominate. Only the weak hate. The weak haters furthermore seek to portray the strong and noble in the harshest possible terms: "evil," "killers," "sinners." But this is ludicrous, of course. The strong are just doing what is appropriate to their nature. The haters might then try to confuse the strong, to guilt them into changing their behavior, to get them to become 'weak' and 'good' like the haters themselves. But this would be the death of them, just as a life of munching grass—so pleasant for a lamb—would mean death for an eagle. Nietzsche emphasizes this very point:

> [I]t's no wonder that the repressed, secretly smouldering feelings of rage and hate use this belief for themselves, and basically even maintain a faith in nothing more fervently than in the idea that *the strong are free* to be weak and that predatory birds are free to be lambs: —in so doing, they arrogate to themselves the right to *blame* the birds of prey for being birds of prey.

Today, weak and lowly haters—Jews, Jewish-inspired Christians, and Jewish lackeys in the media—have been working hard to convince the strong and noble that they are bad, evil, bigoted, racist, and supremacist. And to the extent that they have succeeded, it has been the death of noble humanity. We must resist this tendency with all our might.

Hate Speech in the 20th Century

With growing wealth and financial clout, and with a 2,000-year history of skill in hatred under their belts, organized Jewry began to press the case for legal sanctions against their opponents. With the flood of Jewish immigrants around the turn of the century, it is perhaps not surprising that Jewish legal advocacy took hold in the US. In the first two decades, a number of major pro-Jewish groups emerged, including the American Jewish Committee (1906), the Anti-Defamation League (1913), the American Jewish Congress (1918), and the American Civil Liberties Union (1920). All these groups were *de facto* anti-hate speech advocates, even if the federal legal apparatus did not really exist at that point. Their focus was on so-called "group libel," a novel legal concept that was formulated specifically to benefit Jewish interests.

Meanwhile, across the ocean, Jews were making better legal progress in the proto-Soviet Union. The rise of Jewish Bolsheviks from around 1900, including Leon Trotsky and the quarter-Jewish Vladimir Lenin, brought a new concern with anti-Semitism to the Russian Empire. When they took power in the February Revolution of 1917, they immediately set to work to make life better for Russian Jews. Pinkus (1990) explains that these Bolsheviks "issued a decree annulling all legal restrictions on Jews" in March 1917.[11] He adds that, unsurprisingly, "Even before the October [1917] Revolution, Lenin and the Bolshevik Party were hostile to anti-Semitism. Lenin castigated it in the strongest terms on a number of occasions." As soon as July 1918, the Soviet Council issued a decree (though without legal enforcement) stating that "the anti-Semitic movement and the anti-Jewish pogroms are a deadly menace to the Revolution"; all Soviet workers are called upon "to fight this plague with all possible means".[12] Lenin himself continued to press his pro-Jewish propaganda; in one short but notable speech of March 1919, he said:

> Anti-Semitism means spreading enmity towards the Jews. When the accursed Czarist monarchy was living its last days, it tried to incite ignorant workers and peasants against the Jews. The Czarist police, in alliance with the landowners and the capitalists, organized pogroms against the Jews. The landowners and capitalists tried to divert the hatred of the workers and peasants who were tortured by want against the Jews. ... Only the most ignorant and downtrodden people can believe the lies and slander that are spread about the Jews. This is a survival of ancient feudal times, when the priests burned heretics at the stake, when the peasants lived in slavery, and when the people were crushed and inarticulate. This ancient, feudal ignorance is passing away; the eyes of the people are being opened.
>
> It is not the Jews who are the enemies of the working people. The enemies of the workers are the capitalists of all countries. Among the Jews there are working people, and they form the majority. They are our brothers, who, like us, are oppressed by capital; they are our comrades in the struggle for socialism. ... Shame on accursed Czarism which tortured

[11] Benjamin Pinkus, *The Jews of the Soviet Union* (1990), p. 84.
[12] In Pinkus, p. 85.

> and persecuted the Jews. Shame on those who foment hatred towards the Jews, who foment hatred towards other nations.[13]

As (non-Jew) Joseph Stalin rose to power in the 1920s, he found it expedient to continue working with the Soviet Jews and generally defending their status. Consequently, that decade became a sort of 'golden age' for them; it saw the emergence of the likes of Lazar Kaganovich, Yakov Sverdlov, Lev Kamenev, Karl Radek, Leonid Krasin, Filipp Goloshchekin, and Yakov Agranov—all high-ranking Jews in the Soviet hierarchy.[14] Partly because of this governmental dominance, anti-Semitism among the Russian masses continued to percolate. Eventually, "in 1927, a decision was reached to take drastic steps to repress anti-Semitism".[15] Various forms of propaganda were employed, including books, pamphlets, plays, and films; the process culminated in harsh legal action against anti-Jewish hate, *up to and including the death penalty*. Stalin confirmed this in writing in 1931:

> Anti-Semitism is of advantage to the exploiters as a lightning conductor that deflects the blows aimed by the working people at capitalism. Anti-Semitism is dangerous for the working people as being a false path that leads them off the right road and lands them in the jungle. Hence Communists, as consistent internationalists, cannot but be irreconcilable, sworn enemies of anti-Semitism. In the USSR, anti-Semitism is punishable with the utmost severity of the law as a phenomenon deeply hostile to the Soviet system. Under USSR law, active anti-Semites are liable to the death penalty.[16]

The Jewish Golden Age in the Soviet Union lasted until the late 1930s, when Stalin inaugurated a retrenchment of Jewish power, apparently in response to the National Socialist stance.[17]

But the Soviet (and Bolshevik) philo-Semitic policies of the 1920s and 1930s were not lost on Hitler. He and Goebbels were relentless, and justified, in their critiques of "Jewish Bolshevism" as a dominant threat to Germany and Europe. Goebbels in particular noted the growing push for 'hate speech' and 'hate crime' laws in defense of Jews in both the USSR and the UK; for him, this was proof of (a) a deep-seated and imminent

---

[13] "Anti-Jewish Pogroms," from www.marxists.org.

[14] The parallels to the Biden regime are striking; see chapter 31 in the present volume.

[15] Pinkus, p. 86.

[16] "Anti-Semitism," from www.marxists.org.

[17] Postwar, Stalin's purging of high-ranking Jews accelerated, resulting in a decade-long period of virtual state-sponsored anti-Semitism, ending only with Stalin's death in 1953.

mass uprising against the Jews, and (b) an over-playing of their legal authority. Anti-hate laws are a sign of desperation; they indicate that the end-game is near. In a revealing diary entry of 19 April 1943, Goebbels writes:

> The Jews in England are now calling for legal protection against anti-Semitism. We know that from our own past, in the times of struggle. But even that didn't give them much advantage. We've always understood how to find gaps in these protective laws; and moreover, anti-Semitism, once it rises from the depths of the people, cannot be broken by law. A law against Jew-hatred is usually the beginning of the end for the Jews. We will make sure that anti-Semitism in England does not cool down. In any case, a longer-lasting war is the best breeding ground for it.[18]

The following month, in his published essay "The War and the Jews," Goebbels commented on the legal situation in the USSR—the very law that Stalin described above, and that was still in force some 13 years later:

> We constantly hear news that anti-Semitism is increasing in enemy nations. The charges being made against the Jews are well-known; they are the same ones that were made here. Anti-Semitism in enemy nations is not the result of anti-Semitic propaganda, since Jewry fights that strongly. In the Soviet Union, it receives the death penalty.[19]

The status of anti-Semitic hate speech laws was of importance to Goebbels right to the very end. In his last major essay, "Creators of the World's Misfortunes" (1945), he reiterated the significance of the Soviet law:

> Capitalism and Bolshevism have the same Jewish roots—two branches of the same tree that in the end bear the same fruit. International Jewry uses both in its own way to suppress nations and keep them in its service. How deep its influence on public opinion is in all the enemy countries and many neutral nations is plain to see: it may never be mentioned in newspapers, speeches, and radio broadcasts.
>
> There's a law in the Soviet Union that punishes 'anti-Semitism'—or in plain English, public education about the Jewish Question—by death. Any expert in these matters is in

---

[18] *Goebbels on the Jews*, p. 199.

[19] Ibid., pp. 206-207.

> no way surprised that a leading spokesman for the Kremlin said over the New Year that the Soviet Union would not rest until this law was valid throughout the world. In other words, the enemy clearly says that its goal in this war is to put the total domination of Jewry over the nations of the Earth under legal protection, and to use the death penalty to threaten even a discussion of this shameful attempt. It is little different in the plutocratic [Western] nations.

Even at the bitter end, this theme still impressed Goebbels. In one of his final diary entries, he wrote:

> The Jews have already registered for the San Francisco Conference [on post-war plans]. It is characteristic that their main demand is to ban anti-Semitism throughout the world. Typically, having committed the most terrible crimes against mankind, the Jews would now like mankind to be forbidden even to think about them.[20]

And indeed, they succeeded, at least in part. The postwar German *Volksverhetzung* and the Austrian *Verbotsgesetz* both stand as among the most embarrassing legal capitulations to Jewish interests in the Western world.

Thus we clearly see the origins of hate speech legislation in the 20th century: it was first constructed by Jews and their sycophants (like Stalin), both in the US and in the Soviet Union, to quell any looming opposition to their power structure. So intent were they on stifling objection to Jewish rule that they were willing to kill those who opposed them.

To the Present Day

With the growing dominance of Jewish influence in American government over the past five decades, and ongoing influence in Europe, calls have grown ever-larger to restrict and punish any anti-Jewish commentary via hate speech laws. The US government—or at least the Republicans—have so far mostly resisted such efforts, but social media has come around to the philosemitic stance. Facebook and Facebook-owned Instagram, Twitter (pre-Musk) and Google-owned YouTube, have all taken it upon themselves to censor hate speech, especially of the anti-Semitic variety.[21]

---

[20] 4 April 1945, in *Goebbels on the Jews*, p. 255.

[21] See: "Zuckerberg: Facebook will prohibit hate speech in its ads," "Instagram announces tougher consequences for hate speech in direct messages," "California

Google has altered its search algorithms to de-rank offensive and 'hate' sites.[22] All this is perfectly understandable, given the huge Jewish presence atop Big Tech; we need only mention Mark Zuckerberg, Sergei Brin, Larry Page, Larry Ellison, Michael Dell, Sheryl Sandberg, Safra Katz, Susan Wojcicki, Steve Ballmer, Brian Roberts, Marc Benioff, Craig Newmark, and Jeff Weiner, for starters.

Parallel to Big Tech censorship, Jewish advocacy groups like the SPLC and the ADL continue to press civil cases against those 'haters' who they believe violated the rights or reputation of some aggrieved party. The SPLC has a section of its website dedicated to "anti-Semitism and hate speech," and the ADL—well, that's their *raison d'etre*. Third-party lawsuits and tech censorship serve the purpose of implementing *de facto* pro-Jewish hate speech policies, at least within the US.

But to come full circle: I began this piece with a discussion about the logical vagueness and incoherence of the concept of hate speech. Clearly, though, many powerful, Jewish-inspired corporations and politicians find the concept useful. For them, in the most basic and practical terms, it becomes quite simple: *Hate speech is any speech that Jews hate*. Yes, they may claim to hate anti-Muslim speech or anti-Black speech, but this is so only because it is a necessary corollary to anti-Jewish hate speech. The Jews are not so stupid today as to push for uniquely Jewish, 'anti-anti-Semitism' laws; those are a thing of the past. Today, such laws require cover language that, at least in theory, includes other 'oppressed' groups. Jews and their defenders must appear universal and fair—when in reality most seem to have utter contempt for virtually all non-Jewish groups (there's that "hatred of humanity" again). Hate speech is any speech that Jews hate.

Consider: If you hate what I say, who's the hater? It's *you*, not me. The fact that you may not like what I'm saying does not make me a hater. It makes *you* the hater. And if you happen to be a champion, master-class, world-historical hater, well then—it's all hate to you.

---

court sides with Twitter on right to ban users for speech considered hateful," and "YouTube banning hate speech isn't censorship, it's the bare minimum."

[22] "Google search changes tackle fake news and hate speech," BBC (25 Apr 2017).

— 33 —
THE PROBLEM WITH LEFTISM

Everyone complains about the Left, but no one does anything about it. Or so it would seem. Part of the problem, I suspect, is that many in the public have mistaken notions about what "the Left" is and how it operates, and thus they more or less mindlessly support it, or oppose it, as the case may be. Hence it is high time for a hard look at this nefarious political entity, in order to devise better and more appropriate responses to it.

Let me start with conventional views. A constant theme of right-wing and conservative commentators is that the Left dominates America today. This holds true across nearly the entire spectrum of conservatism, from the dissident- and alt-Right to conventional Republicans, to Pat Buchanan, to Fox News, to the *Wall Street Journal*, to the pro-Trump crowd. In fact, it's about the only thing they all agree on. The primary concern seems to focus on media and on politics, the latter via the Democrats and the Biden regime. Many would include academia, Hollywood, and the public schools as well. Furthermore, this is universally seen on the Right as a disaster—and it *is* a disaster, but for reasons other than they presume—as well as something that poses a fundamental threat to America, to the "American way of life," and to our very health and well-being. The Left, apparently, is the root of all evil.

But what exactly is "the Left," and why are they so evil? This is rarely explained, likely because it is a relatively complicated matter that requires more than the usual 10 seconds of thinking. Given the importance of the topic and the seriousness of the threat, however, we need to dive a bit more deeply into it.

To anticipate my main conclusion: I think "the Left" is largely misnamed and misconceived—it is a kind of diversionary concept invented to distract from the real power-brokers and the real conflicts at hand. "The Left" is actually a kind of *fake Left*, portrayed as opposing "the Right," which is in reality a *fake Right*. The net effect is to create a false antagonism and to encourage the unthinking masses to pick sides, even as they ultimately support the *same* side in the end. Unsurprisingly, the Jewish Lobby plays a large role here, as I will show.

Real Leftism

I think many would be surprised to hear that real leftism is not what is commonly portrayed, and that it is actually (gasp!) not so bad. At the risk of being pedantic, let's look at standard definitions of both "Left" and "liberal," since these seem to nominally be at the heart of the problem. As I like to say, we need to know what we are talking about, if we hope to make any progress on these vital issues. Here, then, is a typical definition of "Left":

> ***Left*** n, cap a: those professing views usually characterized by desire to reform or overthrow the established political order, and usually advocating change in the name of the greater freedom or well-being of the common man. b: a radical (as distinct from conservative) position.

Thus stated, this is relatively benign. Anyone unhappy with an existing political administration will of necessity seek to reform or replace it, and thus we can all agree with this. However, it is surprising to see the Left defined as striving for *increased* freedom for the average individual, when today it is more common to decry the "liberty-loathing left." It is true that those in power are working to diminish or restrict peoples' freedoms—but this doesn't make them leftists. In fact it makes them *anti*-leftists, at least on this definition. More problematically, we can have no doubt that "the Right" in anything like current forms, including neo-con and Judeo-Trumpian conservatism, would certainly (and in some cases did) institute their own forms of liberty restriction; hence 'liberty-loathing' is no hallmark of "the Left."

As to the "radical" aspect, I would argue that this is largely in the eye of the beholder. To be a radical in this sense is simply to press for far-reaching and qualitative change, as opposed to "tinkering around the edges," which can be considered a conservative approach. Clearly one can be a "radical right-winger" as much as one can be a "radical leftist," and so part (b) does not offer much illumination.

What about "liberal," or more generally, "liberalism"? Here's what we might find:

> ***liberalism*** n: a political philosophy based on belief in progress, the essential goodness of man, and the autonomy of the individual, and standing for the protection of political and civil liberties.

Again, we find woefully little to object to here. I think we all are in favor of "progress," even though we may have different ideas about what exactly that means. What about "the essential goodness of man"? That's a strange phrase. It is almost a religious idea, almost like saying we are all "children of God" or something. But that's nonsense. I guess we can agree that *most* people, *most* of the time, are good; but still, there are bad, malevolent, and detestable people out there whom I would never declare to be "essentially good." That phrase might have been better stated as a general optimism about human nature, perhaps. And I can agree to this. I am generally optimistic about humanity; it is primarily aberrant conditions that cause the worst in people to come out. In a mass technological society, "people" can seem incredibly dull, ignorant, and short-sighted, but this is more a consequence of social structure than anything else. Much more needs to be said on this, but I defer that to another time.

"Autonomy of the individual" and "protecting civil liberties" are again, perhaps, a surprise. But they should not be. Liberalism, like liberal, derives from the Latin *liber* (free). A liberal is, literally, a free thinker; a key part of the definition of 'liberal' is the idea of "one who is open-minded." Who among us does not claim to be open-minded? Hence a true liberal is a free-thinking, autonomous, civil libertarian. But doesn't that describe the vast majority of "the Right"? What are we to make of this?

We are beginning to see the nature of the problem. Many of us, based on these definitions, would be forced to call ourselves "leftists" and "liberals." And yet, many would never do this, even on pain of death. Somehow, politics has either become detached from reality, or it has altered the basic meaning of words so much that we, collectively, and quite literally, do not know what we are talking about. Or perhaps a bit of both.

If nothing else, all this suggests that the stereotypical right-left distinction has become almost meaningless, likely as part of a deliberate strategy of obfuscation. Clearly a more precise analysis is called for.

The Structure of the Fake American Left

The Left as commonly portrayed—the fake Left—is in reality a two-tiered system, composed of a small number of ideological leaders and propagators, and a large mass of people who generally self-identify as "Democrats" or "liberals." In America today, 'Democrat' and 'Left' are virtually coextensive; nearly all Democrats are leftists, and nearly all leftists are Democrats. The terms are almost interchangeable. But here, I will focus on 'Left' and 'leftism' since that terminology has a broader international meaning than the American-only party of Democrats.

More revealing is who these people are. The elite leftists today are almost exclusively either Jews—of political, corporate, or academic stripe—or Gentiles, mostly White, working for and on behalf of Jews. (Whether these Gentile lackeys are aware of their subservient status or not, and whether they care, are good questions that I can't address here.) In other words, the elite Left are either Jews or people beholden to Jews. Either way, Jewish interests and Jewish issues predominate.

We know this because, firstly, so many of the Democratic elite are themselves Jews (Bernie Sanders, Chuck Schumer, Adam Schiff, George Soros, Jerry Nadler, Dianne Feinstein, Michael Bloomberg, Tom Steyer, Janet Yellen, Tony Blinken, Rochelle Walensky…) or have Jewish family members (Joe Biden, Kamala Harris, Nancy Pelosi, Donald Trump, Hillary Clinton, the Cuomo family). The pervasive Jewish presence in the Democratic Party is a fact never mentioned in the MSM, and rarely discussed even by their strongest right-wing opponents.[1] This should tell us something.

Secondly, we know that a large majority of Democratic campaign money comes from Jewish sources. Over the past few decades, reported percentages of Democratic totals range from "about half," to 50%, to "as much as 60%," to "over 60%," to as much as 2/3, to "70% of large contributions," to 80-90%.[2] A recent study, "The Jewish Vote 2020," cites a number of relevant statistics, including these:

- In the 2016 cycle, *all of the top seven* biggest donors overall were Jews (p. 11).
- The top 10 donors in 2016 gave $406 million, of which $357 million—an amazing 88%—was from Jews (p. 14).
- Of the top 50 donors in 2016, 20 (40%) were Jews (p. 14).
- And it reconfirms that, today, Jews comprise roughly 50% of "big individual donors" to Democrats, and 25% of the same for Republicans (p. 11).[3]

Late in 2020, in the run-up to the presidential election, it was reported that 15 of the top 25 donors (for both parties combined), or 60%, were Jews.[4] Top Democratic donors were Steyer ($54 million), Don Sussman ($22 million), James Simons ($21 million), Michael Bloomberg ($19 million), Deborah Simon ($12 million), Henry Laufer ($12 million), Josh Bekenstein ($11 million), Stephen Mandel ($9 million), Soros ($8 million—although he funnels many other donations through various nonprofits), and Steve Ballmer ($8 million). These days, anything less than $10 million barely warrants mention.

So much for politics. What about leftist media? We know the main culprits: CNN, MSNBC, the *New York Times*, and the *Washington Post.*

---

[1] It will be a cold day in hell before Tucker Carlson or Sean Hannity ever speak explicitly about the Jews on the Left.

[2] Respectively: *Jewish Power*, by J. J. Goldberg (1996), p. 277; *Jerusalem Post* (27 Sep 2016); *Washington Post* (13 Mar 2003), p. A1; *Jewish Power in America*, by B. Feingold (2008), p. 4; *Jewish Telegraphic Agency* (7 Jun 2011); *The Hill* (30 Mar 2004), p. 1; *Passionate Attachment*, by Ball and Ball (1992), p. 218.

[3] Posted at www.rudermanfoundation.org.

[4] "Meet the top 15 Jewish political donors in this election cycle," JTA.org.

Unsurprisingly, Jews fill top spots at all these organizations or their parent companies. CNN's president was Jeff Zucker, and is owned by Warner Media, with Jason Kilar as CEO. MSNBC is owned by NBC Universal, with CEO Jeff Shell, and top execs Robert Greenblatt, Bonnie Hammer, Noah Oppenheim, and Ron Meyer. The NYT has been Jewish-owned and -operated since 1896; the current owner and publisher is Arthur Sulzberger. The *Washington Post* has been Jewish-owned and -operated since 1933, with the possible exception of current owner Jeff Bezos (status unknown), who acquired it from the Jewish Graham family in 2013 ("at the suggestion of his friend, Don Graham").[5] We could include various other media entities, such as NPR Radio; in Chapter 31 of the present work, I have shown that its on-air staff is over half Jewish.

In support of political and media Jews are the leftist "Big Tech" Jews, who include the likes of Mark Zuckerberg and Sheryl Sandberg (Facebook), Larry Page and Sergei Brin (Google), Larry Ellison and Safra Catz (Oracle), Susan Wojcicki (YouTube), Steve Ballmer, Andy Jassy (Amazon), Marc Benioff, and Michael Dell (Dell computers). Thus, between money, power, media, and technology, the leftist elite—Jews and their sycophants—have a near monopoly on discourse in America and much of the West.

What about the base of the fake Left? This is a large group of individuals, mostly White, who have been deluded as to the true nature of that ideology. We can get a rough idea of numbers by considering the fact that Biden received about 80 million votes, of which some 72% were Whites; thus, there are about 55 million Whites who presumably identify with or favor the leftist Democrats. To this number we can add the 15 million Blacks and 10 million Latinos who also voted for Biden. The leftist base is thus about 80 million people. This is a large number, though not overwhelming in a nation of 330 million.

By contrast, Trump earned about 50 million White votes; another 50 million or so Whites did not vote. Hence, in rough terms, the (fake) Left has a grip on only about one-third of Whites; *two-thirds elude their grasp.* This is a good sign—perhaps the best news among a raft of bad omens. Something like 100 million Whites are either opposed, or potentially opposed, to leftist ideology. There is much to build on here.

In sum, the nominal Left is a *fake Left*, adhering to virtually nothing of the meaning of a true leftism. Rather, it is influenced and run, directly and indirectly, by wealthy and influential Jews. This fake Left is a Jewish Left, ideologically speaking, and it operates largely by and for Jewish

[5] This fact alone is damning; I know of no instance in which Jews have sold a major media company to a non-Jew. And the fact that Bezos turned over operations of Amazon to another Jew, Andy Jassy, is a further indication.

interests. Likewise with liberalism, which today is a *fake liberalism*: an ideology that is fully aligned with Jewish interests. In fact, the marriage of convenience between Jews and liberalism has long been known. Consider this revealing passage:

> Throughout the nineteenth century and later, the fate of the Jews would be linked inextricably with that of liberalism itself. Their loyalty to liberalism would be intense and abiding, nurtured on gratitude for rights received and determination to establish a permanent place for the Jews in the modern European world. Liberals, although scarcely ecstatic over persistent Jewish religious and social particularism, would reciprocate with toleration and increasing measures of equality before the law. Both parties, but especially the Jews, would be acutely aware that Jewish emancipation stood or fell with the fortunes of liberalism.[6]

For well over a century, a majority of Jews have allied themselves with liberalism and leftism *solely because it served their interests*—the welfare of native populations be damned. In a sense, they hijacked an otherwise virtuous ideology and perverted it to their own benefit.

The Real Right

Now that we have done some preliminary analysis of the Left, let's turn to the Right. In a popular sense, the Right has some stereotypical characterizations. We know the catchphrases: "Guns, God, and country"; "Don't tread on me"; "Liberty or death"; and various takes on the notion of freedom. Again, these are constant themes across the conservative spectrum.

But how do these conventional ideas match up with the formal notion of "the Right"? Earlier I cited standard definitions of 'Left' and 'liberal,' and to be fair, I need to do the same for their nominal counterparts, 'Right' and 'conservatism.' Here they are:

> ***Right*** n, cap (1) individuals favoring traditional attitudes and practices, and sometimes advocating the forced establishment of an authoritarian political order. (2) a group or party that favors conservative, traditional, or sometimes authoritarian attitudes and policies.

---

[6] *The Jews in Weimar Germany*, by Don Niewyk (1980), p. 1.

> ***conservatism*** n: a political philosophy based on tradition and social stability, stressing established institutions, and preferring gradual development to abrupt change.

As before, there are some surprises—mostly in what is *not* here. On the one hand, we find an emphasis on tradition and stability, gradual change ("reform"), and potentially anti-democratic policy, if this is how we may interpret 'forced authoritarianism' in this context. On the other, we notice what is missing: God, religion, rights, liberty, freedom. Nothing on "small government." Even terms like 'nation' and 'country' are absent. What are we to make of this?

It would seem that, as with the Left, that the Right has also been distorted from its formal and definitional meaning into a kind of caricature. The current obsession with religion, freedom, patriotism, and formal democracy have been introduced by those who would like to divert people away from the true ruling entities in the US—Jewish money and power, Judeophilic lackeys, the ultra-rich, and a techno-industrial system that is spinning out of control—in order to confuse and distract the masses.

A *true* Right, composed of *true* conservatives, would do the following:

- They would be less concerned about formal, representative democracy and more about the integrity of society, human welfare, and long-term sustainability of their own people. If this demands the use of "undemocratic" policies, so be it.
- They would actively oppose any corrupt and malevolent minority from attacking the basis of society and from seeking to exploit it for their personal gain.
- They would strive for social homogeneity, both racially and ethnically, knowing that multicultural and multiracial societies are inevitably prone to conflict, disruption, instability, and ultimately decay.
- They would oppose an advancing high-tech society, knowing that potent and uncontrollable technologies not only empower our social overlords but also destroy traditional society, damage human health, and promote the destruction of the natural world upon which all real stability is grounded.
- They would support the disintegration of large, unstable political systems like modern America and encourage the devolution and decentralization of political power; large complex societies have, of necessity, more laws, more constraints, and less freedom. They are also more easily manipulated by unscrupulous minorities.

Incidentally, one troubling fact of the January 6 "insurrection" is that most of the people there were pro-America and pro-democracy (or so it is claimed). But true conservatives would not hold these views. True conservatives realize that "America," in both practice and theory, is anti-conservative and unsustainable. America needs to be replaced with something else—something new, something different, something that will protect and defend the social well-being of the American majority and the ecological basis for it. Sadly, very few of the "insurrectionists" seem to have had any conception of the Judeocracy that rules over them and which dictates much of what Trump does and says; this strongly suggests that they severely misread the real basis of American power politics. Most of those people, I would suggest, are members of the "fake Right"—a manipulated and distorted ideology that serves the purposes of the ruling Jewish elite.

The True Problems with "the Left"

Returning to the main theme, the fake Left is a heavily Jewish enterprise. But most people, Left and Right, don't know this or don't acknowledge it, and they therefore don't object to that fact. When those on the Right object to the Left, it is usually to more concrete (but secondary) issues. We can make a short list: leftists are for "big government"; they support "open borders"; they want to take our guns; they stifle our freedom of speech (or freedom generally); they are authoritarian; they conduct "cancel culture"; they demonize Whites; they are anti-Christian; they tyrannize the public, as via their over-hyped Covid panic; they "tax and spend." Maybe even "they hate America" (if we listen to Tucker Carlson). Doubtless we could add more, but I think this covers the main concerns for most on the Right.

I cannot argue with these points; I think all of them are basically true. But there are deeper factors at work that help to explain this collective phenomenon, which is why we need to press a bit harder to really understand the process at work here.

When I consider the many objectionable features of what is called the Left, I compile a different sort of list. For what it's worth, I find it to have the following negative qualities:

A desire to impose their beliefs and values on others. This is the "controlling," "authoritarian," and "liberty-loathing" aspect. Leftist liberals seem to have an inordinate need to compel others to follow their belief-system. They are the antithesis of "live and let live." They have little or no tolerance for dissenting views, especially those that threaten their own positions. They know that rational dissent will severely undermine their credibility, and so they suppress it.[7]

---

[7] Again, the Left has no monopoly on this issue. The Right can be just as imposing.

They are blind to the realities of race, biology, and genetics. For the Left, most all of human nature is a "social construction"—something pliable and malleable, something that can be defined and redefined almost at will. Humans are merely a plastic biology; the many races are rather like different colors of Playdough, all equally moldable into new shapes and forms. This results in an over-inclusive and naïve egalitarianism.

But this is not reality. The fact is that there are profound and unalterable differences between human beings, both between and within races. These are manifest in physical, mental, emotional, psychological, and cultural ways. They are rooted in genetics, and cannot be wished away. But leftists have deeply imbibed the fallacy of human equality. Many are also functional relativists who cannot bear to make value distinctions. (I should note here the difference between the leftist elite, who espouse views that they don't really believe, and the naïve leftist masses, who generally do seem to believe them.) As a result, leftists say incredibly stupid things and make incredibly stupid policy proposals.

No concept of a noble humanity. When one swallows the myth of human equality, one condemns the human race to a miserable mediocrity. If all are equal, then none are better, and in fact no one *can* be better. Equality denies the existence of superior individuals, who are the very ones that drive society forward. When such superior individuals do appear—as they inevitably do—they are suppressed, censored, attacked, perhaps jailed, perhaps killed. Superior individuals put the lie to the myth of equality, which is one reason why they are so dangerous to the Left. Because leftists have repudiated the whole concept of a noble humanity, they represent a profound threat to human well-being. They effectively destroy the future of our race.

A pathology of pity. Leftists are pity-mongers in the extreme. They wallow in pity. They praise pity. And they sell pity.[8] Great individuals and great societies do not wallow in pity. They accept pain, hardship, and loss, and then they move on. They give a fair respect to all of humanity, but they don't elevate the lesser or the weak. They don't allow the lesser to dominate or even to consume inordinate time or resources. The lesser of one's own race are cared for, quietly, and the lesser of other races are excluded. Such an approach can seem harsh, but such is life.

---

[8] One need only watch any episode of popular television shows, especially so-called reality TV. Shows like "American Idol" or "Dancing with the Stars" or "America's Got Talent" are endless parades of sob stories. Crying contestants are *de rigueur*.

Dangerous and possibly fatal naiveté. By accepting false but comforting myths, by failing to address the real threats to society, by adopting a *de facto* philo-Semitism, and by wallowing in an over-socialized and misdirected form of pity, leftists dodge the hard reality of the modern world. In doing so, they doom society to inevitable suffering and decay. Life is hard, evolution can be brutal, and choices are painful. Leftists, though, prefer the easy way out; they seek to avoid all conflict and confrontation, and are happy to surrender control of their lives to, for example, a Jewish elite who would like nothing more than to use them, exploit them, and utterly crush them in the end.

Only by addressing these deeper failings of the Left can we get to the root of the problem.

Where Is the Opposition?

As I mentioned above, all sectors of the Right oppose leftism, but most are half-hearted—or worse. Let me take a specific example. Perhaps the most visible and vocal critic of the Left is Tucker Carlson of Fox News. In Chapter 26 of the present volume, I have critiqued his *modus operandi*, but here I want to emphasize his deeper alignment with the Left.

We can compare Carlson's worldview to that of the typical leftist:

> (A) The leftist, being a naïve egalitarian, is an anti-racist. He believes deeply in human equality. He is pro-democracy (at least verbally) and he supports "America." He is materialistic; he strives for a thriving economy, economic growth, and material prosperity. Most importantly, he is *philosemitic*; he supports Israel, defends Jewish interests, promotes Jewish ideology, and gives free reign to Jewish voices. The leftist never 'outs' Jews, never really criticizes Israel, never seeks to limit Jewish dominance in government, finance, media, or academia, and never calls to restrict their activities. In this way, the leftist maintains his status and material well-being.
>
> (B) Carlson, being a naïve egalitarian, is an anti-racist. He believes deeply in human equality. He is pro-democracy (at least verbally) and he supports "America." He is materialistic; he strives for a thriving economy, economic growth, and material prosperity. Most importantly, he is *philosemitic*; he supports Israel, defends Jewish interests, promotes Jewish ideology, and gives free reign to Jewish voices. Carlson never 'outs' Jews, never really criticizes Israel, never seeks to limit Jewish dominance in government, finance, media, or

academia, and never calls to restrict their activities. In this way, Carlson maintains his status and material well-being.

I trust that we can see the similarities here.[9] And yet Carlson is supposedly an exemplary member of "the Right." Sadly, he is not alone; the above description applies to a large majority of the nominal Right. This is precisely why the alleged Right is a *fake Right*, and why so many populist conservatives are *fake conservatives*.

If Carlson and others were true right-wingers, and true conservatives, they would display the characteristics I cited above. They would be openly and explicitly anti-minority, anti-egalitarian, explicitly "racist" (or "racialist"), anti-Semitic, pro-environment, anti-technology (and not just anti-Big Tech), and perhaps even anti-democratic. They might be anti-capitalist, knowing the disruption caused by unrestrained free-market capitalism. God forbid, they might even be a little socialist! They would be not so much patriotic—which implies a kind of naïve acceptance of the ruling class and the existing political order—but rather truly *nationalist*, in the sense of defending the interests one's own race and ethnicity, which is, after all, the true basis of a "nation".[10]

Where, then, are the true conservatives? Where lies the true Right? It is almost impossible to find, even in the big wide world of the Internet. We can be thankful for organizations like *The Occidental Observer*, *The Unz Review*, and *National Vanguard*, who are willing to call a spade a spade. Thankful for individuals like Kevin MacDonald and Andrew Anglin, William White Williams and David Duke, who are willing to speak openly and intelligently about the Jewish Question. Thankful for the small circle of leading Holocaust revisionists, who work relentlessly to undermine the keystone of Jewish mendacity.[11] Without such individuals, we would be lost. With them, we have hope.

The Way Forward

In sum, the popular Left-Right divide in American politics is a fake dichotomy, constructed by and serving the interests of a Jewish elite and their well-paid Gentile lackeys. When people focus all their attention and

---

[9] There are, of course, differences: Carlson is anti-immigration, pro-Christian, Covid-skeptical, and withering in his critique of the Biden regime. But the similarities are more significant and more consequential than the differences.

[10] 'Nation' comes from Latin *natus* or *natio*, that is, those who are "born together," or of similar birth.

[11] Among whom I would include Germar Rudolf, Carlo Mattogno, and Jürgen Graf. Any discussion of Holocaust revisionism that does not mention these men is not worth its salt—and probably deliberately deceptive.

energy on this contrived distinction, they are distracted from, and thus overlook, the true and deeper causes of social crisis in this country. The fake Right and the fake Left both serve their Jewish masters. Only by moving beyond this superficial divide can we get to the root of things.

There are positive aspects of both real leftism and real conservatism. We should indeed be open-minded, free-thinking, non-dogmatic, and progress-oriented. We should indeed defend individual autonomy, and political and civil liberty, while promoting the better instincts of humanity. At the same time, we should be truly nationalist: that is, defending the integrity and well-being of White Americans. We should work toward a relatively homogenous, monocultural, mono-ethnic nation, which is the only type of nation proven to be stable and sustainable. We should be ardent environmentalists, preserving wild nature, expanding wilderness, and protecting indigenous species; without this, we cannot hope for a flourishing society. We should put sharp limits on free-marketeers, finance capitalists, and financial speculators; if this means moving toward a limited socialism, so be it.

Above all, we should end the constant clamor over the bogus Left-Right confrontation, and focus on what really matters: subverting the dominant Judeocracy, creating a manageable and ethnically-uniform nation (or nations), and getting down to the hard work of restoring a sane society. I fear that we haven't much time to spare.

— 34 —
America Must Die— So That the People Can Live

When you live in a 200-year-old house, you would do well to give it a thorough inspection every few years. Rap on the walls, pull down some old wallpaper, climb into the attic, and get down into the crawl space. Check the roofing, check the exterior walls, check the foundation. You are looking for signs of rot: decay, mold, insects, rodents, or just plain aging. With luck, you find one or two small problems, you patch them up, and all is well. Unfortunately, sometimes all is not well. Sometimes, you find signs of major and irreparable decay. In those cases, and as painful as it may be, you must be prepared to tear the house down and start anew. Anything less would be a lost cause, an act of utter futility.

America today is a 245-year-old house—a grand mansion with many rooms, situated on a wonderfully vast and glorious estate. From the outside, from a distance, it still looks nice: glitzy, glamorous, wealthy, powerful, exciting. It still carries much from its well-intentioned (if flawed) beginnings. But our inspection proves otherwise. When we rap on the walls, or get up in the ceiling, or crawl down to the foundations, we are shocked to find signs of widespread and irreparable decay. The main timbers supporting the building are rife with termites; the roof is leaking; the foundation is cracked, the sands beneath are eroding, and all manner of vermin are running wild, both above and below. In short, it is a horrible mess. We try to plaster over holes here and there, and slap on some new paint once in a while, but the rot inevitably shows through. By any reasonable accounting, the building is on the verge of collapse. It may come down on its own, or we can be proactive and take it down, but down it will come.

Any viable nation is not only an edifice; it is a living entity. It lives and breathes with the people in it. Our house is a living house; but sadly, it is terminally ill. A combination of old age, disease, neglect, and poor hygiene have put it in a terrible state, one that is evidently beyond any hope of recovery or repair. The house must come down; America must die—in order for a new house, a new nation, to arise. Such is life.

It is worthwhile, then, to review my brief 'inspection report' of the American nation, and to diagnose the ailments that we are currently enduring. If I am able to get down to root causes, this will naturally lead to some prescribed courses of action that we can take, both near-term and for the longer haul. No one wants to live in a rotting house. No one wants to live in a decaying nation. No one wants their children and grandchildren to grow up in such conditions. We have better options.

At the highest level, my inspection report finds two major, and related, areas of concern: (1) a false notion of human equality, and (2) misplaced faith in the doctrine of democracy. Further analysis shows that these two aspects have been ruthlessly and malevolently exploited by a potent Jewish lobby to maximize benefit to themselves. In what follows, I will attempt to outline the nature of this far-reaching and deep-rooted crisis, and to suggest some ways forward.

The False and Destructive Concept of Equality

In 1927, and four years before he penned *Brave New World*, famed writer, thinker, and "casual anti-Semite" Aldous Huxley published a compelling little book called *Proper Studies*. It opens with an essay titled "The Idea of Equality." The very first line reads as follows:

> That all men are equal is a proposition to which, at ordinary times, no sane human being has ever given his assent. (p. 1)

Doctors, editors, bureaucrats—any person, in any walk of life, displays evident and obvious inequalities, says Huxley. People are different in every way imaginable: skills, abilities, interests, intelligence, appearance, character. Everyone acknowledges this, and yet at the same time they also want to insist on the essential and intrinsic equality of humans. Hence does Huxley write of the human mind's "almost infinite capacity for being inconsistent." He then describes the basic axiom at work:

> Politicians and political philosophers have often talked about the equality of man as though it were a necessary and unavoidable idea, an idea which human beings must believe in, just as they must, from the very nature of their physical and mental constitution, believe in such notions as weight, heat, and light. Man is "by nature free, equal, and independent," says Locke, with the calm assurance of one who knows he cannot be contradicted.[1] It would be possible to quote literally thousands of similar pronouncements. (p. 2)

He identifies the original source of this fallacy in Aristotle, whose metaphysical assumption of a human essence[2] implies a sort of equality among

[1] *Second Treatise on Civil Government* (1690), chapter 8, section 95.
[2] As "the rational animal"; *Nicomachean Ethics* I.8, 13.

the human species. Against Huxley, we can argue that this does not quite follow; the existence of a common and distinctive quality of all humans need not imply their social, political, or existential equality, any more than the fact that all material objects have mass imply that they all have the same weight.[3] Huxley also fixes some blame on Descartes, but again, this is perhaps an exaggerated claim. In *Discourse on Method* (1637), Descartes writes:

> Good sense is the best distributed thing in the world. … It indicates that the power of judging well and of distinguishing the true from the false—which is what we properly call 'good sense' or 'reason'—is naturally equal in all men. … [A]s regards reason or sense, since it is the only thing that makes us men and distinguishes us from the beasts, I am inclined to believe that it exists whole and complete in each of us.[4]

Even if we allow that reason is equal in all—a highly dubious assertion, to say the least—it still does not imply political, social, or moral equality.

More to the point, Huxley cites Christian doctrine and the position of the Church. Even granting a "brotherhood of men" under Christ, "the brotherhood of men does not imply their equality." He continues: "Neither does men's equality before God imply their equality as among themselves." Even if God, from his divine and lofty standpoint, views us all as equals, any putative inter-human equality "is entirely irrelevant".[5] It is rather like us viewing all ants or mice as identical when in fact they all recognize and acknowledge vast differences among themselves.

All this bodes ill for the "religion of democracy," says Huxley (and as I will elaborate). Its "primary assumption" is that "all men are substantially equal." If the equality falls, so too falls democracy. He summarizes concisely:

> The historical and psychological researches of the past century have rendered the theory which lies behind the practice

---

[3] And in fact, Aristotle's later discussion of the "great-souled man" (*Nicomachean Ethics* IV.3) demonstrates conclusively that he believed in vast difference among men.
[4] *The Philosophical Writings of Descartes*, volume one, Cambridge University Press (1985), pp. 111-112.
[5] Indeed, explicit human equality exists nowhere in the Bible. Paul claims in Galatians (3:28) that "there is neither Jew nor Greek" under Jesus and that "we are all one in Christ Jesus." But this only says that all are welcome into his nascent universalist church; it does not support the idea that all are equal. And more importantly, there are very good reasons for believing that Paul held to the most obnoxious form of Jewish supremacism, and thus did not believe in human equality in the least; see chapters 4 and 25 of the present book.

> of modern democracy entirely untenable. Reason is not the same in all men; human beings belong to a variety of psychological types separated from one another by irreducible differences. (p. 12)

Science, anthropology, philosophy, and common sense all come to the same conclusion: human equality is a fallacy, and any political ideology based on that notion is doomed to failure.

Huxley, of course, was hardly alone in his condemnation of a claimed human equality. Nietzsche viewed the idea with greater contempt and wrote in more scathing terms. We find, especially in *Beyond Good and Evil*, a stunning repudiation of the concept. His elaborations on the "order of rank" among men, the "instinct for rank," the "noble soul," and the necessity for human greatness, pervade the work. A few examples will have to suffice:

> Men, not noble enough to see the abysmally different order of rank, the chasm of rank, between man and man—*such* men have so far held sway over the fate of Europe, with their "equal before God," until finally a smaller, almost ridiculous type, a herd animal, something eager to please, sickly, and mediocre has been bred, the European of today. (sec. 62)

> The highest and strongest drives, when they break out passionately and drive the individual far above the average and the flats of the herd conscience, wreck the self-confidence of the community, its faith in itself, and it is as if its spine snapped. Hence just these drives are branded and slandered most. High and independent spirituality, the will to stand alone, even a powerful reason are experienced as dangers; everything that elevates an individual above the herd and intimidates the neighbor is henceforth called *evil*; and the fair, modest, submissive, conforming mentality, the *mediocrity* of desires attains moral designations and honors. (sec. 201)

> Every enhancement of the type 'man' has so far been the work of an aristocratic society—a society that believes in the long ladder of an order of rank and differences in value between man and man. (sec. 257)

The concept of equality is ultimately destructive because it declares, not only that no one is worse than anyone else, but more importantly that no one is *better* than anyone else—yes, that no one *can* be better. True self-betterment and self-enhancement become impossible if we are all equal. No matter what you do, you will still be only, and always, equal to the very least among men. This doctrine is not merely false; it is utterly contemptible and destructive of higher aims and goals. It means the death of humanity. Where we do not ascend, we decline; this is Nietzsche's basic outlook. Sadly, it conforms to the actual world in which we live today.

In the final passage above, Nietzsche points to a central fact and thus to a possible solution. If every improvement to humanity and to society has occurred in aristocratic societies—that is, rule by *the best*—then we ought logically to use those as our model. Societies that are capable of sorting men into lesser and greater types, and to do so effectively, are the drivers of human evolution. They strive for greatness, and they create greatness. Even the smallest steps in that direction—such as were taken by Hitler in his National Socialist Germany—would be such an improvement over the present day that any nation even attempting it would likely flourish spectacularly; and in fact, this is precisely what happened in Germany, beginning in 1933. The rest of the equality-obsessed, Jewish-inspired world was so aghast that they were compelled to drive the remaining industrial nations against Hitler and to destroy him, so fearsome was the prospect of his success.

Still, entrenched myths die hard. We in the US have our treasured Declaration of Independence, which declares as "self-evident"—with the calm assurance of those who know they cannot be contradicted—that "all men are created equal." As we know, this was disingenuous at best. For one, they indeed meant 'men,' given that women could neither vote nor hold office. And they meant 'White men,' given that all the Founders were White Anglo-Saxons, and many were slaveholders or otherwise endorsed slavery. Hence that famous phrase really meant "all White males are created equal"—though even that is demonstrably untrue, as I have argued.

Original Democracy

Huxley had it exactly right: support for modern democracy is in fact more of a belief system, or even a faith, than something grounded in history, reason, and philosophy. Like many other religions, democracy derives from a core of historical truth—here, in ancient Greece—that was then altered beyond recognition by an accretion of layers of myth, lie, and corruption. Today we have the belief, the *faith*, by all sides, "left" and "right" alike,[6] that democracy is an unquestioned virtue, that it must be defended

---

[6] Though, as I argued in chapter 33, both the Left and the Right are "fakes," which explains why they both adhere to similar nonsense, and why they both supplicate to the Jewish Lobby.

at all costs, and that it must be spread to the world, even at the point of a gun. This is a fundamental political error, founded on an erroneous and detrimental conception of human equality; it must be overcome if we are to survive in the long run.

Democracy wasn't always a religion. At one time, at the beginning, it was a rational and effective (though not unproblematic) means of self-government. Let me take a minute to examine the original democracy of ancient Greece to see what worked and what did not.

Athenian democracy was a remarkable institution, and remarkably different than what passes for democracy today. To begin with, the population of the state (or *polis*) was small—it constituted only some 300,000 people at its peak, which included many slaves and foreigners. By modern standards, this seems tiny but, for the time, it was extremely large. Of this number, the only formal citizens were the adult native-born males, numbering perhaps 30,000, or just 10 percent of the population. These citizens—the *demos*, the people—were the formal basis of political power, rather than some ruling wealthy elite (also known as oligarchs or plutocrats), or some tyrannical dictator, as could be found in other Greek states.

The democratic system, inaugurated by Cleisthenes around 500 BC, functioned in a very different way than we might expect. For one, there were *no elections*; all leadership positions (apart from the military) were chosen by lot, at random, from among the citizens who had put forth their names. This included even the leader of the Assembly—the collected body of citizens—who was effectively the president of the nation, though without much formal power. The Greeks had invented a device called a *kleroterion* into which names were randomly inserted on small tokens; colored dice were then deployed to select names randomly and fairly from among the various tribes or families. The system had several virtues: immediate results, no costly or corrupted election campaigns, fairness, transparency, and an equal involvement of all concerned. The Greeks clearly had to be nice to all their fellow (Athenian male) citizens, any one of whom could someday have a position of prominence.

Secondly, there were *no representatives*. Athens was a famously direct democracy. All interested citizens gathered on a large open hilltop, called the Pnyx, roughly once per month, to listen to the issues of the day. When the time came for decisions, a very public show of hands determined the outcome. Even the gravest of matters, such as going to war, were decided this way. This is all the more striking when we consider that the army was composed of the very men who had themselves just voted for war. In other words, when you voted for war, *you personally went to war*. And many never returned. We can only imagine a similar situation in America today: that the Congressmen and women who support the next illegal and unjust foreign war would be compelled to be on the first combat plane into the warzone.[7] I suspect that we would have very few wars indeed.

In sum, Athenian democracy was small, direct, accountable, and transparent. The wealthy elite had very little power to steer events in their favor. The citizenry comprised only native men; foreigners had literally no voice in the state, even though they outnumbered the actual citizens by a factor of two or three. Greek democracy was thus a racial (White European), ethnic (Athenian), and gendered (men only) system of rule. And it worked incredibly well; it produced and sustained the brilliant Athenian culture that we know today.

Two Famous Critics

For all that, the system had some harsh and prominent critics—notably, Plato and Aristotle. Plato had two main complaints against democracy: First, he asked, why should all the citizens get to vote on key decisions? Why are they all treated as equals, one vote per man? This is illogical and counterproductive. Even in Athens, they had their share of dunces, dimwits, and degenerates. Why let these men vote? Why not let only the best, the wisest, vote? For that matter, why have votes at all? Why not just determine who are your wisest few, *and let them rule?* This was Plato's vision of an aristocracy, the optimal form of government. It is, at least in theory, far superior to anything like a democracy.

Plato's second concern was, ironically, with freedom itself. In a democracy, since "the people" rule, anything goes. Whatever the people want, the people get. And the people—the masses—rarely want the kinds of things that they *should* want, namely, virtue and discipline. Rather, they want to have *fun*: they want to do one thing one day, and something else the next, as it suits their fancy. They are 'free,' after all. They want to play games, engage in various petty amusements, fill their bellies, get drunk, and so on. As it was then, so it is now; human nature has scarcely changed in two millennia.

Plato is scalding in his attack. The "democratic man" is inundated by all manner of trivial and detrimental desires. True and deep thoughts are driven from his soul, and "false and boastful conceits and phrases mount upwards and take their place" (*Republic* Bk 8; 560c):

> And so the young man returns to the country of the [pleasure-seeking] lotus-eaters, and takes up his dwelling there in

[7] Actually, in America we don't have wars anymore; we have "authorized uses of military force" or AUMFs. This is Congress' cowardly way to kill others on behalf of their lobbyists and patrons without having to vote for an actual war.

> the face of all men. ... There is a battle and [the false and boastful words] gain the day, and then *modesty*, which they call 'silliness', is ignominiously thrust into exile by them, and *temperance*, which they nickname 'unmanliness', is trampled in the mire and cast forth. They persuade men that *moderation* and *frugal spending* are vulgarity and meanness, and so, by the help of a rabble of evil appetites, they drive them out.
>
> And when they have emptied and swept clean the soul of him who is now in their power and who is being initiated by them in great mysteries, the next thing is to bring back to their house *insolence* and *anarchy* and *waste* and *impudence* in bright array, having garlands on their heads, and a great company with them, hymning their praises and calling them by sweet names. *Arrogance* they term 'good-breeding', and *anarchy* 'freedom', and *waste* 'magnificence', and *impudence* 'courage'. And so the young man passes out of his original nature, which was trained in the school of necessity, into the freedom and libertinism of useless and unnecessary pleasures. (560d-e)

And if wiser thoughts come calling, and if they struggle for predominance in his soul, he becomes confused; "he shakes his head and says that *they are all alike*, and that *one is as good as another*." He has lost the ability to judge and to discriminate, which degrades his entire life:

> His life has neither law nor order; and this distracted existence he terms 'joy' and 'bliss' and 'freedom'; and so he goes on... [H]e is all 'freedom' and 'equality.'

Hence the democratic man. His precious freedom, given unrestrained license and lack of discipline, devolves into mindless and confused pleasure-seeking. He believes he has freedom, and he believes in equality—but this is a sham; it is a false equality and the freedom of a shallow and vapid libertine. Plato sums up the situation on democracy with one of the most striking sentences in the *Republic*:

> These and other kindred characteristics are proper to democracy, which is a charming form of government, full of variety and disorder, and dispensing a sort of equality to equals and unequals alike. (558c)

"Charming" and "disordered" democracy, so "fair and spangled," is all show and no substance. It encourages undisciplined, unvirtuous lives of hedonistic pleasure. And most importantly, it "dispenses a sort of equality to equals and unequals alike." Such a democracy, he says, can only lead in turn to the lowest form of government, tyranny.

I haven't the space to elaborate, but in short, Aristotle basically agreed with this analysis. He identified three primary forms of government, each of which had good and bad versions. In descending order, the three good systems are *monarchy* (rule by one), *aristocracy* (rule by a small and wise few), and a '*constitution*' (conditional rule by many). The distorted or bad forms of each of these are *tyranny*, *oligarchy*, and *democracy*.[8] In this sense, for Aristotle, democracy is literally 'the worst of the worst.' It is rule by the poor and needy masses, not the best or noblest few.

Industrial Democracy

What, then, of democracy in the world today? We have variations on the democratic theme that are so remote from the Athenian original that they hardly deserve the same name. They have lost all the virtues of the original but retained all the vices. Democracy today has devolved into a crude perversion that I like to call *industrial democracy*. Its primary characteristics are these:

1) Representative (parliamentarian) system—no direct participation.
2) Universal suffrage—all adults can vote.
3) Multiracial—all races can vote.
4) Unlimited population size.
5) Financially corrupt—moneyed interests (especially Jewish) hold great sway.

On every point, this is opposed to the Athenian model. We vote, but typically only for a handful of pre-determined candidates or on a very limited number of referenda. Our representation is scaled down by a factor of thousands or millions; a state as large as California, with almost 40 million people, gets all of two senators.[9] And every half-witted, uneducated ignoramus gets his or her vote—people who vastly outnumber the educated and the wise. (And we wonder why the intellectual level of political campaigns is so low.) People of every race can vote, and they often do so in their own racial interest, thus guaranteeing a divided and conflicted government.

[8] *Politics* III.7.

[9] It does get 53 federal representatives, but even here, each represents the interests of an average of 750,000 very diverse individuals.

Perhaps most critically, the original small size of the Athenian citizen body, some 30,000 individuals, now numbers almost 250 million—the number of eligible American adults.

The vast size and scale of representation ensures that billions of corrupting dollars flow through the system, distorting even the most virtuous lawmaker, and guaranteeing a flood of media confusion, propaganda, and "fake news." Industrial democracy is *rule by money*: those with the most money, and the will to spend it, rule. In America, we know who leads this race: the Jewish lobby, which contributes at least 50% of Democratic campaign funds and at least 25% of Republican funds. Wealthy American Jews spend literally hundreds of millions on campaigns, ads, donations, and various other activities, all to influence the outcome in their favored direction. The situation is comparable in the UK, Canada, France, and Australia, all of which have relatively large and wealthy Jewish populations.[10] The ancient Greeks—most of them, at least—would be appalled to see what their cherished democracy has come to.

As it is, we now have that which Plato predicted: democracy on the brink of degenerating into tyranny of various forms. We have tyrannies of the rich, tyrannies of the Judeocracy, and tyrannies of Big Tech, all vying for power, and all cooperating as needed to ensure that nothing like transparent and accountable government ever comes to pass. The main objective of the rich is to stay rich, and to maintain or grow the wealth gap between themselves and the masses; the larger the disparity, the more relative power they hold. The main objective of the Judeocracy, of the Jewish power-elite, is to weaken and damage the national psyche sufficiently, and to diversify and deplete the nation genetically, so that they can maintain maximum control without completely destroying the wealth-producing capacity of the economy. Under industrial democracy, the future is grim indeed.

America, sadly, has been completely subsumed by this pernicious and insidious form of government. The country is ruled by the lowest, most depraved, most incompetent individuals imaginable. At the same time, it is being flooded by the virtual scum of humanity—in July 2021 alone, over 212,000 arrests ("encounters", in the government's euphemistic propaganda) occurred at the southern border.[11] How many more evaded "encounter"

---

[10] I emphasize "relative." Jewish percentages of these four nations range from 0.4 to 1.0%. Normally this should be inconsequential, but with wealthy and pernicious Jews, it poses substantial problems. The lesson here is that any nation seeking to free itself from the Jewish Lobby had best restrict Jewish numbers to something well below 0.1%.

[11] Of course, not all illegal immigrants are scum. But from everything we know, a very high proportion of them are from the lowest, least intelligent, and most criminal segments of humanity. And since virtually all of them are non-White, even the best will alter the nature of our traditionally White society.

and entered the country illegally, we do not know. And to these numbers we must add the "legal" immigration of large numbers of non-European, non-White individuals who inevitably change the character of the nation for the worse. The combined effect is dramatic. A 2020 study stated that the US now has an astonishing 44 million people who were foreign-born, of which about 75% are legal and 25% are illegal.[12] Nearly half of these millions were born in just five countries: Mexico, China, India, Philippines, and El Salvador. Surely not more than a percent or two of these 44 million are White. The grand edifice that is America is collapsing as we speak.

Therefore, it is time to accept reality and give up America for lost. Put away your flags, your pins, and all your red-white-and-blue paraphernalia. Toss out your MAGA hats; America will never be "great again." Anyone who tells you otherwise is a liar or a fool. The country is rotting from above and below. Vermin are calling the shots from on high, and human detritus washes in over the borders. This was precisely how Ancient Rome fell. Such is the terminal stage of many an empire.

Looking Ahead

If this report on the fatal condition of America is close to the mark, it also suggests corrective actions that must be taken to regain a sane and stable civic life, at least for the White Euro-Americans who established and ran the country for most of its existence. The necessary actions are hardly a secret. The basic ideas are already floating around the Internet. Andrew Anglin, for one, was right on the mark in an essay on immigration. His conclusion:

> The only way we are going to fix this [immigration] problem is through a two-fold solution: 1) Redrawing the borders of the country, and 2) Physically removing tens of millions of people. There is no situation where both of those things are not going to be necessary in the future.[13]

He is absolutely right. Those are two necessary, but not sufficient, conditions for the restoration of rational government among the White population today.

---

[12] "Key findings about U.S. immigrants," Pew Research (20 Aug 2020)—though the actual number of illegals could be much higher than the presumed 11 million. Another study argued that the true figure could be as high as 29 million; see "The number of undocumented immigrants in the United States: Estimates based on demographic modeling with data from 1990 to 2016," PLOS ONE.

[13] "Immigration Is Really Just a Distraction at This Point," 25 Aug 2021.

More specifically, my above analysis suggests the following steps: (a) Break up the existing United States into smaller, more cohesive, more homogenous, and more manageable units. (b) In these new units, encourage all non-Whites, and especially all Jews, to emigrate as soon as possible. (c) Discard the pernicious concept of human equality and replace it by a celebration of the higher, the nobler, and the best. (d) Replace industrial democracy with something like an aristocracy. Let me close by offering a few words of elaboration on each.

More and more people these days seem to be recognizing the desirability and the inevitability of secession of portions of the US, and the establishment of new, independent nation-states. In fact, as the nation continues to disintegrate, at some point people will have no choice; thus, it is better to plan now than to wait for some chaotic future breakdown.

Some of the current talk on secession has the right intent but is woefully weak and misguided. One can find articles like "Is America still our country?" and "The separation," but these are pathetically half-hearted. Breaking up existing states but staying within America is a wholly insufficient form of secession. The "Six Californias" idea is very weak; "Greater Idaho" is well-intentioned but falls way short of the mark. None of these explicitly advocates breaking away from the US and forming new nations. Only full-blown secession can hope to get to the root of the problem. The reigning Judeocracy knows this, which is why they do everything in their power to discredit the idea.

Point (b) is mandatory for restoring effective and rational governance. Blacks, Asians, Hispanics, and Jews all have countries of origin; they need to return there with all due haste. After a short period of voluntary compliance, increasing pressure will need to be applied until they comply. Yes, Whites could theoretically return to Europe, except that Whites created and built up the present civilization (such as it is) of the USA, and thus have earned a right to stay and to evict the interlopers.[14] Native Americans were of course here before the White Europeans, and that precedence needs to be respected, such as via truly autonomous homelands. And since Blacks were forcibly brought here from Africa (with heavy Jewish involvement[15]), I would have no issue with assisting their return to Africa with subsidized travel arrangements, a small one-time cash payment, or with the

---

[14] Yes, Black African slaves and Chinese coolies "built" portions of the early US. But they provided only the low-end brute labor, not the organizational or intellectual basis for the nation. To give them credit for building America would be akin to giving credit to the oxen and draft horses of the early pioneers.

[15] See Louis Farrakhan's book *The Secret Relationship between Blacks and Jews* (3 volumes).

use of political leverage in Africa to aid their repatriation. We can ease the transition, but out they must go.

The hardest to deal with will of course be the Jews. With their political clout, wealth, and bull-headed tenacity, they will be very hard to root out. The task is made all the more difficult because of the inability of our supposedly "conservative Right" to address the Jewish Question in a meaningful way. Most all prominent rightwing individuals and organizations flee from the Question like the devil from holy water. As I have noted elsewhere, Fox News and crew—Carlson, Hannity, et al—never explicitly mention Jews, never out them, and never criticize them in any way; Hannity in fact bends over backward to curry favor. Alex Jones never criticizes or outs Jews. Same with Jared Taylor. *American Renaissance* won't deal with the Jewish Question in a serious way. Breitbart at least discusses them, but always in a neutral or positive light. The real critics are, sadly, few and far between; to reiterate what I wrote elsewhere, we need to be extremely grateful for *The Occidental Observer*, *Unz.com*, *National Vanguard*, and people like Anglin, all of whom are willing to speak the hard truth on the Jewish Question.

Point (c) obviously follows from the above discussion. We must drop all talk of human equality and replace it with a promotion and celebration of human uniqueness and human greatness. This needs to be made explicit in common discourse, media, and school curricula. We need to celebrate and praise human genius while emphasizing the fact that most people are not geniuses and will never achieve greatness, but who can nonetheless have meaningful and valuable lives. When it is understood that humans never were, and never will be, equal, then all become free to achieve their full potential and, for those who succeed in bettering themselves, to reap the rewards of exceptional development. In a just society, exceptional individuals will earn additional rights, but they will also bear additional duties, compared to the lesser. "Equal" performance for the various subgroups of people—as distinguished by gender, age, socio-economic status, ethnicity, etc.—will never be expected or mandated. "Racial equality" will be a nonissue.

On the final point, it is clear that the hopelessly corrupt industrial democracy must go. We can also be confident that something like an aristocracy would be a vast (if imperfect) improvement, even as there is much leeway in the specific details. If we allow that "rule by the wiser" is superior to "rule by the masses," then we have many ways to realize such a system. At the simplest level, we could retain elections for officeholders but permit only the wiser—smarter, more educated, more accomplished—individuals to vote. It could be very basic: require that voters earn a college degree, for example; or score above average on an IQ test; or distinguish themselves in some other relevant way (an exceptional athlete, by contrast, earns no right to a voice on political issues). The disenfranchised would not be made to feel inferior; rather, they would come to accept such a system as in the best interests of all.

At a more sophisticated level, we might move to adopt something like a Platonic education system, as laid out in the *Republic*. There he sketches a 50-year training program involving age-appropriate schooling, skills training, physical fitness, and practical experience that both educates the masses and serves as a filtering process to determine who the truly wisest and most capable leaders are. A series of pass-fail criteria progressively reduce the pool of eligible candidates, leaving, at the end, a mere handful of individuals who have repeatedly proven themselves under pressure. In a future aristocracy, a small pool of "the best" could be added annually to a kind of ruling congress who would then be unconditionally empowered to make and enforce all laws and policies. After a fixed term of governance, each individual would be compelled to retire in turn. Again, this is just one way of realizing such a system. Variations might include finding ways to identify and empower the truly exceptional individuals—or perhaps a single individual—and give them correspondingly exceptional powers to rule.

In any case, the system would need to be recognized by the vast majority of people as an effective and desirable solution. In this sense, it would retain a small flavor of traditional democracy. "Consent of the governed" can work, as long as the population is not too large and as long as we do not have to contend with competing racial minorities or Jewish financial corruption. But such consent is a far cry from universal suffrage or rule by the masses, which can never work, and which always degenerates.

Such is my basic outline of a path forward. Obviously, much more needs to be said. But it is a start, one that addresses the root causes of our present crisis.[16]

I close with this thought: To the extent that America ever was great, this is because, at the start, it was roughly modeled on the Athenian original. The early American government was gendered, racial, and ethnic—White males of a predominantly north European stock. And it stayed that way for nearly 100 years.[17] The celebrated American "diversity" at the beginning was a *diversity among Whites*: English, Scots, Irish, Dutch, Germans, and Scandinavians all would have been represented in those

---

[16] Elsewhere I have argued that Hitler's National Socialism can also be a model going forward. His nationalism created an ethnic-based sense of unity and purpose that far exceeded mindless patriotism, and his socialism served as an antidote to unrestrained finance capitalism. There are many good lessons to be learned there. Interested readers should start with my recent edition of *Mein Kampf*, and with my newly-reworked edition of Alfred Rosenberg's classic, *The Myth of the 20th Century*.

[17] Black males were granted the right to vote in 1866, and women (of all races) in 1920.

early years. Yes, America had significant numbers of Blacks and Jews from the 1600s, but they had limited or no political influence. Religion was of secondary importance. Yes, it was nominally a "Christian nation" at the start, but few among the Founders were deeply religious—Patrick Henry, Samuel Adams, and John Jay being the exceptions—and most were skeptical believers or deists, if not functional atheists.

Hence, early America prospered and flourished *in spite of*, not because of, Christianity; *in spite of*, not because of, Blacks and Jews; and *in spite of*, not because of, the principle of equality. Blacks, Jews, "equality," and Christianity were millstones around the young nation's neck. It is a testament to our initially gendered and racial governance that we accomplished so much in those early years, with such huge burdens to bear. Two centuries later, those millstones proved to be our ruination.

America is dying a slow and painful death. Let us euthanize the long-suffering nation, redraw the boundaries, rethink the guiding principles, and begin again.

— 35 —

The Jewish Hand in World War Three

Thanks to the ongoing conflict in Ukraine, we indeed seem to be rushing headlong into a major war—possibly a World War Three, possibly the world's first (and perhaps last) nuclear war. Ukraine leadership and their Western backers seem hell-bent on fighting to the last man, and Vladimir Putin, as an old-school Cold Warrior, seems equally determined to press ahead until achieving "victory." The cause seems hopeless for Ukraine, who cannot reasonably expect to prevail in an extended conflict with one of the largest militaries on Earth. At best, they may bleed Russia over a period of months or years, but only at the cost of massive blood-letting themselves. It seems that Ukraine will be the loser in this struggle, no matter what comes.

In the Western media, we are presented with a remarkably simplified storyline: Putin is an evil warmonger who simply wants to extend Russian territory; to this end, he is exploiting events in Ukraine, deploying his military ostensibly to support the Russian-speaking districts of Luhansk and Donetsk in the Donbass region of eastern Ukraine. But this is just cover, they say, for his mad quest to rebuild the Russian empire. In pursuit of his goal, he is willing to inflict any amount of material damage and kill any number of civilians. Fortunately, say our media, Putin has thus far been largely contained; the brave Ukrainian fighters are constantly "reclaiming" land, Russia's advance has "stalled," and indeed, Russia seems to be in danger of losing.

Consequently, the US and its allies must do all they can to "aid" and "support" the brave Ukrainians and their beleaguered but heroic leader, Volodymyr Zelensky. No amount of money, no assortment of deadly weaponry, no military intelligence, is too much. Like World War Two, this "war" is an unconditional struggle of Good versus Evil; therefore the West, as the moral paragon of the world, must step up, undergo sacrifice, and ensure that Good prevails.

And indeed, the financial support from just the United States is breathtaking: By May of 2022, Congress approved $13.6 billion in aid, much of it for direct Ukrainian military support. And yet this would only cover costs through September of that year. Thus, president Biden then called for an additional package of $33 billion, which would include over $20 billion in military and security aid, and, surprisingly, $2.6 billion for "the deployment of American troops to the region," in order to "safeguard NATO allies." Incredibly, Congress responded by approving *$40 billion*, bringing the total aid at that point to $54 billion. For perspective, this represents over 80% of Russia's annual defense budget of $66 billion. (By contrast, America allocates well over $1 trillion—that is, $1,000 billion—annually in direct and indirect military expenditures.)

Notably, such unconditional support and defense of Ukraine is a virtually unanimous view across the American political spectrum, and throughout Europe. Right and left, conservative and liberal, working class or wealthy elite, all sectors of society are apparently united in opposition to the evil Putin. In an era when virtually no issue garners unanimous support, the Ukrainian cause stands out as an extremely rare instance of bipartisan, multi-sector agreement. The rare dissenters—such as Fox News' Tucker Carlson and a handful of alt-right renegades—are routinely attacked as "Russian assets" or "tools of Putin." There is no room for disagreement, no space for debate, no opposing views allowed.

In fact, though, this is yet another case of what I might call the "unanimity curse": when all parties in American society are united on a topic, any topic, then we *really* need to worry. Here, it seems that the reality is of a potent Jewish Lobby, exerting itself (again) in the direction of war, for reasons of profit and revenge against a hated enemy. There is, indeed, a Jewish hand at work here, one that may well drive us into another world war, and even a nuclear war—one which, in the worst case, could mean the literal end of much of life on this planet. The unanimity comes when all parties are subject, in various ways, to the demands of the Lobby, and when the public has been misled and even brainwashed by a coordinated Jewish media into believing the standard narrative.

The best cure for this catastrophic situation is unrestricted free speech. The Lobby knows this, however, and thus takes all possible measures to inhibit free speech. Normally, such a struggle ebbs and flows according to the issue and the times; but now, the situation is dire. Now more than ever, a lack of free speech could be fatal to civilized society.

Context and Run-Up

To fully understand the Jewish hand in the Russia-Ukraine conflict, we need to review some relevant history. Over the centuries, there have been constant battles over the lands of present-day Ukraine, with Poles, Austro-Hungarians, and Russians alternately dominating. Russia took control of most of Ukraine in the late 1700s and held it more or less continuously until the break-up of the Soviet Union in 1991; this is why Putin claims that the country is "part of Russia."

For their part, Jews have experienced a particularly tumultuous relationship with Russia, one that ranged from disgust and detestation to a burning hatred. As it happened, Jews migrated to Russia in the 19th century, eventually numbering around 5 million. They were a disruptive and agitating force within the nation and thus earned the dislike of Czars Nicholas I (reign 1825 to 1855), Alexander II (1855 to 1881, when he was assassinated by a partly-Jewish anarchist gang), and especially Nicholas II (1894 to 1917)—the latter of whom was famously murdered, along with his family, by a gang of Jewish Bolshevists in 1918. Already in 1871, Russian activist Mikhail Bakunin could refer to the Russian Jews as "a single exploiting sect, a sort of bloodsucker people, a collective parasite".[1] The assassination of Alexander initiated a series of pogroms that lasted decades, and which set the stage for a lingering Jewish hatred of all things Russian.[2]

For present purposes, though, we can jump to the 2004 Ukrainian presidential election (I note that Ukraine also has a prime minister, but unlike most European countries, he typically has limited powers). In 2004, it came down to "the two Viktors": the pro-Western V. Yushchenko and the pro-Russian V. Yanukovych. The first round was nearly tied, and thus they went to a second round in which Yanukovych prevailed by around three percentage points. But amid claims of vote-rigging, Western Ukrainians initiated an "Orange Revolution"—backed by the Ukrainian Supreme Court—that annulled those results and mandated a repeat runoff election. The second time, the tables were turned, and the pro-West Yushchenko won by eight points. The West was elated, and Putin naturally mad as hell.

The following years witnessed financial turmoil and, unsurprisingly, constant harassment from Russia. By 2010, Ukrainians were ready for a change, and this time Yanukovych won handily, over a Jewish female competitor, Yulia Timoshenko—notably, she had "co-led the Orange Revolution." Russia, for once, was satisfied with the result.

But of course, in the West, Europe and the US were mightily displeased, and they soon began efforts to reverse things yet again. Among other strategies, they apparently decided to deploy the latest in high tech and social media. Thus in June 2011, two of Google's top executives—Eric Schmidt and a 30-year-old Jewish upstart named Jared Cohen—went to visit Julian Assange in the UK, then living under house arrest. It is well-

---

[1] Cited in Wheen, *Karl Marx* (1999), p. 340.

[2] Russia's recent defense of Assad in Syria, against Israel, has obviously not made things better. Nor has the fact that Putin, once thought to be a tool of Jewish-Russian oligarchs, has been able to turn the tables and hold them in check.

known, incidentally, that Google is a Jewish enterprise, with Jewish founders Sergei Brin and Larry Page running the ship.[3]

The nominal purpose of the trip was to conduct research for a book that Schmidt and Cohen were working on, regarding the intersection of political action and technology—in plain words, how to foment revolutions and steers events in a desired direction. As Assange relates in his 2014 book *When Google Met Wikileaks*, he was initially unaware of the deeper intentions and motives of his interviewers. Only later did he come to learn that Schmidt had close ties to the Obama administration, and that Cohen was actively working on political upheaval. As Assange wrote, "Jared Cohen could be wryly named Google's 'director of regime change'." Their immediate targets were Yanukovych in Ukraine and Assad in Syria.

By early 2013, the American Embassy in Kiev was training right-wing Ukrainian nationalists on how to conduct a targeted revolt against Yanukovych. It would not be long until they had their chance.

In late 2013, Yanukovych decided to reject an EU-sponsored IMF loan, with all the usual nasty strings attached, in favor of a comparable no-strings loan from Russia. This apparent shift away from Europe and toward Russia was the nominal trigger for the start of protest actions. Thus began the "Maidan Uprising," led in large part by two extreme nationalist groups: Svoboda and Right Sector.[4] Protests went on for nearly three months, gradually accelerating in intensity; in a notable riot near the end, some 100 protestors and 13 police were shot dead.

As the Uprising reached its peak, at least one American Jew was highly interested: Victoria Nuland. As Obama's Assistant Secretary of State (first under Hillary Clinton, and then under the half-Jew John Kerry), Nuland had direct oversight of events in eastern Europe.[5] And for her, it was personal; her father, Sherwin Nuland (born Shepsel Nudelman), was a Ukrainian Jew. She was anxious to drive the pro-Russian Yanukovych out of power and replace him with a West-friendly, Jew-friendly substitute. And she had someone specific in mind: Arseniy Yatsenyuk. On 27 January 2014, as the riots were peaking, Nuland called American Ambassador to Ukraine, Jeff Pyatt, to urgently discuss the matter. Nuland pulled no

---

[3] Google has been particularly tenacious in altering its search engine results to censor ('de-rank') critics of Jewish power and stifle alternative voices. And Google owns Youtube, another force for censorship, which is currently run by the Jewess Susan Wojcicki. For their efforts, Brin and Page have become among the wealthiest men in the world; each is currently worth in excess of $100 billion.

[4] Svoboda began its existence as the "Social-National Party of Ukraine"—a not-so-subtle allusion to National Socialism. This is, in part, why both Svoboda and their allies have been called 'neo-Nazi.'

[5] Nuland is currently "Under Secretary of State for Political Affairs" in the Biden administration.

punches: "Yats" was her man. We know this because the call was apparently tapped and the dialogue later posted on Youtube. Here is a short excerpt:

> *Nuland:* I think Yats is the guy who's got the economic experience, the governing experience. He's the... what he needs is Klitsch and Tyahnybok on the outside. He needs to be talking to them four times a week, you know. I just think Klitsch going in... he's going to be at that level working for Yatseniuk, it's just not going to work.
>
> *Pyatt:* Yeah, no, I think that's right. OK. Good. Do you want us to set up a call with him as the next step? […]
>
> *Nuland:* OK, good. I'm happy. Why don't you reach out to him and see if he wants to talk before or after.
>
> *Pyatt:* OK, will do. Thanks.

It was clear to both of them, though, that the EU leadership had other ideas. The EU was much more anxious to be a neutral party and to avoid direct intervention in Ukrainian affairs so as to not unduly antagonize Russia. But in time-tested Jewish fashion, Nuland did not give a damn. A bit later in the same phone call, she uttered her now-famous phrase: "Fuck the EU." So much for Jewish subtlety.[6]

But there was another angle that nearly all Western media avoided: "Yats" was also Jewish. In a rare mention, we read in a 2014 *Guardian* story that "Yatsenyuk has held several high-profile positions including head of the country's central bank, the National Bank of Ukraine… He has played down his Jewish-Ukrainian origins, possibly because of the prevalence of antisemitism in his party's western Ukraine heartland".[7] For some reason, such facts are never relevant to Western media.

As the Maidan Uprising gave way to the Maidan Revolution in February 2014, Yanukovych was forced out of office, fleeing to Russia. Pro-Western forces then succeeded in nominating "Yats" as prime minister, effective immediately, working in conjunction with president Oleksandr

---

[6] Another Jew likely involved in this incident was the Hungarian-American investor George Soros. In late 2019, the lawyer Joseph diGenova appeared in the news, openly charging Soros with direct intervention in American policy: "Well, there's no doubt that George Soros controls a very large part of the career Foreign Service at the United States State Department. … But the truth is George Soros had a daily opportunity to tell the State Department through Victoria Nuland what to do in the Ukraine. And he ran it, Soros ran it."

[7] "Who exactly is governing Ukraine?" (4 Mar 2014).

Turchynov. This provisional leadership was formalized in a snap election in May 2014 in which the pro-Western candidate Peter Poroshenko won. (The second-place finisher was none other than Yulia Timoshenko—the same Jewess who had lost to Yanukovych in 2010.)

It was under such circumstances that Putin invaded and annexed Crimea, in February 2014. It was also at this time that Russian separatists in Donbass launched their counter-revolution, initiating a virtual civil war in Ukraine; to date, eight years later, around 15,000 people have died in total, many civilians.

With this American-sponsored coup finished, Ukrainian Jews began to reach out to the West to increase their influence. Thus it happened that just a few months after Maidan, the wayward son of the American vice president got in touch with a leading Ukrainian Jew, Mykola Zlochevsky, who ran a large gas company called Burisma. In this way, Hunter Biden incredibly found himself on the board of a corporation of which he knew nothing, in an industry of which he knew nothing, and which nonetheless was able to "pay" him upwards of $500,000 per year—obviously, for access to father Joe and thus to president Obama. Hunter carried on in this prestigious role for around five years, resigning only in 2019, as his father began his fateful run for the presidency.[8]

Despite a rocky tenure, Yatsenyuk managed to hold his PM position for over two years, eventually resigning in April 2016. His replacement was yet another Jew, Volodymyr Groysman, who served until August 2019. The Jewish hand would not be stayed. All this set the stage for the rise of the ultimate Jewish player, Volodymyr Zelensky.

This situation is particularly remarkable given that Jews are a small minority in Ukraine. Estimates vary widely, but the Jewish population is claimed to range from a maximum of 400,000 to as low as just 50,000. With a total population of 41 million, Jews represent, at most, 1% of the nation, and could be as small as 0.12%. Under normal conditions, a tiny minority like this should be almost invisible; but here, they dominate. Such is the Jewish hand.

Enter the Jewish Oligarchs

In Ukraine, there is a "second government" that calls many of the shots. This shadow government is an oligarchy: a system of rule by the richest

---

[8] For what it's worth, Hunter seems to have a "thing" for Jewesses. In 2016, while married, he took up with his dead brother's Jewish widow, Hallie Olivere Biden. The marriage failed and the illicit affair died out after a year or so, but then the ever-industrious Hunter latched on to another Jewess, "filmmaker" Melissa Cohen, in 2018. They married in 2019.

men. Of the five richest Ukrainian billionaires, four are Jews: Igor (or Ihor) Kolomoysky, Viktor Pinchuk, Rinat Akhmetov, and Gennadiy Bogolyubov. Right behind them, in the multi-millionaire class, are Jews like Oleksandr Feldman and Hennadiy Korban. Collectively, this group is often more effective at imposing their will than any legislator. And unsurprisingly, this group has been constantly enmeshed in corruption and legal scandals, implicated in such crimes as kidnapping, arson, and murder.[9]

Of special interest is the first named above. Kolomoysky has long been active in banking, airlines, and media—and in guiding minor celebrities to political stardom. In 2005 he became the leading shareholder of the 1+1 Media Group, which owns seven TV channels, including the highly popular 1+1 channel. (The 1+1 Group was founded in 1995 by another Ukrainian Jew, Alexander Rodnyansky.) Worth up to $6 billion in the past decade, Kolomoysky's current net wealth is estimated to be around $1 billion.

Not long after acquiring 1+1, Kolomoysky latched on to an up-and-coming Jewish comedian by the name of Volodymyr Zelensky. Zelensky had been in media his entire adult life, and even co-founded a media group, Kvartal 95, in 2003, at the age of just 25. Starring in feature films, he switched to television by the early 2010s, eventually coming to star in the 1+1 hit show "Servant of the People," where he played a teacher pretending to be president of Ukraine. Then there was the notable 2016 comedy skit in which Zelensky and friends play a piano with their penises—in other words, typical low-brow scatological Jewish humor, compliments of Zelensky and Kolomoysky.

By early 2018, the pair were ready to move into politics. Zelensky registered his new political party for the upcoming 2019 election, and declared himself a presidential candidate in December 2018, just four months prior to the election. In the end, of course, he won, with 30% of the vote in the first round, and then defeating incumbent Poroshenko in the 2nd round by a huge 50-point margin. Relentless favorable publicity by 1+1 was credited with making a real difference. Notably, the third-place finisher in that election was, yet again, the Jewess Yulia Timoshenko—like a bad penny, she just keeps coming back.[10]

Zelensky, incidentally, has dramatically profited from his "meteoric rise" to fame and power. His Kvartal 95 media company earned him some $7 million per year. He also owns a 25% share of Maltex Multicapital, a

[9] In a revealing quotation, Ukrainian nationalist Dmytro Yarosh once asked this question: "I wonder how it came to pass that most of the billionaires in Ukraine are Jews?" ("Ukrainian civilians take up arms," *Der Speigel*, 16 Apr 2014). Criminal activity is surely a large part of the answer.

[10] Not long after winning the presidency, Zelensky named another Jew, Andriy Yermak, as "Head of Presidential Administration." (The current prime minister, Denys Shmyhal, seems not to be Jewish.)

shell company based in the British Virgin Islands, as part of a "web of offshore companies" he helped to establish back in 2012. A Ukrainian opposition politician, Ilya Kiva, suggested that Zelensky is currently tapping into "hundreds of millions" in funding that flows into the country, and that Zelensky himself is personally earning "about $100 million per month." A Netherlands party, Forum for Democracy, recently cited estimates of Zelensky's fortune at an astounding $850 million. Apparently the "Churchill of Ukraine" is doing quite well for himself, even as his country burns.

In any case, it is clear that Zelensky owes much to his mentor and sponsor, Kolomoysky. The latter even admitted as much back in late 2019, in an interview for the *New York Times*. "If I put on glasses and look back at myself," he said, "I see myself as a monster, as a puppet master, as the master of Zelensky, someone making apocalyptic plans. I can start making this real".[11] Indeed—the Kolomoysky/Zelensky apocalypse is nearly upon us.

Between rule by Jewish oligarchs and manipulations by the global Jewish lobby, modern-day Ukraine is a mess of a nation—and it was so, long before the current "war." Corruption there is endemic; in 2015, the *Guardian* headlined a story on Ukraine, calling it "the most corrupt nation in Europe." An international corruption-ranking agency had recently assessed that country at 142nd in world, worse than Nigeria and equal to Uganda. As a result, Ukraine's economy has suffered horribly. Before the current conflict, their per-capita income level of $8700 put them 112th in the world, below Albania ($12,900), Jamaica ($9100), and Armenia ($9700); this is by far the poorest in Europe, and well below that of Russia ($25,700 per person). Impoverished, corrupt, manipulated by Jews, now in a hot war—pity the poor Ukrainians.

Hail the American Empire

Enough history and context; let me cut to the chase. From a clear-eyed perspective, it is obvious why Zelensky and friends want to prolong a war that they have no hope of winning: they are profiting immensely from it. As an added benefit, the actor Zelensky gets to perform on the world stage, which he will surely convert into more dollars down the road. Every month that the conflict continues, billions of dollars are flowing into Ukraine, and Zelensky et al are assuredly skimming their "fair share" off the top. Seriously—who, making anywhere near $100 million per month, wouldn't do everything conceivable to keep the gravy train running? The fact that thousands of Ukrainian soldiers are dying has no bearing at all in Zelensky's calculus; in typical Jewish fashion, he cares not one iota for the well-being

---

[11] "A Ukrainian Billionaire Fought Russia. Now He's Ready to Embrace It" (13 Nov 2019).

of the White Europeans. If his soldiers die even as they kill a few hated Russians, so much the better. For Ukrainian Jews, it is a win-win proposition.

Why does no one question this matter? Why is Zelensky's corruption never challenged? Why are these facts so hard to find? We know the answer: It is because Zelensky is a Jew, and Jews are virtually never questioned and never challenged by leading Americans or Europeans. Jews get a pass on everything (unless they are obviously guilty of something heinous—and sometimes even then!). Jews get a pass from fellow Jews because they cover for each other. Jews get a pass from media because the media is owned and operated by Jews. And Jews get a pass from prominent non-Jews who are in the pay of Jewish sponsors and financiers. Zelensky can be as corrupt as hell, funneling millions into off-shore accounts, but as long as he plays his proper role, no one will say anything.

So the "war" goes on, and Zelensky and friends get rich. What does Europe get from all this? Nothing. Or rather, worse than nothing: They get a "hot war" in their immediate neighborhood, and they get an indignant Putin threatening to put hypersonic missiles in their capital cities in less than 200 seconds. They get to deal with the not-so-remote threat of nuclear war. They get to see their currency decline—by 10% versus the yuan in a year and by 12% versus the dollar. They get a large chunk of their gas, oil, and electricity supplies diverted or shut off, driving up energy prices. And they get to see their Covid-fragile economies put on thin ice.

But perhaps they deserve all this. As is widely known, the European states are American vassals, which means they are Jewish vassals. European leaders are spineless and pathetic lackeys of the Jewish Lobby. *Judenknecht* like Macron, Merkel, and now Scholz, are sorry examples of humanity; they have sold out their own people to placate their overlords. And the European public is too bamboozled and too timid to make a change; France just had a chance to elect Le Pen, but the people failed to muster the necessary will. Thus, Europe deserves its fate: hot war, nuclear threat, cultural and economic decline, sub-Saharan and Islamic immigrants—the whole package. If it gets bad enough, maybe enough Europeans will awaken to the Jewish danger and take action. Or so we can hope.

What about the US? We could scarcely be happier. Dead Russians, the hated Putin in a tizzy, and the chance to play "world savior" once again. American military suppliers are ecstatic; they don't care that most of their weapons bound for Ukraine get lost, stolen, or blown up, and that (according to some estimates) only 5% make it to the front. For them, every item shipped is another profitable sale, whether it is used or not. And American congressmen get to pontificate about another "good war" even as they approve billions in aid.

And perhaps best of all, we get to press for an expansion to that American Empire known as NATO. We need to be very clear here: *NATO is simply another name for the American Empire*. The two terms are interchangeable. In no sense is NATO an "alliance among equals." Luxembourg, Slovakia, and Albania have absolutely nothing to offer to the US. Do we care if they will "come to our aid" in case of a conflict? That is a bad joke, at best. In reality, what such nations are is more land, more people, and more economic wealth under the American thumb. They are yet more places to station troops, build military outposts, and run "black sites." NATO always was, and always will be, the American Empire.

The push for Ukraine to join NATO by the West-friendly Zelensky was yet another blatant attempt at a power grab by the US, this one on Russia's doorstep. Putin, naturally, took action to circumvent that. But of course, now the push moves to Sweden and Finland, both of whom are unwisely pursuing NATO membership in the illusory quest for security, when in reality they will simply be selling what remains of their national souls to the ruthless Judeo-American masters. For their sake, I hope they are able to avoid such a future.

And all the while, American Jews and a Jewish-American media play up the "good war" theme, send more weapons, and press ever further into the danger zone. Ukrainian-American Jews like Chuck Schumer are right out front, calling for aid, for war, for death.[12] "Ukraine needs all the help it can get and, at the same time, we need all the assets we can put together to give Ukraine the aid it needs," said Schumer recently, eager to approve the next $40 billion aid package. As Jews have realized for centuries, wars are wonderful occasions for killing enemies and making a fast buck. Perhaps it is no coincidence that the present proxy war against Jewish enemies in eastern Europe began not long after the 20-year war against Jewish enemies in Afghanistan ended. Life without war is just too damn boring, for some.

Public Outrage?

If more than a minuscule fraction of the public knew about such details, they would presumably be outraged. But as I mentioned, the Jewish-controlled Western media does an excellent job in restricting access to such information and in diverting attention whenever such ugly facts pop up. The major exception is Tucker Carlson, who is able to reach some 3 million people each night; this is by far the widest reach for anything like the above analysis. But Carlson falls woefully short—pathetically short—in defining the Jewish culprit behind all these factors. Jews are never outed and never named by Carlson, let alone ever targeted for blame. This crucial

[12] Other Ukrainian-American Jews, like Steven Spielberg and Jon Stewart, and the heirs to the Sheldon Adelson fortune, are surely elated.

aspect is thus left to a literal handful of alt-right and dissident-right websites that collectively reach a few thousand people, at best.

And even if, by some miracle, all 3 million Tucker viewers were enlightened to the Jewish danger here, this still leaves some 200 million American adults ignorant and unaware. The mass of people believes what they see on the evening news, or in their Facebook feeds, or Google news, or on CNN or MSNBC, or in the *New York Times*—all Jewish enterprises, incidentally. This is why, when polled, 70% of the American public say that current aid to Ukraine is either "about right" or even "too little." This, despite the fact that around 50% claim to be "very concerned" about nuclear war; clearly they are unable to make the necessary connections. And for many, it is even worse than this: around 21% would support "direct American military intervention" against Russia, which means an explicit World War Three, with all the catastrophic outcomes that this entails. Our Jewish media have done another fine job in whipping up public incitement.

In sum, we can say that our media have cleverly constructed a "philo-Semitic trap": any mention or criticism of the Jewish hand in the present conflict is, first, highly censored, and then, if necessary, is dismissed as irrational anti-Semitism. Sympathy toward the (truly) poor, suffering Ukrainians is played up to the hilt, and Putin and the Russians relentlessly demonized. Leading American Jews, like Tony Blinken and Chuck Schumer, are constantly playing the good guys, pleading for aid, promising to help the beleaguered and outmanned Ukrainian warriors. Who can resist this storyline? Thus, we have no opposition, no questioning, no deeper inquiries into root causes. Jews profit and flourish, Ukrainians and Russians suffer and die, and the world rolls along toward potential Armageddon.

The reality is vastly different. Global Jews are, indeed, "planetary master criminals," as Martin Heidegger long ago realized. They function today as they have for centuries: as advocates for abuse, exploitation, criminality, death, and profits. This is self-evidently true: if the potent Jewish Lobby wanted true peace, or flourishing humanity, they would be actively pushing for such things and likely succeeding. Instead, we have endless mayhem, war, terrorism, social upheaval, and death, even as Jewish pockets get ever-deeper. And the one possible remedy for all this—true freedom of speech—recedes from our grasp.

On the one hand, I fear greatly for our future. On the other, I feel that we get what we deserve. When we allow malicious Jews to dominate our nations, and then they lead us into war and global catastrophe, well, what can we say? Perhaps there is no other way than to await the inevitable conflagration, exact retribution in the ensuing chaos, and then rebuild society from scratch—older and wiser.

POSTSCRIPT:

To reiterate what I wrote in the Introduction, we can see the vast difficulties faced by contemporary society—especially for those who might wish to live in ethnically homogenous communities, which of course was the normal and natural mode of human society for nearly all of human existence. Whites in particular can achieve great things in all-White nations, but they are badly hindered by the presence of non-Whites and especially of Jews. Given the presence of such people in virtually all nominally White nations today, the pressing questions are, first, the Jewish Question—how to contain and eventually banish the Jews—and second, the larger 'minority question' regarding how to best deport or repatriate non-Whites.

Goebbels was right: we are indeed faced with a steep climb. He understood, as did Hitler and other National Socialists, that Jews posed a mortal threat to social well-being and thus had to be dealt with in a most forceful manner. Hitler's Germany achieved great things in just 12 years and amidst extremely difficult conditions. Whites everywhere can learn from their example and do even better. They need only educate themselves and then summon the necessary will.

I end with a quotation from Schopenhauer that I cited in Chapter 5. He believed that life is endless struggle, that obstacles are nearly ubiquitous, and that any victories are hard-won and short-lived. Despite all this, Schopenhauer argued that we have an obligation to ourselves and to our human nature to oppose the obstacles and to strive for greatness, no matter the prospects and regardless of whether it makes us 'happy.' He wrote:

> A happy life is impossible; the best that man can attain is a *heroic life*, such as is lived by one who struggles against overwhelming odds in some way and in some affair that will benefit the whole of mankind, and who, in the end, triumphs—although he obtains a poor reward, or none at all.

Strive to be heroic. Expect your rewards to be minimal or nonexistent. But act with the faith that your cause is just and that, in the end, you will triumph. In this lies the key to greatness.

BIBLIOGRAPHY

Assange, J. 2014. *When Google Met Wikileaks*. OR Books.

Bacharach, B. 1977. *Early Medieval Jewish Policy and Western Europe*. University of Minnesota Press.

Ball, G. and Ball, D. 1992. *The Passionate Attachment*. Norton.

Ben-Sasson, H. 1976. *A History of the Jewish People*. Harvard University Press.

Chamberlain, H. S. C. 1910/1968. *Foundations of the Nineteenth Century*. H. Fertig.

Dalton, T. 2016. *The Holocaust: An Introduction*. Castle Hill.

Dalton, T. 2019. *The Jewish Hand in the World Wars*. Castle Hill.

Dalton, T. 2019. *Goebbels on the Jews: The Complete Diary Entries, 1924 to 1945*. Castle Hill.

Dalton, T. 2020. *Debating the Holocaust: A New Look at Both Sides* (4th ed.). Castle Hill.

Dalton, T. 2020. *Eternal Strangers: Critical Views of Jews and Judaism through the Ages*. Castle Hill.

Dalton, T. 2020. *Streicher, Rosenberg, and the Jews*. Castle Hill.

Dalton, T. (ed.). 2022. *Classic Essays on the Jewish Question: 1850 to 1945*. Clemens & Blair.

Duke, D. 1998. *My Awakening*. Free Speech Press.

Emerson, R. 1860/1929. *Complete Works: Conduct of Life*. Houghton.

Franklin, B. 1936. *Representative Selections*. American Book Co.

Ginsberg, B. 1993. *The Fatal Embrace*. University of Chicago Press.

Ginsberg, B. 2013. *How the Jews Defeated Hitler*. Rowman & Littlefield.

Goebbels, J. 1944. *Der Steile Aufstieg* (The Steep Climb). Eher Verlag. Online at www.archive.org.

Gordon, S. 1984. *Hitler, Germans, and the Jewish Question*. Princeton University Press.

Griffin, D. 2007. *Debunking 9/11 Debunking*. Olive Branch Press.

Herodotus. 1998. *The Histories*. Oxford University Press.

Hitler, A. 2022. *Mein Kampf* (2 vols.; T. Dalton, ed.). Clemens & Blair.

Hitler, A. 2019. *Hitler on the Jews*. Castle Hill.

Homer. 1990. *The Iliad* (R. Fagles, trans.). Penguin.

Homer. 1996. *The Odyssey* (R. Fagles, trans.). Penguin.

Huxley, A. 1928. *Proper Studies*. Doubleday.

Kaczynski, T. 2019. *Technological Slavery* (vol. 1). Fitch and Madison.

Kant, I. 1978. *Anthropology*. Southern Illinois University Press.

Kohr, L. 1955. *Breakdown of Nations*. Dutton.

Lemkin, S. 1944/2008. *Axis Rule in Occupied Europe*. Lawbook Exchange.

Lindemann, A. 1997. *Esau's Tears*. Cambridge University Press.

Luther, M. 2020. *On the Jews and Their Lies* (T. Dalton, ed.). Clemens & Blair.
MacDonald, K. 1994. *A People That Shall Dwell Alone*. Praeger.
MacDonald, K. 1998. *Separation and its Discontents*. Praeger.
MacDonald, K. 1998. *The Culture of Critique*. Praeger.
Marcuse, H. 2001. *Legacies of Dachau*. Cambridge University Press.
Marx, K. 1978. "On the Jewish Question," in *The Marx-Engels Reader*. Norton.
Maser, W. 1974. *Hitler's Letters and Notes*. Harper & Row.
Mearsheimer, J. and Walt, S. 2007. *The Israel Lobby and US Foreign Policy*. Farrar, Straus, and Giroux.
Mendes-Flohr P. and Reinharz, J. (eds.). 2011. *The Jew in the Modern World*. Oxford University Press.
Nietzsche, F. 1967. *On the Genealogy of Morals*. Vintage.
Nietzsche, F. 1967. *The Will to Power*. Vintage.
Nietzsche, F. 1982. *The Portable Nietzsche* (W. Kaufmann, ed.). Penguin.
Nietzsche, F. 1982. "The Antichrist." In *The Portable Nietzsche*. Penguin.
Nietzsche, F. 1982. "Twilight of the Idols." In *The Portable Nietzsche*. Penguin.
Nietzsche, F. 1996. *Human, All Too Human*. Cambridge University Press.
Nietzsche, F. 1997. *Daybreak*. Cambridge University Press.
Oliphant, L. 1880. *The Land of Gilead*. William Blackwood.
Perry, M. 2000. *Dachau Liberated: The Official Report by the US Seventh Army*. Inkling Books.
Pindar. 2007. *The Complete Odes*. Oxford University Press.
Plato. 1997. "Republic." In *Plato: Complete Works*. Hackett.
Rosenberg, A. 1930/2021. *The Myth of the 20th Century* (T. Dalton, trans.). Clemens & Blair.
Rudolf, G. 2017. *Lectures on the Holocaust* (3rd ed.). Castle Hill.
Schopenhauer, A. 1974. *Parerga and Paralipomena* (2 vols.). Oxford University Press.
Schopenhauer, A. 1969. *World as Will and Representation* (2 vols.). Dover.
Shogan, R. 2010. *Prelude to Catastrophe*. Ivan Dee.
Smith, G. 1893. *Essays on the Questions of the Day*. Macmillan.
Sombart, W. 1911/1982. *The Jews and Modern Capitalism*. Transaction.
Suzuki, I. 2022. *Unmasking Anne Frank: Her Famous Diary Exposed as a Literary Fraud*. Clemens & Blair.
Toaff, A. 2007/2020. *Passovers of Blood*. Clemens & Blair.
Toland, J. 1976. *Adolf Hitler* (2 vols.). Doubleday.
Trawney, P. 2015. *Heidegger and the Myth of a Jewish World Conspiracy*. University of Chicago Press.
Vaksberg, A. 1994. *Stalin Against the Jews*. Knopf.
Wheen, F. 2000. *Karl Marx: A Life*. Norton.

www.ingramcontent.com/pod-product-compliance
Lightning Source LLC
Chambersburg PA
CBHW052107030426
42335CB00025B/2871